The Reference Sources Handbook

(previously Printed Reference Material)

Fourth Edition

Edited by
Peter W. Lea
and
Alan Day

Library Association Publishing
London

Published by
Library Association Publishing
7 Ridgmount Street
London WC1E 7AE

First published 1980 as *Printed reference material*
Second edition 1984
Third edition 1990
This edition 1996

British Library Cataloguing in Publication Data

A catalogue record for this book is available from the British Library

ISBN 1-85604-177-8

Typeset in 12/14pt Elegant Garamond and 10/14pt Helvetica by Library Association Publishing
Printed and made in Great Britain by Bookcraft (Bath) Ltd, Midsomer Norton, Avon

To all students, past, present and future of the Department of Library and Information Studies, the Manchester Metropolitan University, and all its previous incarnations.

No bird soars too high if he soars with his own wings
William Blake

Contents

Contents

Contents

Contents

Contents

Contributors

ELIZABETH ANKER
  University of Warwick
C. PETER AUGER
  Information Consultant
ALLAN J. BUNCH
  Cambridgeshire Libraries and Information Service
TONY CHALCRAFT
  University College of Ripon and York St. John
LYNNE CLITHEROE
  Information Research Network
ALAN E. DAY
  Editor–Compiler *Walford's guide to reference material*
BOB DUCKETT
  Central Library Bradford
JOHN FARROW
  Manchester Metropolitan University
SUSAN V. HOWARD
  Charing Cross and Westminster Medical School
PETER W. LEA
  Manchester Metropolitan University
BARRIE I. MacDONALD
  Independent Television Commission
CHRIS MAKEPEACE
  Consultant
DAVID MORT
  Information Research Network
VALERIE J. NURCOMBE
  Information Consultant
CHRISTINE REID
  University of Strathclyde

DONNA SHILLING
  Central Library, Nottingham
MALCOLM STACEY
  Central Library, Nottingham
ANTHONY HUGH THOMPSON
  Consultant
A. JOHN WALFORD MBE
  (Retired)
STEPHEN WILLIS
  Central Library, Manchester
HAZEL WOODWARD
  Loughborough University of Technology

Preface to the Fourth Edition

The inexorable and irresistible momentum of electronic publishing has finally caused the original title of this work to be replaced by one which more accurately reflects the developments of the past five years. Contributors were asked to include references to relevant publications of appropriate places in their text, rather than to consider them as special examples, in order to emphasize that this form of publishing is here to stay as a permanent feature of the information network. It is hoped that the new title will encompass all current reference publishing processes and be hospitable to any which may appear in the future.

Although the work has retained its original structure in describing and evaluating sources of information, some changes have been deemed necessary in order to keep down its size and, ultimately, its price. Chapters on subject and general encyclopaedias, and current and subject bibliographies, have been combined respectively into single chapters, with some inevitable loss of content. The previous chapter on electronic publishing has been replaced by an overview of reference publishing and, reluctantly, the chapter on indexes has been omitted. A number of our original authors were able to revise their chapters and we are also pleased to welcome the expertise of some new contributors to replace those who, for various reasons, were not able to contribute to this edition. We thank them for all their efforts and for complying with the deadlines. Our particular thanks go to David Mort and Lynne Clitheroe for accepting a late commission.

The question remains what purpose this work serves and to whom it is addressed. Quite simply, the objective has been to provide a practical handbook and guide to reference material in a series of discrete chapters relating to a particular form or type of material, each contributed by a recognized authority or practitioner, for reference librarians to employ in stock editing and evaluation; for library and information professionals experiencing a change of direction into unfamiliar areas; and for new entrants to the profession pursuing courses in departments of library and information studies, grappling with complex and multifarious biblio-graphical sources.

Constructive criticism on the content of *The reference sources handbook* would be welcomed by the editors, not least so that future editions will continue to meet the needs of its targeted audience.

Peter Lea and Alan Day
Manchester
July 1996

1
Reference publishing

Bob Duckett

TRADITIONAL REFERENCE PUBLISHING

Traditional paper-based reference publishing is alive and well; even many of the traditional titles are still going strong. The ghost of reference libraries past will recognize *Whitakers almanack* (first published in 1868), *Pears cyclopedia* (1897), *Statesman's yearbook* (1864), *Oxford English dictionary* (OED, started 1879) and the *Dictionary of national biography* (DNB, 1882). Some of these titles have new editions and formats of course. The user of the 11th (1910) edition of *Encyclopaedia Britannica* might struggle with the current Macro-, Micro-, and Pro- paedias, while the microprint edition and magnifying glass of OED would amuse, but in our consideration of the deluge of IT-hype that is flooding our in-trays, let it be clearly understood that print, user-friendly print, is still the core resource of most library and information services and publishers' catalogues. We still have printed bibliographies, printed dictionaries, printed atlases and yearbooks.

Mega works

Even some of the great Victorian multivolume shelf-benders are still alive and kicking – those survivors from the age of scholarly publishing famous enough to be known by their initials. Indeed, *DNB* is being revised (and will take a leisurely decade or two to complete), *OED* has been revised, and *CBEL* (*Cambridge bibliography of English literature*), now the *New CBEL*, is being revised again. These works set a standard to be emulated. One emulator, the *New Grove dictionary of music and musicians* is in its 6th edition of 20 volumes; the new *Dictionary of art* ('the most comprehensive book about art ever published') will be in 34 volumes, have 41,000 articles by 6700 scholars from 120 countries, and cost £5,300; while the six-volume *World encyclopedia of theatre* currently being published by Routledge, and the *International dictionary of historic places* to be in five volumes of 800 pages each (Fitzroy Dearborn), are two middle order quality publications. The densely packed *Books in print* (the 1995–96 volume has 1.3 million book entries in ten very heavy volumes plus five for the *Subject guide* volumes) and the continuing multivolume Halsbury's series of law, statutes and statutory instruments, will be familiar to most librarians.

Publishers' series are still a feature. Thus ABC-Clio Press's *World bibliographical series* is now at volume 184, and Routledge's *The critical heritage* series on English literature comes in a set of 68 volumes and a special offer price of £4,000. 'Each volume presents contemporary responses to a writer's work' plus introduction, select bibliography and indexes. The work is also available in 13 mini-sets selected by period (in slip cases), and as individual volumes. Bowker Saur's *World database series* is another new publishing venture in the grand design.

Quality

Staying with the classic reference book, one difference our visitor from the past will notice is its improved quality. Although there are some exceptions – the eye-wateringly small print of *Books in print* and the *Clover* newspaper indexes perhaps, and a penchant for grey recycled paper – generally the legibility of typefaces, design of page layouts, the use of colour and the quality of illustrations, graphics and covers are all much improved. The American textbook style of using inserted 'boxes' and 'bullet points' is now widespread, though it is interesting that many US publishers are still wedded to quality hardback book production when a softback would be more appropriate. But just to compare today's editions of, say, *Britannica*, *World book* and *Collier's* encyclopedias, with the *Chambers* and *Everyman* of the 1960s, is to make the point clear. St James Press, Bloomsbury, Thorpe, Reader's Digest, Oxford University Press and even HMSO produce some of the best of today's reference publishing. The books published by the Royal Commission on the Historical Monuments of England, often by HMSO, are outstanding examples of a mix of text and photography. David & Charles' *The encyclopedia of fungi of Britain and Europe* 1995 (1040 colour photographs in

384 pages), and the *Collins new encyclopedia of fishing in Britain and Ireland* 1992, with several colour photographs, drawings or paintings on every page, are two particularly outstanding works. The use of coloured aerial photographs has been used to great effect in Ian Allan's *Aerofilm guides* series: for example in Dave Twydell's *Football grounds*, where car parks, railway stations and ground entrances are clearly shown, while Colin Speakman's *The Yorkshire Dales* cleverly uses aerial photographs overlaid with symbols and close-ups. Such work marks a significant advance in topographical description – a welcome mix of esoteric mapping and the popular guidebook. Computer-produced typefaces have improved, and gone for good, one hopes, are those photoreduced typescripts of the early 1970s that Pergamon and Greenwood presses, among others, used for academic monographs.

In terms of arrangement, however, progress is mixed. The sloppy use of computer-produced indexes has produced many barbarisms never tolerated in the past. The word 'the' used indiscriminately as a filing term is a particularly irritating practice. There is also often a lack of care in the selection of terms: 'Bibles, for example, were entered under a range of different titles including "Giant Print Reference Bible", "Large Print Imperial Reference Bible", and "Personal Size Giant Print Reference Edition (Bible)". These particular titles were not indexed under "Bible"';[1] and 'A colleague gave up looking for Boris Yeltsin – it's under Eltsin! Tchaikovsky is Chaikovskii and Ouspensky is Uspenskii. There are no cross-references from the more popular spellings, not even a transliteration table.'[2]

Factbook wars, the popular market and trivia
Two areas of reference publishing are witnessing fierce battles. These are for the home (house) reference market and in the area of 'factbooks'. The quantity of 'mini', 'pocket' and 'concise' dictionaries, grammars and other compendia pouring from the presses of the likes of Oxford, Collins, Chambers, Helicon and Macmillan is really quite amusing, while the range and variety of 'sourcebooks', 'factbooks' and 'information' works is bewildering. Examples of the latter are *Arts and entertainment fads*, *Pears' book of winners and champions*, *Hutchinson factfinder*, *The Cambridge factfinder*, *Larousse desk reference encyclopedia*, *Chambers' book of facts* ('essential home reference book. 150,000 facts covering 280 fields of interest') and the *Reader's Digest illustrated dictionary of essential knowledge* (self-billed as 'a new type of reference book' this 'revolutionary' work pre-

sents 'all the information you really need' and 'the key facts that everyone ought to know'). This is in addition to the long-serving *Daily Mail yearbook*, *Pears' cyclopedia*, *Enquire within upon everything*, *World almanac and book of facts* and *Whitaker's almanack*.

These are attempts by the mainstream publishers to 'cash in' on the home education market by producing cheaper books and redesigning encyclopedias with more appeal. This burgeoning genre is giving reviewers and selectors a headache. The thematic and individual arrangements are generally quite complex, making direct comparison difficult. They are, in fact, often quite difficult books to use and are more suited to the home or schoolbag where frequent use brings familiarity.

There is also quite a battle for market share in the various developing and popular subjects. The *Rough guides* (Harrap Columbia/Penguin) and *Traveller's world guides* series (published by Trade and Travel of Bath) are two low-priced series catering for the travel market; other popular topics are antiques, where the Tony Curtis-edited *Lyle price guides* are for keeping safe behind the enquiry counter (e.g. *Film and rock 'n' roll collectables*); sport (*Guinness book of world soccer*); contemporary history, a market interest spurred on by curriculum developments (e.g. Blackwell's *Contemporary Britain: an annual review*, Batsford's *Portrait of a decade* series aimed at GCSE students, and the truly remarkable Longman *Chronicle* corpus; and of course popular music (Blandford's *Top twenty book* and the *Guinness book of hit singles*).

Even at the upper end of the market, competition between rival publishers is fierce: witness the clash of books on abbreviations, quotations and contemporary biography. To take some titles in the latter category, there is the St James suite of biographical dictionaries, Debrett's *People of today*, A & C Black's *Who's who* (c.29,000 entrants), Bowker Saur's *Who's who in the world* (35,000), and Europa's *International who's who* (20,000).

Competition in the reference book market is fun to watch, but results in our having to buy more books since each publisher strives to have something in its book that its competitors do not. Thus, St James Press' *Olderr's fiction index* and *Chamber's fiction file* have much that the long-established *Fiction index* of Marilyn Hicken (AAL) does not have, while Hicken's *Sequels* vies with the ALA's *Sequels* compiled by the Husbands, and Bowker Saur's *The whole story: 3000 years of sequels and sequences*.

A popular area of growth is in 'trivia', a development of the quiz and competition market. Guinness have long been market leaders with the

Guinness book of records. Russell Ash's *Top ten of everything* has led to a lucrative niche in this glossy leisure market, with 'top tens' of music, sport and much else ('listomania' has been a useful neologism). We learn from Ash that *The Guinness book of records* is the fourth-best selling book of all time, after *The Bible*, Chairman Mao's 'Little red book' and Noah Webster's *American spelling book*. Other books in this trivia market are crossword and Scrabble dictionaries. Publishers will, it seems, publish anything, and at the risk of showing a reference librarian's prejudices, there does seem to be a burgeoning supply of rather pointless books. *The Bloomsbury book of dedications, The murder guide to Great Britain – 100 bizarre and gruesome murders, The Guinness book of lasts, The Guinness book of naval blunders, Death dictionary* and *The vampire book* perhaps qualify in this category.

Another shot at the domestic market and impoverished reference library is paperback publishing. The percentage of paperback purchases by libraries in general has been increasing steadily as hard-pressed book-funds seek to cope with ever-rising prices and demands. This is true of reference libraries as well, particularly for textbooks and titles that date quickly; thus we now have the 20-volume *New Grove dictionary of music and musicians* in paperback, costing only £320 compared to £750 for the hardback.

There is also fierce competition to develop new subject fields such as Europe (e.g. Cassell's *What's what and who's who in Europe*); the environment (Cassell's *The green index: a directory of environmental organizations*); new technology (Sans.Net's *Navigating the Internet*); and grants and funding (*The awards almanack*, St James Press).

Publishers, sponsors and others

Publishers come and go, and frequently get swallowed up. One of the many newcomers to reference publishing is Bloomsbury, which is carving out a niche for itself in quality production of popular subjects such as names, games and quotations. Many of the well-established regulars, such as OUP, Routledge and Blackwell, are often to be seen wearing new clothes, perhaps none more so than HMSO, a publisher that has come a long way in recent years. Once reliably drab and dowdy, their quality and range of titles is now impressive. From the documentary publication, such as *War with Japan*, the complete official naval staff history which 'provides the full Ministry of Defence account of World War Two events in the Pacific, previously only accessible for official purposes' in six volumes, we go right through the range to *The clans*, a colourful children's book complete with a snakes-and-ladder-type Cattle Reiving Game. Particularly noteworthy is HMSO's *Aspects of Britain* series of 50-plus titles which give useful information pitched at a general level on political, economic and social topics.

Other innovative publishers in the reference field are Facts On File which has developed far beyond its Keesing's-type news service to a major quality reference book provider (a *Dictionary of 20th century allusions* is a recent title) and Chadwyck-Healey, a pioneer in publishing large-scale documentary works. Although now mostly working in the non-print field, their *Catalogue of British official publications not published by HMSO*, first published in 1980, was a boon to the many librarians struggling with quangos and government publications. There continues to be a rich mosaic of small independent publishers who are producing good-quality and innovative work. Examples are Perennial Publications of Oxford (*Focus on Britain*), Kenneth Mason of Emsworth in Hampshire (*Hockings European cups: who won which, where, when*) and, in our own field, LISU, the Library and Information Statistics Unit at Loughborough University, who are developing the much-needed field of library statistics.

One feature which illustrates the complexity of contemporary reference publishing is the interlocking of publishers in joint marketing ventures and takeovers. The volatile 'who owns whom' and 'who distributes whose' markets does confuse. Shelwing, Eurospan and Europa currently distribute a wide range of US publisher's titles, and many are the travelling salespeople who call in carrying several publishers'/distributors' portfolios. In the excellent new rival to *The artists' and writers' yearbook*, Macmillan's *The writer's handbook*, we learn that Gower, Scolar Press and Variorum are part of Ashgate; Mansell, Ward Lock, Gollancz, Studio Vista and Arms & Armour are part of Cassell; that Chambers, Harrap and Macmillan are part of Larousse; and that Reed International includes such stalwart reference imprints as Heinemann, Hamlyn, Methuen, Mitchell Beazley, George Philip and Butterworth. Bowker Saur books carry the cover note that they are part of 'Reed Reference Publishing Group' and the current Prentice Hall catalogue lists no fewer that 22 imprints, including G. K. Hall, Jossey-Bass, Scribners, Simon & Schuster Reference, Twayne, and Harvester Wheatsheaf. No doubt things are changing as I write.

Another developing feature which can confuse is that of the sponsored publication. Shell (*Book of firsts*) and BP (countryside books) were early in the field, but others have followed. Guinness have moved on from their *Records* to many other titles, the six-volume *Guinness encyclopedia of popular music* being described by *The Times* as 'a work of almost frightening completeness'. Other examples of sponsored works are *The Embassy book of world snooker*, *The Benson and Hedges top 10 of everything* (a sponsorship since dropped), *Pears' book of winners and champions* and the *Rothman's football yearbook*.

Prices

Of course, our visitor from reference publishing past will be amazed at prices today. As always, quality costs money; the £100 reference book is a familiar sight today (and the £200 and £300 book not unknown), and multivolume reference sets can go into thousands of pounds. The problem for the reference librarian is that the price of reference books rises considerably faster than the general rate of inflation and of lending library books, with their bulking of paperbacks, discounted bestsellers and student texts: facts which can bring misery to the reference librarian, whose budget is frequently pegged to a global average. Many a reference collection is ageing and deteriorating as a consequence. A spoiling factor here is the cut-throat cost-cutting in the burgeoning home reference market – books which are described as reference books, but not reference *library* books. A quick look through *Reference reviews* reveals titles costing as little as £4.99, such as the Oxford Reference series (e.g. *French grammar*); £3.99, such as the Hutchinson Pocket series (e.g. *Dictionary of geography*); £2.99, as in the Chambers' English Usage Series (e.g. *Chamber's punctuation guide*); even £2.50, as in the Harraps' Study Aids (e.g. *Verbs*). Many of these are 'minis' and 'micros', but not all; thus volumes in the Chambers Compact Reference series (e.g. *Great modern inventions*) are some 230 pages, the Diagram Group's *Ready reference* has 319 pages for £4.99, the *Larousse dictionary of British history* 730 pages for £5.99, and *Harrap's learner mini dictionary* is 614 pages for a mere £2.99! If the larger reference collections will prefer the larger hardback versions, at least the smaller collections can benefit from this cost competition.

At the other end of the market, the *Instat: international statistics sources* costs £185, *World guide to libraries*, 12th edn. £340, *Who's who in America*

£410, and the *International encyclopedia of business and management* £800 (£650 pre-publication).

Alternative formats

Alternatives to hardcopy eye-legible print are developing fast. Microform alternatives have, of course, existed for some time. Indeed, some of the alternative microform formats are now so old that it is hard to find any equipment remaining on which to use them. The Readex Corporation microcards of government documents and the *Books in English* ultrafiche are two such that are still around. After microform came online, which many people thought would be an alternative to print, and for many it was, but, as with microform, there is still value in the printed versions. And so it is with the newer technologies of CD-ROM and networking: some media are better for certain uses than others. Print for quick reference and browsing perhaps, microform for storage and copying from large and fragile volumes, CD-ROM for complex searching on popular databases, online for the less-used ones.

Many reference and information sources are now available in several formats. Thus Bowker's *Books in print* is now available in ten volumes of print, on CD-ROM, on microfiche and online. Other titles available in four formats are *Biography and geneology master index* (print title) or *Biobase* (microfiche version); or *BMI* (DIALOG file 287); and CD-ROM. Bowker offer *Ulrich's international periodicals directory* in five printed volumes and three electronic options: *Ulrich's plus* (CD-ROM with both Windows and Macintosh versions), *Ulrich's on tape* (magnetic tape version), and *Ulrich's online* (updated monthly on DIALOG and OVID). Not many sources are available in quite as many formats as these, but a large number offer two or three. *Treaties and alliances of the world* (6th edition) and *Keesing's record of world events*, are just two of hundreds of titles available in both print and CD-ROM versions, while *The Times collection* is a complete archive of international events, both current and historical, available in microform, CD-ROM and print (Research Publications). *The Times* newspaper itself, like many others, can be had in hard copy, microfilm (from 1785) and fiche (from 1990). The index can be had in print or on CD-ROM.

Journal publishers have long experimented with electronic versions: the early online systems were, and still are, largely journal based, but the development of CD-ROM alternatives is more recent. Sweet & Maxwell's

Legal journals index is one, while MCB University Press supplies a CD-ROM version alongside the hard copy. The fact that the core data for most publications are stored in machine-readable form explains why alternative formats are so easily produced. They can, however, cause confusion, especially when marketed under different titles. The *American book trade directory*, for example, is the same as *Publishing market place reference plus*. Bowker, the publishers of these titles, make the point clear in their publicity, but other publishers may not be so careful. Overlapping databases are another source of confusion, as with *New Zealand books in print* being part of *Bowker/Whitaker global books in print plus*. Bowker's massive book and serial databases spawn a large number of such publications.

ELECTRONIC SOURCES

Alternative electronic formats have been developed from the computer databases used by the major publishers. From these databases come the printed sources. Now publishers are marketing the databases themselves, either by selling direct access online, reformatting on to disk or tape, or leasing to a service provider. Not only do individual reference titles have their computer source which can be formatted and marketed various ways, but publishers and data suppliers have their massive corporate databases from which several different reference works can be generated. This is why so many mainstream publishers such as OUP, Whitaker, Bowker, H. W. Wilson, Helicon and Chambers can have so many variants of their standard texts. This provides a challenge for librarian-selectors who can easily find themselves selecting the same basic text under different titles and in different arrangements.

Complexities

The new formats also provide new challenges to the skills of information selectors. Now they have to evaluate the relative merits of a work itself; they have to decide which of the many formats available to buy – CD-ROM, PC disks, or even tapes; and they have to face a bewildering supply of alternative products by which to access the same data: shall I consult *UKOP* on CD-ROM, *HMSO books in print* on microfiche, the HMSO *Annual catalogues* in hard copy, or use the Internet to find details of government publications? In addition the librarian-selector has to be systems sophisticated (or have supportive systems staff at frequent beck and call). This is not just the need to be familiar with the start-up proce-dures and search strategies of a variety of disparate services: they must be able to determine whether their library has an 'IBM PC/XT/AT or 100% compatible, 512 Kb memory (384K free), one floppy disk, 20 Mb hard CD-ROM drive with appropriate controller card and interface cable hardware with a MS-DOS 3.0 or higher operating system' and under-stand 'The BookFind-CD Developer's Pack uses the new HEADFAST Search Engine which has an easy-to-use Application Program Interface'. Then there are all the licensing agreements to worry about, the adequacy and sufficiency of the equipment, its security, and staff and user training. Beyond the publisher's glossy leaflets lies the reality – using the product.

CD-ROM

We have seen how many publishers now supply electronic alternatives to their hardcopy titles. In fact, they are not true alternatives at all, since they can provide far more sophisticated access to the data they contain than is possible with the printed form. They are a different product. The skill of the librarian now lies in advising the user which of the various for-mats is best for any enquiry. The publishers' blurbs make great play of promoting these extras. Chadwyck-Healey, for example, point out that entries selected in *Palmer's index to The Times* on CD-ROM can be dis-played in chronological order and users can print their search results; Microinfo point out that just four discs can replace two metres of shelf space of *Keesing's record of world events* and access 15.5 million words in seconds; Butterworth proclaim their 'books on screen' software can enable the user to access the 180 volumes of the *All England law reports* from 1936 onwards, that you can add your own notes, and transfer directly into word-processed documents (unlike most publisher's blurbs this shows a laptop computer rather than the usual VDU); Bowker Saur offer *Ulrich's on tape* to provide your own customized system; *Britannica CD* includes not just the text of the encyclopedia but also the *Merriam-Webster's dictionary* and sound effects!; RIBA's *Architectural publication index* includes the British Architectural Library's own subject index; and Kogan Page's *European business data systems* is an electronic version of six of the publisher's business books.

Beyond these enhanced alternative formats lie the increasing number of information sources that the publishers make available *only* on CD-ROM. Many of these products are innovative and powerful. Thus

Chadwyck-Healey's *English poetry plus* contains 165,000 poems from 1250 poets of the English-speaking world, from Chaucer to the end of the nineteenth century. Every poem is coded for easy access by topic, chronological period and author's nationality. Selected poems are coded by poetic form and genre. There are also biographies, portraits and recorded readings. From the mass of new electronic information products just a few examples will have to suffice: the BADGER database of supplementary legal materials, including newspaper articles, European Commission documents and House of Commons Papers (Sweet & Maxwell); *Reference update* to keep abreast of current scientific information, available via disk, modem or the Internet; *Anbar management intelligence* (MCB and the British Library); ECCTIS (Educational Counselling and Credit Transfer Information Service); *Butterworths EC legislation implementor*; *AgeInfo CD-ROM*; and *Facts about Britain 1945–1995* (HMSO). TFPL publish (and issue on disc) *The CD-ROM directory*, the 14th edition (1995) of which gives details of 10,000 CD-ROM and multimedia CD titles – testimony indeed to the energy of publishers in the new CD-ROM market.

Online and the Internet

Suddenly online seems old fashioned, but developments and amalgamations are a feature here too. One very traditional service is offered online by British Book Service, who provide registers of out-of-date and rare publications either wanted or available for sale, and which are updated daily!

Then there is the Internet. At this point we have some problems over the concept of what is 'published', but publishers are busy making use of this resource. For example, Kluwer Academic Publishing has a gopher server covering 11,500 book entries and 260 journals, and Cambridge Scientific is making available 15 of Elsevier's *Excerpta medica* abstract journals and also Microinfo's *Environmental RouteNet* (an encyclopedic reference guide to environmental information). Osborne McGraw-Hill publish *The Internet golden directory*, Random House *Netguide*, Mecklermedia *Internet worlds* and Fawcett Columbine *The Internet directory*.

Such is the pace of change that no sooner has one organized the acquisition and implementation of an information source in a new improved format, and is about to cancel the old, than the new itself is upstaged.

OTHER MEDIA

Electronic publishing is not replacing the book, nor making other forms of media obsolete. In fact, electronics is coming to their aid and enhancing them. Take maps, for example: Ordnance Survey are a fast-moving publisher in the electronic field, and although the familiar printed series remains, folded, flat and 'encapsulated', electronic transmission is becoming the norm. US publisher MapInfo write: 'Connect to your corporate data using the new Query Wizard. In four easy steps you can perform complex spatial queries to remote RDMs and retrieve only the information you requested'. A downside is that no longer are Ordnance Survey printing retrospective copies; though they are not extending copyright cover beyond 50 years.

Microform

> In the great debate about the future of print in the electronic age, the role of microfilm tends to be overlooked – except by the thousands of librarians who use it every day and who continue to make large purchases of micropublications. In spite of predictions to the contrary, micropublishing lives on with no end in sight.[3]

So says Norman H. Williams of CIS, microform publishers of current and historical US Government and intergovernmental documents. Other players in the microfilm field are Research Publications, one of whose titles is *The eighteenth century*, a full text collection of 200,000 titles filmed from the collections of the British Library and other major collections; UMI, whose *Dissertation abstracts* comprise over 1.3 million largely unpublished doctoral and master's theses dating from 1961; and Chadwyck-Healey, whose *The nineteenth century: publishing, the book-trade and the diffusion of knowledge* consists of 2519 microfiches comprising more than 795 English-language texts published between 1801 and 1900. This is part of the publisher's Nineteenth Century microfiche programme.

One of the changes brought about by the application of electronics and image processing within publishing is that the concept of being 'out-of-print' has less relevance. UMI has long been a leader in the provision of otherwise unobtainable materials. It has produced *Book vault*, a new index on CD-ROM giving access to 134,000 out-of-print titles available for reprint through their Books on Demand service. All titles available are copyright cleared. It includes books originally published by university presses, learned societies and trade book publishers around the world.

The catalogue allows for tailored searches using numerous access categories. UMI also offer microform reprints of over 22,000 periodical and newspaper titles worldwide in their *Serials in microform* catalogue. Bowker Saur publish *Guide to microforms in print*, which enables librarians and researchers to locate microform titles, including filmed book editions, journals, newspapers, government publications and archival material. The increasing acceptance of microform has seen a decline in the facsimile reprint, of which Gregg International and Scolar Press were once major players. Trade standardization for fiche at 24-times reduction and 6 in × 4 in size has helped librarians enormously.

THE SPECIALISTS

Coincraft for coins, Brassey's for military history, Croner to 'Cut through the maze of business information', Hans Zell for Africa. Law has Sweet & Maxwell, Blackstone, Barry Rose and Butterworths, and who else but the Royal Horticultural Society for *The plant finder*? After the maze of IT hype, shifting goalposts and turbulent playing fields, it is comforting to get back to the firm ground of Stanley Gibbons, Ian Allen and the Geographical Association. Quality and subjects coverage guaranteed! We have met some of the big generalist reference publishers already, the Gales, the Routledges, Longmans, Europa, Facts on File and Macmillans though even here some have their own specialities. OUP, through its Asian branches, is a major player in the Indic language dictionaries market: Gujarati and Telugu with English have been two recently published dictionaries; HMSO publishes many very specialist works, as its recent *Forestry catalogue* demonstrates by including the Forestry Commission's *Forest recreation guidelines*. Conversely, Butterworths cover far more than just law. On the other hand, the librarian needs to be familiar with a number of small and enterprising publishers and specialist bookshops and mailing agencies.

Contemporary social living and its problems has a large clutch of organizations championing our right to have access to information. ACE (Advisory Centre for Education) publish low-priced information and offer a subscription service; DIG (Disablement Income Group) have just published a new care assessment guide; CPAG (Child Poverty Action Group) issue important handbooks such as those on fuel rights, debt advice and the essential *Non-means-tested benefits legislation*; and the Consumer Association, whose *Which?* magazine and publications on such subjects as making a will are bestsellers. Unsurprisingly, Africa Books specialize in Africa (*Africa who's who* etc.); Jane's, of *Jane's fighting ships*, is the major publisher of books on defence and transport technology (and whose volumes are creeping up to the £200 mark); Gower, often in association with Aslib, rivals The Library Association for information studies (e.g. *Harrod's librarians' glossary*); and the Hilmarton Manor Press publish such specialized works as *International art price annual*, the *International directory of arts* and the *International dictionary of miniature painters, porcelain painters and silhouettists*. The ICA (Institute of Contemporary Arts), apart from their specialist monographs, offer over 1400 talks on audio cassette (700 writers, 200 performers, 70 feminists, 35 new technologists and 21 anarchists, among others), video, CD and CD-ROM. Other special interest groups include *ARLIS (Art and design documentation in the UK: a directory of resources)*, Lloyd's Register of Shipping (*Shipwreck index of the British Isles*) and Almedic Publishing with *The UK alternative & complementary medicines handbook*. On all these specialists, large and small alike, librarians rely.

PUBLISHERS' PROMOTION

The energy and initiative that publishers expend on selling their products is impressive, and the reference library selector needs to be tough-minded, astute and clear of purpose. The commercial world of selling information is no place for the naive, the soft-hearted or the careless. Mistakes can be very expensive.

Publisher pressure

The quantity and quality of publisher's catalogues, leaflets, product cards and blurbs landing on reference librarians' desks and filling their waste bins is daunting. And if the colourful graphics and highflown hype does not impress, then what of the myriad of extra inducements? A trawl through a recent sackful of blurbs produced the following:

- 30 day approval service
- special offer for previous customers: 'Everything half price'
- 5% standing order discount
- 50% off backruns
- pre-publication discounts: 'Save £55 if you order early!'
- limited offer: '£650 until Oct 1, then £800'

- pay by instalments
- advance information
- trade in your old edition for special discount
- special discounts for account holders
- discounts for bulk purchase.

Needless to say, much of this is couched in emotive and beguiling prose: 'Save your organization £500' says one; 'Unique, topical, multidisciplinary, international, easy-to-use' says another, using all the strong buzz-words.

Then there are the gimmicks. *Whitaker's almanack* run a yearly quiz to impress its value on users and library staff, and Oxford University Press ran a general knowledge quiz in a national paper featuring its reference titles, with a £10,000 first prize. And then there are all those genial sales-people who call in and stay until a sale is made; the telephone call that puts you on the spot; the bogus renewal notice or final demand for payment for an unordered title, or for a payment already made, or a book supplied but not ordered. Delayed or abandoned publications and unannounced price increases remind us that publishers are sometimes too optimistic, or too clever by half.

Customer care

Many publishers take care to establish good relations with their customers. MCB University Press, publisher of some 150 journals, provides a Literati Club for its authors (who are also critical users of libraries) and a *Library Link* newsletter telling us of new titles and services. It also offers a variety of services on the Internet: up-to-date journal information searchable by interest area and keywords; current and forthcoming contents pages and abstracts; illustrative articles as a journal selection aid, names of editors and editorial board members; and e-mail discussion groups.

Many publishers mail regular bulletins of new titles they have published, and tell you of special offers etc. Sweet & Maxwell issue *Subscriber news* and Blackwell's *BHB review* is 'the journal for Blackwell's customers worldwide'. Some even provide hotlines and follow-up aftercare for customers, while 'freebies' and 'add-ons' may be sent to keep you sweet. And should you dare to cancel a journal or standing order, then beware the 'I assume this was a mistake!' note, followed by the 'you can't be serious?' letter and the 'how can we help you better?' questionnaire.

Intermediaries

Library suppliers are a common link in the publisher–library chain. In the current volatile area of contracting out of library services, the collapse of the Net Book Agreement, and diminishing bookfunds, the place of library suppliers is changing. Although library suppliers are not publishers, they are important to publishers and there is close liaison between them. Often library suppliers will advertise publishers' titles or provide special discounts. One supplier has upgraded its promotion to librarians in recent years: in addition to the glossy personalized mailings, it has put book images on to CD-ROM as a selection aid. Images of the jackets of spoken-word cassettes, CD-ROMs and videos are included. This service, iMAGE SELECT [*sic*] includes details of up to 800 titles a week. As with other library suppliers, there is an online ordering and enquiry system, stocklists in various arrangements, and showrooms. At least one library supplier has a showroom of CD-ROMs: 'Take a Test Drive. Visit our CR-ROM Test Centre. Over 200 titles to test'.

The wider field

Reference publishers are active in the wider field of book promotion, regularly attending – and often sponsoring – conferences and exhibitions. Whitaker now sponsor the Library Association Reference Awards for outstanding works of reference (McColvin Medal), bibliography or guide to the literature (Besterman Medal), an index (Wheatley Medal), and to bibliography generally (Walford Award), while MCB make annual awards for the best generalist and specialist books reviewed in *Reference reviews*.

SUMMING UP

In this brief look at reference publishing, from the Victorian works of scholarship to the Internet, there are a number of issues to consider.

First, although the medium changes the content is the same. In Chadwyck-Healey's 'Special Offer: Microform and Printed Publications', the *Birmingham Reference Library catalogue 1879–1963* is for sale in microform. When it was used in the now-demolished Birmingham Reference Library, the catalogue was in heavy folio volumes. It is significant that the publisher thought it worth preserving. They also offer on CD-ROM the 221 folio volumes of Migne's *Patrologia Latina*, the classic collection of the Latin Church Fathers. It is important, not just that such work is preserved for the next millennium, but also that, recast in the new technology, it has the potential for enhanced use: new knowledge may yet come from the old.

Secondly, there is a danger that publishers using the new technology will focus more on the form than the content. A major criticism of the Internet is that the source, accuracy and authority of much of the information available is unclear. Although there are some excellent new reference sources being published, exhibiting close attention to detail, indexing and presentation, there is, sadly, a loss of quality, especially in choice of terms and subject access in many new services. The electronic capabilities may give us access to the title words, and even text words, not easily done in pre-computer days, but the intellectual effort needed to choose consistent and sought terms, especially for concepts, is often lacking. Doubtless publishers find it cheaper to let the computer compute, even if it does make a lot of 'noise', but it cannot compute terms which are not there.

Thirdly, there is the problem of bibliographical control. From the reference publishing perspective, this relates to problems of copyright and legal deposit.

> As the number of scholarly journals continues to increase, it has become increasingly difficult for university libraries to maintain comprehensive research journal collections. As 'journals' appear on the Internet, requiring neither publisher nor librarian, serious problems have been identified, such as lack of bibliographic control, access, training of users, for example.
> (Blurb to *Project Elvyn: an experiment in electronic journal delivery*. Bowker Saur, 1995.)

Jacques Paul Migne, the editor of *Patrologia Latina*, and the generations of cataloguers in Birmingham's Reference Library, were concerned to identify and record knowledge as a prelude to its use. The *American book publishing record 1994* is a record of the books catalogued by the Library of Congress during that year – 40,400 records. *Books In print 1995/96* details some 155,000 new and forthcoming titles. The work of publishing and bibliography continues, and the problems increase. Librarians and publishers must work hard and use the technology to maintain this essential work.

Fourthly, already mentioned has been the blurring of the term 'publishing'. Not only is the new technology superseding the dominance of the standard published book for information work, but it also enables authors and editors to be their own publishers. Desktop publishing and the Internet are making radical changes to the way we regard publishing.

Lastly, in 1992 Oryx Press published *Distinguished classics of reference publishing* edited by James Rettig. Thirty-three classic reference books are featured, from the *Baedeker Guidebooks and Brewer's dictionary of phrase and fable* to *Science citation index* and *The national union catalog*: a veritable reference librarian's bedside reading. What will feature in a follow-up? *Classics of database construction and gopher servicing?*

REFERENCES AND CITATIONS

1 Review of 'The complete directory of large print books & serials', 1991, in *Reference reviews*, **5** (3), 1991.
2 Review of 'The biographical dictionary of the former Soviet Union', in *Library Association record*, **95** (5) May 1993.
3 Williams, N. H., 'Microform publishing: alive and well in the electronic age', *LOGOS*, **6** (3), 1995, 138.
4 Rettig, J., *Distinguished classics of reference publishing*, Phoenix, Oryx Press, 1992.

SUGGESTIONS FOR FURTHER READING

In the fast-moving world of publishing, information is quickly out of date. The weekly *Bookseller* is the main organ of the book trade and is essential reading for book selectors. *The Author* and *The electronic author* give useful and informed comment. *LOGOS*, 'the journal of the book world community', has quickly established itself as the leading journal of informed comment among publishers and librarians. Publishers' own announcements, catalogues and product publicity are major sources of information. Rettig's book, quoted above, gives a historical perspective.

2
Bibliographies

Tony Chalcraft

Bibliographies are central to the reference and information process. Most of the chapters in this book include some bibliographies. In this chapter the aim is to outline the main types of bibliographies and, specifically, to identify and discuss some of the most important bibliographical tools. Before beginning, a few words of clarification are necessary. The bibliographies considered here are primarily those listing books and related monograph material. Bibliographies mainly concerned with periodical articles, that is, indexing and abstracting sources, are largely excluded. Because the range of bibliographies available is so enormous the emphasis has been firmly placed on general works, especially listings compiled on a national basis. Subject and other specific bibliographies are included, but are not treated in depth. Apart from these qualifications, 'bibliographies' of all types are covered. Thus book trade lists and library catalogues are included, as are bibliographies of bibliographies. It should also be noted that as electronic sources are especially prominent in the bibliographical world particular attention has been given to online and CD-ROM databases.

NATIONAL BIBLIOGRAPHIES

A natural basis on which to list books is by country. Some of the earliest bibliographical listings were organized in this way. Two examples are John Bale's *Illustrium Majoris Britanniae scriptorum hoc est Angliae, Cambriae ac Scotiae*, published as long ago as 1548, and Andrew Maunsell's *Catalogue of English printed books*, issued in 1595. By the end of the twentieth century most countries will have produced some form of national bibliography. These can be conveniently divided into two main types, retrospective and current. Retrospective national bibliographies are those which list material published in the past. Current national bibliographies are concerned with listing material as it is published. A number of guides, or 'bibliographies of national bibliographies', have appeared. The most useful of these are:

Bell, B. L. AN ANNOTATED GUIDE TO CURRENT NATIONAL BIBLIOGRAPHIES. Alexandria, Virginia: Chadwyck-Healey, 1986.

Contains lengthy annotated entries commenting on matters such as scope and coverage, classification scheme, arrangement and indexes.

Gorman, G. E. and Mills, J. J. GUIDE TO CURRENT NATIONAL BIBLIOGRAPHIES IN THE THIRD WORLD. 2nd edn. London: Zell, 1987.

Includes 12 regional bibliographies. Generally more detailed than Bell.

Beaudiquez, M. (ed.) INVENTAIRE GÉNÉRAL DES BIBLIOGRAPHIES NATIONALES RÉTROSPECTIVES. München: Saur, 1986.

English title *Retrospective national bibliographies: an international directory*. Some entries in French, a few in German, but the majority in English. Does not cover ex-Soviet Bloc countries.

Current national bibliographies

Most current national bibliographies confine their coverage to books, significant pamphlets, initial issues of periodicals and perhaps doctoral dissertations and important government publications. Reasonable comprehensiveness is normally underwritten by legal deposit, that is, a requirement on publishers to submit at least one copy of all books published to an official receiving body, most commonly the national library. To be effective as an up-to-date record a current national bibliography must appear at frequent intervals, preferably on a regular basis. The appropriateness of this interval depends to some extent on publishing activity. Most major states of any size produce a monthly listing. Some, for example, Great Britain and Germany, publish weekly issues. Other smaller countries, for example Luxembourg and Iceland, make do with annual lists. Nearly all major national bibliographies are now also available as online and CD-ROM databases. Indeed, it is possible that many will cease to appear in printed form altogether, finding electronic publication more convenient and economical. Already a number have abandoned paper in favour of microfiche.

BRITISH NATIONAL BIBLIOGRAPHY. Boston Spa: British Library National Bibliographic Service, 1950– . Weekly etc.

Britain's national bibliography, commonly referred to as *BNB*, is a relative infant compared with some of its continental cousins, which can trace their origins well back into the nineteenth century. Based on items received at the British Library's Legal Deposit Office, it excludes music (covered by *British catalogue of music*), maps, Parliamentary publications and many items produced by government departments, especially those of a routine or specialized nature. Since its inception the arrangement has been according to the Dewey Decimal Classification. Printed issues now appear weekly in the form of a classified subject catalogue with an author/title index. Cumulated indexes are provided in the final issue for each month. Interim softback cumulations are produced for January–April and May–August, with a hardback annual cumulation comprising a separate index and classified volumes. *BNB* is also available in microfiche with cumulations for 1981–92 and 1950–84 (the latter is author/title only). The online version *BNBMARC*, searchable through BLAISE-Line, is updated weekly. *BNB on CD-ROM* comprises three CD-ROM discs, a current file from 1986 and two back files for 1950–76 and 1977–85.

As nearly all significant post-1950 items with a British imprint are recorded, *BNB* is usually the first source consulted when details of a British published book need to be verified. Records are of a generally high standard, although it is disappointing that certain categories of material, for example fiction, are now only catalogued according to AACR level 1. It must also be said that application of Dewey classification has at times been idiosyncratic. Items appear in *BNB* promptly, heavy use being made of cataloguing-in-publication (CIP) data. The arrangement of the weekly lists in classified arrangement facilitates browsing by subject specialists, making it useful as a current awareness and acquisitions tool. With the online and CD-ROM versions rapid searches for material back to 1950 are easily performed. *BNB* has no equal and for the UK librarian is the pre-eminent general bibliographic source.

Similar bibliographies produced by national libraries appear in most other English-speaking countries:

CANADIANA. Canada's national bibliography. Ottawa: National Library of Canada, 1950– . Microfiche: monthly, with annual cumulation.

AUSTRALIAN NATIONAL BIBLIOGRAPHY. Canberra: National Library of Australia, 1961– . Monthly, with annual cumulation.

Canadiana includes French-language material from Quebec. Printed issues were discontinued at the end of 1992. *Australian national bibliography* lists serials in a separate section, but otherwise closely resembles *BNB*. Unlike *BNB* both national bibliographies include material relating to the country published overseas, in the case of *Canadiana* in a separate sequence. Both are also available in database versions.

The situation in the United States is rather different in that there is no officially sponsored national bibliography. The equivalent of a national library, the Library of Congress, does produce the microfiche service *US books* as an offshoot of the *National union catalog*. The nearest equivalent of *BNB* is, however, a commercially produced listing:

AMERICAN BOOK PUBLISHING RECORD. New Providence, NJ: Bowker, 1960– . Monthly, with annual cumulation.

Based on Library of Congress cataloguing with full records. Arrangement is by Dewey with separate sections for adult and juvenile fiction. About 60,000 items are listed annually. A cumulation is available as *American book publishing record cumulative 1950–1977*. New York: Bowker, 1978. 15v. A further retrospective set is *American book publishing record cumulative 1876–1949*. New York: Bowker, 1980. 15v.

A number of other bibliographies record current US publishing output. The most important of these is:

THE CUMULATIVE BOOK INDEX. A world list of books in the English language. New York: Wilson, 1898– . Monthly, with annual cumulation.

Author, title and subject entries in one A–Z sequence. Excludes items with fewer than 50 pages. Records 1982 to date are searchable online through Wilsonline and BRS. CD-ROM also available. *Cumulative book index (CBI)* differs from *American book publishing record* in that it is not confined to US books, recording material published in other English-speaking countries, especially Great Britain and Canada. It also has much shorter records, being intended primarily as a checklist. Despite this it is widely used for American published titles and must be regarded as a component of the US national bibliographical apparatus.

Current national bibliography in Europe largely follows the British model. Publication is usually under the auspices of the national library, with legal deposit legislation to ensure comprehensive coverage. One of the oldest-established national bibliographies is that of France, which can trace its origins back to 1811. From 1976 publication has been under the title:

BIBLIOGRAPHIE NATIONAL FRANÇAISE: bibliographie établie par la Bibliothèque Nationale de France . . .. Paris: Bibliothèque Nationale, 1976– . Semi-monthly etc.

As in several European countries the French national bibliography is issued in a number of separate series. The main listing, appearing every two weeks, is devoted to monographs. Less frequently produced series cover periodicals, government publications, music and maps and atlases. German current national bibliography has a somewhat similar publication structure, with separate trade and non-trade listings issued weekly, complemented by a CIP service and various other listings. The bibliography in its current form dates from 1991, when the East German current national bibliography was subsumed into its West German rival to create:

DEUTSCHE NATIONALBIBLIOGRAPHIE: und bibliographie der im Ausland erschienenen deutschprachigen Veröffentlichungen. Frankfurt am Main: Buchhändler-Vereinigung, 1991– . Weekly etc.

Other important European national bibliographies are the Italian *Bibliografia nazionale italiana* and the Spanish *Bibliografia española*. Both these services and *Bibliographie national française* are available as CD-ROM databases from Chadwyck-Healey. Various collaborative projects are being investigated by European national bibliographic agencies with a view to cooperation, especially in the production of electronic listings.

Retrospective national bibliographies

These present a more complex picture than current national bibliographies. Whereas the majority of current listings are officially sponsored, many retrospective bibliographies have been privately produced. As a result progress has been haphazard, dependent on the efforts of individual scholars or publishing houses. Although recent years have seen considerable effort, many countries still lack a complete retrospective bibliographical record. Another complication is that a retrospective bibliography is in a sense created by the cumulation of a current bibliography. Here we will attempt to avoid confusion by considering as retrospective only those works deliberately compiled with the objective of listing books published in the past. In the majority of cases this means bibliographies dealing with material dating from before the start of the present century. Compared with some countries Great Britian has a relatively complete national bibliographical record. Coverage of the period from the beginning of printing, around the late fifteenth-century, to the end of the seventeenth-century, is provided by two works:

Pollard, A. W. and Redgrave, G. R. A SHORT-TITLE CATALOGUE OF BOOKS PRINTED IN ENGLAND, SCOTLAND AND IRELAND: and of English books printed abroad 1475–1640. 2nd edn. London: Bibliographical Society, 1976–1991. 3v.

V. 1–2 lists c.37,000 items alphabetically by author (26,500 1st edn.). V.3 provides comprehensive indexing, including printers and publishers and places. Like Wing (below), and many other catalogues of this type, gives locations in nearly 500 libraries, including many in the United States.

Wing, D. G. (comp.) SHORT-TITLE CATALOGUE OF BOOKS PRINTED IN ENGLAND, SCOTLAND, IRELAND, WALES AND BRITISH AMERICA AND OF ENGLISH BOOKS PRINTED IN OTHER COUNTRIES 1641–1700. 2nd edn. revised and enlarged. New York: Index Committee of the Modern Language Association of America, 1972–88. 3v.

Contains about 120,000 entries (50,000 1st edn.) A–Z by author. As with Pollard and Redgrave, locations are provided in British and Northern American libraries. A revised and updated edition of v. 1 covering A–E was issued in 1994.

Pollard and Redgrave and Wing are monumental works which give as complete a picture of early British printing as possible. Both employ a numbering system which has been widely adopted by librarians and scholars as a shorthand method of referring to the books themselves. These are 'short-title catalogues' only because the excessive length of many early book titles makes complete transcription impractical. In all other respects bibliographical detail is adequate. Wing, for example, gives author, edition statement, imprint, date, format and occasionally pagination. Both bibliographies, but especially Wing, include material in

English published outside the British Isles. This is a feature shared with other British retrospective bibliographies. The development of British colonies and the consequent spread of English-language publishing after 1700 means that listings for later periods are in many ways international bibliographies of English-language books in which items published in the British Isles predominate.

The main source for bibliographical information on eighteenth century English books is unusual in that it is one of the few retrospective bibliographies of its type to be available only in database form.

EIGHTEENTH CENTURY SHORT TITLE CATALOGUE. London: British Library.

Available online via BLAISE-Line and RLIN and on CD-ROM, widely known as *ESTC*. An ongoing project, the file contained about 360,000 records in late 1995, derived from 500 participating organizations worldwide. Searching is by author, title, imprint, date, notes etc. Subjects are not searchable, but the notes field may contain some form of subject statement. *ESTC* is also available in several microfiche editions. The latest produced, in 1990 and listing 284,000 items, is accompanied by a useful 30-page explanatory pamphlet. A far less comprehensive and accurate alternative to *ESTC* which should be noted is:

Robinson, F. J. G. (comp.) EIGHTEENTH CENTURY BRITISH BOOKS: an author union catalogue extracted from the British Museum general catalogue of printed books, the catalogues of the Bodleian Library and of the University Library, Cambridge. Folkestone: Dawson, 1981–2. 5v.

Given the explosion of publishing activity that occurred in the nineteenth century it is not surprising that this is the last period to be tackled by a retrospective bibliographical listing. What is surprising is that, unlike with the eighteenth century, the method chosen is printed volumes.

NINETEENTH CENTURY SHORT TITLE CATALOGUE: extracted from the catalogues of the Bodleian Library, the British Library, Harvard University Library, the Library of Congress, the Library of Trinity College Dublin, the National Library of Scotland and the university libraries of Cambridge and Newcastle. Newcastle-upon-Tyne: Avero, 1984– .

Publication is in three series. I, covering 1801–15, is complete in 5v. II, covering 1816–70, is nearing completion 1995. III is to cover the period 1871–1918.

Nineteenth century short title cataogue is an ambitious project which appears set to continue doggedly to its conclusion. Like *ESTC* it is not geographically restricted to Great Britain, British books being 'taken to include all books published in Britain, its colonies and the United States of America'. It is, however, not without flaws either in conception or in execution. Being based on the catalogues of major libraries, it cannot be expected to be fully comprehensive. This is especially the case for books published outside the British Isles. There are also indexing problems with such a massive undertaking. Subject indexes for example, which appear in every fifth volume, contain many extremely long sequences. As the *British library general catalogue of printed books (BLC)*, which has the added advantage of being available electronically, includes a very substantial proportion of the listed items, one must question whether the project was needed in the first place.

Until *Nineteenth century short title catalogue* is complete it is largely to *BLC* that we must look for coverage of British publishing output 1871–1950. Other sources which might be consulted are *The English catalogue of books* (issued as a current listing 1864–1969, mainly valuable for the period to 1914) and *Whitaker's book list* (previously *Whitaker's cumulative book list*, which gives coverage from 1924). It is also important to remember that English is not the only British language. Although most of the bibliographies so far discussed include some books in Welsh and Gaelic, specialist works are still useful. Chief among these are:

Rees, E. (comp.) LIBRI WALLIAE: a catalogue of Welsh books and books printed in Wales 1546–1820. Aberystwyth: National Library of Wales, 1987. 2v.

Ferguson, M. and Matheson, A. SCOTTISH GAELIC UNION CATALOGUE: a list of books printed in Scottish Gaelic from 1567 to 1973. Edinburgh: National Library of Scotland, 1984.

While titles produced on the other side of the Atlantic are included in sources such as *ESTC*, it is generally best to consult specialist bibliographies when details of older American books are required. One source already noted is *American book publishing record cumulative 1876–1949*. A new work, which may be one of the last bibliographies on such a scale to appear in printed form, is

BIBLIOGRAPHY OF AMERICAN IMPRINTS TO 1901: compiled from the database of the American Antiquity Society and The Research Libraries Group. New York: Saur, 1993. 92v.

V.1–42 contain MARC-style records in title order. V.43–56 author index, v.57–71 subject index, v.72–82 place index and v.83–92 date index. This accomplished listing of 400,000 entries includes pamphlets and leaflets. Coverage is especially strong for the period to 1820. After this date an alternative and generally better source is the ongoing:

A CHECKLIST OF AMERICAN IMPRINTS . . . 1820– . Metuchen, NJ: Scarecrow Press, 1964– .

Issued in annual volumes. Has now reached the 1840s, will eventually cover to 1875.

The period 1801–19 is covered in the similar 23-volume *American bibliography: a preliminary checklist*. Other important American retrospective bibliographies are:

Evans, C. AMERICAN BIBLIOGRAPHY. Chicago: Evans, 1903–34. 14v., including indexes.

Sabin, J. A DICTIONARY OF BOOKS RELATING TO AMERICA. New York: 1868–92. 29v.

Lack of space precludes detailed consideration of the retrospective bibliographical listings of other nations. Like the United States, most other major English-speaking countries have produced their own compilations. These are usually more thorough than sources such as *Nineteenth century short title catalogue*. Australia, which has two main retrospective listings, provides a good example:

Ferguson, Sir J. A. BIBLIOGRAPHY OF AUSTRALIA, 1784–1900. Sydney: Angus & Robertson, 1941–70. 7v.

National Library of Australia. AUSTRALIAN NATIONAL BIBLIOGRAPHY, 1901–1950. Canberra: National Library of Australia, 1988. 4v.

The listing by Ferguson aims to include 'every publication relating in any way to Australia printed anywhere outside Australia as well as any imprint made in Australia'. The 1901–50 compilation produced by the National Library of Australia is intended to fill the gap between Ferguson and *Annual catalogue of Australian publications*, forerunner to the current *Australian national bibliography*.

European states with a long publishing history often rely on former current listings to trace items published over the last 100–150 years. Frequently these have been upgraded and improved by recent efforts. A good example is the German:

Geils, P. and Gornzy, W. (eds.) GESAMTVERZEICHNIS DES DEUTSCHSPRACHIGEN SCHRIFTTUMS (GV) 1700–1910. München: Saur, 1979–87. 160v.

This massive compilation combines entries from three listings, Heinsius, Hinrichs and Kayser, published on a current basis throughout the nineteenth and early twentieth centuries. Entries are arranged in one alphabetical sequence, German-language material from Austria and Switzerland is included. A further compilation, *Gesamtverzeichnis des deutschsprachigen Schrifttums (GV) 1911–1965*, extends coverage.

In other European countries similar initiatives to create and improve the retrospective bibliographical record continue to be undertaken. A good recent example is the Italian:

CLIO: CATALOGO DEI LIBRI ITALIANI DELL'OTTOCENTO (1801–1900). Roma: Editrice Bibliografica, 1991. 19v.

If current trends continue most larger European states will soon have a reasonably complete retrospective national bibliographical listing. As many of these will be based on machine-readable records there exists the prospect of creating some form of Europe-wide retrospective 'national' bibliography combining records from all languages.

BOOK TRADE OR 'IN PRINT' LISTS

Apart from national listings, probably the most commonly used type of general bibliography is the book trade list. Despite being largely structured on a national or language basis, this differs fundamentally from national bibliography in that it is limited to books, regardless of date of publication, currently available or in print from publishers. Although primarily intended for booksellers and others engaged in the book trade (hence the term 'trade list'), such bibliographies have considerable value in reference and information work. Trade listings need to be up to date, and often include new and forthcoming titles not recorded elsewhere. Because many important titles remain in print for a long period, or are reprinted, trade lists can also be used to trace older books. Other uses are checking current prices and ISBNs in connection with acquisition work, or verifying details such as publisher. By and large trade lists tend to be revised in printed form on an annual basis, often with updating supplements. Most are produced by commercial publishers or associations of publishers rather than national libraries. Almost all 'in print' listings are also available as online or CD-ROM databases.

WHITAKER'S BOOKS IN PRINT: the reference catalogue of current literature. London: Whitaker, 1874– . Annual.

Whitaker's, or *British books in print* as it was known from 1965–87, lists books published in the United Kingdom 'freely available to the general public'. English-language titles issued elsewhere are also included, provided they are 'available to the trade through a sole stockholding agent based in the United Kingdom'. Published annually, the printed version of *Whitaker's* now runs to five large volumes. Arrangement is in one A–Z sequence of authors and titles. Keyword subject entries are added where the subject forms part of the title or subtitle. Records contain generally full bibliographical detail with edition statement, pagination, size, series, price and ISBN. Microfiche versions are issued monthly and quarterly. *Whitaker's* is available online and on CD-ROM as *Bookbank* (monthly or bimonthly updating).

The American equivalent of *Whitaker's* is:

BOOKS IN PRINT. New York: Bowker, 1948– . Annual.

This is now published as a ten-volume set comprising separate author and title listings with recently out-of-print and publisher volumes. A *Subject guide to books in print,* currently issued in five volumes, provides access under modified Library of Congress subject headings. Supporting services are *Books in print supplement,* an interedition update, and *Forthcoming books,* a bimonthly listing of titles scheduled for publication within the next four months. Microfiche, online and two CD-ROM versions, *Books in print plus* and *Books in print with book reviews plus*, are also available. The latter CD-ROM is particularly notable in that full book reviews from sources such as *Library review*, *Choice* and *School library journal* are added for a number of titles.

An important recent innovation in the development of trade listings has been cooperation between Whitaker's and Bowker to produce a joint CD-ROM combining records from both databases:

WHITAKER/BOWKER GLOBAL BOOKBANK. London: Whitaker, 1993– .

Available as a CD-ROM only, issued monthly. In addition to *Whitaker's books in print* and *Books in print* records are added for Australian, New Zealand and other English-language titles. The Bowker version is marketed under the title *Global books in print Plus*.

Global BookBank provides a valuable single listing for current English-language books. Although different data structures can hinder searching, this is the largest database of current English-language books and deserves to be more widely used as a reference source. A similar CD-ROM product is:

BOOKFIND CD-ROM. Twickenham: Book Data, 1991– .

Issued monthly or bimonthly. Contents listings or title descriptions are provided for many books included. Three service levels offered: *BookFind standard*, containing UK records with title descriptions; *BookFind world*, providing international coverage but without title descriptions.

Like *Global BookBank*, *BookFind* has potential as a reference source. It is, however, generally less comprehensive, especially for more obscure items. The provision of title descriptions on *BookFind* and the addition of review extracts on the *Books in print* CD-ROM are indicative of an emerging trend. Trade lists are exploiting CD-ROM to add title descriptions and similar additional data. This will increase their usage as reference tools, possibly at the expense of more traditional sources such as national bibliographies.

A number of other English and foreign-language trade lists need a brief mention:

INTERNATIONAL BOOKS IN PRINT. Munich: Saur, 1979– . Annual.

Issued as a four-volume author/title and subject set or on CD-ROM. Despite title, confined to English-language titles published outside the

US and UK. English books from outside English-speaking countries are included.

Most English-speaking countries have nationally based trade lists. Titles include *Australian books in print, Canadian books in print, Indian books in print* and *New Zealand books in print*. These, especially the Canadian and Indian titles, generally give more comprehensive coverage for the country than *International books in print*. Two of the more important established European trade lists are:

VERZEICHNIS LIEFERBARER BÜCHER. [German books in print]. Frankfurt am Main: Buchhändler-Vereinigung, 1971– . Annual.

LIVRES DISPONIBLES. [French books in print]. Paris: Editions du Cercle de la Librairie, 1977– . Annual.

Author, title and subject sequences are provided for the print versions. Both are also available as CD-ROM databases with English-language search interfaces.

An interesting new trade list available only on CD-ROM is:

RUSSIAN BOOKS IN PRINT PLUS. London: Bowker-Saur, 1993– . Annual.

LIBRARY CATALOGUES

When considering major bibliographical tools it is important not to overlook library catalogues. The most valuable in general reference work are the catalogues of the great libraries of the world, especially national libraries or equivalent collections. Also increasingly significant are the newer, computer-based union lists which have been developed over the last few decades. Because the materials included are not bounded by geographical frontiers like national bibliographies, the largest library catalogues might almost be considered universal bibliographies. This is certainly the case with the catalogues produced by the largest library in the world, the Washington DC-based Library of Congress.

The first major published Library of Congress catalogue appeared between 1942 and 1946 in 167 volumes as *A catalog of books represented by Library of Congress printed cards issued to July 31, 1942*. This was continued by a series of further multivolume sets, beginning with 1953–7, under the title *National union catalog*. This change of title reflected the inclusion of books held in other major North American libraries. A major cumulation of the *National union catalog* has been issued as:

NATIONAL UNION CATALOG, PRE-1956 IMPRINTS: a cumulative author list representing Library of Congress printed cards and titles reported by other American libraries. London: Mansell; Chicago: American Library Association, 1968–81. 754v.

One of the greatest bibliographies ever produced in printed form, containing 11,000,000 entries. The main sequence occupies the first 685 volumes, the remainder of the set covers items added since compilation began in 1967.

At the end of 1982 printed publication of the *National union catalog* ceased, coverage continuing in the microfiche:

NATIONAL UNION CATALOG. BOOKS. Washington, DC: Library of Congress, 1983– . Monthly.

Appears in 'register' format, with indexes by name (main and added entry), title, series and subject. Indexes cumulate, with final annual cumulations plus additional cumulations such as 1983–7.

The *National union catalog* has become a bibliographical bedrock, a first port of call when details of books, particularly more obscure titles of uncertain national origin and date, are required. Its use has been greatly encouraged by various database versions. Subscription-based online access is available through BLAISE-Line, DIALOG and WilsonLine, and on CD-ROM as CD-MARC. Searching is also possible through the Internet and other networks free of charge, as *LOCIS*.

The other great universal library catalogue is that of the British Library. Like the *National union catalog*, this appeared in a number of editions. The main set is now:

BRITISH LIBRARY GENERAL CATALOGUE OF PRINTED BOOKS TO 1975. London: Saur (initially Bingley), 1981–7. 360v.

Incorporates records from the 263-volume *General catalogue of printed books* to 1955, published 1960–6. An author, or 'name' catalogue, it adopts many of the practices of its predecessors and can be confusing to the uninitiated. Online access is available through BLAISE-Line, and a CD-ROM version on five discs is available from Chadwyck-Healey.

The British Library current catalogue – that is, of material acquired since 1975 – is available in microfiche sets or in printed volumes. The latter, published by Saur as *The British Library general catalogue of printed books*, currently comprises five sequences covering 1976–82, 1982–5, 1986–7, 1988–9 and 1990–2. The online equivalent is the BLAISE-Line file *Humanities and social sciences*. A number of subject indexes to the British Library catalogue have appeared, the latest being:

BRITISH LIBRARY GENERAL SUBJECT CATALOGUE 1886 TO 1990. London: Saur, 1991–2. 42v.

It should be noted that at the time of writing the British Library catalogues are available free of charge on a networked basis to a number of mainly academic UK libraries. It is unclear whether this access, part of the *BL OPAC* experiment, will be continued and extended to other libraries.

Among the other published catalogues of the world's great libraries are:

Bibliothèque Nationale (France). CATALOGUE GÉNÉRAL DES LIVRES IMPRIMÉS DE LA BIBLIOTHÈQUE NATIONALE. Paris: Imprimerie Nationale, 1897–1981. 231v.

Supplemented by a microfiche set from Chadwyck-Healey listing material added since 1897 not included in the printed volumes.

New York Public Library. Research Libraries. DICTIONARY CATALOG OF THE RESEARCH LIBRARIES OF THE NEW YORK PUBLIC LIBRARY 1911–1971. New York: New York Public Library, 1979–83. 800v.

The only great library catalogue in dictionary format. Contains about 10,000,000 reproduced cards.

Other important general library catalogues – or, more properly, union lists – are the bibliographical databases developed by library cooperatives and similar consortia. Originally intended to support shared cataloguing these now provide a rich bibliographical resource. The best-known and largest database of this type is:

OCLC ONLINE UNION CATALOG. Dublin, Ohio: OCLC.

Available to subscribing libraries through the FirstSearch service as *WorldCat*. Contains over 30,000,000 records contributed by 14,000 libraries in nearly 50 countries.

Exceeding even the *National union catalog* in size, *WorldCat* is the ultimate union catalogue. For those libraries which access it it is an extremely powerful and flexible reference tool, the greatest single database of books and other bibliographical material so far assembled.

Although it is the major library catalogues and union lists that have most reference value, many specialized catalogues based on the holdings of individual or groups of libraries can also be useful. Worthy of mention, as they are likely to be found in major British libraries, are the British Library short-title catalogues of older foreign language books. A recent example is:

British Library. CATALOGUE OF BOOKS PRINTED IN THE GERMAN-SPEAKING COUNTRIES . . . 1601–1700 NOW IN THE BRITISH LIBRARY. London: British Library, 1994. 5v.

Library catalogues are most likely to have been published where a collection is particularly rich or notable in its field. Two examples from the sphere of children's literature are:

Toronto Public Libraries. THE OSBORNE COLLECTION OF EARLY CHILDREN'S BOOKS, 1566–1910: a catalogue. Toronto: Toronto Public Libraries, 1975–6. 2v.

University of Reading. CATALOGUE OF THE COLLECTION OF CHILDREN'S BOOKS 1617–1939 . . .. Reading: University of Reading, 1988.

A good source for further information on available library catalogues, although now somewhat dated, is:

Nelson, B. R. A GUIDE TO PUBLISHED LIBRARY CATALOGS. Metuchen, NJ: Scarecrow Press, 1982.

With the advance of computer technology and ready access to library catalogues through the Internet and other networks, it seems unlikely that many further printed multivolume library catalogues will be published. If major libraries make their catalogues freely available for network access, it is probable that reference enquiries will be increasingly directed at these sources, perhaps in preference to national bibliographies and similar listings.

SUBJECT AND SPECIALIST BIBLIOGRAPHIES

So far we have focused on bibliographies which do not restrict their scope and content to a particular subject area or topic. Although it is not the intention to deal in detail with listings compiled from a subject or other specialist approach, some consideration needs to be given to this form of bibliographical endeavour, and several types of specialist bibliography can be identified. The most obvious is the subject bibliography, in the sense of a listing devoted to material on a particular discipline or topic. Works exist on virtually every subject of significance, and many more besides. Some are published as separate 'stand alone' titles; others are issued as part of a wider series or on a periodic basis as indexing and abstracting services. The latter tend to focus on material appearing in academic journals, and as such are really beyond the scope of this chapter. Books and book chapters are, however, included in a number of the major serially published subject bibliographies. A representative and notable example is:

MLA INTERNATIONAL BIBLIOGRAPHY: of books and articles on the modern languages and literature. New York: Modern Languages Association of America, 1921– . Annual.

Dissertations also included. One of the main bibliographical sources in literature, language and related fields. A CD-ROM version is available from SilverPlatter.

In terms of style and content subject bibliographies are highly variable. Many adopt some form of internal subject arrangement and provide detailed indexes. One major stand alone bibliography, again from the field of literature, is:

Watson, G. *et al.* (eds.) THE NEW CAMBRIDGE BIBLIOGRAPHY OF ENGLISH LITERATURE. Cambridge: Cambridge University Press, 1969–77. 5v.

A bibliography of literature in a 'literary' rather than a wider sense. Arrangement is by broad periods, with subdivisions for literary forms and genres. Coverage, which extends to 1950, is confined to 'authors native to or mainly resident in the British Isles'.

A further major subject bibliography, this time from the field of history, is the *Bibliography of British history* published by Clarendon Press. This covers from earliest times to 1989 in seven period volumes. An example is:

Davies, G. and Keeler, M. F. STUART PERIOD 1603–1714. 2nd edn. 1970.

Both these bibliographies deal with wide subject areas. Works focusing on more specialist topics usually seek to provide comprehensive coverage of the subject matter and often add annotations to entries. An excellent example of this type of listing is:

Linton, D. and Boston, R. (eds.) THE NEWSPAPER PRESS IN BRITAIN: an annotated bibliography. London: Mansell, 1987.

Only significant compilation in its field, 2909 critically annotated entries clearly set out A–Z by author. Good subject, newspaper title and person indexes. A further work by Linton, *The twentieth-century newspaper press in Britain: an annotated bibliography*. London: Mansell, 1994, adds 3779 items.

Another form of specialist bibliography which might be distinguished are those listing works relating to a particular geographical location or country. These should not be confused with national bibliographies. Whereas the latter list the publishing output of a country, geographically based bibliographies list books relating to a specific country or other location wherever published. Although bibliographies of this type are relatively few in number, many are very useful from a reference point of view. The most valuable and best-known bibliographical source structured on a geographical basis is Clio's ongoing *World bibliographical series*. Aiming for eventual global coverage, each title lists and briefly annotates significant, mainly English-language, works on a particular country. Two recent but contrasting contributions are:

Day, A. ENGLAND. Oxford: Clio, 1994.

Bradt, H. MADAGASCAR. Oxford: Clio, 1993.

England contains nearly 2400 entries. *Madagascar* has around 400, a fair proportion of the important English-language sources available.

Another useful example of a geographically based bibliography is:

Konn, T. (ed.) SOVIET STUDIES GUIDE. London: Bowker Saur, 1992.

First in the publisher's *Area studies guides* series, identifies about 1000 works in discursive chapters.

Finally, it needs to be remembered that geographically based bibliographies are not always structured on a country basis: regional and other listings are also available. A British example is:

Steward, A. V. (comp.) A SUFFOLK BIBLIOGRAPHY. Ipswich: Suffolk Records Society, 1979.

3812 numbered entries with the emphasis on history; full index.

A variation on the subject bibliography frequently encountered are listings based on material relating to particular persons. Many such bibliographies deal with famous writers, artists or musicians. Frequently these include not only critical, secondary material, but also works produced by that individual. As bibliographies of this type are plentiful only a few illustrative examples can be given. A work on the grand scale is:

Namenwirth, S. M. GUSTAV MAHLER: A CRITICAL BIBLIOGRAPHY. Wiesbaden: Harrassowitz, 1987. 3v.

A more modest offering from Garland, a publisher specializing in bibliography, is:

Bryant, H. B. ROBERT GRAVES: AN ANNOTATED BIBLIOGRAPHY. New York: Garland, 1986.

Another approach to bibliography is to list material on the basis of form of publication. Some major examples, such as listings covering government publications, dissertations and conference proceedings, will be dealt with elsewhere in this book. One or two useful bibliographies of this type do, however, merit attention. A source for tracing reprinted material, often not readily located in general listings, is:

GUIDE TO REPRINTS: an international bibliography of scholarly reprints. Kent, Connecticut: Guide to Reprints, 1967– . Annual.

Directories are a further publication form for which a number of specialist bibliographical listings have been developed. For current titles the most comprehensive is:

DIRECTORIES IN PRINT. Detroit: Gale, 1980– . Annual.

Recent editions have included over 15,000 entries from all countries, although US published titles predominate.

Non-current directories are listed in a variety of specialist sources. An important but incomplete British source is:

Shaw, G. and Tipper, A. BRITISH DIRECTORIES: a bibliography and guide to directories published in England and Wales (1850–1950) and Scotland (1773–1950). Leicester: Leicester University Press, 1988.

Pre-sixteenth century printed books, or incunabula, are another distinct form of printed material for which specialist bibliographical tools are available. The most ambitious printed listing is still ongoing, and if it continues at its present pace will take many years to complete:

GESAMTKATALOG DER WIEGENDRUCKE. Kommission für der Gesamtkatalog der Wiegendrucke. Stuttgart: Hiersmann, 1925– .

Intended as an author union catalogue. Currently records around 12,000 titles of an estimated 40,000.

An alternative and increasingly preferred source is the British Library's:

INCUNABULA SHORT TITLE CATALOGUE. London: British Library, 1984– .

Available as a BLAISE-Line database. Records over 27,000 works held in libraries in Britain, North America and Europe.

One could continue to identify additional bibliographies based on form of publication, and indeed other types of specialist bibliographies such as those devoted to literary genres, historical epochs etc. So immense is the amount of bibliographical material produced that even those with good subject knowledge cannot be expected to know all the important sources within their area of expertise. Fortunately, there are a number of tools which can be consulted when it is necessary to navigate in unfamiliar bibliographical waters. It is to a brief summary of the most important of these that the remainder of this chapter is devoted.

TRACING BIBLIOGRAPHIES

Sources for tracing bibliographies can be divided into a number of broad types. Bibliographies of bibliographies – that is, works devoted to listing bibliographies – are an obvious category. Another source is guides to reference sources. Despite listing many other types of material, these usually provide information on the major bibliographical tools in any specific area. Finally, given the growing importance of electronic sources in bibliography, guides to online and CD-ROM databases are useful pointers to bibliographies available in electronic formats.

Bibliographies of bibliographies

The best-known and greatest non-specialist bibliography of bibliographies is:

Besterman, T. A WORLD BIBLIOGRAPHY OF BIBLIOGRAPHIES: and of bibliographical catalogues, calendars, abstracts, digests, indexes and the like. 4th edn. Lausanne: Societas Bibliographica, 1965–6. 4v. and index.

A monumental work recording over 117,000 separately collated volumes of bibliographies in more than 40 languages. Arranged under 16,000 subject headings, cited material is not described although the number of items listed is normally stated. Updated by *A world bibliography of bibliographies 1964–1974: a list of works represented by Library of Congress printed catalog cards*, Rowmann & Littlefield, 1977. 2v.

The best source for locating recent bibliographies of bibliographies is:

BIBLIOGRAPHIC INDEX: a cumulative bibliography of bibliographies. New York: Wilson, 1937– . 3pa., final issue annual cumulation.

Lists predominantly English-language bibliographies containing 50 or more citations. Not confined to separately published works: bibliographies appearing as part of books, pamphlets, periodicals etc. are also included.

Few other worthwhile or relatively recent English-language based general bibliographies of bibliographies exist. Most listings of bibliographies tend to be based on either particular countries or specialist subjects. A recent example of a country-based bibliography of bibliographies is:

Ingles, E. G. (ed. & comp.) BIBLIOGRAPHY OF CANADIAN BIBLIOGRAPHIES. 3rd edn. Toronto: University of Toronto Press, 1994.

General guides to reference sources

There are really only two major English-language guides to reference sources. In both, bibliographies account for a substantial proportion of the listed material. The most comprehensive source in terms of size is:

WALFORD'S GUIDE TO REFERENCE MATERIAL. 6th edn. London: Library Association, 1993–5. 3v.

V.1 Science and technology, v.2 Social and historical sciences, philosophy and religion; v.3 Generalia, language and literature, the arts. Entries are classified by UDC and have brief critical annotations.

The American Library Association produce a similar work:

Sheehy, E. P. (ed.) GUIDE TO REFERENCE BOOKS. 10th edn. Chicago: American Library Association, 1986.

Tends to be less international in coverage than *Walford*, but otherwise has in-depth annotated entries. A supplement, *Guide to reference books: covering materials from 1985–1990*, was published in 1992. A full updated edition is expected in 1996.

To trace very recently published bibliographies of bibliographies it is generally necessary to rely on standard bibliographical listings such as *BNB*. Where information beyond a bibliographical citation is required it is sometimes possible to obtain details from sources devoted to the reviewing of current reference materials. The most comprehensive general title in this area is:

AMERICAN REFERENCE BOOKS ANNUAL. Englewood, Col: Libraries Unlimited, 1970– . Annual.

Reviews over 2000 titles each year, including a good number of bibliographies.

The only British source to specialize in the reviewing of reference material, and therefore newly published bibliographies, is:

REFERENCE REVIEWS. Bradford: MCB University Press, 8pa.

About 500 titles reviewed annually.

Guides to databases

Although general works on reference materials, such as *Walford's guide*, attempt to cover electronic sources of information, detail is not always complete. For fuller coverage of bibliographies available electronically it is necessary to consult specialist sources. The pre-eminent listing of online databases is:

GALE DIRECTORY OF DATABASES. V.1. ONLINE DATABASES.
Detroit: Gale, 1993– . Semi-annual.

Each issue fully updated and revised. About 6000 entries A–Z by database name 1995; databases of a bibliographic nature specifically identified. Also available online through DataStar and as a CD-ROM from SilverPlatter.

The companion volume covering databases available on CD-ROM is:

GALE DIRECTORY OF DATABASES. V.2. CD-ROM, DISKETTE, MAGNETIC TAPE . . . . Detroit: Gale, 1993– . Semi-annual.

Rival listings of CD-ROM databases are:

THE CD-ROM DIRECTORY. London: TFPL, 1986– . Annual.

CD-ROMS IN PRINT: an international guide to CD-ROM, multimedia and electronic book products. Westport, Conn: Mecklermedia, 1987– . Annual.

A number of other subject-based online and CD-ROM database guides are also available. A notable new source is Bowker Saur's *World database series*, begun in 1993, which provides comprehensive treatment of online files on a broad subject basis.

ASSESSING AND EXPLOITING BIBLIOGRAPHIES

A bibliographical search can be considered successful if it gives an adequate quantity of citations on a topic of interest in a reasonable time. To meet this objective bibliographies must be well designed and structured. Particular attention needs to be given to coverage. Few works, other than the major national listings, can be expected to be comprehensive. It is critical, however, that scope is clearly defined and the material included well balanced. Also crucial is the avoidance of errors. Ghost entries and other inaccuracies, often carried over from the past, are all too frequently encountered and can lead to much frustration. If a bibliography is dealing with current material the extent to which material is up to date is a further critical consideration. Other general factors to take into account are the provision and suitability of complementary apparatus, such as indexes, and whether additional helpful information, such as library locations and annotations, is added.

Evaluating bibliographies and knowing which are the best to use when faced with a particular research need is a skill largely acquired through experience. The ever-expanding wealth of bibliographical resources offers new challenges and opportunities. Online and CD-ROM in particular have greatly increased the range and flexibility of bibliographical tools. The key to successful exploitation is developing a broad understanding of the major bibliographical tools available. A good knowledge of bibliographies in all their forms remains at the core of successful reference and information work.

SUGGESTIONS FOR FURTHER READING

Berger, S. E., *The design of bibliographies: observations, references and examples,* London, Mansell, 1991.

Gates, J. K., *Guide to the use of libraries and information services*, 7th edn. New York, McGraw-Hill, 1994.

Grogan, D., *Case studies in reference work. Vol. 3. Bibliographies of books,* London, Bingley, 1987.

Harner, J. L., *On compiling an annotated bibliography*, New York, Modern Languages Association of America, 1985.

Katz, W. A., *Introduction to reference work*, 6th edn. New York, McGraw-Hill, 1992. 2v.

Krummel, D. W., *Bibliographies: their aims and methods*, London, Mansell, 1984.

Mann, T., *Guide to library research methods*, Rev. pbk edn. New York, Oxford University Press, 1990.

Robinson, A. M. L., *Systematic bibliography: a practical guide to the work of compilation*, 4th edn. London, Bingley, 1979.

3
Dictionaries

Stephen T. Willis

INTRODUCTION

The word 'dictionary' is derived from the Latin dictionarium, which was a mediaeval book containing lists of words and phrases (*dictiones*). Today the word has two basic meanings: a reference book dealing mainly with words, and any alphabetically arranged reference book. This chapter will deal with the former meaning and the emphasis will be on the English language; many other alphabetically arranged reference books (often with the word 'dictionary' in their title) are covered in other chapters. Coverage of both varieties has to be highly selective, given the phenomenal numbers of dictionaries which are published: a keyword-in-title search of *Whitaker's bookbank* in December 1995, using the word 'dictionary' yielded over 17,000 references.

It may be useful first to explain some other names given to word-related reference books. 'Lexicon' is derived from the Greek *lexikon* (*biblion*) – 'word book' – and is usually applied to dictionaries of the classical and scriptural languages, the best-known example being *A Greek–English lexicon* by H. G. Liddell and R. Scott (Oxford: Clarendon Press, 1843). 'Glossary', from the Latin *glossarium*, 'a collection of glosses or explanatory notes', generally refers to a list of specialist terminology with explanations. An example is *Harrod's librarian's glossary* (8th edn, compiled by R. J. Prytherch. Aldershot: Gower, 1995). 'Thesaurus', which has passed into the language through Latin from Greek and means 'storehouse' or 'treasury', has been used by many dictionary compilers, and because of the success of *Roget's thesaurus of English words and phrases* (described later in this chapter), it is most often applied to dictionaries of synonyms, especially those presented thematically. In recent years it has acquired a new meaning as a stored list of terms used in a computerized information retrieval system.

Linguists and publishers use standard abbreviations when citing the titles of major dictionaries, such as *OED2* for the second edition of the *Oxford English dictionary*, and these conventions will be followed in this chapter when reference is made to a dictionary which has already been given a full citation.

HISTORY

The earliest known forerunners of the modern dictionary are West Asian wordlists of the second millennium BC. The Akkadians, who had inherited through conquest the culture and traditions of Sumer, inscribed in parallel columns on clay tablets thematically arranged lists of Sumerian and Akkadian words and used these as a means whereby their scribes could learn what was, in effect, the classical language of writing.[1] Similarly, in mediaeval Europe scribes learned to read Latin and added glosses in their own language between the lines of texts to explain difficult words. The first dictionaries developed as these Latin words and vernacular glosses were collected together.

The idea of producing a work in which difficult English words were explained by the use of other English words developed in the late sixteenth century, and the first published English dictionary, Robert Cawdrey's *A table alphabeticall*, with about 3000 entries, appeared in 1604. The first substantial attempt to compile a full list of English words was Nathaniel Bailey's *Universal etymological English dictionary* (London, 1721), which had 40,000 entries. The most famous pre-twentieth century work of English lexicography is Samuel Johnson's *Dictionary of the English language*, published in London in 1755. Johnson's work is a milestone in lexicography because in it he sought to encapsulate what he considered to be the best usage of the time, basing the dictionary on the language of a range of texts produced during the period 1560–1660, including literary works by Shakespeare and other major writers. Johnson's dictionary thus became accepted as the authoritative work on the English language, and the idea of a dictionary as a prescriptive tool in matters of spelling, meaning and usage was born. A deluxe facsimile edition was issued by Longmans in 1990 which incorporated Johnson's *The plan of a dictionary of the English language* (1747).

The first comprehensive account of American English was *An*

American dictionary of the English language by Noah Webster (New York: S. Converse, 1828), with 70,000 entries. *Webster's* remains one of the most important dictionaries of English and the latest edition is described below. The next major development in Britain was the compilation of the *Oxford English dictionary (OED)*. James Murray, a Scottish schoolmaster, began work in the 1870s on what was originally called *A new English dictionary on historical principles*. His approach was modelled on that advocated by the German classicist Franz Passow, and used by the Grimm brothers in the compilation of their pioneering *Deutsches Wörterbuch* (Leipzig: Hirzel, 1852–1960), in which definitions are supported by textual citations organized chronologically. The first part (*A–Ant*) was published in 1884, and by the time the dictionary was completed in 1928 there were 125 parts and the name had been changed. Although three other editors had become involved, Murray having died in 1915, it is very much Murray's work as he had set the standards and was personally responsible for over 7000 of the *OED*'s 15,500 pages.

The twentieth century has seen a move away from the prescriptive approach, with modern dictionary compilers generally trying to present their language as it is actually used rather than dictating to users on matters of correct usage. There has also been a proliferation of different editions for use in schools, colleges, libraries and homes, with single-volume, monolingual desk dictionaries and bilingual translating dictionaries among the bestselling items in bookshops. During the last 20 years new technology has brought about rapid and far-reaching developments in dictionary publishing. Publishers now maintain vast lexical databases which can be continuously updated, and from these a dictionary of a given size and scope can be easily produced in a fraction of the time it used to take. The end product need not be a printed book: it may be a CD-ROM for stand alone or network access, or a floppy disk which an author can install in his or her computer and integrate with a word-processing program. Many of the dictionaries described in this chapter are currently available in electronic as well as printed formats, and most of those which are not are likely to be eventually.

DICTIONARIES OF THE ENGLISH LANGUAGE

Unabridged dictionaries

The most comprehensive dictionaries are referred to as 'unabridged', and although there is more than one English dictionary which assumes this epithet the most definitive record of the written language can be found in:

THE OXFORD ENGLISH DICTIONARY. 2nd edn. *(OED2)*. Oxford: Clarendon Press, 1989.

The first complete edition of the *OED*, comprising ten volumes, was published in 1928. In 1933 this edition was reissued in 12 volumes, with a supplementary volume containing additional entries and a bibliography of cited works. *A supplement to the Oxford English dictionary*, recording new words and meanings, was published in four volumes over the period 1972–86. The second edition *(OED2)* integrates the *Supplement* and adds a further 5000 new entries, bringing the total to over 290,000, in which over 600,000 words are defined. Among the important changes made was the replacement of Murray's system for indicating pronunciation with the International Phonetic Alphabet (IPA). It must be borne in mind that *OED2* is not a quick-reference tool, its sheer size daunting many library users who innocently ask to be directed to 'the Oxford dictionary' only to find that several pages may be devoted to a single word. For example, the entry for 'set' runs to 60,000 words, in which 430 senses and subsenses are explained and illustrated.

As a research tool, however, *OED2* is unrivalled, as it offers a historical account of the development of each sense of each word since its first recorded appearance, illustrated by nearly 2,500,000 quotations with precise references. The CD-ROM version, which includes 5000 more words than the printed work, may be searched in a variety of ways which enable users to exploit this vast storehouse of information, the quotations forming a database in their own right to supplement standard quotations dictionaries. Specialized searches may be undertaken to ascertain, for instance, which words were first recorded in a particular year, or which author first used a particular word in literature. The results can be surprising: Jane Austen's citations include 'baseball', first recorded in *Northanger Abbey* (1818).[2] Computer technology enables continuous revision to take place and a full new edition should appear early in the next century. In the meantime, two volumes have appeared in the *Oxford English dictionary additions series* (Oxford: Oxford University Press, 1993–) covering new and newly researched words. The *OED* is widely regarded as one of the greatest of all reference books, and is one of the few for which a full-scale user's handbook has been separately published.[3] Like any national institution, however, it has had its critics. John Willinsky has recently revealed what he considers to be its inherent prejudices in an iconoclastic, sociopolitical history,[4] and James Rettig has highlighted three priorities for the compilers of the third edition: 'many of the definitions need to be brought up to date; additional reported antedatings and postdatings need to be recorded; and the English of Great Britain's former colonies needs to be more fully represented'.[5]

Two other important unabridged dictionaries are American publications:

WEBSTER'S THIRD NEW INTERNATIONAL DICTIONARY OF THE ENGLISH LANGUAGE *(W3)*. Springfield: Merriam, 1961.

W3 is actually the eighth in a distinguished line of dictionaries dating back to 1828. This edition aroused a great deal of controversy when it was first published because it differed radically from its forerunners in adopting a descriptive rather than a prescriptive approach, and including, without qualification, many terms that might be regarded as incorrect or vulgar. It is now, though, 'widely recognized as the most authoritative general American dictionary of its kind'.[6]

As in the *OED*, the different senses of words are given in chronological order (earliest first) and illustrated by quotations, although these are mostly from contemporary sources and are undated. Unusually for an unabridged dictionary, this edition, with some 450,000 entries, is significantly smaller than its predecessor (published 1934) as it omits many obsolete and rare words and foreign terms. Later printings carry addenda with new words, and three supplements covering new terms and meanings have been separately published, the latest, entitled *12,000 words*, appearing in 1986.

THE RANDOM HOUSE UNABRIDGED DICTIONARY OF THE ENGLISH LANGUAGE. 2nd edn. *(RHD2)*, revised and updated. New York: Random House, 1994.

RHD first appeared in 1966 and was promoted as a home reference work for non-specialists which was both cheaper and more user-friendly than *W3*. The second edition (first published 1988) has over 315,000 entries in the main sequence, plus a great deal of encyclopedic information in 300 pages of supplementary sections. Unlike *OED2* and *W3*, it orders senses by contemporary frequency (commonest first) and uses specially created phrases rather than quotations for illustrative purposes. Many entries have appended synonym lists and notes on usage and regional variations. The updated second edition, which has 1500 new entries, is also available on CD-ROM.

Abridged dictionaries

An abridged version of *OED2* and a substantial work in its own right is:

THE NEW SHORTER OXFORD ENGLISH DICTIONARY ON HISTORICAL PRINCIPLES. Oxford: Clarendon Press, 1993. 2v.

This is the fourth edition in a series which began with *The shorter Oxford English dictionary* in 1933, and a welcome replacement for the outdated third edition (1944; revised and reset 1973). Like the parent work it includes many quotations, but these are generally limited to one per major sense and are used primarily to illuminate semantic distinctions and to exemplify grammatical constructions, rather than to trace etymological development.

Desk dictionaries

Evaluation

The dictionaries most commonly used in libraries, offices and homes are single-volume abridged works which are often referred to as 'desk dictionaries'. As it is in this sector of the market that librarians have the most competing titles to choose from, it is worth considering the criteria against which they should be evaluated.

1 *Authority*. Dictionaries from well-established publishers, such as Oxford University Press in the UK and Merriam-Webster Inc. in the USA, can always be relied upon, but it should not be automatically assumed that they are the best. OUP, for example, was until recently noted for a conservative style of presentation which enabled competitors with more attractive, user-friendly products to gain the ascendancy.

2 *Number of entries*. It is often difficult to make direct comparisons of the size of dictionaries because publishers use different terms when describing their products, claiming to have a certain number of 'entries', 'references' or 'definitions', or using combinations of these terms. A good English desk dictionary will have well over 100,000 entries.

3 *Currency*. Each new edition of a desk dictionary should contain a substantial proportion of new words and meanings, and publishers often focus on these innovations in their publicity. However, whereas a dictionary should always be as up to date as possible, an overemphasis on vogue words which quickly fall out of fashion is not desirable.

4 *Coverage of varieties of English*. A British desk dictionary should cover American English in depth, with differences in spelling, pronunciation, meaning and usage clearly indicated, and provide reasonable coverage of other major varieties such as Australian English.

5 *Layout*. A clear page layout and the use of a range of different typefaces are essential, and several publishers have moved to larger page sizes with recent editions to enable them to improve layout and use larger type without having to reduce the number of entries.

6 *Organization of entries*. It is much easier to use a dictionary in which every word or phrase covered has its own individual entry. Dictionaries which subsume lengthy lists of related words and phrases under a single headword slow down the user and can be very confusing for non-native speakers, but they will probably be more comprehensive in their coverage. The data *within* entries should be consistently organized, and numbering the different senses of a word is particularly helpful. Senses can be ordered either chronologically, starting with the oldest, or by frequency, with the commonest meaning first. The latter arrangement is more convenient for general reference work.

7 *Contents of entries*. The minimum requirements in a desk dictionary entry for an English word are (excluding the headword and not necessarily in this order): pronunciation; part of speech label; definitions of its different senses; and etymology. Additional labels should be included to identify words or senses which are colloquial or obscene; which belong to a particular regional variety of English; or which are used in a specific profession or discipline. A good dictionary will also provide a range of phrases to illustrate the different senses, plus notes on grammar and usage.

8 *Clarity of entries*. Clarity is essential in all the elements of an entry. Pronunciation should be indicated by the IPA or an easily understood alternative method; definitions should be written in unambiguous language; and etymologies should be comprehensible to users who are not expert in linguistics.

9 *Guidance for users*. Introductory material should include clear explanations of the entries, their conventions and abbreviations, the system used

for showing pronunciation, and any special features.

10 *Encyclopedic entries.* There has been a trend recently towards the inclusion in desk dictionaries of brief entries under proper names, usually of people and places. These can be very handy for checking facts such as the age of the Prime Minister, or the population of Norway, and considerably enhance a dictionary's value for home and office users, but in most libraries such information will be available in other sources and so they may not be such an important factor in selection.

11 *Supplementary information.* Many dictionaries have appendices which include useful information such as tables of weights and measures, lists of monarchs and presidents, and even maps. These add to the work's quick reference value but, as with encyclopedic entries, may not be crucial in a library context. Abbreviations and acronyms, which used generally to be appended, are now often included in the main sequence.

Examples

The market in the UK is dominated by four titles:

THE CHAMBERS DICTIONARY. Edinburgh: Chambers, 1993 (frequently revised, but editions not numbered).

COLLINS ENGLISH DICTIONARY. 3rd edn, updated. Glasgow: HarperCollins, 1994.

CONCISE OXFORD DICTIONARY. 9th edn. *(COD9)* **Oxford: Clarendon Press, 1995.**

LONGMAN DICTIONARY OF THE ENGLISH LANGUAGE. 2nd edn. Harlow: Longman, 1991.

Each of these titles has its strengths and the most basic reference collection should contain more than one of them.

Chambers first appeared in 1901, and several editions bore the title *Chambers twentieth-century dictionary*. Because of the sheer number of words it contains (the latest edition claims 215,000 references and 300,000 definitions) and its coverage of dialect, Scots and archaic terms, it is the preferred source of word-game and crossword enthusiasts. However, in order to maintain such coverage, words derived from the same root have to be grouped under one headword rather than given their own entry, making searching slower, and the number of illustrative phrases is limited. A

CD-ROM version is available.

First published in 1979, *Collins* quickly established itself as a leader in the field, breaking new ground by including brief encyclopedic entries. The current edition has some 16,000 of these among its 180,000 entries, enough to be useful but not so many as to deflect from the dictionary's main purpose or to make it unwieldy. Derivatives and compounds are usually entered as separate headwords and definitions are augmented by illustrative phrases and usage notes. It is available on CD-ROM, coupled with *Collins thesaurus in A–Z form*, under the title *Collins electronic dictionary and thesaurus.*

COD has been one of the leading desk dictionaries since 1911, but it was never very easy to use until increased competition brought about the adoption, in the eighth edition, of a much more user-friendly format and style. This features numbered definitions written in continuous prose rather than the terse 'telegraphese' favoured by earlier editors, reduced reliance on symbols and abbreviations, and the provision of more information on grammar and usage. The ninth edition claims 140,000 meanings and a CD-ROM version is available.

Longman is another relative newcomer, first appearing in 1984, and is noted for its coverage of contemporary English throughout the world and for a number of features which reflect the publisher's long involvement in producing materials for teachers and learners of English as a foreign language (EFL). These include extensive guidance on grammar and usage, placed within boxes scattered throughout the dictionary, and generous use of illustrative phrases taken from a corpus of twentieth century texts. The second edition claims 100,000 headwords, including some proper names, and 220,000 definitions.

There is similar competition in the American desk dictionary market, where the leading titles include *The American heritage dictionary* (3rd edn. Boston: Houghton Mifflin, 1992), which is the largest with around 200,000 entries; *Merriam-Webster's collegiate dictionary* (10th edn. Springfield: Merriam-Webster, 1993); *Random House Webster's college dictionary* (New York: Random House, 1991); and *Webster's New World dictionary of American English* (3rd college edn. New York: Simon & Schuster, 1988). This list clearly illustrates how the name 'Webster's' is used by other publishers to lend authority to their dictionaries. The CD-ROM version of *Merriam-Webster's collegiate dictionary* includes digitally recorded pronunciations of each main entry word.

Encyclopedic dictionaries

Some European countries have a long tradition of publishing encyclopedic dictionaries, probably the best-known example being *Le Petit Larousse illustré*, first published in France in 1856. The popularity of the inclusion of brief encyclopedic entries in recent editions of certain British desk dictionaries has led some publishers to produce what they describe as 'encyclopedic' or 'reference' dictionaries, such as:

CHAMBERS ENCYCLOPEDIC ENGLISH DICTIONARY. Edinburgh: Chambers, 1994.

THE OXFORD ENGLISH REFERENCE DICTIONARY. *(OERD)* Oxford: Oxford University Press, 1995.

Encyclopedic entries here are longer than those in desk dictionaries, giving, for example, potted biographies for historical figures rather than merely dates and a brief description. *Chambers* claims 14,000 out of a total of 70,000 entries, whereas *OERD* claims 120,000 dictionary definitions plus over 12,500 'definitions in depth' offering encyclopedic information. Both supply extra data by means of appended maps and tables, which in *OERD* run to over 100 pages. The amount of basic linguistic information has to be limited in order to accommodate the encyclopedic articles, but these dictionaries are large enough to satisfy all but the most esoteric word enquiries and represent good value.

Illustrated dictionaries

Some publishers, particularly American ones, include occasional line drawings in standard dictionaries, but these are inevitably limited in size and number and add little to the definitions. A dictionary based completely on labelled illustrations can, however, be extremely useful to anyone seeking the precise meaning of a technical term and, in particular, to language learners.

Corbeil, J. C. and Manser, M. THE FACTS ON FILE VISUAL DICTIONARY. Oxford: Facts on File, 1988.

THE OXFORD–DUDEN PICTORIAL ENGLISH DICTIONARY. Oxford: Oxford University Press, 1981.

ULTIMATE VISUAL DICTIONARY. London: Dorling Kindersley, 1994.

The OUP title listed here is based on the German publisher Duden's *Bildwörterbuch der deutschen Sprache* (3rd edn, 1977). It has 384 sets of labelled drawings (all but six in black and white), each covering the vocabulary of a particular subject, which identify some 28,000 objects or activities. An alphabetical index of terms follows the illustrations. Unfortunately, most of the illustrations have not been updated since they were first drawn, and although this does not matter in some subjects (e.g. flora and fauna or musical instruments), in many areas they look distinctly old-fashioned.

The Facts on File visual dictionary is a British edition of a dictionary developed in Canada. It has over 3000 labelled illustrations arranged thematically under 28 main headings, followed by general and thematic indexes to the 25,000 terms illustrated. The high-quality drawings include detailed cutaways and cross-sections. A full-colour four-language edition, with new computer-generated artwork, is due to be published by Oxford University Press in 1996 as *The visual dictionary*. Dorling Kindersley specialize in high-quality illustrated reference works, particularly for young people, and their *Ultimate visual dictionary* is a very attractive product. It has 6000 colour pictures (many of them photographs) on 320 elegantly produced page openings, with 30,000 terms labelled and indexed.

SPECIALIZED ENGLISH DICTIONARIES

English learners' dictionaries

These are dictionaries intended for the use of foreign- and second-language learners but are printed entirely in English. They are also known as 'EFL dictionaries' and 'ELT dictionaries'. This is an area of English lexicography where much progress has been made in the last 20 years towards easier access and more lucid presentation. 'Such dictionaries have not only become a genre in their own right but have begun to influence the organization of mother-tongue dictionaries'.[7] The traditional leader in the field is:

Hornby, A. S. THE OXFORD ADVANCED LEARNER'S DICTIONARY OF CURRENT ENGLISH. 5th edn. *(OALDCE5)*. Oxford: Oxford University Press, 1995.

This dictionary first appeared in 1948 as *A learner's dictionary of current English*, and for 30 years had few rivals. The current edition has over 60,000 entries, and is noted for its extensive coverage of idiomatic expressions and generous provision of corpus-based illustrative phrases. Recent publications which offer an alternative to *OALDCE* include:

COLLINS COBUILD ENGLISH DICTIONARY. 2nd edn. London: HarperCollins, 1995.

THE CAMBRIDGE INTERNATIONAL DICTIONARY OF ENGLISH. Cambridge: Cambridge University Press, 1995.

LONGMAN DICTIONARY OF CONTEMPORARY ENGLISH. 3rd edn. Harlow: Longman, 1995.

Each of these dictionaries has its own innovations in terms of layout, pronunciation guidance, usage notes etc., but a common feature is the move towards definitions written in complete sentences, often using a strictly controlled 'defining vocabulary'. Illustrative sentences are drawn from massive computerized corpuses of contemporary texts to ensure that actual current usage is reflected, *COBUILD*, for instance, using the 200 million-word Bank of English. *COBUILD on CD-ROM* (Worthing: HarperCollins Electronic Reference, 1994) incorporates the dictionary, grammar and usage guides from the same publisher, and a Word Bank containing five million words from the corpus.

Regional dictionaries of English

English is spoken by 377 million people as their first language, by 98 million as a second language, and is the dominant or official language in over 60 countries.[8] Larger general reference collections should include dictionaries of the major national varieties, such as:

Branford, J. and Branford, W. A DICTIONARY OF SOUTH AFRICAN ENGLISH. 4th edn. *(DSAE4)* Cape Town: Oxford University Press, 1991.

DSAE records words which have originated in South Africa or have a special significance there, with quotations from a range of sources supporting the definitions. It has had to be updated three times since it first appeared in 1978, in order to keep pace with the changes in the language brought about by the rapidly developing political situation, and the latest edition includes many quotations from black writers/speakers and from sources previously banned. A more comprehensive dictionary 'on historical principles' is in preparation.

Etymology

Etymology is the study of the history of words. Whereas all good desk dictionaries include basic information on word origins, specialist works are required to deal with more complex enquiries.

THE OXFORD DICTIONARY OF ENGLISH ETYMOLOGY. *(ODEE)* Oxford: Oxford University Press, 1966.

THE BARNHART DICTIONARY OF ETYMOLOGY. New York: Wilson, 1988.

ODEE is the standard work, covering over 38,000 words and word elements such as prefixes and suffixes. Entries indicate in which century the word was first recorded in English and trace developments in form and meaning since then. Based on contemporary American English, *Barnhart* includes many words not covered by *ODEE*. Its 30,000-plus entries are written in a very accessible style, avoiding technical terminology and confusing abbreviations, and coverage of word elements is particularly comprehensive.

Pronunciation

A specialist pronunciation dictionary lists words in Roman letters followed by their equivalents in a phonetic transcription, with stress-marked and variant pronunciations given.

Jones, D. ENGLISH PRONOUNCING DICTIONARY, CONTAINING OVER 59,000 WORDS IN INTERNATIONAL PHONETIC TRANSCRIPTION. 14th edn, revised with a supplement. *(EPD14)* Cambridge: Cambridge University Press, 1991.

Wells, J. C. LONGMAN PRONUNCIATION DICTIONARY. *(LPD)* Harlow: Longman, 1990.

Jones; *EPD* first appeared in 1917 and quickly came to be regarded as the standard source on received pronunciation (RP), the accent generally associated with educated British English. A. C. Gimson's 14th edition

(1977) represents a comprehensive revision, with the definition of RP broadened to cover a wider sample of contemporary speakers. Over 15,000 proper names and abbreviations are included. Wells uses essentially the same transcription system as Jones, but he gives recommended American as well as British pronunciations for 75,000 words, including technical vocabulary and proper names. Good use of colour, typefaces and symbols makes *LPD* a user-friendly source which is particularly useful for students and teachers of English as a foreign language.

Loanwords

As English has borrowed extensively from other languages, it is not surprising that several dictionaries of loanwords have been compiled. The best of these provide etymological information and guidance on pronunciation, as well as definitions and explanations.

Bliss, A. DICTIONARY OF FOREIGN WORDS AND PHRASES IN CURRENT ENGLISH. London: Routledge, 1966.

Ehrlich, E. (ed.) LE MOT JUSTE: THE PENGUIN DICTIONARY OF FOREIGN TERMS AND PHRASES. 3rd edn. New York: Harper & Row; London: Viking, 1988.

Bliss has over 5000 informative entries, giving the date of first introduction (where possible), many illustrative quotations, and guidance on usage, spelling and transliteration. Ehrlich provides less information on each term, but defines over 15,000 words and phrases and has many new entries in the latest edition, which was reprinted in 1993 as simply *The Penguin dictionary of foreign terms and phrases.*

Neologisms

By releasing new editions more frequently, publishers of general dictionaries are nowadays keeping track of new coinings better. Nevertheless, dictionaries devoted to new words also appear regularly and are able to provide much more contextual information.

THE OXFORD DICTIONARY OF NEW WORDS. *(ODNW)* Oxford: Oxford University Press, 1991.

THIRD BARNHART DICTIONARY OF NEW ENGLISH. New York: Wilson, 1990.

ODNW deals with only 2000 neologisms from the 1980s, but the lengthy entries provide a great deal of information on pronunciation, etymology and usage, and include chronologically arranged illustrative quotations from international literature and journalism. *Third Barnhart* supersedes similar works published in 1973 and 1980, and lists some 12,000 new terms and meanings recorded in the English-speaking world since 1960. Entries include substantial quotations with full bibliographical information.

Slang

The key feature of slang is that it is constantly changing and the pace of change is so rapid, particularly among young people, that lexicographers cannot possibly keep up with it. This has not stopped them from trying, and many slang dictionaries have appeared since J. C. Hotten's pioneering *Dictionary of modern slang, cant and vulgar words* . . . (London: Hotten, 1859), most notably:

Partridge, E. A DICTIONARY OF SLANG AND UNCONVENTIONAL ENGLISH: COLLOQUIALISMS AND CATCH PHRASES, FOSSILISED JOKES AND PUNS, GENERAL NICKNAMES, VULGARISMS AND SUCH AMERICANISMS AS HAVE BEEN NATURALISED. 8th edn. *(DSUE8)* London: Routledge, 1984.

The subtitle gives some indication of the scope of this extraordinary work, which first appeared in 1937. Early editions were notable for the inclusion of sexual and scatological vulgarities which were at that time omitted from the *OED* and standard desk dictionaries, with asterisks replacing vowels in order to comply with the obscenity laws. The latest edition, edited by Paul Beale, has approximately 55,000 entries in the main sequence plus nearly 100 appended articles on specific types of slang and related topics such as nicknames.

DSUE covers English slang at all periods and should be supplemented by a record of contemporary slang, such as:

Ayto, J. and Simpson, J. A. THE OXFORD DICTIONARY OF MODERN SLANG. *(ODMDS)* Oxford: Oxford University Press, 1992.

Thorne, T. BLOOMSBURY DICTIONARY OF CONTEMPORARY SLANG. London: Bloomsbury, 1990.

Green, J. THE MACMILLAN DICTIONARY OF CONTEMPORARY SLANG. Basingstoke: Macmillan, 1995.

ODMS has over 5000 entries for words and meanings which have been current in the twentieth century, most of them taken from *OED2*. In most cases there is at least one illustrative example from a published source, which is unusual in a slang dictionary. Thorne covers the period 1950–90 and has entries for over 5000 words likely to be encountered in contemporary literature, popular music and the media. Green crams 14,000 entries into an inexpensive paperback, and although he is unable to provide more than a brief definition for each term, he does cite sources (books, films, TV programmes) in many cases.

All of the works cited above include American slang, but for specific coverage of that subject see R. L. Chapman's *New dictionary of American slang* (New York: Harper & Row, 1986). This work has been criticized because it seldom gives even approximate dates for the first appearance of terms and its illustrative quotations are undated, but a more scholarly approach to the subject is taken by the *Random House historical dictionary of American slang* (New York: Random House, 1993–), which is based on dated examples from written and oral sources. Volume One (A–G) of this projected three-volume set appeared in 1994.

Synonyms

Dictionaries of English synonyms have been popular since George Crabb's *English synonymes explained* was published in 1816. It is still occasionally reprinted, but the best-known synonym dictionary is:

Roget, P. M. ROGET'S THESAURUS OF ENGLISH WORDS AND PHRASES. New edn. Harlow: Longman, 1987.

Peter Mark Roget was a physician when the work which was to make him a household name was published in 1852. Rather than to give the meaning of words, his object was (as he states in the Introduction) 'the idea being given, to find the word, or words, by which that idea may be most fitly and aptly expressed'. To achieve this end, he grouped terms within six main 'classes', which were further subdivided into numbered 'sections' 'subsections' and 'heads of signification'. The latter form the basic units of the book, and this edition has 990. The 'heads' are divided into paragraphs, beginning with an italicized keyword, within which terms are grouped according to meaning, context or stylistic level, and there are numerous cross-references to other 'heads'. An alphabetical index of 45,000 terms provides access via references to headwords and keywords. In all, 250,000 words and phrases are included, 11, 000 of them new to this edition, which has improved coverage of technology and includes the notorious 'four-letter words' for the first time.

Roget's thesaurus has never lost its popularity, but most readers, rather than access it in the way Roget intended, head straight for the index, which he saw as a safety net for anyone having difficulties. As Sydney Landau points out, 'however ingenious the hierarchy of concepts, it was pure fantasy to suppose that any conceptual arrangement of the vocabulary of English was natural to most native speakers'.[9]

BLOOMSBURY THESAURUS. London: Bloomsbury, 1993.

Most recent synonym dictionaries have been alphabetically arranged but this one embraces Roget's subject approach, with a new classification scheme which is more relevant to contemporary English and allows better coverage of science and technology. 350,000 terms, including labelled American and Australian words, are grouped under 879 headwords and alphabetically indexed.

Urdang, L. THE OXFORD THESAURUS: AN A–Z DICTIONARY OF SYNONYMS. Oxford: Oxford University Press, 1991.

This is probably the best of the many alphabetically arranged thesauri on the market. It lists 275,000 terms under 8500 headwords, giving lists of synonyms for each sense of the headword and an illustrative sentence for each sense group. These sentences, which are lively and idiomatic, together with the clear labelling of words typical of a particular geographical or stylistic variety of English, elevate this dictionary above the many basic collections of word lists on the market. A CD-ROM version is available.

None of the works listed above provides very much guidance to the user who wants to distinguish carefully between the various synonyms for a particular term. Dictionaries which do so are described as discriminatory, and are particularly useful for non-native speakers grappling with the subtle nuances of meaning that distinguish apparently synonymous words. Two examples are:

CASSELL GUIDE TO RELATED WORDS. London: Cassell, 1994.

WEBSTER'S NEW DICTIONARY OF SYNONYMS. Springfield: Merriam, 1968.

Webster's has discursive entries dealing with many thousands of terms under 7000 alphabetically arranged headwords. Differences in meaning are illustrated by sample sentences and quotations from literature. The *Cassell guide* deals with around 6000 terms under 1400 keywords, using illustrative sentences but no quotations. Both works include useful lists of autonyms with each entry.

Usage guides

Guidance on matters of usage, including grammar, spelling, pronunciation, morphology and distinctions of meaning, is often presented in dictionary form for ease of reference. The best examples will have numerous examples, extensive cross-references and possibly even an index.

Fowler, H. W. A DICTIONARY OF MODERN ENGLISH USAGE. 2nd edn. *(MEU2)* Oxford: Clarendon Press, 1965.

Manser, M. H. (ed.) BLOOMSBURY GUIDE TO BETTER ENGLISH. 3rd edn. London: Bloomsbury, 1994.

Fowler is noted for his well-written and occasionally humorous articles on contentious issues, and the first edition of *MEU* (Oxford: Clarendon Press, 1926) has been described as 'a blend of prescription, tolerance, and idiosyncracy'.[10] It has also been asserted, however, that 'in spite of a few instances where his interpretations can be called progressive, he remains a defender of the attitudes of the well-educated, upper-class Englishman' and that the usages he recommends do not reflect the language of educated people in Britain or America today.[11]

The second edition, which includes revisions by Sir Ernest Gowers and makes some concessions to American usage, is still in print but has many competitors, of which Manser's *Bloomsbury guide* (formerly entitled *Bloomsbury good word guide*) is a very accessible example. Like other contemporary guides it pays due attention to American usage and gives advice on the avoidance of discriminatory language. For more comprehensive guidance in these areas see *Webster's dictionary of English usage*, edited by E. W. Gilman (Springfield: Merriam-Webster, 1989), and R. Maggio's *The dictionary of bias-free usage* (2nd edn. Phoenix: Oryx Press, 1991), both of which are alphabetically arranged.

DICTIONARIES OF SPECIALIST TERMS

Every profession, occupation and academic discipline has its own vocabulary, consisting of words and phrases which are used exclusively by its practitioners and of standard English terms which have a different meaning in that particular sphere of activity. For example 'gigabyte' is unique to information technology, whereas 'mouse' has been given a specific meaning within that context. There are hundreds of dictionaries of specialist vocabulary and the best ones, as well as defining terms, give explanations of their origin and development, illustrate their use, and are fully cross-referenced. Two well-established examples are:

Crystal, D. A DICTIONARY OF LINGUISTICS AND PHONETICS. 3rd edn. Oxford: Blackwell, 1991.

Cuddon, J. A. A DICTIONARY OF LITERARY TERMS AND LITERARY THEORY. 3rd edn. London: Blackwell, 1991.

Crystal defines, explains and exemplifies around 1500 linguistic terms and provides references to standard textbooks where further information can be found. Cuddon gives similar treatment to nearly 3000 literary terms.

NAMES

A group of specialist dictionaries which has grown markedly in recent years is that covering proper names, and one man who has made a major contribution to this proliferation is Adrian Room, who has produced over 20 authoritative reference works on the subject, including dictionaries of pseudonyms, place names, trade names and animal names. There are so many name dictionaries available that only a few examples can be described here.

Room, A. CASSELL DICTIONARY OF PROPER NAMES. London: Cassell, 1994 (first published 1992 as *Brewer's dictionary of names*).

Payton, G. THE PENGUIN DICTIONARY OF PROPER NAMES. London: Viking, 1991 (revised edn. by J. Paxton of *Payton's proper names*, first published London: Warne, 1969).

These two works complement each other, there being so many proper names worthy of an entry that overlap is limited. Payton has about 11,000 entries and Room over 8000, covering a wide range of names that are likely to be encountered in literature and the media, including places, events, titles of artistic works, buildings, vehicles, political and religious organizations and many more. Entries explain the significance of the name, and Room is particularly strong on etymology.

Apart from place names, which are covered in the chapter on local history, the categories of names most likely to generate enquiries are forenames and surnames.

Hanks, P. and Hodges, F. A DICTIONARY OF FIRST NAMES. Oxford: Oxford University Press, 1990.

This dictionary covers over 7000 names, its main sequence having entries for names used in Britain, Europe and North America, tracing each name back to its linguistic root and listing variant forms, such as diminutives and pet versions. The entries include information about the fluctuations in popularity of individual names and there are supplementary sequences of names used in the Arab world and on the Indian subcontinent.

Hanks, P. and Hodges, F. A DICTIONARY OF SURNAMES. Oxford: Oxford University Press, 1988.

Reaney, P. H. A DICTIONARY OF ENGLISH SURNAMES. 3rd edn. London: Routledge, 1991.

Reaney is the acknowledged authority on specifically English surnames and gives the meanings of over 16,000, with scholarly notes on etymology. Hanks and Hodges cover a much wider field, dealing with 70,000 surnames from the English-speaking world and Europe, in 10,000 entries which explain the linguistic origins of each name and provide information on its history and current distribution.

QUOTATIONS AND ALLUSIONS

Quotations dictionaries

The quotations dictionary is one of the most heavily used specialist dictionaries in any reference library, but no single work can hope to include all the quotations about which enquiries are received. There are plenty to choose from, with new compilations appearing regularly to challenge the hegemony of the established standard works.

The most common arrangement for a quotations dictionary is by author/speaker, either alphabetically or chronologically, but some are arranged thematically, a format which is useful for writers and speakers seeking quotations on a particular topic. Whichever layout is adopted, a thorough keyword index is essential to give plenty of access points for each quotation. It is particularly important for reference purposes that citations are precise, giving dates for publications and speeches, and chapter (or even page) numbers for quotations from novels, stanza numbers for poems, and act/scene/line numbers for plays. Additional contextual information (e.g. the place where a speech was made) and biographical details of authors/speakers increases the dictionary's usefulness.

Three general compilations are very well established:

OXFORD DICTIONARY OF QUOTATIONS. 4th edn. *(ODQ4)* Oxford: Oxford University Press, 1992.

Barlett, J. FAMILIAR QUOTATIONS: A COLLECTION OF PASSAGES, PHRASES AND PROVERBS TRACED TO THEIR SOURCES IN ANCIENT AND MODERN LITERATURE. 16th edn. Boston: Little, Brown, 1992.

Stevenson, B. E. THE HOME BOOK OF QUOTATIONS, CLASSICAL AND MODERN. 10th edn. New York: Dodd, 1974.

Arranged alphabetically by author, the *ODQ* was first published in 1941. The latest edition contains some 17,500 quotations, by 2500 authors, and has around 75,000 entries in its keyword index. The *ODQ* and its companion work, *The Oxford dictionary of modern quotations*, are also available on a single CD-ROM.

Bartlett, which is one of the oldest continuously published reference books, first appeared in 1855. It is arranged chronologically by author, provides extra information in footnotes, and is noted for its precise citations and thorough indexing. The 16th edition has over 22,500 quotations from 2550 people. A multimedia version is available on *Microsoft bookshelf* (Microsoft, 1993).

First published in 1934, *Stevenson* is one of the biggest compilations, with over 50,000 entries listed under alphabetically arranged subject headings. The tenth edition was published in the UK as *Stevenson's book of quo-*

tations (London: Cassell, 1974).

Quotations dictionaries, where keyword indexing is so important, lend themselves to electronic publishing and a new source which is likely to establish itself quickly is:

GALE'S QUOTATIONS: WHO SAID WHAT? Detroit: Gale Research, 1995.

This CD-ROM contains 117,000 quotations and is available in network and stand alone versions. Author and keyword searches may be carried out, alphabetical lists of quotations can be browsed, and an extended search function allows users to employ multiple qualifiers (e.g. name, occupation, nationality, keyword) from any part of the record. An alternative electronic source is *Microsoft bookshelf*, which offers a multimedia version of *Bartlett* and *The concise Columbia dictionary of quotations*, along with other reference tools on the same CD-ROM.[12]

Andrews, R. THE COLUMBIA DICTIONARY OF QUOTATIONS. New York: Columbia University Pres, 1993.

BLOOMSBURY TREASURY OF QUOTATIONS. London: Bloomsbury, 1994.

Rees, N. BREWER'S QUOTATIONS: A PHRASE AND FABLE DICTIONARY. London: Cassell, 1994.

Andrews lists over 18,000 quotations under 1500 subject headings, claiming that 11,000 of them have never previously appeared in a general quotations dictionary. *Bloomsbury* has over 20,000 quotations by 3000 people in one alphabetical sequence of thematic and biographical entries, the latter including notes about the person's life, quotations by and about him or her and cross-references to other relevant entries. Although *Brewer's quotations* has only 2000 entries, arranged A–Z by author, it is extremely useful because it deals with 'the most commonly misquoted, misattributed, misascribed, misremembered and most disputed sayings that there are': in other words, those which are very frequently sought. Entries include lengthy contextual notes, precise citations and details of variant forms and misattributions.

As so many enquiries relate to recent quotations, general quotations dictionaries should be supplemented by more specialized works listing sayings of the twentieth century, such as *The Penguin dictionary of twentieth-century quotations* by J. M. and M. J. Cohen (3rd edn. London: Viking, 1993). Larger reference libraries should also include works listing quotations by particular groups of people, e.g. E. Partnow's *The new quotable woman: from Eve to the present day* (revised edn. New York: Facts on File, 1992; London: Headline, 1993).

Allusions

Allusions are indirect references (as opposed to direct quotations) which are frequently used by authors and journalists. The potential for allusion to literature, mythology, folklore, history and popular culture is endless and a range of sources is required, of which the best known is:

BREWER'S DICTIONARY OF PHRASE AND FABLE. 15th edn. London: Cassell, 1995.

The first edition was compiled by Ebenezer Cobham Brewer, a Victorian clergyman and schoolmaster, and published by Cassell in 1870. Its subtitle talks of 'giving the derivation, source, or origin of common phrases, allusions, and words that have a tale to tell'. Those terms of reference have been largely adhered to in subsequent editions, and the book has become one of the best-loved reference works, perhaps because it so often provides the answer to an enquiry when other sources have been exhausted. For the latest edition, which has 20,000 entries, Adrian Room has revised and updated the entire text, provided more precise citations and expanded the eytmologies.

BREWER'S DICTIONARY OF TWENTIETH CENTURY PHRASE AND FABLE. 2nd edn. London: Cassell, 1994.

Because allusions are so often made to contemporary culture, a purely twentieth-century version, with 8000 entries in the style of the parent work, was published in 1991. A selection of entry words from two pages gives some idea of the scope: Prohibition, proms, Pru (man from the), Prufrock, pseud, Psmith, psychedelia. Also strong on popular culture is Nigel Rees's *Bloomsbury dictionary of phrase and allusion* (London: Bloomsbury, 1991).

Concordances

A concordance is the ultimate quotations dictionary as it lists every occurrence of each significant word in a particular text, or in the works of a specific author, with references to passages in which each indexed word appears. Computer technology has greatly facilitated production and concordances of the works of a wide range of authors are now available, but the ones most frequently encountered are those covering the Bible and the works of Shakespeare. J. Bartlett's *Complete concordance to Shakespeare* (first published London: Macmillan, 1894) remains popular and is regularly reprinted, although *The Harvard concordance to Shakespeare* by M. Spevack (Cambridge: Harvard University Press, 1973), an abbreviated version of a computer-generated three-volume work, is the most comprehensive single-volume Shakespeare concordance. A. A. Cruden's *Complete concordance to the Old and New Testament*, first published in 1737, remains the best-known Bible concordance and is based on the Authorized Version of 1611. Choice of a concordance will depend on which of the many versions of the Bible is to be accessed.

DICTIONARIES OF FOREIGN LANGUAGES
It is not within the scope of this chapter to describe the available dictionaries across the whole range of foreign languages, but the main types of dictionaries will be exemplified with reference to French.

Comprehensive monolingual
LE GRAND ROBERT DE LA LANGUE FRANÇAISE: DICTIONNAIRE ALPHABETIQUE ET ANALOGIQUE DE LA LANGUE FRANÇAISE. 2nd edn. Paris: Robert, 1985. 9v.

This is an outstanding *OED*-style dictionary, giving comprehensive coverage of French since the fifteenth century with entries supported by precisely referenced quotations. A CD-ROM version, *Le Robert électronique*, provides rapid and flexible access to all elements of the 80,000 entries.

Single-volume monolingual
LEXIS: DICTIONNAIRE DE LA LANGUE FRANÇAISE. New edn. Paris: Larousse, 1992.

One of the many Larousse dictionaries, this is strong on contemporary vocabulary and includes words from Belgian, Canadian and other varieties of French. When using a bilingual dictionary for translation work it is often necessary to refer to a monolingual dictionary like this to verify nuances of meaning.

Comprehensive bilingual

For serious translators a multivolume work is essential, and for French this has for many years meant:

HARRAP'S STANDARD FRENCH DICTIONARY. London: Harrap, 1977–80. 4v.

This dictionary, with 250,000 headwords, could once claim to be the largest bilingual reference work in existence, but it now faces competition from the *Larousse French dictionary* (unabridged edn. Paris: Larousse, 1994), which packs 300,000 entries (including encyclopedic ones) into a single volume and is also available in a more manageable two-volume edition, and the *Collins-Robert comprehensive French–English/English–French dictionary* (2v. Glasgow: HarperCollins, 1995), which has 400,000 entries and includes a thesaurus of each language.

Single-volume bilingual

For most reference collections single-volume bilingual dictionaries are adequate, and for French there are a number of excellent examples, including:

COLLINS–ROBERT FRENCH DICTIONARY. 4th edn. Glasgow: HarperCollins, 1995.

HARRAP'S SHORTER FRENCH DICTIONARY. New edn. London: Harrap, 1991.

LAROUSSE STANDARD FRENCH DICTONARY. Paris: Larousse, 1994.

OXFORD–HACHETTE FRENCH DICTIONARY. Oxford: Oxford University Press, 1994.

As with English desk dictionaries there is intense competition in this sector of the market, which serves teachers and students as well as libraries. The dictionaries cited are from publishers who all produce reliable bilingual dictionaries for several European languages and, as some of the titles suggest, collaboration between British and foreign publishers is common. Each dictionary has at least 220,000 entries and the criteria for evaluation are essentially the same as for an English desk dictionary, with clarity and ease of use paramount. In addition, it is essential that plenty of examples of words and phrases in use are provided in both sections. Supplementary material on grammar and usage adds value to many dictionaries in this category. CD-ROM versions are becoming available, the first to appear being *Harrap's French shorter electronic dictionary* (London: Harrap, 1994).

Specialist translating

There are countless specialist translating dictionaries available, covering broad subject areas such as business, and more specific topics like banking. Dictionaries of this kind, which have a limited market, are usually produced by specialist publishers and tend to be very expensive.

ROUTLEDGE FRENCH DICTIONARY OF BUSINESS, COMMERCE AND FINANCE. London: Routledge, 1995.

This is the first of a new series of specialist dictionaries to be published by Routledge, all of which will also be available in electronic formats (CD-ROM and diskette), allowing translators to integrate them with their word-processing software.

Polyglot dictionaries

Dictionaries covering several languages have long been available in specialist subject areas, and the Dutch firm Elsevier is one of the leading publishers. A major example is the International Electrotechnical Commission's *Electricity, electronics and telecommunications multilingual dictionary* (5v. Amsterdam: Elsevier, 1992), which covers nine languages.

The advent of computer technology has enabled the production of general polyglot dictionaries on CD-ROM, such as:

HARRAP'S CD-ROM MULTILINGUAL DICTIONARY DATABASE. London: Harrap, 1989.

This is actually 18 separate bilingual dictionaries on one CD-ROM, giving access to 7 million words in 12 languages. The dictionaries include both general and specialist words and may be searched separately or jointly.

SOURCES OF INFORMATION ABOUT DICTIONARIES

Encyclopedias

The most comprehensive source of information on all aspects of lexicography is *Dictionaries: an international encyclopedia of lexicography*, edited by

F. J. Hausman and others (Berlin: de Gruyter, 1989–91). Its three volumes contain 334 articles by specialist contributors writing in either German, French or English, including 114 essays on the lexicography of individual languages. Each article has a bibliography. Although few reference libraries are likely to stock this monumental work, all should have *The Oxford companion to the English language*, edited by T. McArthur (Oxford: Oxford University Press, 1992) whose coverage of lexicography is exemplary. It contains entries on lexicographical terms, major lexicographers, the lexicography of varieties of English, dictionary publishers and over 50 individual dictionaries.

Bibliographies

In addition to general sources such as *Walford's guide to reference material, vol. 3: Generalia, language and literature, the arts* (6th edn. London: Library Association, 1995) and the *Guide to reference books* (10th edn. Chicago: American Library Association, 1986; *Supplement*, 1992), there are a number of specialist bibliographies of dictionaries. A potentially useful, but rather idiosyncratic, source is T. Kabdebo's *Dictionary of dictionaries* (London: Bowker-Saur, 1992), which evaluates 6000 mainly English-language dictionaries and encyclopedic reference works (both current and historical) under A–Z headings for languages, subjects and key titles. It must be treated with caution, as although the entries are lively and readable the selection of material varies widely between subjects. Probably the most comprehensive listing is A. M. Brewer's two-volume *Dictionaries, encyclopedias and other word-related books* (4th edn. Detroit: Gale, 1988), which includes reproductions of Library of Congress catalogue cards for some 35,000 works, arranged by author and indexed by title and subject.

Selection tools

Which dictionary? a guide to selected English language dictionaries, thesauri and language guides, by B. Loughridge (London: Library Association, 1990), gives advice on dictionary evaluation, reviews both general and specialist works, and makes recommendations for purchase. However, electronic sources are excluded and it is unfortunate that the second edition planned for 1995, which would have extended coverage to these, has been delayed. *Kister's best dictionaries for adults and young people*, by K. F. Kister (Phoenix: Oryx Press, 1992) performs a similar function for American publications, reviewing and evaluating 300 titles, including electronic sources. The most detailed reviews of new English-language dictionaries are to be found in the periodical *English today* (Cambridge: Cambridge University Press. Quarterly). The best sources of information on the availability of foreign-language dictionaries are the catalogues produced by specialist dealers such as Grant & Cutler Ltd. The major publishers of dictionaries, such as Collins and OUP, regularly produce very informative specialist catalogues which indicate at which sector of the market each title is aimed.

Perhaps the last word on dictionary selection should be left to the most celebrated English lexicographer, Dr Johnson: 'Dictionaries are like watches; the worst is better than none, and the best cannot be expected to be quite true'.[13]

REFERENCES

1 McArthur, T. (ed.), *The Oxford companion to the English language*, Oxford, Oxford University Press, 1992.

2 Hartston, W., 'Jane Austen hits a home run', *Independent*, 23 November 1995.

3 Berg, D. L., *A guide to the Oxford English dictionary*, Oxford, Oxford University Press, 1991.

4 Willinsky, J., *Empire of words: the reign of the OED*, Princeton, Princeton University Press, 1994.

5 Rettig, J., 'The jewel in the crown: the *Oxford English dictionary*', in Rettig, J. (ed.), *Distinguished classics of reference publishing*, Phoenix, Oryx Press, 1992, 180–97.

6 Sader, M. (ed.), *General reference books for adults: authoritative evaluations of encyclopedias, atlases and dictionaries*, New York, Bowker, 1988.

7 McArthur, T., *op. cit.*, 594.

8 Crystal, D., *The Cambridge encyclopedia of the English language*, Cambridge, Cambridge University Press, 1995.

9 Landau, S., *Dictionaries: the art and craft of lexicography*, New York, Scribner, 1984.

10 McArthur, T., *op. cit.*, 1076.

11 Landau, S., *op. cit.*, 211.

12 Reviewed in *RQ*, **35** (1), 1995, 105–6.

13 Johnson, S., *Letters of Samuel Johnson: vol. 3*, Oxford, Clarendon Press, 1952.

SUGGESTIONS FOR FURTHER READING

Bailey, R. W. (ed.), *Dictionaries of English: prospects for the record of our language*, Ann Arbor, University of Michigan Press, 1987; Cambridge, Cambridge University Press, 1989.

Burchfield, R. (ed.), *Studies in lexicography*, Oxford, Clarendon Press, 1987.

Crystal, D., *The Cambridge encyclopedia of language*, Cambridge, Cambridge University Press, 1987.

Green, J., *Chasing the sun: dictionary makers and the dictionaries they made*, London, Cape, 1996.

Grogan, D., *Grogan's case studies in reference work: vol. 5, Dictionaries and phrase books*, London, Library Association, 1987.

McArthur, T., *Worlds of reference: lexicography, learning and language from the clay tablet to the computer*, Cambridge, Cambridge University Press, 1986.

Murray, K. M. E., *Caught in the web of words: James Murray and the Oxford English dictionary*, New Haven, Yale University Press, 1977.

Osselton, N. E., *Chosen words: past and present problems for dictionary makers*, Exeter, University of Exeter Press, 1995.

Rettig, J. (ed.), *Distinguished classics of reference publishing*, Phoenix, Oryx Press, 1992 (lengthy chapters on *Brewer's dictionary*, Fowler's *Dictionary of modern English usage*, *OED*, *Roget's thesaurus* and *Webster's dictionary*, with detailed publishing histories and extensive bibliographies).

4

Encyclopedias

A. John Walford

The term 'encyclopedia' implies a complete system of learning, a comprehensive reference work covering either all branches of knowledge, as in the *New encyclopaedia Britannica*, or a particular subject area like *World of art*. The quick-reference A–Z order of entries is usual; for sustained reading thematic chapters, plus a detailed analytical index, may well be the answer. The title 'encyclopedia' could be equated to 'dictionary', as in *The new Grove dictionary of music and musicians*, or simply as 'companion', as in *The Oxford companion to chess*. Titles of some subject encyclopedias can be deceptive: a compendium such as *Merck index* has the subtitle 'an encyclopedia of chemicals, drugs and biologicals'.

CRITERIA

Authority

One test of an encyclopedia's worth is its reputation for longstanding excellence. *Black's medical dictionary*, now in its 38th edition, began publication in 1906. Moreover, the present editor, G. Macpherson, was formerly assistant editor of the *British medical journal* and is now Vice-President of the British Medical Association. M. Eliade's *Encyclopedia of religion* (1987. 16v.) comprises signed articles by an international team of 150 specialist contributors.

Arrangement

The first edition of *Encyclopaedia Britannica* (1771. 3v.) consisted of 45 treatises. That on 'surgery' ran to 238 pages, with definitions of technical terms, A–Z. The *New encylopaedia Britannica* splits its alphabetical sequence into two main parts: 'ready reference' (Micropaedia. 12v.) and 'knowledge in depth' (Macropaedia. 17v.). An introductory survey, 'Outline of knowledge' (Propaedia, 1v.) precedes, and an extensive two-volume index completes the 32-volume set. The *Oxford illustrated encyclopedia* – primarily for youngers – assigns eight of its nine volumes to separate subject areas (1. The physical world . . . 8. People and cultures). Entries in each volume are in A–Z order. Volume 9 is the cumulated 'index and ready reference'.

Level

The *World book encyclopedia* is intended primarily for elementary and secondary school readers, with suitable vocabulary and colour illustrations. Its accuracy and readability make it equally acceptable to adults and librarians as a ready-reference source. The *Fontana dictionary of modern thought* 'steers a middle course between an ordinary dictionary and an encyclopedia' (*Preface*). Clearly written, it is addressed to both the ordinary person and the specialist reading outside his particular area. On the other hand, Professor Eysenck's *Blackwell dictionary of cognitive psychology* is clearly for the professional.

Slant

Imbalance can take two forms. The first is disproportionate allocation of space to a particular field. National pride is a leading factor. American encyclopedias devote several pages to the lives and achievements of US presidents, and US states are each given preferential treatment, with double-page spread maps and gazetteers. The great Spanish 'Espasa' encyclopedia devote a whole volume to 'España'. The second imbalance is often ideological. The *Great Soviet encyclopedia* is one example. Another is the 1924–33 edition of *Meyers neues Lexikon*, whose producers openly hailed the coming of National Socialism in the Germany of 1933. In 1946 the Meyer concern was liquidated, but subsequently revived.

Currency

There are various devices for keeping encyclopedias up to date. Annual revision of 10% of the text is normal practice. *Academic American encyclopedia* claims 20% annual revision. *Compton's encyclopedia* has annual revision of selected subjects. The *New encyclopaedia Britannica* had complete overhauls in 1974 and 1985, apart from 'annual revision'. Yearbooks mainly highlight events of the previous year, but subject encyclopedias fare better. *McGraw-Hill encyclopedia of science and technology*'s yearbook (1961–) helps to update selected topics in the encyclopedia and is well indexed.

One-volume encyclopedias can overhaul their text more promptly. *The Cambridge encyclopedia* has had two editions, in 1990 and 1994, and *Hutchinson's encyclopedia* (now in larger format) has virtually annual 'touching up'.

Visual appeal

The first part of the Royal Horticultural Society *Gardeners' encyclopedia of plants and flowers* (1993) consists of 4000 colour photographs of flowers arranged by colour or by season of interest. The second part is an A–Z dictionary of 8000 plants, cross-referenced, where appropriate, to the colour photographs. *The Pelican history of art*, in about 50 volumes, uses both monochrome and colour to illustrate architecture, sculpture and paintings. The photographs are placed adjacent to the relevant text. This similarly applies to the pictorial work in *A world history of art*, by H. Honour and J. Fleming (King, 1992. 766p). The illustrations number 1151, including 472 plates in full colour, 20 maps, 106 grounds plans and 21 time charts. The 2000 illustrations and maps in *Hutchinson's encyclopedia* are also placed close to the relevant text, but they are nearly always squeezed into three colour pages. Graphics are well exploited, in the forms of stills and animations in the multimedia encyclopedia.

Biographies

The new Grove dictionary of music and musicians (1980. 20v.) includes 16,300 biographical entries for composers, instrument makers etc. *The new Grove dictionary of women composers* (1993) selects 875 composers, from Sappho to Ethel Smythe: it claims to cover women composers at every level and for every purpose.

St James Press *Contemporary poets* (5th edn. 1991) comprises profiles of over 800 English-language poets in the form of bibliographies – works by and about them, signed critical assessments and, at times, 'self-portraits'.

Bibliographies

Ideally, bibliographies in encyclopedias should contain lists of books, citations of periodical articles and other source materials. When lengthy they should be annotated, and they should include notes 'for further reading'.

The article in Eliade's *Encyclopedia of religion* on 'Chinese religion' runs to 30 pages and has a four-column annotated bibliography. The 200-page bibliography in volume 24 of *Collier's encyclopedia* is grouped into clearly defined subject fields, giving the reader an understanding of the relationship of one branch of knowledge to another. The general index to *Collier's encyclopedia* includes subjects that figure in the 'Bibliography'.

Typography and format

The phrase 'small print' has ominous overtones. The magnifying glass that accompanies the compact edition of the *Oxford English dictionary* could well be applied when searching through indexes. They include the index to the *Oxford dictionary of quotations* and the *Mitchell Beazley Joy of knowledge*. Adoption of a two-column page for the *New encyclopaedia Britannica's* Macropaedia volumes is better for prolonged reading than the three-column page of the Micropaedia quick-reference volumes (1995). The 1996 *Hutchinson's encyclopedia* not only has a three-column page but also has a margin to accommodate quotations. The *Cambridge encyclopedia*, with a wide page, can more comfortably accommodate location maps, diagrams and tables.

The flimsy paper used in the *Columbia encyclopedia*, with its 3072 pages, makes it unsuitable for constant handling – apart from the fact that its weight is over 10 lb (for consultation purposes a lectern should be available). The *New encyclopaedia Britannica* itself is not immune from the charge of flimsy paper.

Spine lettering of encyclopedias calls for some attention, especially when a set is placed on a bottom shelf. *World Book encyclopedia* has allocated single letters of the alphabet to volumes in its set, whenever possible, and the brightly-coloured spine of the *Encyclopedia Americana* has unerringly drawn students to its presence on the shelves. *Collier's encyclopedia* also has a pleasing appearance.

ENGLISH-LANGUAGE ENCYCLOPEDIAS

THE NEW ENCYCLOPAEDIA BRITANNICA has a long history. The *New encyclopaedia Britannica* (15th edn. 1974, 1985 editions) reflects complete overhaul and restructuring.

It first appeared in 1788–91 as *Encyclopaedia Britannica* in three volumes. The 11th edition of 1910–11 was the last British version, at the peak of its scholarly reputation. Change of publisher and editor does not always augur well. In the 1929 edition, articles marked 'x' after the original contributor's initials meant that the scissors had been applied, sometimes injudiciously. Division of the main text into Micropaedia ('ready-reference') in 12 volumes, and Macropaedia ('knowledge in depth') in 17 volumes, was a basic innovation. The 60,000 entries in the Micropaedia average 275–300 words. They are either self-contained or summarized for quick reference, pointing to the Macropaedia for fuller treatment. Thus, 'French literature' in the Micropaedia has three columns; in the Macropaedia it runs to 30 pages. The article on USA in the Macropaedia also runs to 30 pages. The two-volume index (v.31–32) has over 500,000 entries and is a vital key to the whole. The prefatory volume 1, Propaedia ('outline of knowledge'), is less frequently consulted. The *Britannica*, with its 5000 contributors, still leads the encyclopedia field in authority and comprehensiveness. *Britannica book of the year* (1938–) included 'The year in review, statistical data, feature articles, and an occasional reprint, updated from Macropaedia'. *Britannica electronic index* and a CD-ROM version are available. 'Annual revision' continues.

ACADEMIC AMERICAN ENCYCLOPEDIA (Grolier, 1980– . 21v.) is also published in the UK as *Macmillan family encyclopedia* (now *Lexikon universal encyclopedia*).

Its aim is fourfold: to provide quick access to information; general accuracy; as a starting-point for further research; and as an aid to regularization. The set is intended for secondary schools, colleges and the 'enquiring' mind. Its 30,000 articles are usually signed, with brief references. Volume 21 has 21,000 index entries. Illustrations, mostly in colour, number 17,000. This Grolier encyclopedia, as it is also called, has a CD-ROM version and a *Grolier multimedia encyclopedia* (qv).

COLLIER'S ENCYCLOPEDIA, with bibliography and index (New York: Macmillan, 1949– . 24v.)

Has 25,000 signed articles by some 5000 contributors. Illustrations, mostly monochrome, number 14,500. Articles on US states figure prominently, with double-page spreads, map and gazetteer. The text is engagingly written and addressed to advanced students and adults. A leading feature is volume 24, with a 200-page bibliography – 24,000 briefly annotated entries, assembled under broad subjects. The 400,000 entry index

includes references to illustrations as well as items in the bibliography.
Collier's international yearbook (1950–) is well organized, being based on
an A–Z sequence. It records events of the previous year, plus topical essays
and statistics. Cross-references link yearbook and the parent set.

**EVERYMAN'S ENCYCLOPEDIA (6th edn. Dent, 1978. 12v.) first appeared
in 1913–14.**

The small octavo format accommodates shortish articles by 350 contributors. Illustrations are all monochrome. A British slant is reflected in
the outline maps of countries and entries for London, Oxford and
Cambridge colleges. Longer articles are sectionalized. Volume 1 lists contributors, although articles are unsigned. Easy to handle, *Everyman's*
seems intended for desk and home use. The absence of an index –
although there are cross-references – is a definite drawback. (An atlas is
appended to volume 12.) *Everyman's* is online through DIALOG.
Compensation for the lack of coloured illustrations is neatly met in the
New illustrated Everyman's encyclopedia (1978), first issued in 80 weekly
parts. This has about 1000 illustrations, largely in colour. Articles in the
parent set appear in condensed form, but there is still no index.

A recent British contender in the middle-sized range of general encyclopedias is *Hutchinson's unabridged encyclopedia* (Helicon Publishing,
1995. 8v.).[1] It has 34,000 entries (*Everyman's* 50,000), including dictionary
defintions. All illustrations are in colour. The index provides 60,000
entries. Helicon Publishing also produce *Hutchinson's multimedia encyclopedia*.

ONE-VOLUME ENCYCLOPEDIAS
**THE COLUMBIA ENCYCLOPEDIA (5th edn. Columbia University Press,
1993. 3048p.) first appeared in 1935; 4th edition 1975.**

The 5th edition claims 60% revision. Editorial staff number nearly
100; academic advisers 114. The *Columbia* is declared to be an 'American
encyclopedia for the Americans', but coverage is international. The
50,000 entries are in three-column form on flimsy paper. A feature is the
inclusion of short bibliographies (e.g. 'West Indies: five book items).
Illustrations are limited to some 500 black and white line drawings and
diagrams, plus maps. Chief lack is an index, although there are some
65,000 cross-references. The weight of the volume is about 12 lb, surely
calling for the provision of a lectern.

THE CAMBRIDGE ENCYCLOPEDIA (1990. 2nd edn. 1994. 1337p.) edited by D. Crystal.

Has 30,000 unsigned entries. Over 100 specialists contributed. There are 75,000 cross-references but no index. The 750 line drawings include neat two-column location maps. The final 128 pages on yellow-tinted paper provide a wealth of ready-reference data, from 'Deaf and dumb alphabet' to 'The northern sky'. End-papers illustrate *c*.180 national and international flags. A weighty quarto, with a pleasing two-column page.

THE HUTCHINSON ENCYCLOPEDIA, 1996 (Helicon, 1995, 1132p.)

First appeared in 1948. This 1996 edition has a larger format, with over 26,000 short unsigned entries but over 60 contributors are listed. Not only is the page three-column but margins are used for citing quotations. Provision of cross-references is inadequate.

CHAMBERS ENCYCLOPEDIC ENGLISH DICTIONARY (1995. 1424p.)

This also adopts a three-column page. There are 60,000 entries in all. Dictionary entries occupy 1–3 lines; biographies and subject entries average ten lines. ('South African Republic': half a page including a map). There are also 12 colour maps.

JUNIOR ENCYCLOPEDIAS

WORLD BOOK ENCYCLOPEDIA (Chicago and London: World Book, 1917– . 22v. Annual revision).

Has over 3000 contributors. Articles number 17,000 and illustrations 29,000 (80% in colour). The main aim is to provide information for elementary and secondary schools. It also functions as a handy reference tool for adults and librarians. Format and layout are attractive, and single letters of the A–Z sequence are allocated to most volumes. Currency, accuracy and readability are well maintained. Volume 22 is the 'index and research guide'. Technical terms are italicized and explained. *World Book yearbook* organizes entries in A–Z sequence, updating the parent set. *World Book encyclopedia* has CD-ROM and multimedia versions (qv).

CHILDREN'S BRITANNICA (London: Encyclopaedia Britannica. 4th edn. 1988. 20v.)

Has slim volumes, each indexed. There are 4230 articles and 130 pages of maps. The set is intended for upper forms in primary schools and offers a British approach. Volume 20, the consolidated index, has 30,000 entries. Over 50% of the illustrations are in colour. This is a widely used set for home and school use.

COMPTON'S ENCYCLOPEDIA and fact index (1922–92. Encyclopaedia Britannica, 1993– . Chicago: Compton's Learning Co. 26v.)

Has 22,500 entries and as many illustrations (36% in colour). *Compton's* is intended for young people aged 9–18, with a reading list prefacing each volume. Bibliographies on major subjects number about 400. The set is available on CD and multimedia.

OXFORD ILLUSTRATED ENCYCLOPEDIA (Oxford: Oxford University Press, 1985–93. 9v.)

For youngsters aged 12 and upwards. Each volume, purchasable separately, covers a major subject field: 1. The physical world; 2. The natural world; 3/4. History; 5. The arts; 6. Invention and technology; 7. The universe; 8. People and cultures. Each volume has some 400 pages in A–Z sequence. Volumes 3 and 4 each have 130 colour illustrations and 60 line drawings. Volume 9 is 'Index and reading reference'. Well produced and authoritative, this set is written by specialists for the non-specialist.

NEW BOOK OF KNOWLEDGE (Grolier, 1912– . 21v.)

Continuous revision) has 9000 entries, usually signed, and is intended for youngsters aged 7–14. Illustrations are abundant. Each volume has an index, cumulated in volume 21. Five-yearly overhaul of the set is under way. Available on CD-ROM.

FOREIGN-LANGUAGE ENCYCLOPEDIAS

'The forefront of encyclopedia progress has passed overseas', wrote H. Einbinder,[2] the American critic, in 1980. He based this impression on (a) the striking visual appeal of *La grande encyclopédie, Encyclopedia universalis,* and the Dutch *Grote Winkler Prins encyclopedie;* and (b) their depth of treatment of current topics, plus new devices in presenting data. Thus, *Grote Winkler Prins* (8th edn. Amsterdam: Elsevier, 1979–82. 25v.) offers well documented and illustrated information in coloured panels and tables. It includes details of events of a succession of centuries (e.g. Volume 2, the events of the second century AD). *Encyclopedia universalis* devotes its final volume, 'Symposium', to essays on controversial world

issues. Einbinder condemns the so-called 'annual revision' of US encyclopedias – selective patching up of the text – and the eye-catching yearbooks that offer little systematic updating of encyclopedia text.

German

German encyclopedias have a long history. Although international in
scope, they give preferential treatment to Central Europe.

BROCKHAUS ENZYKLOPÄDIE (19th edn. 1986–) follows a main A–Z sequence (volume 1–24; v.25), *Personenregister*, is followed by part 1 of a German-language dictionary (A–GLUG. 1995. 1360p.).

The stout octavo volumes make much use of marginal illustrations.
The protracted publication of the main text is partly compensated for by
adding new material at the end of every sixth volume. *Der Brockhaus in
einem Band* (6th edn. 1994) has 55,000 brief entries and mostly marginal
illustrations.

MEYERS ENZYKLOPÄDISCHES LEXIKON (9th edn. 1972–84)

Generally considered to be the most comprehensive German encyclopedia. Volumes 1–25, A–Z, have a supplement (volumes 26–27), *Personen-
register*; volume 28; *Weltatlas* plus volume 29; *Bildwörterbuch* (illustrated
trilingual dictionary: Deutsch–English–Französich) and volume 30:
Deutsches wörterbuch. The main set is well illustrated and documented,
with a two-column page (less congested than *Brockhaus*). Biographies
include living persons. The set is updated by a yearbook, 1973– .

French

The pride taken by the French in their language, its precision and style, is
reflected in the diversity of French dictionaries and encyclopedias.

LA GRANDE ENCYCLOPÉDIE LAROUSSE (Larousse, 1971–8. 20v. and index) supplements (1981, 1985, 1990).

Stresses twentieth-century achievements and 8000 lengthy signed articles give prominence to French places and personalities. Its ample pages
accommodate 14,000 illustrations, and the index has 400,000 entries. *Atlas
générale Larousse* (1976) provides 184 pages of maps, a gazetteer of 34,000
place names and a statistical section. *La grande encyclopédie* appeals to a
wide public, and the dearth of French public libraries adds to its value as

a working tool for students who need to obtain their baccalaureate as a stepping stone to a career.

GRAND DICTIONNAIRE ENCYCLOPÉDIQUE LAROUSSE (1982–5. 10v.)

Updated but condensed version of *La grande encyclopédie Larousse* for quick reference. Its format is less generous, with a three-column page, small illustrations and marginal drawings. Bibliographies – 190,000 in all – are at the end of each volume, where they could be overlooked. Maps number 250.

ENCYCLOPEDIA UNIVERSALIS (Paris, 1985. 20v.)

Has some features in common with the 1985 *Britannica*, breaking with the Larousse tradition. Thus, *Corpus* (18v.) is a kind of Macropaedia, the substantial entries having 60,000 references attached to them. *Thésaurus* (3 volumes) resembles the Micropaedia in having an abundance of short entries in small print on a four-column page. Volume 20, *Symposium*, contains essays on the contemporary world. One article 'Espace (conquête de l')' occupies 32 pages, with 51 illustrations (21 in colour) and four columns of bibliography. The encyclopedia has a yearbook that includes a cumulative index covering 1974–85 issues.

PETIT ROBERT 2: dictionnaire universal des noms-propres alphabétique et analogique (new edn. 1988. 1932p.)

The fullest of the French one-volume encyclopedias. The 38,000 entries cover historical, geographical, art, literary and science proper names. *Petit Robert 2* is, in fact, a single-volume version of the five-volume *Dictionnaire universal alphabétique et analogique* of 1984. *Petit Robert 2* is superior to the corresponding second part of *Petit Larousse en couleurs* (annual).

Italian
ENCYCLOPEDIA ITALIANA DI SCIENZE, LETTERE ED ARTE (Rome: Istituto della Enciclopedia Italiana, 1929–39. 36v. Appendices 1–5, 1938–92)

Authoritative signed articles and fine-quality illustrations. Humanities and social sciences are particularly well covered. In the main set 87 pages cover 'Inghilterra': history, language, ethnography and folklore, art, music and literature. Bibliographies attached to articles are extensive and include periodical article references. Appendices become more international, more concerned with scientific and technical achievements. The ample page size accommodates not only illustrations but also maps (by Touring Club Italiano). *Grande dizionario enciclopedico UTET* (4th edn. Turin, 1984–93. 25v.) has a standing similar to that of the *Enciclopedia italiana*. Volume 21, *Grande atlante geografico e statistico*, has 387 pages of general maps and 178 of historical maps. The index runs to 785 pages.

Spanish
ENCICLOPEDIA UNIVERSAL ILUSTRADA EUROPEO–AMERICANA (Barcelona: Espasa, 1905–33. 80v. in 1981. Appendices 1–10)

The largest twentieth-century encyclopedia, with over one million unsigned articles. 'Espasa', as it is called, goes beyond the functions of a general encyclopedia by including a multilingual dictionary (French, Italian, English, German, Catalan, Esperanto and Spanish equivalent terms) plus a gazetteer and biographical dictionary. Emphasis throughout is on the Iberian peninsula. Volume 21: 'España' is revised at ten-yearly intervals. Latin America is also well covered. An annual supplement (1924–) has a cumulative index 1934–80 (1980).

Russian
THE GREAT SOVIET ENCYCLOPEDIA: a translation of the 3rd edition of *Bol'shaya sovetskaya entsiklopediya*, **was published by Macmillan (New York: 1973–83. 31v.).**

It is a volume-by-volume English translation. Each volume has its own A–Z sequence of articles, usually with bibliographies. All the original maps and most of the illustrations have been omitted. To locate specific topics the cumulative index must be consulted. Volume 31 of the translation is devoted to the Soviet Union.

SUBJECT ENCYCLOPEDIAS
In order to show the diversity of types of subject encyclopedia, the following examples are arranged in Dewey class order.

THE ENCYCLOPEDIA OF LIBRARY AND INFORMATION SCIENCE (New York: Dekker, 1969–), known as *ELIS*, is virtually a serial publication.

Volume 52 appeared in 1994, and supplements come out at intervals. As the only English-language encyclopedia of its kind, *ELIS* is invaluable, even if haphazardly edited. Volumes 46–47 contain *c*.60,000 author and subject index entries to a wealth of contributions on librarianship theory and practice, on individual libraries and institutions worldwide, plus profiles of deceased librarians. Volume 52, supplement 12 (1992) has 18 articles on a range of topics. The essay 'CD-ROM in libraries' occupies pages 89–136, including 15 pages of references.

THE ENCYCLOPEDIA OF PHILOSOPHY (Collier-Macmillan, 1993. 4v.)

1450 signed, well-documented articles, A–Z, by 500 contributors from 24 countries. The editor, P. Edwards, says of the first edition (1967. 8v.) that 'some of the longer articles are in effect small books and even the shorter articles are long enough to allow a reasonably comprehensive treatment of the subject under discussion'. This allows contributors to express opinion, sometimes controversially. The detailed subject index has 38,000 entries.

Eliade, M. (ed.) ENCYCLOPEDIA OF RELIGION (Collier-Macmillan, 1987. 16v.)

Intended for the 'educated non-specialist reader'. It contains 2000 articles, including 130 biographies and is truly international in scope. Whereas D. Hastings' *Encyclopedia of religion and ethics* (1908–27. 12v. and index) has a western approach, Eliade's encyclopedia gives some weight to eastern religions. This is a 'no-nonsense' compilation: it omits illustrations and maps but is rich in bibliographies. The index (332 pages) includes a directory of contributors, an A–Z list of articles and a synoptic outline of contents.

INTERNATIONAL ENCYCLOPEDIA OF THE SOCIAL SCIENCES (New York: Macmillan, 1968. 18v. 8v. reprint 1977) Includes biographical supplement)

Designed to supplement, not to supplant, the earlier *Encyclopedia of the social sciences* (Macmillan, 1930–5). It contains 1900 entries by 1500 specialists. Whereas the 1930–5 set had 4000 biographies, these are now reduced to a few hundred, excluding living persons born after 1890. Emphasis is on theory and methodology, psychology and sociology. Articles average 1500 words: that on Karl Marx has seven pages. The many cross-references supplement a 40,000-entry index, which includes a classified list of articles. The one-volume *The social science encyclopedia* (Routledge & Kegan Paul, 1985. 516p.) gives a more contemporary approach. Coverage is wide-ranging and multidisciplinary, discussing social issues. Most articles carry references and suggestions for further reading. There is no index.

THE NEW PALGRAVE: a dictionary of economics (Macmillan, 1986. 4v.) is edited by W. Eatwell and others.

The original Palgrave dictionary of political economy appeared in 1923–6, and a new edition was certainly overdue. The 1988 version, with 2000 articles by some 900 specialists, is impressive. Every entry has references. Biographies number about 900. Cross-references are ample and the detailed analytical index has a classified list of articles and an appendix. However, treatment is scholarly and mathematical, beyond the scope of the average economics students. Again, a one-volume *Macmillan dictionary of modern economics* (4th edn. 1992) fills a gap for the reader in economics, business and social sciences, although this lacks references and further reading.

Crystal, D. THE CAMBRIDGE ENCYCLOPEDIA OF LANGUAGE (1987. 479p.)

Focused on the history and structure of language, how children acquire languages, and languages around the world. The 11 chapters have 85 sections. A visual approach is stressed, with 50 maps and 500 other graphics. Eight appendices include further reading, references and three indexes.

Comrie, A. (ed.) THE WORLD'S MAJOR LANGUAGES (Croom Helm, 1987. 1033p.)

Has over 40 contributors. It offers a grammatical and linguistic survey of 50 language groups, each with bibliography and references. The language index covers about 800 languages – a rich quarry for the researcher. Diagrams, tables and maps also feature.

THE McGRAW-HILL ENCYCLOPEDIA OF SCIENCE AND TECHNOLOGY (7th edn. 1992. 19v. and index)

Over 7500 entries by 3000 contributors. Revision of the 1987 edition includes medicine, chemistry, environmental sciences and engineering. Signed articles have short bibliographies. Biographical and historical articles are excluded. The *McGraw-Hill yearbook* (1962–) updates entries in the main set between editions. There are spin-offs of the *McGraw-Hill encyclopedia*, ranging from astronomy, physics, chemistry, the geological sciences, ocean and atmospheric sciences, energy, engineering, electronics, environmental sciences, to food, agriculture and nutrition. The *McGraw-Hill dictionary of scientific and technical terms* defines 100,000 terms, each categorized with pronunciation, making this dictionary the best single-volume source for definitions in all areas of science.

VAN NOSTRAND'S SCIENTIFIC ENCYCLOPEDIA (7th edn. 1988. 2v. 3180p.)

First published in 1968, embraces mathematics, physics, chemistry, biological sciences and medicine. Special contributors number 200; photographs and line drawings over 2000. Major entries are documented. The 9500 cross-references supplement the 109-page index. In its day *Van Nostrand* was reckoned to be the world's most used one-volume scientific reference.

BLACK'S MEDICAL DICTIONARY (38th edn. 1995. 656p.)

First issued 1906, includes new material on hospital medicine, genetics, immunology, medical tests and travel health. Widely used by the general public, *Black's* has notes on causes, symptoms and treatment. It follows British practice. *The Oxford companion to medicine* (1986. 3v.) separates British and US practice in such areas as dentistry, hospitals and nursing. *The Oxford companion* has documented entries (e.g. 'Law and medicine in the UK' has two columns of references).

ALEXIS LICHINE'S NEW ENCYCLOPEDIA OF WINES AND SPIRITS (7th edn. Cassell, 1987. 771p.) started in 1967.

The ten chapters of the present edition range from the history of wine and spirits to the distillation of spirits, listing of wines and a vintage chart. A select bibliography precedes the detailed index, pp.731–77. There are 60 maps. Alexis Lichine is a wine grower and former wine merchant and this encyclopedia is considered to be the leading work in its field.

INTERNATIONAL ENCYCLOPEDIA OF COMMUNICATIONS (New York: Oxford University Press, 1988. 4v.) has 400 specialist contributors.

The 569 A–Z entries cover mass media, theatre, language, literature and cinema. 'Communications' is defined as 'all ways in which information, ideas and attitudes pass among individuals, groups, nations and generations'. Articles are documented, and there are 1100 black-and-white photographs plus line drawings. The approach is academic, and some articles are too specialized for the lay person. Cross-references link subjects, and the analytical index has 15,000 entries.

KIRK, R. E. AND OTHMER, R. F. (eds.) ENCYCLOPEDIA OF CHEMICAL TECHNOLOGY (3rd edn. Wiley, 1978–84. 26v., supplement and general index) began in 1947 (15v. plus two supplements).

About half of the 1300 articles in the third edition concern chemical substances. Whereas the second edition had an entry 'Literature on chemical technology', this now appears as 'Information retrieval' (50 references) and 'Patent literature' (80 references). Chemical Abstracts Service Registry Numbers are cited throughout, making 'Kirk–Othmer' the first point of reference on properties, manufacture and use of any chemical, industrial process, method of analysis etc. The third edition is on CD-ROM. The fourth edition (1991–) proceeds at the rate of one new volume every three months. The *Concise* edition (3rd ed. 1986p.) has extensive cross-references as well as an index.

HALLIWELL'S FILM GUIDE (10th edn. HarperCollins, 1990. 1400p.)

A standard source for data on 13,000 films, arranged A–Z by title. Information on each film states country of origin, year of release, running time, black-and-white/colour production, credits, alternative titles, synopsis, assessment, and credits. Emphasis is on British and US films. By contrast, E. Katz's *The Macmillan international film encyclopedia* (2nd edn. 1994. 1496p.) concentrates on the film business. Over 7000 entries deal with the film industry, country by country, film organizations, people, events, inventions, techniques, processes and equipment. This encyclopedia was first published in 1979. Coverage of many minor performers is an asset.

INTERNATIONAL DICTIONARY OF THEATRE (London: St James Press. 1992. 3v.) deals with the theatre from ancient Greece to modern times.

Volume 1 considers 600 of the most performed plays in the world theatre, the works of 350 dramatists, plus bibliography, a lengthy, authoritative assessment and further reading list. Volume 2 gives profiles of 485 playwrights, A–Z, with bibliographies. Volume 3 concerns actors, directors and designers, with bibliographies and signed critical essays. A well-organized survey.

Drabble, M. (ed.) THE OXFORD COMPANION TO ENGLISH LITERATURE (new edn. 1995. 1155p.)

First published in 1932, with a second edition in 1983. The later two editions omit most of the illusions in the first editions. There are 7000 entries covering authors, works, literary schools and movements, genres, terms, characters and literary periodicals A–Z. Drabble includes major authors born prior to 1940. An effective dot system provides cross-references, avoiding an index. No attempt is made to be comprehensive on Commonwealth literature. *The Cambridge guide to literature in English* (Clio, 1985) covers the literature of Canada, Africa, Australia and New Zealand, India and the Caribbean. Well over 4000 entries, A–Z.

PELICAN HISTORY OF ART (Yale University Press, 1953–) was originally published by Penguin Books.

Of the some 50 titles now available, about half are in both hardback and paperback. *Architecture of Britain 1530–1830* (9th edn. 1993. 558p.) has 377 monochrome and 75 colour plates. The focus is on architecture, sculpture and painting; each volume covers a particular country or region over a given period. All volumes have a bibliography and index. Scope is international.

THE ENCYCLOPEDIA OF WORLD ART (McGraw-Hill, 1959–69. 15v. Supplements, v.16–17. 1983–7)

Also concerns the art of all countries and periods in a historical setting. The text comprises 1000 scholarly monographs, with detailed bibliographies. The text occupies the first part of each volume, and the second part consists of monochrome plates. Lack of colour and failure to place illustrations adjacent to the relevant text are distinct drawbacks. Volumes 16–17 are updating supplements and can be purchased separately.

Sadie, S. (ed.) THE NEW GROVE DICTIONARY OF MUSIC AND MUSICIANS (6th edn. Macmillan, 1980. 20v.) first appeared in 1871–89.

The New Grove has 22,000 entries and 2426 contributors (76% American, British and German). The 4500 illustrations are in addition to 3000 music examples. Biographies number 16,500 (J. S. Bach (Volume 1, columns 962–1074) includes a list of works, bibliography (columns 935–47), facsimiles and autographs). There is no index, but 9000 cross-references help. Volume 20, Appendix A, is an index of terms in non-western languages. *The New Grove* has been acclaimed as the leading music reference tool. A further tribute to it is the appearance of the separate monographic *New Groves*, on musical instruments (1994. 3v.), American music (1986. 4v.), jazz (1988), Gospel blues and jazz, with spirituals and ragtime (1988), opera (1992) and women composers (1994). *The New Grove* on jazz has 90% new material, by 90 contributors, with bibliographies and discographies. *The Grove concise dictionary of music* (Macmillan, 1985. 850p.) is designed for a wide public: 'All articles in this new dictionary have been written afresh to a length befitting a single volume work.' Unlike *The New Grove*, it includes 'more than 1000 entries under the names or nicknames of individual works' (Preface).

Hammond, N. G. L. and Scullars, H. H. (eds.) THE OXFORD CLASSICAL DICTIONARY (1970. 1176p.)

Concerns all aspects of Greek and Roman civilization up to the death of Constantine (AD 337). Signed articles, many with extensive bibliographies, cover biography, literature, geography and history. This is essentially a reference work for the scholar. It has not been superseded and is still in print.

DICTIONARY OF THE MIDDLE AGES (New York: Scribner, 1982–9. 13v.)

An interdisciplinary encyclopedia spanning the years 500–1500. It has over 5000 entries, A–Z, unlike the chronological order of the *Cambridge medieval history*. It gives due attention to Byzantine, Islamic and Jewish contributions to mediaeval culture, as well as the European. Some entries provide definitions and identifications, whereas others offer background and analogies concerning political religious and social life. There are over 1000 illustrations, charts and maps.

THE OXFORD COMPANION TO THE SECOND WORLD WAR (1995. 1343p.)

A timely single-volume compendium with over 1750 entries, A–Z. The general editor and assistant editor both took part in World War II. Five advisory editors, all academics, cover the main theatres of the war, including one from the University of Freiberg, Germany. Longer articles carry bibliographies (e.g. 'Japan', p.609–32, has 25 references). All aspects of the war are considered: grand strategy, intelligence, battles, weapons, people and politics. Articles are unsigned. Campaign maps, with legends, are a feature. Photographs and diagrams number about 250. There are 1750 cross-references, compensating to some extent for the lack of an index.

THE CAMBRIDGE ENCYCLOPEDIA OF AUSTRALIA (1994. 384p.)

One of several Cambridge University Press quarto volumes on countries and regions of the world. The editor in this case has an all-Australian team of contributors. The seven parts are: The physical continent; The Aboriginal heritage; The history since European contact; Government; The economy; Society; Science and Technology; Culture and the arts. Forty-six coloured maps and 200 photographs, tables and information panels add to the attractive layout. The seven-part bibliography of *c*.300 items precedes the detailed analytical index.

BUYERS' GUIDES

The fullest and most rewarding guide to encyclopedias is *Kister's best encyclopedias: a comparative guide to general and special encyclopedias* (Phoenix, Arizona: Oryx Press, 1994, xix, 506p.). It covers both multiple and single-volume encyclopedias in English, plus foreign-language and subject encyclopedias, as well as those for children and young people. Lengthy evaluations grade 77 publications by accuracy and clarity. CD versions also figure.

Another weighty guide is B. S. Wynar's *ARBA guide to subject encyclopedias and dictionaries* (Littleton, Colorado: Libraries Unlimited, 1986. xvi. 570p.). This work has 43 subject chapters (Agricultural sciences . . . Zoology). It includes general encyclopedias and dictionaries, place-name and biographical dictionaries.

The American Library Association's *Purchasing an encyclopedia: 12 points to consider* (4th edn. Chicago, 1992. 42p.) evaluates English-language encyclopedias, both adult and junior. Equally practical and moderately priced is the British *The buyers' guide* by M. Tucker and C. Price (4th edn. Cheltenham: Simply Creative, 1991. 14p.). This concentrates on multivolume sets widely purchased in Britain: *Children's Britannica, New encyclopaedia Britannica, Encyclopedia Americana, New book of knowledge, Oxford illustrated encyclopedia* and *World Book encyclopedia*.

The annual *Reference books bulletin* (American Library Association)[3] regularly features an 'Omnibus review: annual encyclopedias update'. It forms a six-page survey of ten leading US general encyclopedias, with a summary chart under five headings. 'Encyclopedia annuals and yearbooks' similarly reviews six US encyclopedia yearbooks of the previous year.

MULTIMEDIA ENCYCLOPEDIAS

Multimedia English-language general encyclopedias have created a vogue in recent years.[4] Grolier's *Academic American encyclopedia* was the first CD-ROM version to appear in 1980. The *New Grolier multimedia encyclopedia* of 1995 contains over 33,000 articles, 8000 still pictures, and some six hours of sound. *Compton's interactive encyclopedia* (1995) is based on the 20 volumes of *Compton's encyclopedia and fact finder* (for many years published by Encyclopaedia Britannica Inc.). *Compton's interactive* of 1995 has nearly 35,000 articles, 8000 stills and maps, 100 videos and animation, and 15 hours of sound. The set is intended for students from secondary school to university level.

A third multimedia encyclopedia is the *Microsoft Encarta multimedia*, based on *Funk and Wagnall's new encyclopedia*, a 29-volume family set. The 1995 *Encarta* includes 26,000 articles, 7800 stills and maps, 100 videos and animation, and nearly nine hours of sound. All three of these multimedia sets are $100 or less, against the printed versions of $500 for *Compton's* and $200 for *Encarta*.

World Book encyclopedia, a current bestseller at junior and adult level, launched a multimedia version at the end of April 1995. It covers the entire text of *World Book encyclopedia*, a dictionary and a modest amount of videos, animation and sound (against $595 for the printed set).

The *New encyclopaedia Britannica* continues to operate a CD-ROM version, incorporating *Merriam-Webster's collegiate dictionary* and *Merriam-Webster's thesaurus*. A version that includes graphics is in preparation.

A 'multimedia release schedule'[5] gives details (publisher, date of release, price) of four multimedia encyclopedias: *Hutchinson's*, *Groliers*, *Encarta* and *Compton's*.

REFERENCES

1 *The good book guide*, 85, November 1995, 12.
2 Einbinder, H., 'Encyclopedias: some domestic and foreign encyclopedias', *Wilson library bulletin*, 58 (4), 1980, 257–61.
3 *Reference books bulletins 1993–1994*, 1995, 1–16.
4 Kister, K., 'The multimedia encyclopedia takes off', *Wilson library bulletin*, 69 (5), 1995, 42–4.
5 Shingleton, D. and Dunn, B., 'Towards a multimedia culture', *The bookseller*, 34, 17 November 1995, 36–7.

5
Biographical sources

Barrie I. MacDonald

The *Concise Oxford dictionary* definition of 'biography' is 'the written life of a person'. It can be described more fully as the recreation of a person's life, drawing upon memory and written and oral evidence. However, the ideal biography should not be merely a narrative of the facts but should also give the flavour of personality, as well as the person's achievements, in relation to the times in which they lived and events in which they participated. 'The aim of biography' according to Sir Sidney Lee, the editor of the *Dictionary of national biography*, 'is the truthful transmission of personality'. Certainly it should be accurate, balanced and as objective as possible. 'By telling us the true facts', wrote Virginia Woolf, 'by sifting the little from the big, and shaping the whole so that we perceive the outline, the biographer does more to stimulate the imagination than any poet or novelist.'[1]

Broadly speaking, biography can be divided into two categories: individual biography, at its best the highly creative and interpretive literary form described by Virginia Woolf; and collected biography, now usually intended for reference purposes and the subject of this chapter.

BIOGRAPHICAL REFERENCE PROCESS
Requests for biographical information are among the most frequent enquiries a librarian will receive. Many will be straightforward enough to be answered from such standard works as *Chambers biographical dictionary* or *Who's who*; others will require a sound knowledge of biographical reference works, print or electronic, as well as the biographical resources of general reference works and various bibliographical guides to biography, and will result in lengthy searches.

Most important in the reference process is the initial interview, during which the librarian will clarify the enquiry by asking sufficient questions to establish an understanding and common objective with the enquirer.

The first step is to find out any supplementary details the enquirer has about the subject to enable an assessment as to the most likely sources of the required information. Is the person living or dead? What nationality is the subject? What is his or her profession or occupation? For what achievements is he or she best known? Enquirers often know more than they initially volunteer. The less that is known about the subject of the enquiry the more searching is required and the more sources to be consulted. This initial assessment process requires experience and a knowledge of appropriate reference material.

The next, essential, step before undertaking the enquiry is to ascertain the amount, level and type of information required. These will further enable the librarian to decide which sources are most suitable. It would, for example, be as inappropriate to supply *Chambers' biographical dictionary*, rather than the *Dictionary of national biography*, to an academic requiring a scholarly article with full bibliography on Queen Elizabeth I, as to offer *DNB* and not *Chambers* to a 12-year-old school pupil wanting to find out about Good Queen Bess.

Not all enquiries will be for complete biographies: some will be for selected, often obscure, facts or physical characteristics. Did George III speak with a German accent? In which leg was Byron lame? Which museums have works by Leonardo da Vinci? What do Jane Austen's handwriting and signature look like? How tall is the Prince of Wales? A thorough knowledge of biographical sources will enable quick decisions as to which of the many entries for these persons is likely to contain the particular item of information. For example, of the entries for Prince Charles in *Burke's peerage, Debrett's peerage and baronetage, International who's who* and *Current biography*, only the latter would give his height. Denis Grogan gives many useful examples of biographical enquiries.[2] The reliability and accuracy of even the most authoritative reference works can occasionally be in doubt; therefore, potentially suspect details, such as birthdate or education, should be double-checked in as many sources as possible. Herbert Woodbine, editor of the *Library Association record* from 1936 to 1944, wrote, 'there are no geniuses in reference work, but that experience does time after time, show the way to the solution of a problem'.[3]

MANAGEMENT OF A BIOGRAPHY COLLECTION

Thorough preparation for enquiry work, by considered book selection, by updating and correction of reference books, by compilation of user guides, and by general good management of the collection, is as essential as research skills.

Increasingly, biographical reference works are available in both hard-copy and electronic formats, so an important part of stock selection and management is considering the relative merits of hard copy with online, CD-ROM or even microfiche alternatives, taking into account ease of use, availability of reading facilities, frequency of updates and cost. Microfiche and CD-ROM archive collections of important and scarce earlier biographical dictionaries now enable comprehensive biography sections to be created.

Ensuring prompt acquisition of the latest editions of current works, through standing orders and direct contact with publishers, is essential.

In deciding on the best arrangement of the collection, the question of whether to classify specialized biographical dictionaries (e.g. *Who's who in art*) with general biography or with the subject will be determined by library usage.

Enquirers and trainee librarians should be warned about inaccurate works, perhaps with a note on the book itself. A problem with current biographical works is the currency of the information, such works as *Who's who* being out of date when published owing to the time lapse between compilation and publication; they should therefore be updated by amendment from newspaper appointments, honours and obituaries columns.

ASSESSMENT OF BIOGRAPHICAL REFERENCE WORKS

The following points are some of the criteria for assessing biographical reference works:

1 *Purpose.* The title or preface will normally indicate the purpose and scope of the work; whether it is intended to be general, international, national or specialized in coverage; and, within these categories, retro-spective or current.

2 *Authority.* An important point in evaluating biographical dictio-naries is their authority, as indicated by the sponsoring body (often a uni-versity or learned society), the author or contributors. Reputable

publishers, particularly well-established biography specialists such as A & C Black (*Who's who*), Debrett, and Marquis (*Who's who in America*), also guarantee authority.

3   *Coverage.* Is the work comprehensive within its chosen area (as *Crockford's clerical directory* is for Church of England clergy), or highly selective, as with many subject 'Who's whos'.

4   *Selection policy.* The criteria used for selection of biographees are particularly important with current works: whether inclusion is solely on merit, as decided by the publisher or editor (as with *Who's who*), or by application, or even for payment, as in the case of 'vanity' publications.

5   *Sources of information and method of compilation.* Many 'Who's whos' use the questionnaire method of compiling the entries, whereby biographees write and later correct their own entries, which result in generally more accurate and comprehensive information, though this is occasionally subject to omission or falsification, e.g. of birth date, education, early career, divorces or other sensitive details. In other cases the publisher researches the material; both methods have advantages and disadvantages.

6   *Frequency of publication.* An important consideration for current works is their frequency of issue (annual, biennial or irregular), and therefore how up to date is the information. If the work is irregular and claims to be a new or revised edition, it is advisable to check it against the previous one. If the work is retrospective does it have regular supplements to update the main set?

7   *Accuracy and reliability.* These are mostly established through experience, although routine examination of the work and reviews in the professional press may help.

8   *Arrangement.* Most biographical dictionaries are arranged alphabetically by name, some with professions or geographical indexes, although chronological or subject order can provide an alternative approach to biography.

9   *Format and style.* The entries should be clearly presented in an easy-to-use format, though the style can vary from the quick-reference sketches of 'Who's whos', or outline biographies of *Chambers' biographical dictionary*, to the lengthy scholarly essays of the national biographical dictionaries.

10   *Indexes and cross-references.* Alphabetically arranged works are self-indexing, although classified indexes in such works can be useful.

Classified or chronologically arranged works must have alphabetical indexes. Cross-references are important, especially for foreign or variant forms of names.

11 *Special features.* Bibliographies, portraits, autographs and lists can greatly enhance the value of a biographical reference work.

12 *Comparison with similar works.* After examining a work by these criteria, comparison can be made with similar works for duplication, authority, accuracy and ease of use, in order to assess its value relative to comparable works.

BIOGRAPHICAL DICTIONARIES

Louis Shores defines a biographical dictionary as 'essentially a directory of notable persons, usually arranged alphabetically by surname, with biographical identification that ranges from brief outline to extended narrative'.[4] There are three broad categories of biographical dictionaries: general or universal, containing persons from all countries; national, area or local, for persons from a specified continent, country, region or locality; and specialized, for specific social classes, occupations, professions or subject areas; and within these categories, retrospective or current.

UNIVERSAL BIOGRAPHICAL DICTIONARIES

General

Chalmers, A. THE GENERAL BIOGRAPHICAL DICTIONARY. New edn. 32v. London: Nichols, 1812–17; Liechtenstein: Kraus, reprint 1976.

Michaud, J.F. BIOGRAPHIE UNIVERSELLE ANCIENNE ET MODERNE. 2nd edn. 45v. Paris: Desplaces, 1843–65; Graz: Druck- und Verlaganstalt, reprint 1964.

Hoefer, J.C. NOUVELLE BIOGRAPHIE GENERALE. 46v. Paris: Didot, 1852–66; San Francisco: A. Wofsy Fine Arts, 1981.

These three works are important in the history of biographical literature, and are now available in facsimile reprints. *The general biographical dictionary*, edited and revised by Alexander Chalmers for publication from 1812 to 1817, after several earlier editions, contains more than 8000, often lengthy and discursive, articles on 'persons of all nations, eminent for genius, learning, public spirit and virtue', with footnote references to other sources. The earlier and more authoritative of the two French works, the *Biographie universelle ancienne et moderne*, was originally published by Jean Francois and Louis Gabriel Michaud of the Royalist printing house in Paris. Alphabetically arranged, its signed articles are scholarly, often very long, and with some sources for further reading. The Roman Catholic and Royalist bias of its first edition, reputedly later corrected, is still occasionally apparent in the lack of objectivity: Henry VIII, for example, is described as 'ce tyran voluptueux'. Certainly a French bias is evident in the length of articles, and those on British persons are generally less satisfactory. The 'rival' *Nouvelle biographie générale*, started in 1852 under Johann Hoefer's direction, was intended as a complement to the publisher's *Encyclopédie moderne*; many of its articles are taken from that, and other Didot publications, as well as pirated from Michaud, for which the publisher was promptly sued.[5] The articles, though shorter and less scholarly than those in Michaud, are better presented, with more bibliographical references. It is overall a more comprehensive work.

The most accessible and comprehensive general biographical dictionaries, apart from the general encyclopedias, are the single-volume dictionaries.

CHAMBERS' BIOGRAPHICAL DICTIONARY. 5th edn. Edinburgh: Chambers, 1990.

MERRIAM-WEBSTER'S BIOGRAPHICAL DICTIONARY. Latest edn. Springfield, Massachusetts: Merriam-Webster, 1995.

The entries in these two single-volume works are necessarily short, but their comprehensive coverage often provides quick and convenient verification of a person's dates, achievements or occupation, nationality and outline of his or her life, and are therefore a useful starting-point for a biographical enquiry. *Chambers' biographical dictionary*, first published in 1897, now contains over 20,000 sketches, providing names, dates, and a brief outline of the person's life and work, with occasional bibliographical references. Persons referred to in entries, who have their own main entry are indicated in bold type. *Merriam-Webster's biographical dictionary* is very comprehensive, with over 30,000 brief biographies; it contains pronunciation guidance and useful lists of world leaders and monarchs. It now omits living persons because of the difficulty of keeping their entries up to date.

Some general biographical dictionaries are intended primarily for study purposes or for younger readers.

THE MCGRAW-HILL ENCYCLOPEDIA OF WORLD BIOGRAPHY. 12v. New York and London: McGraw-Hill, 1975.

'Designed to meet a growing need in school and college libraries', this work contains 5000 clearly arranged, signed short illustrated biographies of contemporary and Third World, as well as historical, personages. It has a 'study guide' volume of biographees listed within a structured, curriculum-related subject and historical outline, with indexes of biographees and subjects. A similar one-volume work, *The Cambridge biographical encyclopedia*, edited by David Crystal (Cambridge: Cambridge University Press, 1994) adds an encyclopedic element to its biographical section of over 15,000 living and dead persons, with chronologically arranged lists of contemporaries, a thematic rearrangement of names providing connections between them, and a ready-reference section of tables of monarchs, heads of state, Popes etc.

Current

Current international biographical dictionaries, which offer quick-reference sketches for important contemporaries, are useful because, if the nationality of the person is not known or obvious, they save searching through numerous national 'Who's whos'.

THE INTERNATIONAL WHO'S WHO. 1935– . 59th edn. 1995–6. London: Europa, 1995. Annual.

THE INTERNATIONAL YEAR BOOK AND STATESMEN'S WHO'S WHO. 1953– . 43rd edn. East Grinstead: Reed Information Services Ltd, 1995. Annual.

WHO'S WHO IN THE WORLD. 1st edn. 1971–2; 11th edn. 1993–4. Chicago: Marquis, 1992. Irregular.

The international who's who contains over 20,000 entries, representing worldwide coverage of heads of state, government and military officials, diplomats and prominent persons from the law, business, arts, sciences and the professions. The entries, arranged alphabetically, give name, title, nationality, date of birth, parentage, marriage, children, education, profession, career, present position, honours, publications, leisure interests and address. Lists of world reigning royal families and the year's obituaries precede the biographies section. A reliable work that is a first source for internationally renowned contemporaries. *The international year book and statesmen's who's who* is a general reference work on international and national organizations, and countries of the world; its third section is a 'Who's who' of over 8000 biographies. Biased towards those 'who have had a demonstrable impact upon international affairs' – government officials, politicians, diplomats and businessmen – this has only a small overlap with the previous work. *Who's who in the world*, published by Marquis, the American biography specialists, is very comprehensive, with entries for over 31,000 persons selected for their position, occupational stature or achievements. Most entries are compiled from biographees' own data; those by Marquis staff (because of the failure of individuals to supply information) are denoted by an asterisk.

Biographical articles in magazines and newspapers can be a valuable source on people currently in the news:

CURRENT BIOGRAPHY. 1940– . New York: H. W. Wilson. Monthly; annual cumulation. (CD-ROM)

Current biography contains lively, well-researched articles on between 15 and 18 international celebrities a month, mostly statesmen, politicians, writers, performers and sports personalities. The entry contains brief data of full name, birth date and address, and a recent photograph, followed by a chatty article quoting liberally from the biographee and others, including personal information unlikely to be found elsewhere (e.g. height and colour of eyes), and concludes with bibliographical references, mostly to periodical and newspaper articles. After publication in the monthly issue articles are submitted to biographees for additions or corrections before inclusion in the annual volume. Each monthly issue has a cumulative index for the current year; the annual volume, which reprints all the year's articles in one alphabetical sequence, contains a cumulative index to the preceding volumes of the decade, a professions' index and obituaries of the year. *A Current biography cumulated index, 1940–90* (New York: H. W. Wilson, 1991) has appeared. Biographical articles, interviews and obituaries from the *New York Times* are now available online through NEXIS or on CD-ROM as *New York Times profiles*.

NATIONAL OR AREA BIOGRAPHICAL DICTIONARIES

Today the standard pattern of biographical dictionaries for most countries is a retrospective dictionary of deceased notables, and quick-reference 'Who's whos' of eminent contemporaries.

Retrospective

Most important within this category are the 'official' national biographical dictionaries, usually multivolume works of unimpeachable authority containing lengthy, scholarly articles researched from original sources and including substantial bibliographies. Such works are seen as symbols of national prestige.

DICTIONARY OF NATIONAL BIOGRAPHY. 63v. London: Smith, Elder, 1885–1901; reissue: 22v. 1908–9; 2nd–11th supplements, 1901–89. Oxford: Oxford University Press, 1912–96.

This fine achievement of Victorian ambition, perseverance and attention to detail is the most important reference work of British biography, and a pioneer of national biographical dictionaries. The historian G. M. Trevelyan described it as 'the best record of nation's past that any civilization has produced'. It was initiated by the original publisher, George Smith, whose heirs presented it in 1917 to the Oxford University Press, which has published it and the various later supplements ever since.[6] Sir Leslie Stephen was appointed the first editor in 1882, to be succeeded by Sir Sidney Lee in 1891. The original work contains over 28,000 notable persons from Great Britain, Ireland and the colonies (including America during the colonial period), from early Britons to the present century. The lengthy signed articles, researched wherever possible from original sources and private papers, have extensive bibliographies, often with portraits and memorials indicated. Such distinguished writers as Wilkie Collins and James Ramsey MacDonald were among the 600 specialist contributors. The original work is revised by *Corrections and additions to the Dictionary of national biography, cumulated from the Bulletin of the Institute of Historical Research, University of London, covering the years 1923–63* (Boston: G. K. Hall, 1966) and has been updated with ten-year, and latterly five-year, supplements, each containing a cumulative alphabetical index to all editions since 1901. A micrographic edition of the basic set, plus the supplements up to 1960, is now available as *The compact edition of the Dictionary of national biography* (Oxford: Oxford

University Press, 1975. 2v.). The *1986–1990* Supplement (1996) is the final volume of the *DNB*. A *New dictionary of national biography* is planned for publication early in the next century. *The concise dictionary of national biography* (Oxford: Oxford University Press, 1992. 3v), originally the *Index and epitome*, contains brief versions of all entries from the full set up to 1985, and is therefore both an index to the work and an abstract of its articles, as well as a stand alone biographical dictionary. *The contributors' index to the Dictionary of national biography, 1885–1901*, by Gillian Fenwick (Winchester: St Paul's Bibliographies, 1989) contains statistical analysis and lists of contributors and their biographical sketches. *The dictionary of national biography. Missing persons*, edited by C. S. Nicholls (Oxford: Oxford University Press, 1993) is intended as a 'catch-up' volume of lives of those who were not in the original work because they became famous posthumously, such as Mrs Beeton and Wilfred Owen.

The national biographical dictionaries for Germany, France, Italy and the United States are similar in scope to DNB, offering long, well-researched signed articles with bibliographies. Germany has two overlapping sets: the *Allgemeine deutsche Biographie* (Leipzig: Duncker und Humblot, 1875–1912. 56v.), containing 23,000 biographies of famous persons who died before 1899; and the *Neue deutsche Biographie* (Berlin: Duncker und Humblot, 1953–), which is currently updating the earlier work with articles on persons who have died since 1899. The French and Italian national biographical dictionaries are still in progress: the *Dictionnaire de biographie française* (Paris: Letouzey, 1933–) and the *Dizionario biografico degli italiani* (Rome: Istituto della Enciclopedia Italiana, 1960–). The *Dictionary of American biography* (1928–37. New York: Scribner. 21v.; *Supplements 1–10, 1935–80* 1944–95) was initiated by the American Council of Learned Societies. The term 'American', widely interpreted, includes persons born in the United States or the older colonies, naturalized Americans and those identified with America through association or contribution. The dictionary and its supplements contain over 18,000 signed biographies by such notable contributors as Carl Sandburg. An index volume consists of six indexes: to biographees, contributors, contributors' articles, birthplaces of biographees, occupations, and 'distinctive topics'. The *Concise dictionary of American biography: complete to 1970* (3rd edn. New York: Scribner, 1990) abridges the biographies of the original set and is a useful quick-reference biographical dictionary.

Not all national biographical dictionaries adopt an alphabetical arrangement: some more recent projects have opted for a chronological approach. The *Australian dictionary of biography* (Melbourne: The University Press, 1966– ; Vols. 1–2: 1788–1850. 1966–7; Vols. 3–6: 1851–90. 1969–76; Vols. 7–12: 1891–1939. 1979–90; Vols 13–16: 1940–80. 1993–) is a truly national project, supported by the Australian National University. The selection, from convict settlers to politicians and administrators, is very egalitarian. A person is placed within the period in which they did their most important work; if this overlaps two periods then the earlier is chosen. A general index volume to the 10,422 biographies in the 12-volume set covering 1788–1939 appeared in 1991. A similar chronological arrangement is adopted by the *Dictionary of Canadian biography* (Toronto: The University Press, 1966–), in which each volume covers a specified period from AD 1000 to the present, with the biographee placed according to the period in which they died. Selection, as with the Australian work, is very wide, from pioneers and fur-traders to Governors-General. Each volume contains excellent historical introductions to the period covered, putting the biographies in context. The advantage of a chronological approach is historical perspective: the works become historical as well as biographical, reflecting Thomas Carlyle's view that 'History is but the essence of innumerable biographies'.

There are extensive works for many countries that are not the 'official' national biographies, but because of their scope and comprehensiveness are as highly valued:

Boase, F., MODERN ENGLISH BIOGRAPHY. 6v. Truro: Netherton, 1892–1921. London: Frank Cass, reprint, 1965.

Contains over 30,000 short biographies, more national and local celebrities for 1850–1900 than *DNB*, with portraits in books, periodicals and newspapers listed.

The United States has two similar works, both comprehensive, with lengthy articles, portraits and autograph facsimiles: *Appletons' cyclopedia of American biography* (New York: Appleton, 1888–1900. 7v.; Gale, reprint 1968), now largely superseded by *DAB*; and the *National cyclopedia of American biography* (Permanent series, 1892– ; Current series, 1930– ; New York: White).

Another type of retrospective national dictionary is the 'Who was who', consisting of entries removed from the current 'Who's who' on the biographee's death:

WHO WAS WHO, 1897–90. 8v. London: Black, 1920–91; WHO WAS WHO: A CUMULATED INDEX 1897–1990. 1991.

WHO WAS WHO IN AMERICA, 1897–93. 10v. Wilmette, Illinois: Marquis, 1942–93; HISTORICAL VOLUME, 1607–1896. 1963; CUMULATIVE INDEX. 1993.

These works bridge the gap between the current 'Who's who' and the older retrospective national biographical dictionaries, and often contain people not included in *DNB* or *DAB*. *Who was who* contains biographical sketches, basically unchanged since their last inclusion in *Who's who*, with date of death added and occasional editing and updating. *Who was who in America* (1942–), has added a historical volume covering 1607–1896 to pre-date the main set of removed entries from *Who's who in America*. Later volumes, which also include entries from Marquis 'regional' 'Who's whos', add details of date of death, place and name of cemetery where the person was buried. Now available on CD-ROM in *The complete Marquis who's who plus*.

Obituaries from newspapers, periodicals and yearbooks are invaluable biographical material. Many quality newspapers and journals, for example *The Times, Guardian* and *New York Times*, publish their own indexes for research purposes:

OBITUARIES FROM 'THE TIMES', 1951–75. 3v. Reading: Newspaper Archive Developments, 1975–9.

THE NEW YORK TIMES OBITUARIES INDEX, 1858–1968. New York: New York Times, 1970; NEW YORK TIMES OBITUARIES INDEX, 1969–79. Glen Rock, New Jersey: Microfilming Corporation, 1980.

Obituaries from 'The Times' is both an index to all the newspaper's obituary notices and a collected biography of selected full obituaries for national and international figures, reprinted without rewriting, and therefore representing the contemporary view of the subject before later reassessment. Subsequently continued as *'Times' lives remembered* (Didcot, Oxfordshire: Blewbury Press, 1991– . Annual), which selects between 120 and 180 obituaries a year. The *New York Times obituaries* is a straightforward index to over 350,000 obituary notices from 1858 to 1979.

Specially written obituaries appear in *The annual obituary* (1980– . Detroit and London: St James Press, 1981–), which covers internationally prominent persons who have died during the year. Its evaluative obituaries, containing a descriptive essay followed by a 'Who's who'-style sketch and bibliography, are arranged chronologically according to date of death. Each volume contains cumulative alphabetical indexes of entrants and professions in the series. Many general yearbooks also contain obituaries, for example *The annual register* (London: Longman, 1758 –).

A recent development is the archive of photoreproduced original biographical dictionaries or articles from them:

BRITISH AND IRISH BIOGRAPHIES 1840–1940, Jones, D. L. (ed.), Cambridge: Chadwyck Healey, 1985–91. (Microfiche)

BRITISH BIOGRAPHICAL ARCHIVE. Munich: K. G. Saur, 1984. (Microfiche)

British and Irish biographies republishes on microfiche 272 general, professional and regional collected biographical works originally published between 1840 and 1940, and contains a total of 6,500,000 articles on over 4 million people. It is particularly rich in the regional and county 'Who's whos', and therefore people hardly represented in *DNB*. The *British biographical archive* reproduces articles from 324 important English-language biographical reference works published between 1601 and 1929, including John Aubrey's *Brief lives*, *The general biographical dictionary* (q.v.), and *Bryan's dictionary of painters* (q.v.) A sequence of reproductions of title-pages and prefaces from all the source works included, is followed by the main set of over 200,000 original biographical articles rearranged into one alphabetical sequence, each with brief identifying bibliographical citation. Its value is in providing biographies on persons who appear only in these important but elusive collected works, and not in *DNB* or *Who was who*. The *British biographical index* (Munich: K. G. Saur, 1990. 4v.) is a printed index to the *British biographical archive* as well a standalone reference work. K. G. Saur has now published similar photoreproduced biographical archives and printed indexes for America, Australasia, France, Germany, Italy, Scandinavia, Spain and Portugal, Baltic States, Poland and the Czech Republic and

Slovakia, most of which are included in *The world biographical index* (Munich: K. G. Saur, 1994. CD-ROM).

Finally, a category of works which offer different, often highly specialized, approaches to retrospective biography. Interesting examples answer specific questions: 'What did they really look like?', 'What was their handwriting like?', 'Who was it who gave their name to that word?'. *They looked like this* by G. Uden (Oxford: Blackwell, 1965), and its companion volume *They looked like this (Europe)* (Oxford: Blackwell, 1966) aim to 'give eyewitness accounts of the physical appearance of the great figures of history' through extracts from contemporary diaries, letters and journals. Finding reproductions of the signatures of historical personages has been made easier by *Four hundred years of British autographs* by R. Rawlins (London: Dent, 1970), which gathers 1000 facsimile signatures of monarchs, statesmen and the famous, with brief biographies, a descriptions of the autograph and its date and source. *The Penguin concise dictionary of biographical quotation*, edited by J. Wintle and R. Kenin (Harmondsworth: Penguin Books, 1989), contains 10,000 contemporary or later quotations about 1300 deceased Britons and Americans. Those whose names became commonly used words or product names (e.g. Biro, Bowler, Dow-Jones and Sandwich) can be found in *A dictionary of eponyms* by C. L. Beeching (3rd edn. London: Library Association, 1989). Listing 12,000 literary pseudonyms and giving the real names of around 7500 authors is *A dictionary of literary pseudonyms in the English language*, compiled by Terence Carty (London: Mansell, 1995).

Current

The standard current biographical dictionary in most countries is the 'Who's who', a regularly published collection of biographical sketches of important contemporaries from all walks of life.

WHO'S WHO. 1849– . 148th ed. 1995. London: Black, 1996. Annual.

This notable 'first', the model for all later 'Who's whos', began in 1849 as a slim handbook of the titled and official classes, containing only lists of names; it changed to its present format of an alphabetical sequence of biographical sketches in 1897. Currently it contains more than 29,000 biographies, mostly of United Kingdom and Commonwealth citizens, although some internationally prominent figures from other countries are included. It represents a broad spectrum of achievement in politics, central and local government, the armed forces, commerce, industry, the professions, sports, entertainment and the arts, as well as some holders of hereditary titles. Selection is by the publisher solely according to merit and, once included, the entry remains until the biographee's death, so inclusion is of considerable prestige, recognizing the person's distinction and influence. The entries are compiled from information supplied by the biographee, both for the first-time entry and then subsequently by their checking and revising the annual proofs. This method usually results in accurate, up-to-date entries, although it is occasionally subject to the idiosyncrasies of the biographee – birth dates, education, divorces and early career being the usual casualties. The standard-format entry usually contains full name, title, honours with dates received, current position, birthplace and date, parents' names, marital state, name of spouse and number of children, education, career, publications, recreations, address and clubs. *People of today* (1988– . 1995 edn. Debrett's Peerage, 1995. Annual), covering 35,000 people, also drawn widely from British society, includes many not in *Who's who*.

Modelled on *Who's who*, the following works have the same arrangement and type of entry, with slight variations in scope, frequency of publication and method of compilation. The very term 'Who's who' has become completely international: for example, *Who's who in France* (1953– . 26th ed. 1994–5. Paris: Lafitte, 1994), despite its English title, is in French. Germany has two works: *Who's who in Germany* (1955– . 1994 edn. Essen: Who's Who Verlag, 1994. 2v.) in English as 'the world's first language'; and *Wer ist wer?* (1905– . 34th edn. 1995–6. Lubeck: Schmidt-Romhild, 1995), containing over 33,000 biographies in German.

Who's who in America (1899– . 49th edn. Chicago: Marquis, 1995. 3v. Biennial) includes more than 90,000 notables from the United States, Canada and Mexico, with lists of those deleted in the latest edition owing to retirement or death, and of those in the Marquis companion regional volumes for America. Many entries end with an italicized 'mission statement' from entrants. Accompanying it are a supplement of 20,000 new or revised entries for the intervening year, and a geographical, professions and retiree index volume. Marquis 'Who's who' data are now available online from DIALOG, on the Internet through CompuServe in conjunction with Telebase, and on CD-ROM as *The complete Marquis who's who plus.*

Special features, such as lists and illustrations, can be useful additions to the traditional 'Who's who' format. *Who's who in Australia* (1906– . 28th edn. Melbourne: Information Australia, 1991) contains, in addition to its 10,000 biographies, lists of Australian Government officials, diplomats, Nobel-prize winners and recipients of honours. *Who's who in Canada* (1907– . 86th edn. Toronto: Global Press, 1995. Annual), has photographs for two-thirds of its biographees, unlike its more comprehensive and authoritative rival, the *Canadian who's who* (1910– . Vol. 30. Toronto: University of Toronto, 1995).

Another type of geographical area 'Who's who' covers a continent or groups of countries associated through race, culture, language or region:

AFRICA WHO'S WHO. 2nd edn. London: Africa Books, 1991. Irregular.

WHO'S WHO IN THE ARAB WORLD. 1966– . 11th edn. 1993–4. Beirut: Publitec/K. G. Saur, 1993. Irregular.

For the African continent, *Africa who's who* covers 12,000 persons in all the Organization of African Unity states from Algeria to Zimbabwe, and including South Africa.

Spanning two continents, *Who's who in the Arab world* is a general work in English, with an outline of the Arab world, a survey of 19 Arab League countries from Algeria to Yemen, and a biographical section of 6000 prominent living Arabs.

A final category of area coverage work in the local 'Who's who' for region, administrative area or town:

WHO'S WHO IN SCOTLAND. 4th edn. Ayr: Carrick, 1992.

Prominent living Scots from all walks of life, either living within Scotland or playing a significant or active role in the country's life, are included in *Who's who in Scotland*.

In Victorian Britain local and civic pride found expression in the illustrated county biographical works, such as *Norfolk notabilities* (1893) or *Suffolk celebrities* (1893). Later, series of town and county 'Who's whos' appeared: *Who's who in Cheltenham* (1910) and *Who's who in Berkshire* (1939), for example, now almost non-existent in Britain apart from occasional occurrences such as *The Birmingham Post & Mail year book and who's who* (Birmingham: Kingslea Press. Annual). Regional or local 'Who's whos' still regularly appear in the United States, such as *Who's who in New York* (1960) and *Who's who in California* (1976), and the

Marquis series of regional companion volumes to *Who's who in America* (q.v.)

SPECIALIZED BIOGRAPHICAL DICTIONARIES

Specialized biographical dictionaries are probably the largest and most diverse group discussed in this chapter, covering almost every subject, occupation and profession.

Retrospective

Collected biographies of special groups of persons have a long and interesting history dating back to Greek literature, with early examples – Plutarch's *Parallel lives* (of statesmen and generals) and *Lives of eminent philosophers* by Diogenes Laertius – establishing the genre of 'short lives'. By the eighteenth and nineteenth centuries collections of biographies, such as Samuel Johnson's *Lives of the poets* (1779–81), were an established literary form, and many appearing then are still standard works, including Alban Butler's *Lives of the saints* (1756–9) and *Lives of the engineers* (1862) by Samuel Smiles. From these developed the scholarly biographical dictionaries for various subjects.

Thieme, U. and Becker, F. ALLGEMEINES LEXIKON DER BILDENDEN KÜNSTLER VON DER ANTIKE BIS ZUR GEGENWART. 37v. 1st edn. Leipzig: Seeman, 1907–50; reprint 1965.

Bénézit, E. DICTIONNAIRE CRITIQUE ET DOCUMENTAIRE DES PEINTRES, SCULPTEURS, DESSINATEURS ET GRAVEURS . . . 1st edn. 1911–23; 3rd edn. 10v. Paris: Grund, 1976.

DICTIONARY OF SCIENTIFIC BIOGRAPHY. 16v. New York: Scribner's, 1970–80; new edition, 1985.

The German and French works are the most comprehensive biographical dictionaries for the graphic arts. Thieme/Becker, with its supplementary work *Allgemeines lexikon der bildenden kunstler des XX. jahrhunderts* by Hans Vollmer (Leipzig: Seeman, 1953–62. 6v.), is the more comprehensive of the two, containing approximately 50,000 entries. The articles, the longer of which are signed by the contributor, give brief personal details, a narrative of the artist's life and works, and an exhaustive bibliography. The *World biographical dictionary of artists* (2nd edn.

Munich: K. G. Saur, 1995), on CD- ROM, now includes Thieme/Becker, Vollmer and the first eight volumes of their successor, *Allgemeines künstlerlexikon*. The entries in Bénézit include brief personal details, an outline of the artist's life, a list of museums which contain the artist's works, sale prices fetched at auctions and galleries, and occasional sketchy bibliographies. Despite a European bias Oriental artists are also included. Both works are largely retrospective. There is no comparable English-language work: *Bryan's dictionary of painters and engravers* (4th edn. London: Bell, 1903–4. 5v.; Washington: Kennikat Press, reprint 1964), despite having 20,000 entries, is not as comprehensive. A similar work for scientists is the *Dictionary of scientific biography*, an authoritative work sponsored by the American Council of Learned Societies. It contains essays on over 5000 scientists from more than 60 countries and all scientific disciplines, which contain brief personal details followed by signed articles with quotations, diagrams and formulae illustrating the subject's work, and a bibliography of original and secondary sources.

Subject dictionaries can be useful sources of biographical information.

Sadie, S. (ed.) THE NEW GROVE DICTIONARY OF MUSIC AND MUSICIANS. 20v. London: Macmillan, 1980.

First planned and edited by Sir George Grove, and published from 1878 to 1889, this dictionary, now in its sixth edition and almost completely rewritten, is universal in scope and encyclopedic in coverage, with detailed entries for composers, performers, music scholars and writers, librettists, music patrons and others in the music business. The smaller single-volume subject dictionaries and companions can also be useful, an example being the *Oxford companion to the theatre*, edited by Phyllis Hartnoll (4th edn. London: Oxford University Press, 1983) and described by Walford as 'the standard one-volume encyclopedia for the theatre'.

Current

Many specialized 'Who's whos' are not regular and are frequently short-lived, owing to the often limited market of the chosen occupation or area of activity. Only longer-established works will be covered here.

First, current biographical dictionaries for those working within broad categories of occupation – the 'arts' or 'sciences'.

WHO'S WHO IN ART. 1927– . 26th edn. Havant: Art Trade Press, 1994. Biennial (latterly).

AMERICAN MEN AND WOMEN OF SCIENCE. 1906– . 1995–96 edn. 8v. New York: Bowker, 1994. Triennial. (Also online and CD-ROM.)

Who's who in art aims to produce a comprehensive list of living artists in Britain, but is actually limited to those who wish their names to appear. For artists working in all forms of painting, drawing, graphic art and sculpture, the entries include art qualifications, type of work, art college attended, exhibitions, work in permanent collections, publications, signature and address. Broader in scope is *Who's who in American art* (1935– . 21st edn. 1995–6. New York: Bowker, 1995. Biennial), profiling over 11,000 American, Canadian and Mexican artists, art historians, critics, teachers, dealers and museum personnel. For scientists working in American and Canadian universities, industry, foundations and Government projects, *American men and women of science* in its latest edition contains biographies on 'leaders in the physical, biological and related sciences'. The criteria for selection are: achievement in the particular science; important published research; or organizational position. Entries contain birth date, specialization, education, career, details of research, publications and address. Online through DIALOG, BRS and TECH DATA. *Who's who in science in Europe* (1967– . 8th edn. Harlow, Essex: Longman, 1993. 2v.) contains shorter entries for scientists and engineers from eastern and western Europe (excepting the former Soviet Union) working in universities, research establishments and industry.

Current biographical dictionaries for the professions – traditionally the church, the law and medicine, but now most occupations for which qualifying examinations are necessary, are of a standard type, giving general information about the profession as well as brief biographies of its members.

CROCKFORD'S CLERICAL DIRECTORY. 1858– . 94th edn. 1995–6. London: Church House, 1995. Irregular.

THE BAR DIRECTORY. 1991– . 4th edn. London: Legalease, 1994. Annual.

THE MEDICAL DIRECTORY. 1845– . 151st issue. London: Cartermill, 1995. Annual.

Professional directories, as in these for the professions of the United Kingdom, rarely give personal details in the biographical entries, only information relevant to professional practice. *Crockford's*, the standard reference work on the Anglican clergy, has information on how to address the clergy, a biographical section, and indexes of the churches, benefices and cathedrals of the Church of England. The biographies of the clergy, both active and retired, give name, birth date, education, degree, date of ordination, career outline of parochial and other appointments and current address. *The Bar directory*, published under the authority of the General Council of the Bar, is a comprehensive listing of barristers giving name, degree, Inn of Court and date called to the Bar, address and circuit. *The medical directory* provides lists of health authorities, medical schools and hospitals in the United Kingdom, and a biographical section of qualified members of the medical profession, giving details of degrees, medical school attended, current post, previous posts and professional publications.

Collected biographies of writers often contain essay-style entries with critiques and bibliographies:

CONTEMPORARY AUTHORS. 1962– . Vol. 143. Detroit: Gale, 1994; NEW REVISION SERIES. 1980– . Vol. 44. 1994; PERMANENT SERIES. 1975– . Vol.2, 1978. (CD-ROM)

THE WRITERS DIRECTORY. 12th edn. 1996–8. Detroit: St James Press, 1996.

As writers now 'move more rapidly from one area of communication to another, the medium is less significant than the communicator', so the American *Contemporary authors* aims to be a current source on over 100,000 non-technical writers from all media, including the press, broadcasting and films. Entries include personal details, career, awards, checklist of writings, work in progress, comments from the author, and further sources of biography and criticism. *The writers' directory* covers 17,500 fiction and non-fiction authors, having at least one book published, from Australia, Canada, Ireland, New Zealand, South Africa, the United Kingdom and the United States. Entries, which cover dates, genres, career and publications, are compiled by the publishers but sent to entrants for approval and corrections. Similar works from St James Press, giving standard-format entries of biographical sketch, full bibliography, critiques and comments by the author, include *Contemporary novelists* (6th edn. 1995), *Contemporary dramatists* (5th edn. 1993), and *Contemporary poets* (5th edn. 1991). Increasingly there are also 'Who's whos' for writers in particular literary genres, for example *St James guide to science fiction writers*, edited by Jay P. Pederson (4th edn. Chicago: St James Press, 1995).

'Who's whos' for British politicians illustrate differing but equally valid approaches to the same material.

DOD'S PARLIAMENTARY COMPANION. 1832– . 176th edn. 1995. London: Dod's, 1995. Annual.

'THE TIMES' GUIDE TO THE HOUSE OF COMMONS. 1880–. April, 1992. London: Times Books, 1992.

BBC-VACHER'S BIOGRAPHICAL GUIDE. 1987– . 7th edn. London: A.S.Kerwill, 1995. Annual.

PARLIAMENTARY PROFILES. Edited by Andrew Roth. 1984–. 3rd edn. 1992–7. 4v. London: Parliamentary Profiles, 1994– .

Dod's parliamentary companion contains illustrated biographical sketches for members of both Houses of Parliament, concentrating on their parliamentary careers. *'The Times' guide to the House of Commons*, issued after each general election, contains for each Parliamentary constituency a biography and photograph of the MP, and shorter sketches for the unsuccessful candidates from the main political parties. *BBC-Vacher's biographical guide*, stablemate to the long-established *Vacher's parliamentary companion* (1832–), contains sketches of MPs, peers and UK Members of the European Parliament, together with cross-reference lists of personal and political interests. More informative, and certainly more irreverent, is Andrew Roth's *Parliamentary profiles*, which aims to provide insight into the position, political outlook, character and 'traits' of MPs through standard biographical information, but also from their contributions to parliamentary debates and writing for the press, quoting liberally from press profiles and interviews (producing such quotable descriptions as 'Iron Maiden in blue chiffon' about Margaret Thatcher, and of Tony

Blair as a 'rising Boy Scout').

The biography and lineage of royalty and aristocracy are covered by some long-established genealogical works:

BURKE'S GENEALOGICAL AND HERALDIC HISTORY OF THE PEERAGE, BARONETAGE AND KNIGHTAGE. 1826– . 105th edn. London: Burke's Peerage, 1970; 4th imp. 1980. Irregular.

DEBRETT'S PEERAGE AND BARONETAGE. 1769–. 1990 edn. London: Debrett's Peerage/ Macmillan, 1990. Irregular.

Burke's peerage contains full heraldic details of each member of the Royal Family, followed by biographies and lineage of peers, baronets and knights. *Debrett's peerage* gives information on the life, arms and families of peers and baronets and, although not as detailed as *Burke's peerage*, it has useful sections on orders of knighthood, chiefs and clans of Scotland, and advice on forms of address for titled persons.

Biography and lineage of world royalty and aristocracy are contained in *Burke's royal families of the world*: Vol. 1, *Europe and Latin America*; Vol. 2, *Africa and the Middle East* (London: Burke's Peerage, 1977, 1980); and *Genealogisches handbuch des Adels* (1951– . Limburg: C. A. Starke).

Lists of members of societies, exhibitors in art exhibitions, and university and public school alumni, can be useful biographical sources. *The biographical memoirs of the Fellows of the Royal Society* (1955– . Annual), continuing *Obituary notices of Fellows of the Royal Society* (1932–54), contains lengthy essays, with portraits and complete bibliographies. An example of a list of exhibitors is A. Graves, *The Royal Academy of Arts: a complete dictionary of contributors and their work from its foundation in 1769 to 1904* (London: Henry Graves, 1905; reprint, Weston-Super-Mare: Kingsmead Press, 1989. 4v.), and its supplement *Royal Academy exhibitors 1905–1970* (Calne, Wiltshire: Hilmarton Manor Press, 1986. 4v.). Notable historical lists of students of universities are: *Alumni oxonienses: the members of the University of Oxford, 1500–1714/1715–1886*, by Joseph Foster (Oxford: Parker, 1891–2. 4v.; Liechtenstein: Kraus Reprint, 1968); and *Alumni cantabrigienses: a biographical list of all known students, graduates and holders of office at the University of Cambridge from the earliest times to 1900*, compiled by J. and J.A. Venn (Cambridge: University Press, 1922–54. 10v.; Liechtenstein: Kraus Reprint, 1974). An example of a listing of former school pupils is: *Rugby School register*

1675–1921 (Rugby: The School, 1901–29. 5v.).

Finally, not all biographical enquiries will be about 'real' people, but characters from folklore, mythology or fiction. Written by a foremost authority on British and Irish folklore, Katharine Briggs, the *Dictionary of fairies, hobgoblins, brownies, bogies and other supernatural creatures* (London: Allen Lane, 1976; new edn. Penguin Books, 1993) gives 'biographies', with quotations and bibliographies. Characters from Greek and Roman legends can be found in *Who's who in classical mythology*, by Michael Grant (London: Routledge, 1994). For tracing fictional characters, and in which book they appear, *Dictionary of fictional characters*, by W. Freeman (4th edn. London: Dent, 1991) is a valuable source, from which one can then progress in many cases to a reader's guide or companion to a particular author's works, offering fuller biographies of the characters, such as *Who's who in Thomas Hardy*, by G. Leeming (London: Elm Tree Books, 1975).

BIBLIOGRAPHICAL GUIDES AND INDEXES TO BIOGRAPHY

Collected biographies

This section surveys guides and indexes to the contents of biographical dictionaries, which provide invaluable short-cuts to lengthy searches. Although they may refer to rather elusive works not immediately available, they can identify the subject of the search and lead to further sources.

ALMANACK OF FAMOUS PEOPLE. Stetler, S. L. (ed.) 5th edn. Detroit: Gale, 1994.

Hyamson, A. M. A DICTIONARY OF UNIVERSAL BIOGRAPHY OF ALL AGES AND ALL PEOPLES. 2nd edn. London: Routledge, 1951; Detroit: Omnigraphics, reprint 1994.

Riches, P. M. AN ANALYTICAL BIBLIOGRAPHY OF UNIVERSAL COLLECTED BIOGRAPHY. London: Library Association, 1934; Detroit: Gale, reprint 1980.

Three works which list the names of biographees, with dates and brief identifying description, and citations for the biographical dictionaries in which they appear. The *Almanack of famous people* is a guide to 'newsmakers from Biblical times to the present' who appear in 325 collected biographical works, from the *DAB* to the *International motion picture almanac*. Hyamson contains references to approximately 100,000 biographies appearing in 24 major biographical dictionaries and general reference works, including *The annual register* (1850–1949), *DNB* and the *Allgemeine deutsche Biographie*. Phyllis Riches cites 56,000 biographies in over 3000 English-language collected biographies, with a full bibliography of works analysed and chronological and subject indexes.

Similar indexes to sources of biography in progress:

BIOGRAPHY AND GENEALOGY MASTER INDEX. 2nd edn. 8v. Detroit: Gale, 1981. Annual supplements, 1981– ; Five-year cumulations, 1985– . (Online through DIALOG and CD-ROM.)

ESSAY AND GENERAL LITERATURE INDEX. 1900– . New York: H. W. Wilson, 1934– . Six-monthly, annual and five-year cumulations. (CD-ROM).

Lobies, J-P. INDEX BIO-BIBLIOGRAPHICUS NOTORUM HOMINUM. Osnabruck: Biblo Verlag, 1972– .

The *Biography and genealogy master index*, originally the *Biographical dictionaries master index* (1975), locates biographical entries in over 500 American, Canadian and British current and retrospective biographical dictionaries, subject encyclopedias, indexes and volumes of literary criticism. Now available in electronic formats: online access on DIALOG as *Biography master index* file, equivalent to the main work and annual supplements to date; the CD-ROM version provides over eight million citations, with annual updates. The *Essay and general literature index* cites over 4000 essays and articles annually, many of them biographical, analysed from collected essays and miscellaneous works, published mainly in Britain and the USA, arranged in one alphabetical sequence of authors, titles and subjects, followed by a list of works indexed. *Index bio-bibliographicus notorum hominum*, a massive work gradually appearing in fascicules, and anticipated to list 3–5 million people worldwide, is both a bibliography of some 4500 collected biographical works from all countries and languages, and an analytical index of their contents.

Individual biographies

Bibliographical details of individual biographies or autobiographies can, of course, be traced in the national bibliographies and 'books-in-print' services; however, some useful specialized bibliographies of them exist.

Subject bibliographies, computer-generated from publishers or national library databases, now appear:

BIOGRAPHICAL BOOKS 1876–1949, and 1950–80. New York: Bowker, 1983, 1980.

BIBLIOGRAPHY OF BIOGRAPHY 1970–84. London: British Library National Bibliographic Service, 1985. 44 microfiches. (CD-ROM)

INTERNATIONAL BIBLIOGRAPHY OF BIOGRAPHY 1970–87. 12v. London: K.G.Saur, 1988.

Computer-produced from all Bowker databases, *Biographical books* lists 45,000 individual biographies, autobiographies, letters and diaries published or distributed in the USA, with vocation, author and title indexes. *The bibliography of biography* is compiled from the British Library and Library of Congress MARC catalogue records for biographical works published in all languages throughout the world, arranged in two sequences of biographees and an author-title index. The Bibliography of biography, on CD-ROM, provides 14 search indexes to the 220,000 entries selected from national and international databases. Unfortunately, *Bibliography of biography on CD*-ROM ceased publication with the 1994 issue. Also compiled from MARC records, the *International bibliography of biography 1970–87* overlaps the previous work, and has over 100,000 entries in two sequences of subject/biographee (giving full bibliographical details, Dewey and Library of Congress class numbers) and author/title.

Catalogues to specialist or general libraries can also be useful guides to individual biography:

National Maritime Museum, CATALOGUE OF THE LIBRARY. Vol. 2: BIOGRAPHY. 2v. London: HMSO, 1969.

Simpson, D. H. Royal Commonwealth Society. BIOGRAPHY CATALOGUE OF THE LIBRARY, by Donald H. Simpson. London: The Society, 1961.

These handsomely produced catalogues are invaluable sources of biography within their specialist subject area. The National Maritime Museum catalogue covers naval and maritime biography, and contains lists of collected biographies, navy lists, individual biographies, autobiographies and journals, with a reference index to 15,000 names appearing in 21 collected works, including *DNB*, Boase, and James Ralfe's *Naval biography of Britain*. The Royal Commonwealth Society Library catalogue has an alphabetical sequence of 6500 persons born in, or actively associated with, the Commonwealth, giving brief identification and references to books and periodicals in the collection, followed by country and author indexes.

The *British Library general catalogue of printed books* with its *Supplements* is primarily an author catalogue, but it does list books both by and about an author. The *British Museum subject index of the modern works added to the Library, 1881–1960*, extended as the *British Library general subject catalogue* to 1985, does list individual biographies under specific names; however, collected biographies would be listed under subject headings for 'Biography', 'Autobiography', 'Portraits', and such subheadings as 'Music: Composers'.

Guides to specific types of biographical or autobiographical works are important:

Matthews, W. BRITISH DIARIES: AN ANNOTATED BIBLIOGRAPHY OF BRITISH DIARIES WRITTEN BETWEEN 1442 AND 1942. Berkeley, California: University of California Press, 1950.

This excellent source for biography researchers is a chronological listing of published and unpublished diaries, with annotated entries and an author index. William Matthews also compiled *American diaries* (1945), *Canadian diaries and autobiographies* (1950) and *British autobiographies* (1955), now updated by *And so to bed: a bibliography of diaries published in English* by Patricia P. Havlice (Metuchen, New Jersey: Scarecrow Press, 1987). A similar work, *The autobiography of the working class: an annotated critical bibliography*, edited by John Burnet, David Vincent and David Mayall (Brighton: Harvester Press, 1984–89. 4v.), the result of an eight-year Leverhulme Foundation research project, lists published and unpublished autobiographical accounts between 1790 and 1945, giving biography, family life, occupation and activities of each writer, with indexes to place, occupations, education and dates.

Portraits

Finding portraits can be a difficult part of biographical research, and although many encyclopedias and biographical dictionaries refer to portraits, and occasionally reproduce them, other specialist guides to portraits will be necessary.

ALA PORTRAIT INDEX. 3v. Washington: Library of Congress, 1906; New York: Burt Franklin, reprint 1964.

This index contains references to reproductions of approximately 120,000 portraits of over 40,000 people in books and periodicals. The entry includes a brief identifying description followed by works containing a portrait of the person.

Catalogues of portraits in art galleries, museums and academic or professional bodies are also useful. Two examples are *National Portrait Gallery: concise catalogue, 1856–1969, 1970–76* (London: The Gallery, 1970, 1977), which contains 3000 entries with details of sitter, portrait and artist; and *The Royal College of Physicians of London: portraits* (London: J. & A. Churchill, 1964), and *Portraits: catalogue II* (Amsterdam: Elsevier/Excerpta Medica, 1977), with photographs and documentation of over 300 portraits.

Periodicals
BIOGRAPHY INDEX. 1946– . New York: H. W. Wilson. Quarterly, annual, and three/two-year cumulations. (Online; CD-ROM)

International in scope, though with an American bias, this currently analyses periodicals, newspapers, collected and individual biographies, diaries, letters and obituaries. Entries contain brief identification of the biographee, followed by citations, with portraits and illustrations indicated, and an index of professions and occupations. Now online back to 1984 through WILSONLINE, and on CD-ROM. The general and specialist periodical indexes, *British humanities index*, *Readers' guide to periodical literature*, *Art index* and *Music index*, also have biographical references.

Primary sources
Much valuable biographical material, such as correspondence, diaries and private papers, is still unpublished and only in the original manuscript, stored in archives and record repositories. Locations can be found

through the National Register of Archives, in the 'Index of persons' in *Guide to Royal Commission on Historical Manuscripts 1870–1911, 1911–1957* (London: HMSO, 1914, 1966), and newly acquired papers in *Accessions to repositories and reports added to the National Register of Archives* (London: HMSO, 1957–92. Annual), and the Royal Commission for Historical Manuscripts; *Annual review*.

Subject bibliographies
Slocum, R. B. BIOGRAPHICAL DICTIONARIES AND RELATED WORKS. 2nd edn. 2v. Detroit: Gale, 1986.

This definitive subject bibliography contains details of 16,000 biographical dictionaries, bio-bibliographies, biographical indexes, historical and subject dictionaries, and portrait catalogues. International in scope, it is arranged in three sections – universal biography, national or area biography, and biography by vocation – with author, title and subject indexes. A useful subject-arranged bibliography, *Biographical sources: a guide to dictionaries and reference works*, by Diane J. Cimbala, Jennifer Cargill and Brian Alley (Phoenix, Arizona: Oryx Press, 1986), provides annotated entries on a wide range of biographical dictionaries.

REFERENCES AND CITATIONS
1 Woolf, V., 'The art of biography', in *The death of a moth and other essays*, London, Hogarth Press, 1942, 126.
2 Grogan, D., *Grogan's case studies in reference work*, Vol. 6: *Biographical sources*, London, Bingley, 1987.
3 Woodbine, H., 'Reference libraries', *Library Association record*, **39** (3), March 1937, 119–20.
4 Shores, L., *Basic reference sources*, Chicago: American Library Association, 1954, 99.
5 Christie, R. C., 'Biographical dictionaries', *Quarterly review*, **157**, January 1884, 187–230.
6 'George Smith and the DNB', *Times literary supplement*, 24 December 1971, 1593–5.

SUGGESTIONS FOR FURTHER READING
Bachelor, J. (ed.), *The art of literary biography*, Oxford, Clarendon Press, 1995.
Edel, L., 'Biography: a manifesto', *Biography*, **1** (1). Winter 1978, 1–3.

Ellman, R., *Golden codgers: biographical speculations*, London, Oxford University Press, 1973.

Garraty, J. A., *The nature of biography*, London, Cape, 1958.

Gittings, R., *The nature of biography*, London, Heinemann, 1978.

Maurois, A., *Aspects of biography*, Cambridge, Cambridge University Press, 1929.

Shelston, A., *Biography*, London, Methuen, 1977.

6

Geographical Sources

Susan V. Howard

Mapmaking has a long history, dating back to the prehistoric era when materials such as rocks, wood and clay tablets were used to create depictions of the known environment; Bagrow dates the earliest extant Babylonian map, at *c.* 3800 BC, and maps were also produced in ancient China, Egypt, Greece and Rome.[1] Progress in cartography was sporadic until the great advances during the Renaissance in Europe. Geographical discoveries and technological innovations enabled more accurate maps to be drawn, and the development of printing led to their dissemination to a wider audience. Until the eighteenth century mapmaking was principally a private concern, but a need for accurate, up-to-date maps of large areas stimulated the establishment of national surveys. Early maps were usually topographical and were commissioned for a variety of practical purposes, including land-ownership claims, trade routes, military campaigns and colonial expansion; thematic mapping did not develop on a large scale until the nineteenth century.

Modern cartography is firmly established on a scientific basis and maps are produced by national survey organizations, commercial publishers, specialist institutes and private companies. Traditionally a map was a two-dimensional representation of all or part of the earth's surface or substrata on a sheet of paper, but today maps are available in other media, such as CD-ROM, microform and magnetic tape, and large collections are available via the Internet.

Maps do, of course, play an important role in educational and business activities, but they are also an essential tool in everyday life and as such have a place in the collections of all types of library, where they will be used to answer a wide range of enquiries, from complex academic and planning problems to a simple request for the best route from A to B.

Selection will depend upon the perceived and expressed needs of the users of a particular library. This chapter seeks to illustrate the various types of map available in various formats; also included is a consideration of gazetteers, which are often used in conjunction with maps. Representative examples only can be given: for fuller listings, specialist bibliographies and standard works such as Walford's *Guide to reference material* should be consulted. The librarian will also need to make use of other works for guidance on the storage, acquisition, cataloguing and classification of maps; Nichols,[2] and Larsgaard[3] have both written excellent guides.

SELECTION

Present-day production of maps and atlases is enormous, thus presenting the librarian with a major problem in the selection of current material. No single guide can be claimed to be entirely satisfactory and a number of sources will need to be consulted.

GEOKATALOG. Stuttgart: Geocenter Internationales Landkartenhaus. Vol.1 1972– ; Vol.2 1976– .

This is the sales catalogue of Europe's largest map supplier and is the most comprehensive source available for international mapping. The first volume is an annual publication, listing maps, atlases and guidebooks which are mainly of use for recreational and tourist purposes. The looseleaf second volume is a continuous publication and includes official cartographic publications, arranged by country. Index sheets for map series are included. The entries are in German, but English translations of the abbreviations used are given and there are notes for use in English. *Geokartenbrief*, which is published about three times a year, acts as a supplement.

A less comprehensive but more accessible work is:

Parry, R.B. and Perkins, C.R. (eds.), WORLD MAPPING TODAY. London: Butterworths, 1987.

Arranged alphabetically by country within continents, it lists the principal maps, atlases and gazetteers which were available at the time of publication. Introductory essays give an overview of mapping in each country, and it includes key maps for map series and addresses of the main national and commercial map producers. A revision of this extremely useful work is in preparation.

Bohme, R. (comp.), INVENTORY OF WORLD TOPOGRAPHIC MAPPING. 3v. London: International Cartographic Association, 1989-1993.

This ambitious undertaking gives an historical account of official topographic mapping in each country and a listing of map scales and series. It is illustrated with monochrome reproductions of index sheets and representative maps which vary considerably in legibility. The revised edition of *World mapping today* will probably be a wiser and considerably cheaper purchase, given the narrow scope of the *Inventory*.

GEOBASE. Amsterdam: Elsevier Science. 1980– .

A bibliographic database on CD-ROM, GEOBASE contains the equivalent of a number of printed sources such as *Geographical abstracts*. It is updated quarterly, and does include atlases.

Catalogues and accessions lists of major map collections are another useful source of information, for both current and retrospective acquisition.

British Library, CATALOGUE OF PRINTED MAPS, CHARTS AND PLANS. 15v. London: British Museum, 1967. TEN-YEAR SUPPLEMENT, 1965–74. 1978.

This catalogue contains entries for the maps, atlases, globes and related materials held in one of the world's largest cartographic collections. Items are listed under the names of specific places, areas and geographical features. For more current acquisitions, consult:

BRITISH LIBRARY CARTOGRAPHIC MATERIALS FILE: CURRENT ACCESSIONS 1975– . London, British Library, 1975– .

This microfiche catalogue, which is updated monthly, is divided into three sequences: geographical names; names/titles; subjects. As well as listing current map accessions, it also includes entries for United Kingdom remote-sensing and digital databases. Cartographic materials are not yet available on the BL-OPAC.

American Geographical Society, INDEX TO MAPS IN BOOKS AND PERIODICALS. 10v. New York: American Geographical Society, 1970. FIRST SUPPLEMENT, 1971; SECOND SUPPLEMENT, 1976; THIRD SUPPLEMENT, 1987.

These volumes are arranged alphabetically by geographical area and subject, and give full bibliographic details of the source of the maps. Also available is the *Research catalogue of the American Geographical Society* in 15 volumes (Boston: G. K. Hall, 1970; supplements 1972, 1974 and 1978), which in part acts as a cumulation of:

American Geographical Society, CURRENT GEOGRAPHICAL PUBLI-CATIONS. New York: AGS, 1938– .

Issued ten times a year, this periodical covers all accessions to the library and is divided into four sections: topical; regional; maps; selected books. The maps section is arranged regionally, according to the AGS map classification scheme.

Bodleian Library, Map Section, SELECTED MAP AND BOOK ACCESSIONS. Oxford: Bodleian Library, 1958– .

This monthly listing from a legal-deposit library arranges entries by country within continents.

The review sections of cartographic and geographical journals provide critical evaluations of new material. Significant examples include the *Cartographic journal* (Cambridge: British Cartographic Society, 1964–); *Bulletin of the Society of Cartographers* (Middlesex: Society of Cartographers, 1990– ; formerly Society of University Cartographers, 1965–1989); *Geographical journal* (London: Royal Geographical Society, 1893–) which includes a section on cartography and remote sensing in its reviews.

A number of national bibliographies include sheet maps, as well as atlases and gazetteers, and the catalogues of both official and commercial map publishers should be scanned.

ASSESSMENT OF GEOGRAPHICAL SOURCES

Several criteria need to be considered in the evaluation of geographical sources.

1 *Currency*. Unless the work is specifically historical, the information presented should be as up to date as possible. An atlas containing Rutland or Rhodesia will not be suitable for answering quick-reference enquiries. Political changes over the last decade have relegated many maps and atlases to the historical category.

2 *Accuracy*. This is most easily checked by studying an area with which you are familiar, and by comparison with other sources.

3 *Scale*. The scale should be clearly stated on all maps, and should be large enough to provide sufficient detail. In an atlas, consistency of scale between maps is important, so that comparisons can be made.

4 *Legibility*. Clarity of typography and colour, and the appropriateness of cartographic symbols should be considered.

5 *Accessibility of contents*. In atlases, a comprehensive and easy to use index is essential.

6 *Authority*. If the author (whether an individual or organization) or sponsoring body is well known, their reputation can be considered. Certain publishers are renowned for the quality of their publications.

7 *Comparability*. Comparison between similar sources will identify those which provide the most up-to-date, accurate and comprehensive coverage.

TOPOGRAPHICAL MAPS

Maps can be divided into two major groups: thematic, which will be discussed later in this chapter, and topographical maps. Topographical maps are representations of the land surface, including both natural and man-made features. They are produced at a variety of scales but are not usually smaller than 1:100,000. These maps are used for a number of recreational, educational and business purposes, and as such will form the basis of any map collection.

In many countries, these general topographic maps are produced from original data by national survey organizations. In western Europe a number of these had their origins in the late eighteenth century, when there was a need for accurate mapping for military purposes.

In Britain, the Ordnance Survey was first established in 1791 as the Trigonometrical Survey, and produced its first one-inch map in 1801. After various editions and revisions, the Ordnance Survey moved over to metric maps in 1974. A detailed history has been compiled by Seymore,[4] and a more recent popular history was published by the Ordnance Survey to mark the 200th anniversary of its foundation.[5]

The publications of the Ordnance Survey are listed in its annual *Maps, atlases and guides: catalogue*; this is updated monthly by the *Publication report*. Indexes are available for all series and should be made accessible to library users for identification of the required sheets. The map series produced are listed below:

Pathfinder Scale 1:25,000. These maps, which include public rights of way for England and Wales and delineate field boundaries, are suitable for walking, planning and educational purposes. They provide complete coverage of Great Britain for areas not covered by the Outdoor Leisure and Explorer maps.

Outdoor leisure Scale 1:25,000. These 34 maps cover National Parks and popular areas of outstanding natural beauty. In addition to the topographical detail of the Pathfinder series, they also include tourist information, such as campsites and picnic areas.

Explorer Scale 1:25,000. These cover well-known recreational areas such as the Chiltern Hills and Lands End, and again give tourist information. Ten have been published so far, and more are planned.

Landranger Scale 1:50,000. These 204 sheets, which replaced the one-inch series, are the Ordnance Survey's best-known publication. They include tourist information and contours at 10 m intervals and are suitable for both walking and motoring.

Routemaster Scale 1:250,000. Nine sheets cover the country. Tourist information and road distances are included. They are suitable for touring and business and are regularly updated.

Routeplanner Scale 1:625,000. This covers Great Britain on one sheet, printed on both sides, with inset maps of scenic areas, motorway junctions and major urban areas. It is updated annually, and has been available as a digital map since 1986. In addition, plans are available at 1:1250, 1:2500 and 1:10,000.

The Ordnance Survey has been very active in the field of digital mapping, and by 1995 had digitized all surveyed mapping at scales of 1:1,250, 1:2,500 and 1: 10,000. Agents, such as Stanfords Superplan, use this data to provide customised mapping services on paper or film.

The map series produced by the Ordnance Survey have been described in some detail, since they will be of greatest use in most British libraries. However, most national survey organizations in Europe publish map series at scales of 1:25,000, 1:50,000 and 1:100,000, as well as larger-scale maps for more specialist use.

Cartobibliographies listed at the beginning of this chapter include addresses for these organizations, from which current catalogues can be obtained. Examples of other European national survey organizations include:

France: *Institut Géographique National*
Italy: *Istituto Geografico Militare*
Spain: *Instituto Geográfico Nacional*.

In the United States the principal mapping agency is the United States Geological Survey, which produces geological and resource maps as well as being responsible for topographical mapping. The basic 1:24,000 series is being replaced in some states at the metric scale of 1:25,000. Details of the maps produced can be found in *New publications of the US Geological Survey*, a monthly publication with annual cumulations.

THEMATIC MAPS

Thematic maps are representations of a particular feature or spatial distribution. Data can be derived from physical surveys, as in the case of geological and land-use maps, or statistical data, used in the production of socioeconomic maps.

Geological

Most of Europe had been covered by detailed geological maps by the late nineteenth century.[6] As is the case with topographical maps, most geological series are produced by national survey organizations.

In Great Britain, the body now responsible for geological mapping is the British Geological Survey; most maps are published by the Ordnance Survey, and are obtainable from either organization. The basic map series is:

GEOLOGICAL SURVEY OF GREAT BRITAIN. Scale: 1:50,000.

The maps are published in three editions: drift, solid and combined. The maps have accompanying monographs known as the *1:50,000 sheet memoirs*, which in most cases are entitled *Geology of the country around [place name]*. Other series also exist, including maps of the United Kingdom and its continental shelf at a scale of 1:250,000 in three editions: solid geology, seabed sediments and quaternary. Details of the maps available are listed in the British Geological Survey's *Geological report*; the memoirs and other publications can be located in *HMSO sectional list 45*.

Other geological survey organizations include:

France: Bureau de Recherches Géologiques et Minières. *Cartes géologiques de la France*. Basic series: 1:50,000.

Italy: Servizio Geologico d'Italia. *Carta geologica d'Italia*. Basic series: 1:50,000.

United States: United States Geological Survey. *Geologic quadrangle maps*. Scale 1:24,000.

Land-use maps

Land-use maps employ a number of categories to represent the use of the earth's surface at a given time. Land-use surveys have been carried out, or are in the process of being carried out, in much of the world, following the establishment of the World Land-Use Survey Commission by the International Geographical Union in 1949.

In Great Britain, the first land-utilization survey was organized by Sir L. Dudley Stamp in the 1930s; the *Second land utilization survey* (London: Second Land Utilization Survey, 1961–1966) was carried out under the direction of Dr A. Coleman.[7] The maps identify 70 categories of land use, overprinted in colour on the Ordnance Survey 1:25,000 series.

There has been no full revision of the *Second land utilization survey*, although in 1996 the Geographical Association will act as the prime agent in *Land Use – UK*, a survey of over 1000 1 km Ordnance Survey map grid squares.

Another recent development has been the *Land Cover Map of Great Britain*,[8] made available in 1993 and based on satellite sensor imaging. This was compiled by the Institute of Terrestrial Ecology and is available to order in digital or paper form, or as the Countryside Information System on a microcomputer.

Closely related to land-use surveys are soil surveys. The resultant maps classify soil types and also give some indication of their agricultural potential. In Britain, soil maps are produced by the Soil Survey and Land Research Centre (formerly the Soil Survey of England and Wales) and the Macaulay Land Use Research Institute in Scotland. England and Wales are covered by six sheets at a scale of 1:250,000, with accompanying *Regional bulletins*. Maps of selected areas are also available at 1:63,360, 1:50,000 and 1:25,000. Similar series are available for Scotland. Other soil-map publishers include:

Italy: Touring Club Italiano
France: Service d'Études de Sols et de la Carte Pédalogique de France
United States: Soil Conservation Service.

Charts

Traditionally, the term 'chart' has been used to describe maps used by navigators: the earliest extant chart dates from *c.* 1300. Marine charts show coastlines, water depths, rocks, channels and other features of importance to sea traffic. They are compiled by a number of national hydrographic survey organizations and oceanographic research establishments. The Admiralty Hydrographic Office has produced charts covering the whole world, at a wide variety of scales. These fall into three categories: small-scale charts of large areas, such as the Atlantic Ocean; larger-scale charts of coastal areas; and detailed charts of harbours and estuaries. Details can be found in the annual *Catalogue of Admiralty charts*.

More recently aeronautical charts have been produced, which show surface-relief features as a guide to navigation. World aeronautical charts are published by the United States Defense Mapping Agency at scales ranging from the *Tactical pilotage chart* series at 1:500,000 to the *Jet navigation chart* series at 1:2M.

Road maps

Road maps are intended for the purposes of recreational and business motoring. Although people tend to buy such maps rather than consult them in libraries, they may have a place in a library collection for the purpose of study, or as a guide to availability for library users. It is important that the collection be kept up to date, in view of the number of bypasses and motorway extensions that are continually under construction. In many countries the principal publishers of road maps are commercial organizations, and it is advisable to buy maps produced by the country itself, for they are likely to be more accurate and up to date. Some examples are:

Great Britain: *National and leisure map* series published by Bartholomew. Scale: 1:100,000; coverage of tourist areas only.
Italy: *Grande carta stradale d'Italia* series published by the Touring Club Italiano. Scale: 1:200,000; Italy is covered in 15 sheets.

France: *Cartes IGN* published by the Institut Géographique National. Scale: 1:100,000; 72 sheets.

Other publishers for Europe include the Automobile Association, RAC Publications and Michelin. The Ordnance Survey publishes road maps of Britain, including motorway maps for the M25 and London, and for Manchester, Sheffield, Leeds and York, at a scale of 1:126,720.

ATLASES

Traditionally atlases could be defined as collections of maps of uniform dimensions bound together in a single volume or volumes. Today, many are published serially in a looseleaf format or are available electronically.

Whereas more specialized atlases will be required for the study of geography and history, any public library will need a selection of world atlases for general reference use.

The basic contents of an atlas are of course the maps and an index for the location of places, but other features will also be found. The amount of accompanying text will vary from a brief introduction to lengthy essays; in some cases, the text:map ratio is such that it is doubtful that the work should be called an atlas at all. On the whole, the essays on topics such as earth sciences and the statistical data found in many general atlases will be little used: for these, readers will refer instead to standard reference works. In the case of historical atlases, substantial amounts of text may be necessary to explain properly what is depicted in the maps.

General reference atlases

The general reference atlas, containing topographic coverage of the whole world, and often also containing a thematic section, is the most familiar form of atlas and will form a major part of the collection in non-specialist libraries.

TIMES ATLAS OF THE WORLD: Comprehensive ed. 9th edn. London: Times Books, 1992. Reprinted with revisions 1994.

This is undoubtedly the major general reference atlas and has gone through a number of revisions since it was first published in 1967. This edition contains 123 plates of maps at a variety of scales. Continental scales range from 1:12.9M for Europe to 1:15M for the USSR and Australasia. Larger scales are used for individual countries and regions:

the London area is mapped at 1:100,000, China at 1:5M. A variety of projections are used and the mapping has good clarity. The index contains 210,000 names, spelt according to the principles of the British Permanent Committee on Geographical Names. In many cases English conventional names have been added. This edition includes a large number of name changes.

NATIONAL GEOGRAPHIC ATLAS OF THE WORLD. 6th edn. Washington, National Geographic Society, 1990. Revised 1995.

This edition has been revised twice since 1990, a reflection on the large number of changes which have taken place in recent years. The mapping is clear, with attractive typography.

The scales are often smaller than those in the *Times atlas*, although the mapping of the Americas is especially good. The *Times atlas* is also superior for large-scale maps of urban areas. However, two outstanding features of this atlas are its superb satellite images of the world, and the number of place names included on the maps. For example, its map of England and Wales at 1:1251M contains more Herefordshire village names than does the *Times* map at 1:850,000. The index contains over 150,000 place names.

There are a number of second-tier atlases which are useful for quick-reference enquiries. The *Times atlas* is available in a concise edition, and John Bartholomew and George Philip publish a range of atlases for use at a variety of levels. One good example is:

PHILIP'S GREAT WORLD ATLAS. London: George Philip, 1995.

This contains clear, up-to-date information, using scales ranging from 1:80M for world maps to 1:1M for The Netherlands, Luxembourg and Belgium. Scales used vary between continents, but are comparable within continents. The index has over 45,000 entries and there is a thematic section.

THE TIMES ELECTRONIC WORLD MAP AND DATABASE. Glasgow: HarperCollins, 1994.

This program runs on a PC, is easy to use, attractive to look at on the screen and reasonably priced. From a world map at 1:96M it is possible to move to a particular area and enlarge the scale up to a maximum of 1:4M. Clearly, detailed mapping at this scale is not possible, but the program does contain statistical data which can be used to produce thematic maps, tables and barcharts. It also contains an index.

Multimedia atlases

A number of multimedia atlases have been published recently which combine maps with photographs, statistical data, video clips and sound. They can be enjoyable to use, flexible and attractively presented. However, the Mac or PC specifications given with the products tend to be the minimum required, and the performance can be frustratingly slow. However, with full and powerful multimedia capability, excellent results can be obtained.

NATIONAL GEOGRAPHIC CD-ROM PICTURE ATLAS OF THE WORLD. Washington, DC: National Geographic Society, 1995.

This can be used on Macs and PCs and contains over 800 maps, 50 video clips, 1200 photographs, and sounds including examples of indigenous languages and songs.

ITN EUROPEAN VIDEO ATLAS. Oxford: Attica Cybernetics, 1994.

This is a CD-ROM atlas with maps, 30 video clips, photographs, a gazetteer and a databank which can be used to produce graphs. The mapping is at a large, unspecified scale so that detail is poor, but overall this is an attractive package.

Thematic atlases

A wide variety of thematic atlases is available. Some are global in scale, whereas others deal with a particular topic in a country or region. Many contain a considerable amount of text, especially those dealing with human geography, and they may be lavishly illustrated with diagrams and photographs. Although written from an American perspective, D. K. Podells' *Thematic atlases for public, academic and high school libraries* (Metuchen, New Jersey and London: Scarecrow Press, 1994) describes many British products, and is a handy selection guide for the non-specialist.

An excellent example of a thematic atlas at a local and detailed scale is:

UNITED KINGDOM DIGITAL MARINE ATLAS. 2nd edn. Birkenhead: British Oceanographic Data Centre, 1992.

Based on the *Atlas of the sea around the British Isles* (Lowestoft: MAFF, 1981) this is in IBM PC format, and contains a wealth of data, including Admiralty charts, thematic maps and text on geology, conservation and marine biology and a section on fishing. It is relatively easy to use, and good documentation is provided.

At a global scale and for a wider audience is:

Pernetta, J. PHILIP'S ATLAS OF THE OCEANS. 2nd edn. London: George Philip, 1994.

Pitched at a suitable level for sixth-formers and undergraduates, this well-written, attractively presented atlas is divided into six sections which together provide comprehensive coverage of the ocean environment.

An example dealing with human geography is:

Segal, A. AN ATLAS OF INTERNATIONAL MIGRATION. London: Hans Zell, 1993.

Drawing on data from the United Nations, the World Bank and various national governments, this atlas considers international migration from the origins of man to the present, with a concentration on contemporary movements. The monochrome maps are extremely clear, and are amplified by the accompanying text.

National atlases

National atlases are collections of topographic and thematic maps presenting an overview of a particular country, often using data derived from official censuses. The earliest were produced during the late nineteenth century, and by the Second World War several European countries had national atlases. Production in the rest of the world was stimulated by the establishment by the International Geographical Union in 1964 of the Commission on National Atlases. Several have since gone out of print without intended revisions being made.

National atlases are generally published with the aid of government sponsorship, necessitated by the level of funding required to accumulate up-to-date, detailed information. In recent years computer technology has been used in their production, although most are still published in the traditional format.

NATIONAL ATLAS OF CANADA. 5th edn. Ottawa: Energy, Mines Resources Canada, 1985– .

The first edition of the *National atlas of Canada* was published in 1906; this latest edition is being prepared digitally, with the intention of creating a Digital National Database giving public access to the research material. It is a serial production of looseleaf sheets which will eventually give a comprehensive coverage of 44 subject areas, including topography, climatology, ecology, agriculture, tourism and industry. Most of the maps published so far are on a scale of 1:7.5M, with a good use of colour and very clear cartography. New editions and revisions will be published when the necessary data are available; consequently, the production of a finite set of maps is not envisaged.

ATLAS DER SCHWEIZ. 2nd edn. Wabern, Bundesamt für Landestopographie, 1981– .

The trilingual national atlas of Switzerland is a serial looseleaf publication, with maps at a scale of 1:500,000 and accompanying text.

No comparable atlas exists for Great Britain. The production of such an atlas was under discussion for many years, and in 1975 the first sheets of the Department of the Environment's *Atlas of the environment* were published. Based on the 1971 census at a scale of 1:1.7M these sheets could be regarded as the beginning of a national atlas but the project was abandoned in 1979.

Road atlases

A wide variety of road atlases is published, mainly by commercial organizations. The same general points apply here as were outlined for road maps. A good example at European scale is:

MICHELIN ROAD ATLAS OF EUROPE. 6th edn. London: Hamlyn, 1995.

This road atlas covers Europe at scales intended to reflect the density of the road network: western Europe is mapped at 1:1M, Scandinavia at 1:1.5M and eastern Europe at 1.3M. All motorways and major roads are included, as well as many minor roads, space permitting. Tourist information and holiday routes are included and there are 70 maps of major towns, plus plans of the Channel Tunnel termini. A useful section gives information on the driving regulations of the European countries.

A number of publishers produce annually updated road atlases of Britain. Most are at a scale of 1:190,080 (three miles to the inch). A good example is:

ORDNANCE SURVEY MOTORING ATLAS OF GREAT BRITAIN. 13th edn. Southampton and London: Ordnance Survey and Temple Press, 1995.

This clear and attractively presented atlas includes 45 town plans.

Collins publish a number of road atlases, including the English edition of the Rand McNally atlas of the USA, Canada and Mexico, and road atlases of France and Italy, produced in association with the Institut Géographique National and Instituto Geografico de Agostini, respectively. The Automobile Association and John Bartholomew are other reliable publishers of road atlases.

Street atlases are available for closer detail. A series of Ordnance Survey street atlases is being published at a scale of $3\frac{1}{2}$ inches to the mile, with regular revisions and new additions. So far, 22 are available, such as *Ordnance Survey street atlas: South Hampshire* (2nd edn. Southampton and London: Ordnance Survey and Philips, 1994). The *A–Z London street atlas* (London: Geographers' A–Z Map Company, 1995) is well known. This is now available in digital format as the *A–Z London CD-ROM*; finding the required street is much quicker than with the hard copy, but it is expensive.

Historical atlases

Historical atlases are contemporary mappings of historical data and as such are dependent on the available research for their accuracy and completeness of coverage. Some are thematic in approach: Times Books, for example, have produced atlases of the Bible and the Second World War. Others seek to present the historical development of the world, or of a particular country or administrative unit. The most comprehensive example on a global scale is:

Baraclough, G. and Stone, N. (eds.) TIMES ATLAS OF WORLD HISTORY. 4th edn. London: Times Books, 1993.

This atlas is worldwide in concept and seeks to depict broad movements, such as the spread of religions and European colonial expansion, rather than to compete with national historical atlases. It provides a good overview of world history from the origins of man to the present and, unlike many older world historical atlases, is not strongly Eurocentric in its coverage. The 500 maps use a variety of projections and display the clarity of mapping and good use of colour associated with other Times Books publications. A glossary gives information about particular peoples and events, and there is an extensive index.

Several national historical atlases exist. One outstanding example is:

HISTORICAL ATLAS OF CANADA. 3v. Toronto: University of Toronto Press, 1987–93.

This authorative and attractively presented atlas considers the history of Canada from prehistoric times to 1961. Divided thematically, each section has a series of double-page map spreads enhanced by a concise, clearly written text and numerous illustrations.

For several years the University of Oklahoma Press has been publishing a fine series of state historical atlases. These are all similar in format, and a recent example is:

Goins, C. R. and Caldwell, J. M. HISTORICAL ATLAS OF LOUISIANA. Norman: University of Oklahoma Press, 1995.

This atlas traces the history of Louisiana from prehistoric times to the twentieth century. It is divided into ten thematic sections, covering topics such as native American tribes, political development and agriculture. The mapping is clear and attractive, with good use of colour.

In contrast, little attention has been given to the production of historical atlases of English counties. One example is:

Bennett, S. and Bennett, N. (eds.) AN HISTORICAL ATLAS OF LINCOLNSHIRE. Hull: University of Hull Press, 1993.

This atlas, which presents a wealth of information for the local historian, plots the history of Lincolnshire from early settlement to the present day in 71 maps, with an accompanying text provided by over 30 contributors. The mapping is extremely detailed, showing parish boundaries.

Good examples of historical atlases of towns are:

Lobel, M.D. (ed.) HISTORIC TOWNS. 2v. London: Scolar Press, 1974–5.

The volumes trace the history and development of 12 British towns, including Glasgow, Hereford and Cambridge. For each town, an essay on its development is followed by a series of maps tracing the history from medieval times to *c.* 1800. From the third volume, *The City of London from prehistoric times to c.1520* (Oxford: Oxford University Press, 1989) the series became *The British atlas of historic towns.*

EARLY AND LOCAL MAPS

Early and local maps are the subject of considerable interest: they can be regarded as investments, as works of art and as tools for historical research. As representations of the earth's surface they are inevitably less accurate than contemporary publications, reflecting as they do both the geographical knowledge and cartographic techniques of the time in which they were created; it is also important to bear in mind the purpose for which the maps were made, since there may well exist bias in the information which is portrayed.

Many national and university libraries have built up outstanding collections of early maps and there are several catalogues and bibliographies which can be consulted for details. It should be noted that before the nineteenth century the majority of printed maps appeared in atlases, rather than as individual sheets.

Shirley, R. W. THE MAPPING OF THE WORLD: EARLY PRINTED WORLD MAPS 1472–1700. London: Holland Press, 1983.

During the period 1472–1700 approximately 650 maps of the world are known to have been printed. This bibliography is arranged chronologically with an index of map-makers. The maps, many of which are illustrated, are described and locations are given for those held in the British Library, the Library of Congress and the Bibliothèque Nationale; other locations are given for very rare maps only.

Useful general lists include the published catalogue of the Map Library of the British Library, the Library of Congress's *List of geographical atlases* (8v. Washington, DC: Library of Congress, 1909–74) and the National Maritime Museum's *Catalogue of the Library, Vol.3: Atlases and cartography* (2v. London: HMSO, 1971).

Listings also exist at the national level. The centre of map production from the late sixteenth century was The Netherlands, and a very fine bibliography exists:

Koeman, I. C. ATLANTES NEERLANDICI. 6v. Amsterdam: Theatrum Orbis Terrarum, 1967–85.

This is a bibliography of atlases and pilot books published in The Netherlands. The first five volumes cover the period up to 1880, and Volume 6 is a supplement covering the period 1880–1940. Well over 1000 atlases are described, listed alphabetically by map-maker and publisher, with indexes by year of publication, author, engravers and geographical names.

French maps can be located in:

Pastoreau, M. LES ATLAS FRANÇAIS XVI–XVII SIECLES. Paris: Bibliothèque Nationale, 1984.

This contains descriptions and locations of the atlases produced in France from 1500 to 1700, using present-day France as the boundary for inclusion. It is arranged alphabetically by cartographer, providing a brief bibliography for each. It has a geographical index and list of locations.

English cartography dates from the thirteenth century, with the maps of Matthew Paris. Little development occurred until the mid-sixteenth century, when Christopher Saxton published the first complete set of county maps between 1574 and 1579. Over the next three centuries other county maps appeared, which can be traced in the following bibliographies:

Skelton, R.A. COUNTY ATLASES OF THE BRITISH ISLES, 1579–1850. Vol. 1. Folkestone: Dawson, 1978 (reprint).

Hodson, D. COUNTY ATLASES OF THE BRITISH ISLES PUBLISHED AFTER 1703, 2v. Tewin: Tewin Press, 1984–9.

Chubb, T. THE PRINTED MAPS IN THE ATLASES OF GREAT BRITAIN AND IRELAND 1579–1870. Folkestone: Dawson, 1974 (reprint).

Skelton's work was intended as a multivolume description of county maps from Saxton to the Ordnance Survey. The first volume covers the period up to 1703; Hudson carried on the work after Skelton's death and his two volumes cover 1704–63. Chubb's work can be used for the later period.

Skelton's descriptive bibliography follows a strictly chronological approach, with cross-referencing to other editions; Hodson, like Chubb, brings all editions of an atlas together within a basically chronological format. These volumes provide an extensive bibliography of British atlases.

A number of county cartobibliographies have been produced, such as:

Kingsley, D. PRINTED MAPS OF SUSSEX 1575–1900. Lewes: Sussex Record Society, 1982.

This gives descriptive entries for 200 maps in a chronological arrangement. An appendix lists the 18 comprehensive county cartobibliographies which were published between 1901 and 1977.

Early local maps were generally made for practical purposes, the most common example being estate maps, which date from the sixteenth century. About 30,000 are extant, and they display great differences in scale, detail and accuracy. Other examples of local maps are enclosure maps, tithe maps and town plans. Repositories of such maps include the British Library, Public Record Office, National Library of Wales and The Scottish Record Office: their catalogues should be consulted. A good general location guide is:

Chibnall, J. (comp.) DIRECTORY OF UK MAP COLLECTIONS. 3rd edn. London: British Cartographic Society, 1995.

Other countries hold local maps in their national libraries: they will be listed in the appropriate catalogues.

Early Ordnance Survey maps have been reprinted. David and Charles have published individual sheets, and the old series has been published in book form:

Margary, H. THE OLD SERIES ORDNANCE SURVEY MAPS OF ENGLAND AND WALES. 8v. Lympne Castle: Harry Margary, 1975–91.

Each volume contains an essay on the mapping of the particular area, and reproduction of early 1:63360 sheets.

GAZETTEERS

A gazetteer is an alphabetical list of placenames, including both natural and manmade features. The entries in a gazetteer give some reference to the locations of the features, and in many cases will also be annotated with additional information. Gazetteers are used for two main purposes: locating places and checking the approved names and places.

The standardization of geographical names has long been a problem. In 1960 the United Nations established a Group of Experts on Geographical Names, and in 1967 the UN recommended the creation of standard gazetteers, but so far few countries have produced them. Two other organizations concerned with the standardization of names are the United States Board on Geographical Names and the British Permanent Committee on Geographical Names for Official Use, which have produced a large number of gazetteers for foreign countries.

Gazetteers are published both by national organizations and by commercial firms. They range in scale from world gazetteers to those of a national or local nature; in general, the smaller the scale the more extensive the coverage will be.

The indexes to atlases fit the basic definition of a gazetteer and can be used as such, for example the index of the *Times atlas of the world*, with its 210,000 entries. It does not give descriptive annotations, but provides locations by means of latitudinal and longitudinal coordinates.

Many libraries will still hold a copy of *The Times index–gazetteer of the world* (London: The Times, 1965), based on the mid-century edition of the *Times atlas*. With 345,000 entries, this was the largest available world gazetteer, but it is now so out of date that it should be used with caution.

Separately published gazetteers include:

WEBSTER'S NEW GEOGRAPHICAL DICTIONARY. Revised edn. Springfield: Massachusetts, Merriam, 1986.

Despite its title, this is in fact a gazetteer. It contains about 50,000 entries, with a USA bias; entries include a guide to pronunciation.

Munro, D. (ed.) CHAMBERS WORLD GAZETTEER. 5th edn. Cambridge: Chambers, 1988.

Much smaller than *Webster's* with 20,000 entries, this work does give statistical information as well as brief descriptions. Both of these are now in need of revision.

Throughout the twentieth century there have been numerous place-name changes in some parts of the world. For example, it has been estimated that of the 700,000 populated places in the old USSR, about 50% changed names in the 60 years after the Revolution, and of course many have changed again in recent years. A valuable guide which can be used to update older gazetteers is:

Room, A. (comp.) PLACE NAME CHANGES 1900–1991. Metuchen, New Jersey and London: Scarecrow Press, 1993.

This book lists place-name changes worldwide in one alphabetical sequence.

An electronic world gazetteer is available:

THE GLOBAL GAZETTEER. Watford: ALLM Systems and Marketing, 1994.

The complete database contains over 500,000 place names, and gives population data, latitude, longitude and telephone area codes. It is easy to use but extremely expensive.

Examples of gazetteers at national and continental level include:

ORDNANCE SURVEY GAZETTEER OF GREAT BRITAIN. 3rd edn. London: Macmillan, 1992.

As a locational aid this is outstanding: all of the names shown on the 1:50,000 *Landranger* series are listed. Over 250,000 places are given, with their grid references, sheet number and a feature code. The microfiche version, last published in 1994, has been discontinued.

Mason, O. (comp.) BARTHOLOMEW GAZETTEER OF PLACES IN BRITAIN. 2nd edn. Edinburgh: Bartholomew and Son, 1986.

With its 40,000 entries this gazetteer cannot complete with the *Ordnance Survey gazetteer* for extent of coverage, but it does give brief descriptions of the places included, with a locational reference to the 120 pages of maps. For quick-reference enquiries it is a valuable tool.

NATIONAL GAZETTEER OF THE UNITED STATES. Reston, Virginia: US Geological Survey, 1983– .

This serial gazetteer, many volumes of which are available on microfiche or computer tape as well as in hard copy, is being published state by state.

OMNI GAZETTEER OF THE UNITED STATES: CD-ROM VERSION. Detroit: Omnigraphics, 1992– .

This uses Silverplatter retrieval software and is updated annually. It lists over 1.5 million places, and with Boolean operators can be used to execute complex searches. It can, for example, produce a list of towns in

California with populations over 100,000. It is, however, extremely expensive, and needs better documentation.

Older gazetteers should be selectively retained for information on places which no longer exist, or which have changed their names, since they will be useful for the purposes of historical research. One nineteenth-century work which is still consulted for its use to local historians is S. A. Lewis' *Topographical dictionary of England* (7th edn. 4v. London: Lewis, 1848–9); this gives fairly detailed descriptions for a large selection of places. Some historical gazetteers have been published, such as:

Darby, H. C. and Versey, C. R. DOMESDAY GAZETTEER. Cambridge: Cambridge University Press, 1975.

This gives Domesday placenames, variant spellings and modern equivalents for over 13,000 places which are mentioned in the Domesday Book, arranged by county.

Ellis, H. J. and Brickley, F. B. (eds.) INDEX OF THE CHARTERS AND ROLLS IN THE DEPARTMENT OF MANUSCRIPTS, BRITISH MUSEUM. 2v. London, British Museum, 1900–12.

This lists the placenames and religious houses, with their modern equivalents, which occur in manuscripts acquired up to 1900.

The English Place-Name Society was founded in 1923 to survey English placenames and issue annual volumes, county by county; coverage is not yet complete. Names are arranged by civil parishes within hundreds, with an alphabetical index. Street and field names are included as well as settlements, and non-current placenames are also listed. One recent example is:

Cox, B. THE PLACE NAMES OF RUTLAND. Nottingham: English Place-Name Society, 1994.

Geographical sources of information may be used singly, together, or in conjunction with other works, not necessarily of a geographical nature. For this reason it is not appropriate to house maps separately from other sources of information. The precise contents of any collection must obviously be attuned to local needs, and although collections should be constantly updated to provide accurate, current information, older material should not automatically be discarded because it may be of relevance to historical enquiries.

REFERENCES AND CITATIONS

1 Bagrow, L., *History of cartography*, Revised and enlarged by R. A. Skelton, 2nd edn, Chicago, Precedent Publishing, 1985, 31.
2 Nichols, H., *Map librarianship*, 2nd edn, London, Bingley, 1982.
3 Larsgaard, M. L., *Map Librarianship*, 2nd edn, Littleton, Colorado, Libraries
Unlimited, 1987.
4 Seymore, W. A. (ed.), *A history of the Ordnance Survey*, Folkestone, Dawson, 1980.
5. Owen, T. and Pilbeam, E., *Ordnance Survey: mapmakers to Britain since 1791*, Southampton, Ordnance Survey, 1992.
6 Ireland, H. A., 'History of the development of geologic maps', *Bulletin of the Geological Society of America*, **54**, 1943, 1227–80.
7 Coleman, A. and Balchin, W. G. V., 'Land-use maps', *Cartographic journal*, **16** (2), 1979, 97–103.
8 Fuller, R. M., Sheail, J. and Barr, C. J., 'The land of Britain, 1930–1990: a comparative study of field mapping and remote sensing techniques', *The geographical journal*, **160** (2), 1994, 173–84.

SUGGESTIONS FOR FURTHER READING

Crone, G. R., *Maps and their makers*, 2nd edn, Folkestone, Dawson, 1978.
Harley, J. B. and Woodward, D. (eds.), *The history of cartography, vol.1*, Chicago and London, University of Chicago Press, 1987.
This is the first volume of a projected six-part work, and covers pre-historic, ancient and medieval Europe and the Mediterranean. Volume 2, in two parts, covers East and Southeast Asia (published 1992–4).
Hindle, B. P., *Maps for local history*, London, Batsford, 1988.
A very readable volume describing the different types of maps and plans which are available.
Hodgkiss, A. G. and Tatham, A. F., *Keyguide to information sources in cartography*, London, Mansell, 1986.
This contains an extensive cartobibliography and the addresses of major map publishers.
Hodgkiss, A. G., *Understanding maps*, Folkestone, Dawson, 1981.
Isaacs, M. 'Mapping the Internet: map-related Internet resources and the tools to access them', *Bulletin of the Society of Cartographers*, **28** (1), 1995, 1–6.
A clear introduction to tapping resources worldwide.

Perkins, C. R. and Parry, K. B., *Information sources in cartography*, London, Bowker-Saur, 1990.

Potter, J., *Collecting antique maps*, London, Studio Editions, 1992.

Thrower, N. J. W., *Maps and man*, Englewood Cliffs, New Jersey, Prentice-Hall, 1972.

A history of cartography in relation to the development of civilization.

7
Local history

Chris Makepeace

When local history departments were first established in the 1950s, they were often regarded as the Cinderella department of the reference library service, meeting a limited demand with a small stock and material which was sometimes difficult to catalogue and to store. However, from these small beginnings, local history libraries, or local studies departments as they have often been renamed, have been very successful in attracting readers and creating collections of local material, which is often unique. The growth in local studies collections has not been restricted to major reference libraries, but has spread out to embrace branch libraries of all sizes. It is often the branch libraries where the first approaches are made, especially if it is by children working on a project for school. The importance of local studies has been recognized by its inclusion in the national curriculum.[1]

Local history is not merely the study of dates and events relating to a particular area but as Alan Rogers has defined it, 'the study of the past of some significant local unit, developing as a community, in its context and compared with other such units . . . (it) may be a village or it may be some other unit, such as an estate or a firm. Any association of men . . . concerns the historian and where these fall below the national level, they are properly the concern of the local historian'.[2] More recently, Rogers and Smith put it slightly differently when they wrote that 'Local history begins with place, with an identifiable unit that may range from a hamlet to a city. The object of study is to explore its history, to understand its modern form and topography, its changing character over the centuries and the lives that have been lived there.'[3] In other words, the local history of an area includes not only its political and religious history, but also the

144

history of subjects such as the transport of the area, its social conditions, education and leisure actitivies.

Since 1945 interest shown in all aspects of the history of the individual communities has grown, so that, according to Rogers and Smith, it is 'second only to genealogy in its ability to attract large numbers of devotees'.[4] The growth of interest in the local community, and people tracing their family histories, has led to increased pressure on local studies departments, their resources and staff. The limited amount of printed material which was available when the first local studies departments were established has been supplemented not only by a growth in local history publishing, but also by the availability of primary source material, as either good-quality photocopies, or in microform, and presumably in the future some will appear on CD-ROM. As a result, local studies staff need to be aware of the problems and pitfalls associated not only with the traditional type of material found in local studies collections, but also with material which would formerly have only been consulted in record offices and archives departments.

LOCAL STUDIES LIBRARIANSHIP

Local studies work can be one of the most complex parts of librarianship because of the many different types of material which are used, some of which require detailed indexing in order that the information contained in them may be fully exploited. It is also a subject where the material which exists varies from area to area. There are standard works on local studies souorces and their use which can apply to the whole country; there are few standard works which form part of a series covering the whole country, and those which do exist vary in quality of coverage and detail. Much of the material in a particular local collection is unique to that district. Local studies department staff also need to be aware of national events as well as those which happened in their own area, so that these events can be placed in their proper historical context. Some of the more useful titles relating to national history which local historians might find helpful are listed in *Sources of local history*,[5] *Local history handlist*[6] and in the first section of *A companion to local history research*.[7]

There are several publications which examine local studies librarianship:

Carter, G. A. A. J. HOBBS' LOCAL HISTORY AND THE LIBRARY. 2nd edn. London: Deutsch, 1973.

Dewe, M. A. (ed.) MANUAL OF LOCAL STUDIES LIBRARIANSHIP. 2v. Aldershot: Gower, 1987 and 1991.

Lynes, A. HOW TO ORGANISE A LOCAL COLLECTION. London: Grafton, 1974.

Nichols, H. LOCAL STUDIES LIBRARIANSHIP. London: Bingley, 1979.

Local history and the library takes account of the rapid growth of interest in the subject and the increasing number of local studies librarians. Although it is now over 20 years since Carter revised *Hobbs*, many of the problems it examines, such as the relationship between local studies collections, archives departments and record offices, and the wide range of material found in local studies departments, still holds true today, although in some places local studies libraries have been merged with either archive departments or record offices. Carter includes chapters on various aspects of the organization of a local studies library, such as staffing, cataloguing and classification, as well as chapters on the use of local material for research purposes, photography and the care of archives. However, more modern sources, such as tape recordings and videos, are not included as these have only made their appearance relatively recently. Carter also includes an example of a classification which might be used by a local studies library as well as an extensive bibliography, although this is now dated in view of the amount of publishing that has taken place in recent years.

The *Manual of local studies librarianship* takes account of developments in local studies librarianship since *Hobbs* was revised. Volume 1 examines such subjects as management, finance, acquisition, bibliographical control and indexing; Volume 2 deals with such subjects as information technology, maps, publishing and display, genealogy, books and pamphlets. Taken together, the two volumes provide local studies librarians with the basic information required to run a local studies library or department.

The other two publications, by Lynes and Nichols, concentrate on the problems associated with the development and running of local studies departments. Lynes includes chapters on types of material, their treatment and staffing, whereas Nichols examines these areas as part of more general chapters, which look at some of the differentc types of work that local studies librarians need to undertake to fully exploit the department's stock to its fullest extent. Both books include useful bibliographies.

Comment and discussion on current problems of local studies librarianship, as well as short articles on various aspects of the professional approach to the subject, are to be found in *Local studies librarian*[8] and *Locscot*.[9]

Local history for beginners

Those using local material sometimes require assistance when they start out on their researches, often asking the local studies staff for advice on where to start. One of the difficulties is explaining that the information they seek may be found not only in books and archival and other primary source material, but also in a wide range of non-book material, such as maps, broadsheets and illustrations.

For the person starting out on a local history project, or even for local studies department staff who are new to the subject field, two useful introductory books which examine local history and some of the sources which can be used are:

Celoria, F. TEACH YOURSELF LOCAL HISTORY. London: English Universities Press, 1958.

Iredale, D. DISCOVERING LOCAL HISTORY. Princes Risborough: Shire Publications, 1977.

Celoria's book is wide-ranging and can be used by both the beginner and those with some experience. Iredale, on the other hand, states that his book is intended for someone 'wanting to discover, though not necessarily to write, local history'.[10] Both authors draw attention to the various types of material which can be consulted and make suggestions as to the way research projects can be developed.

The importance of consulting a wide range of both local and national sources was first advanced by Hoskins:

Hoskins, W. G. LOCAL HISTORY IN ENGLAND. Rev. edn. London: Longman, 1988.

When this book was first published in 1959 it was regarded as an important step forward in the study of local history, as it drew attention to the fact that both local and national sources could be used. Although Hoskins did not outline the origins of the various sources, his carefully chosen examples illustrate their potential uses by local historians. He has also included an extensive bibliography of general works which he considers local historians should use and, by implication, which should be available to those using local collections.

Whereas Hoskins discussed local history in terms of the various sources that exist, a different approach has been taken by Tiller:

Tiller, K. ENGLISH LOCAL HISTORY: AN INTRODUCTION. Stroud: Sutton, 1992.

After a general introduction on local history, Tiller takes various historical periods such as the middle ages and early modern communities, and examines the sources for local history that exist for them. Each chapter has a general introduction and concludes with a brief summary of the sources which can be used to trace information on settlements in the period under review. There is a short bibliography of useful background works.

In one of his later publications, *Fieldwork in local history*,[11] Hoskins not only expands some of the themes advanced in his original book, but also suggests that local historians should undertake research not only in libraries and record offices but also in the field, and that fieldwork is a vital element in local studies work. Others who have argued along similar lines include:

Dunning, R. LOCAL HISTORY FOR BEGINNERS. Rev. edn. Chichester: Phillimore, 1980.

Ravensdale, J. R. HISTORY ON YOUR DOORSTEP. London: BBC, 1982.

Riden, P. LOCAL HISTORY: A HANDBOOK FOR BEGINNERS. London: Batsford, 1983.

These three publications concentrate on the sources which can be used to investigate a limited number of 'popular' subjects, and suggest that as well as undertaking research in libraries and record offices, there is much information to be gathered by going out and looking for evidence on the ground. Dunning has included only a limited number of sources to assist 'the beginner who is looking for material near at hand . . . to give a fair coverage . . . and to demonstrate that an important part of local studies involves working out of doors'.[12] On the other hand, Riden seeks to provide 'a simple introduction to the study of local history . . . for part-time amateur enthusiasts with no previous experience of historical research'.[13] Ravensdale's book, published to accompany a television series, follows up points made in the programme in more detail, but at a level to encourage the beginner. All three books contain useful bibliographies of general background works on history generally and local history in particular.

Some other sources which local historians might need to consult are examined in more detail in:

Campbell-Kease, J. A COMPANION TO LOCAL HISTORY RESEARCH. Sherborne: Alphabooks, 1989.

Rogers, A. APPROACHES TO LOCAL HISTORY. 2nd edn. London: Longman, 1977.

Stephens, W. B. SOURCES FOR ENGLISH LOCAL HISTORY. 2nd edn. New impression. Chichester: Phillimore, 1994.

Sources for English local history is not a general bibliographical guide but 'an introduction to the detailed study of the general history of a region . . . or local area'.[14] Stephens takes eight subject areas and examines national and local sources of printed and manuscript information for these areas. However, his coverage of non-book material is limited to maps, with the result that some important and often valuable sources could be overlooked.

Approaches to local history is an in-depth examination of the various sources that exist for mid-Victorian England and provides a framework for research on the period. Rogers includes among his sources not only books and pamphlets, but also non-book material such as broadsheets and illustrations, which adds to the book's usefulness. Although there is no bibliography, the extensive chapter notes can be used to create a list of additional reading material.

Campbell-Kease states that his principal aim is to 'describe the principal material available for the study of local history, indicate where it may be found, and set it against the broader framework of national and regional events'.[15] The various sections examine national sources as well as those for historical periods, particular subjects, and related areas such as palaeontology and archaeology. There is also an interesting section which examines the writing of a local history. Further advice on this subject can be found in:

Iredale, D. LOCAL HISTORY RESEARCH AND WRITING. Chichester: Phillimore, 1980.

Dymond, D. WRITING LOCAL HISTORY: A PRACTICAL GUIDE. London: Bedford Square Press, 1981.

Iredale and Dymond examine the question of writing local histories from different standpoints. Iredale looks at the research techniques and the sources that can be used, whereas Dymond concentrates on the technique of writing a good book. Iredale also includes a useful section on advice when working in libraries and record offices, as well as a bibliography and a long list of helpful addresses. However, with the advent of desktop publishing both these books are in need of revision to include recent developments in the field of publishing.

General series on local history places

When it comes to publishing books on local areas, it tends to be local publishers, societies or organizations who undertake this, rather than national publishers. It is difficult for a national publisher to publish a detailed history of a small town, and so where they have produced town histories they tend to be of major cities or towns. For examples, the series published by Hale entitled *Portrait of* . . . dealt with towns, whereas Phillimore have been engaged since about 1951 in publishing their *Darwen county histories of* . . . series. Where series on towns do exist, they tend to be in the form of photographic albums such as those published by the European Library in Holland and Alan Sutton in England. It should be noted, however, that even local publishers, such as Willow and Hendon, used this approach very successfully.

Many of the county histories are not very detailed in their examination of the growth of the county. One exception to this is the *Victoria county histories*. The project was started in 1899 with the intention of publishing a definitive history of every county in England.[16] However, although the project is almost 100 years old, there are still counties which have not been covered. The length of time taken to produce each county has also meant that the changing emphasis in local history has been reflected in the contents of different volumes. For example, in the earlier volumes there is more on the landed gentry and the established church than on social history. Although there are many footnotes, only one county, Essex,[17] has a bibliographical volume.

Some publishers have produced series of titles on particular subjects using a county basis. An example of this type of publication is Penguin's *Buildings of England*, which includes material helpful to local as well as architectural historians. Other publishers have adopted a regional approach, as in the publications of David and Charles, e.g. *Industrial archaeology of the British Isles*, which is arranged by county, *Canals of the British Isles*, which is regional, as also is *Regional history of the railways of Great Britain*. All of these series not only make important contributions to the history of the subject, but are also valuable sources of secondary information for local historians.

More recently, however, some national publishers, such as Batsford, have extended their range of local history publishing to include books on various sources such as maps[18] and illustrations,[19] which are areas on which there were no adequate books in print. Batsford have also recognized the fact that there is a difference between English, Scottish and Irish local history sources, and have included titles that relate specifically to Scotland or Ireland.[20] Other publishers who have embarked on similar projects dealing with sources are Phillimore, among whose titles are books on manorial court records and church court records,[21] and Sutton, with a publication on probate records.[22]

It is not only new works which have attracted the attention of publishers. Reprints of source material such as the *Domesday book*, reprinted by Phillimore, the first edition of the one inch to one mile Ordnance Survey maps by David and Charles, or the larger-scale turn of the century maps by Alan Godfrey in Newcastle upon Tyne, have become commonplace since the late 1960s.

Those involved in social and urban history at a national level often draw on information which has been collected and published on local communities for examples to support their cases. The result is that many books on social history often contain local material, and some even devote considerable sections to local communities, although the title might not give a clue to this, for example *Building the industrial city*,[23] which includes important contributions on Huddersfield, the West Riding of Yorkshire, Scotland and Liverpool, and *The poor and the city:*

the English poor law in its urban context,[24] which has chapters on Sunderland, Bradford, northeast England and east London. It is therefore important that local studies librarians appreciate the fact that local information may also be found in general historical studies as well as in purely local and regional publications.

Record offices and societies

Another area on which local information may be sought concerns the addresses and locations of record offices and repositories and details of local societies. Addresses of record offices are relatively easy to trace, but the exact location within the town is often more difficult to ascertain. A useful publication which includes address, telephone number and a sketch showing the location is *Record offices and how to find them*.[25]

Information on local societies can be difficult to trace, especially if they are outside the immediate area of the library. The difficulty with information on societies is that details of the secretary can change regularly and societies come and go. Pinhorn's *Historical, archaeological and kindred societies in the United Kingdom* is a useful starting point, but it is now ten years old, although some amendments have been published in *Local history*.[26]

An omission from the information given about societies is whether they have material on their area. Some societies have built up extensive collections of local material, but information on where it is held and how to access it can be difficult to trace. In the northwest this problem has been partially overcome by the publication of a *Directory of local studies in north west England*,[27] which includes not only details of the society, when it meets and date of foundation, but also whether it has a collection of material and who to contact to use it. The publication also includes details of libraries and museums, their opening times and brief details of their local collections.

Periodicals

There are two periodicals published specifically for local historians which are of value to local studies libraries:

THE LOCAL HISTORIAN.[28] London: British Association for Local History,[29] 1952 – . Quarterly.

LOCAL HISTORY. Nottingham: The Local History Press, 1984 – . Six issues per annum.

The local historian was started to assist local historians 'to progress more surely and swiftly and to achieve more reliable results'.[30] As well as articles on sources, each issue includes articles on research that has been undertaken which is considered to be of a wider interest than just the locality to which it relates. Since 1982, the British Association for Local History has also published *Local history news*,[31] which consists of short news and information items, such as detals about courses. When *Local history* was first published, its stated objective was to provide a journal which included 'both scholarly works and news stories'[32] on local history. This is the policy it still follows, and as a result it has made a significant contribution to local history and to the amount of general information about sources, societies and publications which is available.

Tracing new publications

One of the more difficult areas of local studies librarianship is to trace what has been published and where. Many local publications are published by societies and may not have an ISBN or be recorded in *British national bibliography*, or, if they are included, as print runs tend to be short they may be out of print. *The local historian* tends to have longer reviews and list other works, whereas *Local history* has an extensive section of short reviews, arranged by county and giving details of where the publication can be obtained from.

As well as the two periodicals mentioned, details of new publications can appear in local newspapers and are sometimes included in more general periodicals, such as *Urban history yearbook*[33] or regional publications such as the *Manchester region history review*.[34] Both publications also include general articles and an annual bibliography of new publications received. Both include analytical entries for articles appearing in periodicals and journals, some of which the library might not take and which would otherwise have been overlooked.

Bibliographies

Although bibliographies are an important means of tracing what has been published on a particular subject, those published for local studies tend to be of less importance than for many other subjects, as many are produced by libraries for use by either their staff or their readers. Published bibliographies tend to cover a region or a specific county or group of counties, such as Lancashire,[35] Dorset[36] or Cumberland and Westmorland,[37] or for a local event which has national significance, such as Peterloo.[38]

There is no modern local history bibliography like that compiled in the late nineteenth century by Anderson,[39] which listed all the local history publications up to 1881. Nor is there a current bibliography of local history bibliographies like *A handbook of county bibliographies ... relating to the counties and towns of Great Britain*, compiled by A. L. A. Humphreys.[40]

Although local history bibliographies tend to be 'place specific', those which are published and which cover a county or even wider area require good place and subject indexes. They need to be updated regularly by the issue of supplements, like those which were once issued for the *East Anglian bibliography*,[41] but unless these supplements are incorporated into a revised edition or cumulated the bibliography can become unwieldy. However, with modern electronic means of collating information and material, updating and cumulating bibliographies is much easier than it once was.

The growth of interest in urban history has resulted in an increase in the level of bibliographical work that has been undertaken on the subject, and older bibliographical works have been reprinted and revisions started. For instance, in 1900 Goss compiled a *Bibliography of British municipal history*[42] in which he attempted to list not only works on individual towns, but also relevant archival material and periodical articles. He also included sections on archival material and general works on urban history, as well as an index for specific places so that entries which do not appear in the location section of the bibliography can be traced. Goss's work has become the starting point for modern bibliographical work on urban history, such as:

Martin, G. H. and McIntyre, S. A BIBLIOGRAPHY OF BRITISH AND IRISH MUNICIPAL HISTORY. Leicester: Leicester University Press, 1972.

According to the introduction, this volume is intended to be the first in a series of bibliographies on urban history and as such is merely an introductory work listing general works on urban history. There are five sections, including one for bibliographies and another on guides to libraries and record offices. Although some of the information relating to libraries and record offices will have changed, this book is a useful starting point for tracing what has been published on specific places and where to begin to look for material. The index appears to be comprehensive and is arranged in such a way as to enable entries on specific places to be quickly identified.

In addition to those bibliographies which related to particular districts or to urban history generally, some of the more general historical bibliographies also include a limited number of publications that relate to local places. For instance, *Bibliography of historical works issued in the United Kingdom*[43] and *Writings on British history*[44] have both included sections on local history from the beginning. Others, however, like the *Oxford bibliography of British history*,[45] have introduced such sections in their later volumes, and when the earlier volumes are revised local history sections are being added. Local material can also be found in those bibliographies that cover specific historical periods, such as Bonser's bibliographies on Roman[46] and Anglo-Saxon Britain[47] and Keeler's on the Stuart period.[48] Nor should it be forgotten that specialist subject bibliographies such as Ottley's *A bibliography of British railway history*[49] may also include references to local material.

Many important contributions to local history are to be found in the publications of societies which are not of local origin. However, it can be difficult to trace, especially if the society's publications are not taken by the library. The problem can be partially overcome by consulting *Writings on British history*,[50] which has included analytical entries from 1933, when it was first published. However, for the period between 1901 and 1933 it is necessary to consult:

Mullins, E. L P. A GUIDE TO THE HISTORICAL AND ARCHAEOLOGICAL PUBLICATIONS OF SOCIETIES OF ENGLAND AND WALES 1901–1933. London: Institute of Historical Research, 1966; Athlone Press, 1968.

This publication lists the contents of 6560 volumes published by societies between 1901 and 1933. Under the name of each publishing society is given a list of their publications and, where necessary, notes indicating the contents of particular volumes. The comprehensive index allows the user to identify relevant local material without difficulty.

Encyclopedias

Encyclopedias can be a useful quick-reference tool. For local studies staff and local historians, there is:

Richardson, J. THE LOCAL HISTORIAN'S ENCYCLOPEDIA. Rev. edn. New Barnet: Phillimore, 1993.

This is the only proper encyclopedia available in this field. It is divided into sections such as agriculture, architecture, heraldry, dates of market charters, schools and railways. However, to make full use of this important work it is necessary to use the index as some entries are to be found in areas where they would not be expected. The encyclopedia also includes helpful sections on dating and archaic and Latin words, although it is not as comprehensive as some other publications.

A similar publication, although not covering such a wide field, is:

Friar, S. THE BATSFORD COMPANION TO LOCAL HISTORY. London: Batsford, 1991.

This book provides definitions of words and phrases which local historians might encounter in the course of their researches.

There are, however, occasions when the general information included in encyclopedias is not sufficient to deal with a specific query, such as trying to equate eighteenth and nineteenth century prices with modern equivalents. In these cases it is necessary to try and trace a work which is more detailed, such as (in this case) Mumby's *How much is that worth?*[51]

Theses

Another important source of information for local history is to be found in these which have been submitted for higher degrees. Details of these can be found in:

HISTORICAL RESEARCH FOR UNIVERSITY DEGREES IN THE UNITED KINGDOM. London: Institute of Historical Research, 1971– . Annual (2v. per annum).

Horn, J. M. HISTORY THESES, 1970–1980. London: Institute of Historical Research, 1984.

Jacobs, P. M. HISTORY THESES, 1901–1970. London: Institute of Historical Research, 1976.

The two volumes of *History theses* brings together information on theses submitted between 1901 and 1980, which previously had to be traced in a number of different sources. The entries are divided into broad historical periods and then further subdivided according to subject, including local history. Each entry provides information such as title of the thesis, the author's name, date of submission and the university which awarded the degree, together with information on how copies of the thesis can be obtained. The index allows theses on particular areas or subjects to be easily traced.

Details of theses submitted after 1980 and those which are registered are to be found in the annual two-volume *Historical research for university degrees*. The first part of this work details theses which have been completed and submitted and includes an index similar to that in *History theses*. The second part lists those which are in progress, the name of the researcher, the title of the thesis, and to which university the researcher is attached. Unfortunately there is no index, so it can be difficult to trace theses in progress on particular areas.

RECORDS FOR LOCAL HISTORY

It is important that those working in local studies collections should be aware of the existence and content of local material which is held in repositories such as the Public Record Office or county record offices, and to have some knowledge about primary sources, their use and interpretation. This has become increasingly necessary with the increased accessibility of some types of archival material, either in microform or as photocopies. A very useful work in helping to discover what various archive repositories of all types have is:

Foster, J. and Sheppard, J. BRITISH ARCHIVES: A GUIDE TO THE ARCHIVE RESOURCES OF THE UNITED KINGDOM. 3rd edn. London: Macmillan, 1995.

This volume lists all the institutions in the United Kingdom which have archival material. For each entry there is the address, telephone number, opening times, access arrangements, a brief historical background, details of acquisition policy and significant collections and any relevant publications.

National records

National records, found mainly in the Public Record Office, are often overlooked as sources of important local information simply because they are regarded as being national. The guide to the Public Record Office's holdings[52] merely lists the various types of record to be found there and the period covered, there is no information as to their origins or content. However, this information can be found in a series of PRO leaflets.[53] These have now been renumbered and rearranged into four groups relating to records information, general information, census information and family fact sheets.[54] Information is also to be found in *An introduction to the use of public records*.[55]

Two publications which indicate which national records are most useful to local historians are:

Morton, A. and Donaldson, G. BRITISH NATIONAL ARCHIVES AND THE LOCAL HISTORIAN: A GUIDE TO OFFICIAL RECORD PUBLICATIONS. London: Historical Association, 1980.

Riden, P. RECORD SOURCES FOR LOCAL HISTORY. London: Batsford, 1987.

Morton and Donaldson's pamphlet concentrates on material in the Public Record Office and the Scottish Record Office for which calendars have been compiled and published or which have been transcribed and published. A brief outline of the origins of the document is given, together with information on the arrangement of the calendar. The appendix provides a useful list of published calendars for national records.

Riden, on the other hand, gives a detailed account of the local information which can be found in national records, laying stress on 'centrally preserved sources' up to 1974. The book also includes details of the classification system used by the Public Record Office and gives an indication of the subjects covered in the records. This book has many useful footnotes as well as an extensive bibliography.

Private records

Private records, that is, those which are not in the public domain, can also be important sources of local information as many relate to private estates, but it was not until the establishment of the Royal Commission on Historical Manuscripts in 1869 that the full extent of these collections was investigated and made public. The Royal Commission's *Guide to the reports*[56] lists collections which have been surveyed, but it does not go into detail about the contents, which information is to be found in the detailed reports on specific collections.

As well as collections of archival material in private hands, academic institutions also hold archival material and some have published guides to their holdings. For example, Warwick University's *Guide to the modern records centre*[57] shows that there are many records there which relate not only to Coventry and Warwickshire but also to other parts of the country, and whose locations would not have been known had the guide not been published.

Businesses also produce records, some of which go back to the eighteenth century. Many are still held by the company or its successors, but others have found their way into the public domain. In recent years there has been a series of publications which have examined and listed the archives of various companies. For instance, there is Richmond and Stockford's *Company archives: a survey of the records of 1000 of the first registered companies in England and Wales*.[58] When it comes to specific types of company, there have been several detailed surveys on industries such as brewing, insurance and banking.[59] These publications are usually arranged by company, with details of their records and how they can be consulted, and often include an index of places as well. If the term 'business' is extended to include sport, there is also an important compilation of records held by various sporting organizations and sports clubs.[60]

Another useful aid in tracing private and non-public collections is the National Register of Archives, which was established in 1945 to coordinate the production and distribution of archival calendars, to advise individuals and institutions on where they could deposit their archives, and to assist researchers in tracing particular archival collections.[61]

Local records

Local records, found in the county record offices or archives departments in larger libraries, constitute the archival material that local historians will most frequently encounter. Guides to the holdings of local record offices are essential to local studies departments, as they list the various classes of document they hold. As new material is always being added, copies of the record office's annual report should also be close at hand as these usually list new acquisitions and deposits. Useful guides to the type of material found in local record offices are:

Emmison, F. G. ARCHIVES AND LOCAL HISTORY. 2nd edn. Chichester: Phillimore, 1978.

Emmison, F. G. and Smith, W. J. MATERIAL FOR THESES IN LOCAL RECORD OFFICES AND LIBRARIES. 2nd edn. London: Historical Association, 1980.

Archives and local history is a general introduction to the various classes of archives found in record offices, but it also includes a helpful section on using a local record office. Although many types of material are mentioned there is little information as to their origins or use, with the result that it is left to the reader to decide the potential usefulness of the material and what type of information can be found in the documents. Nor is there any indication of the holdings of various record offices, although this information is to be found in Emmison and Smith's *Material for theses in local record offices*.

West, J. VILLAGE RECORDS. 2nd edn. Chichester: Phillimore, 1982.

West, J. TOWN RECORDS. Chichester: Phillimore, 1983.

Porter, S. EXPLORING URBAN HISTORY. London: Batsford, 1990.

John West's two books, *Village records* and *Town records*, examine the various sources which can be used when working on village and town histories. West indicates the type of information which can be gleaned from the various types of documents and, in the case of *Village records*, includes examples of original documents, transcripts and notes about the more difficult parts of the text and handwriting. There is also a useful list of volumes which include transcripts of original source material, a glossary of unfamiliar or archaic words and an extensive bibliography. In *Town records* he examines the various sources which can be used when working on urban history, such as newspapers and directories. As with *Village records*, there is an extensive reading list and details of urban records which have been published. Together, these two volumes refer to most of the records local historians use and which librarians will be asked about or will need to know about.

Porter's book on urban history examines the sources urban historians might consult in the course of their researches and gives some indication of how they came into existence. However, there is no indication of their use by historians and others, nor are there examples of the type of material he is referring to. Although there is no bibliography, there are extensive footnotes to each chapter which could be used to construct one.

Parochial records

Parochial records are also an important source of local information up to the early nineteenth century, as parishes were responsible for such things as highway maintenance and the Poor Law. Details of the various types of parochial record and their use are discussed in:

Tate, W. E. THE PARISH CHEST. 3rd edn. Cambridge: Cambridge University Press, 1969 (reprinted 1983).

This important book examines the origins of the various types of parochial record concerned with local administration and explains their use by local historians and others. There is a helpful glossary of unfamiliar terms and an extensive bibliography.

There are many other types of archival material which may be of use to local historians. Background information on their origins and use of some of these different sources has been published in pamphlet format. Among these are ones dealing with title deeds,[62] quarter sessions,[63] tithes[64] and local taxation.[65] Other pamphlets which make reference to archival material illustrate the use of particular types of material when answering queries on a particular subject, such as the history of a house.[66] Where such guides have been produced by libraries or record offices they tend to be place specific, whereas those published by publishers tend to be general in their approach.

During the nineteenth century many original documents were transcribed and published, thus making original material more widely available. A list of such transcripts is to be found in:

Mullins, E. L. F. TEXTS AND CALENDARS: AN ANALYTICAL GUIDE TO SERIAL PUBLICATIONS. London: Royal Historical Society, 1958–83. 2v.

These two volumes list those transcripts and archival calendars which have been published by national, regional or local societies. The entries are arranged under the society's name and, where appropriate, details of the contents of individual volumes are listed. The index enables individual places, persons and types of document to be traced irrespective of the publishing body.

USING ARCHIVAL SOURCES

The use of archival sources can create problems for those unfamiliar with them, for instance regarding dating, handwriting, phraseology and Latin words. Some of these problems can be overcome by using *The local historians' encyclopedia* (qv), which includes helpful sections on dating, archaic and Latin words. However, it is not as comprehensive as *Handbook of dates for students*[67] and *Latin for local history*.[68] Recently, a new volume has been published on the use of Latin for local historians and family historians which claims to be 'user friendly'.[69]

Although many libraries may not have a great deal of manuscript or archival material, accessibility to such material has increased through the medium of microfilm and microfiche. As a result, local studies staff may be asked to give readers some assistance with things such as handwriting. Simple guides to reading sixteenth- and seventeenth-century handwriting include *How to read local archives 1550–1700*[70] and *Reading Tudor and Stuart handwriting*.[71]

NEWSPAPERS AND PERIODICALS

Newspapers

Newspapers and periodicals are important sources of local information. Newspapers contain not only news but also public announcements, editorial comment on the news and events, feature articles and advertisements. A useful introduction to the importance of newspapers for local historians is *Newspapers and local history*.[72] Although libraries should have back files of local newspapers, often there are gaps in the holdings. Helpful in establishing these is:

British Library CATALOGUE OF THE NEWSPAPER LIBRARY. London: British Library Board, 1975. 8v.

This eight-volume catalogue is divided into three sections: London newspapers, newspapers and periodicals published in provincial towns, and an alphabetical list of titles. The volumes covering the provincial towns are arranged alphabetically by town, and under each town the papers are also arranged alphabetically. The catalogue includes many papers which existed for only a short time and which have only been preserved in the British Library. Although this catalogue is the most comprehensive list of newspapers and periodicals which has been published, it is not fully comprehensive as there are local papers which are not to be found in the British Library. However, regional lists do exist. In an attempt to list all extant copies of newspapers, the British Library sponsored a regional programme referred to as 'Newsplan', which aimed to list all newspapers which were in libraries and newspaper offices together with the extent of their coverage and where they could be consulted.[73]

To be able to fully exploit the contents of newspapers, it is necessary to have an index or some description. Most indexes are local in coverage, such as *The Leicester newspapers 1850–1870*.[74] There is only one published national newspaper index for *The Times*,[75] which includes some local references where major events are concerned.

Periodicals

Periodicals are also important sources of local information. Although local periodicals may be indexed by libraries, national periodicals tend to be overlooked in spite of the fact that titles such as the *Illustrated London news*[76] include many local news items. Nor should the periodicals published for specialist sections of the community be overlooked. For instance, *The builder*, published between 1842 and 1956,[77] includes a wealth of local information, some of which relating to architectural competitions has been included in *Victorian architectural competitions*.[78] Neither should periodicals which cater for the special interest market be missed, such as *Back track*,[79] *Industrial archaeology review*[80] or *Archive*.[81] Information on current periodicals is relatively easy to trace, but for those which have now ceased publication the British Library's *Catalogue of the newspaper library* can be very helpful.

PARLIAMENTARY PAPERS

Parliamentary papers, that is, public and private Acts of Parliament, reports of Royal Commissions, sessional papers and evidence passed to Parliamentary Committees, often contains local material. Useful introductory guides to the various types of material include:

Bond, M. S. GUIDE TO THE RECORDS OF PARLIAMENT. London: HMSO, 1971.

Bond, M. F. THE RECORDS OF PARLIAMENT: A GUIDE FOR GENEALO-GISTS AND LOCAL HISTORIANS. Canterbury: Phillimore, 1964.

Ford, P. and Ford, G. A GUIDE TO PARLIAMENTARY PAPERS. 3rd edn. Shannon: Irish Universities Press, 1972.

Powell, W. R. LOCAL HISTORY FROM BLUE BOOKS. London: Historical Association, 1962.

Bond's *Guide to the records of Parliament* is a comprehensive guide to the manuscript and printed Parliamentary papers in the Palace of Westminster, some of which are to be found nowhere else. However, he does not include information on the origins of the material or their use by local historians. For this type of information it is necessary to consult one or other of the books on the subject, some of which include accounts of how Parliamentary papers are numbered. The only publication which gives information on those papers which might be of interest and use to local historians is *Local history from blue books*, which gives details of libraries with extensive holdings and lists sessional papers which local historians might find useful.

DIRECTORIES

Directories are another important source, containing local information on residents and businesses, information about the district and advertisements for local firms, which may include information not found elsewhere. Although directories for London were published in the late seventeenth century, those for the rest of the country do not start until the late eighteenth century. Many of the early directories are regional in their coverage, although there are some that cover specific towns, such as Liverpool and Manchester. By the mid-nineteenth century, directories covering single towns or counties became the norm. Useful guides to published directories are:

Norton, J. E. GUIDE TO THE NATIONAL AND PROVINCIAL DIRECTO-RIES OF ENGLAND AND WALES . . . PUBLISHED BEFORE 1850. London: Royal Historical Society, 1950.

Shaw, G. and Tipper, A. BRITISH DIRECTORIES: A BIBLIOGRAPHY AND GUIDE TO DIRECTORIES PUBLISHED IN ENGLAND AND WALES (1850–1950) AND SCOTLAND (1773–1950). Leicester: Leicester University Press, 1988.

These two bibliographies list the majority of the directories that have been published in England, Wales and Scotland between the mid-eighteenth and mid-twentieth centuries. Both also include a section on how directories were compiled and why only certain people were included. Norton lists 878 provincial directories held by major libraries, but as Scotland, London and the holdings of smaller libraries have been excluded, the coverage is not comprehensive.[82] For those directories which are listed there is a full bibliographical description which enables different editions to be identified. The index lists only counties, so it is not possible to check whether a particular town is included, although this problem can be resolved by using one of the published regional lists, such as that for the West Midlands.[83]

Shaw and Tipper's work continues where Norton ends, listing directories published up to the mid-twentieth century, but has the added advantage in that it includes Scotland and has an index which lists individual towns by county. The bibliography's coverage is more comprehensive than Norton in that the holdings of all libraries have been included, resulting in the inclusion of directories published by small local directory publishers as well as well-known national ones.

GENEALOGICAL RESEARCH

In the last 20 years there has been a tremendous growth of interest in family history, with research being undertaken not by professional record searchers, but by individuals whose knowledge of sources and the problems that can be encountered in interpreting the information can be limited. As a result, it has become necessary for the local studies librarian to have some knowledge of the methodology and sources that can be used when undertaking genealogical research. There are many books on the subject, such as *In search of ancestry*,[84] *Genealogy for beginners*,[85] *Tracing your ancestors*,[86] *Tracing your family tree*,[87] *Genealogical research in England and Wales*,[88] *Discovering your family tree*[89] and *Basic sources for family history: 1 Back to the early 1800s*,[90] all of which seek to explain the various sources that can be used and how research can be undertaken. In addition to books, many libraries, for example Knowsley and York, have published pamphlets and leaflets which give details of some of the sources that are to be found locally, as well as how to undertake such research.[91]

An important genealogical bibiography for librarians is:

Harvey, R. GENEALOGY FOR LIBRARIANS. 2nd edn. London: Library Association Publishing, 1992.

The aim of this publication is to provide some guidance to librarians who might be asked to assist amateur genealogists and family historians. It examines the problems faced by librarians and the sources family historians use. Although there is no bibliography, the text provides details of many important sources which can be of use.

For dealing with some of the problems which family historians encounter and for which they expect the library staff to know the answers, there is:

Rogers, C. D. THE FAMILY TREE DETECTIVE. 2nd edn. Manchester: Manchester University Press, 1985.

Sometimes the local studies staff are called upon to resolve these problems and explain why the information content of the same type of record varies. This book sets out to explain these problems in a comprehensible manner. There is a useful bibliography, which includes many publications dealing with some of the less well-known sources.

Parish registers are one important source of information for family historians. In recent years, parish registers have become more widely available on microfilm. A useful guide to registers and their format is to be found in:

THE NATIONAL INDEX OF PARISH REGISTERS. London: Phillimore, 1968.

This series of volumes aims to list all parish registers which are available for consultation in libraries and record offices. The first three volumes of the series form an introduction to the various types of register and ancillary sources such as monumental inscriptions and wills. The remaining volumes cover the country on a regional basis, but within each regional volume the parishes are arranged by county. Unfortunately, there is no indication as to where the registers can be consulted, but this information is recorded in *Parish register copies*,[92] which lists those registers held within the library of Society of Genealogists as well as in libraries and record offices. However, as it is now over 20 years since this was first published, the information is somewhat out of date as many other registers have been microfilmed.

To locate where various parishes were and what registers are available there is:

Humpherey-Smith, C. THE PHILLIMORE ATLAS AND INDEX OF PARISH REGISTERS. Chichester: Phillimore, 1995.

This volume consists of two sections. The first is a series of maps showing the various parishes on a regional basis, whereas the second part lists, by county, the various registers which are available, where they can be consulted, whether they are included in the International Genealogical Index (IGI), in Boyd's index or whether Bishop's transcripts exist. The main use of the volume is to establish adjacent parishes if the obvious place does not yield results.

Printed sources which might be helpful to genealogists and librarians are listed in:

Humpherey-Smith, C. R. A GENEALOGIST'S BIBLIOGRAPHY. Rev. edn. Chichester: Phillimore, 1985.

This bibliography is arranged by county, and gives details of the local record repositories before listing published transcripts on a wide range of subjects, such as feet of fines and marriages licences. The book also includes a helpful guide to sources which might be overlooked and a glossary of terms, as well as an extensive bibliography.

For a more extensive definition of unusual terms, as well as general information on genealogy such as when records began in certain parts of the United Kingdom, helpful publications are:

Saul, P. TRACING YOUR ANCESTORS: THE A–Z GUIDE. 5th edn. Newbury and Birmingham: Countryside Books and Federation of Family History Societies (Publications) Ltd, 1995.

Pine, L. G. THE GENEALOGIST'S ENCYCLOPEDIA. Newton Abbot: David and Charles,1969.

Fitzhugh, T. V. H. THE DICTIONARY OF GENEALOGY. Sherbourne: Alphabooks, 1985. 4th edn revised by S. Lumas on behalf of the Society of Genealogists. London: A. & C. Black, 1995.

These three publications are all very similar in that they arrange their material alphabetically and are intended to provide their users with a basic answer relatively quickly and easily. As Saul comments in her introduction: 'No book could possibly give you the answers to all the questions which arise in family history research. It should be helpful . . . to know where to find specialist advice . . . Hence the emphasis . . . is on sources of information in bookform or indexes'.[93] From the point of view of the librarian, Saul's book is probably the most useful as it brings together much of the material included in the other two in a clear, concise format, and has the added advantage that it includes a note of relevant published works for various entries. There is also a helpful list of Public Record Office guides, a list of various regiments, their number and subsequent name, and maps of the counties before and after local government reform in 1974.

As well as genealogical material in local libraries and record offices, there is also some genealogical material in the Public Record Office, details of which are given in:

Cox, J. and Padfield, T. TRACING YOUR ANCESTORS IN THE PUBLIC RECORD OFFICE. 4th edn. Bevan, A. and Duncan, A. (eds.) London: HMSO, 4th impression, 1995. Public Record Office Handbooks No. 19.

This publication examines the various sources which exist in the Public Record Office for genealogists. It includes well-known sources such as the census, but also sources where information can be found on people born abroad or who have served in the armed services, records of the Church of England, criminal trials and emigration. Each section includes a short account of the origin of the source, details of some of the published works on them, unpublished guides and brief details of the dates covered by the records. There is also a list of useful addresses as well as a comprehensive index. As well as guides to general sources in the Public Record Office, there are publications that deal with particular categories of people. Often, the guides to these sources have been published by the Public Record Office in conjunction with a commercial publisher. For example, Hawkins's work on railway staff records provides information on extant railway records as well as on who was employed by the various companies.[94]

In order to help understand some of the sources, and guide researchers to sources they might not think about, the Federation of Family History Societies has an extensive publishing programme which includes pamphlets on a wide range of sources, as well as county genealogical bibliographies. The latter include details of printed histories, parish registers, directories and official lists of names.[95]

Research into family history can sometimes lead individuals to research into the type of community in which the people lived, in other words they become local historians. The Open University course on 'Community and the family' implies that this is the logical step and, to accompany the course, has published four volumes, the first three of which take the reader from family tree to community history, whereas the fourth volume deals with sources and methods.[96]

CENSUS REPORTS

Census returns and reports are also important sources of local information. The census reports, published shortly after the census was taken, are simply a statistical account of the population of an area, whereas the enumerators' returns give personal information which is not released until 100 years after the census was taken. Many libraries have acquired microfilm and microfiche copies of the returns for their own areas for the years 1841–91. Sometimes it is necessary to know where copies of other enumerators' returns can be consulted. This information can be found in J. S. W. Gibson's *Census returns 1841–1891 on microfilm: a directory of local holdings*,[97] which lists not only libraries and record offices with copies of the census, but also where there are indexes as well.

For background information on the way the various censuses have been conducted there are:

Office of Population, Censuses and Surveys. GUIDE TO CENSUS REPORTS: GREAT BRITAIN 1801–1966. London: HMSO, 1977.

Higgs, E. MAKING SENSE OF THE CENSUS: THE MANUSCRIPT RETURNS FOR ENGLAND AND WALES 1801–1901. London: HMSO, 1989.

Luman, S. MAKING USE OF THE CENSUS. London: PRO, 1992.

Lawton, E. (ed.) THE CENSUS AND SOCIAL STRUCTURE. London: Cass, 1978.

The census is one of the most widely used sources as it enables a picture of a community to be built up, especially if the enumerators' returns are used. It is therefore necessary to be aware not only of the way the various censuses were taken, but also their accuracy and the meaning of some of the terms used. An account of how the census was taken is included in *Guide to census reports*, which also includes examples of the forms which were used, and in *Making sense of the census*, which includes a section on the make-up of a nominal page and a glossary of terms used. Luman's book has been described as 'a companion to Higgs' and is a practical guide to using the census. For those who require the census to be placed in context, together with its contribution to developing an understanding of the nineteenth century, there is Lawton's book.

It can be difficult to obtain accurate information on population before the first census in 1801, but there are some sources which can be used. These are outlined in *Sources for the history of population and their uses*,[98] which also includes an explanation of the difficulties and problems encountered when using these sources. For definitions of some of the terms that are used in demographic studies and how some of the calculations are made, there is *A glossary for local population studies*.[99] Many of the results of research using pre-1801 sources, as well as details of analytical work carried out on the enumerators' returns, are reported in *Local population studies*.[100]

PLACE NAMES

Sometimes the occasion arises when it is necessary to trace information on the origins of place names. The English Place Name Society has undertaken much research on this subject, and published its results in a series of volumes for many of the English counties. For each county there is an introductory volume which is followed by a series of volumes covering place and field names for the various districts. For a less detailed account of place names and their origins there is:

Ekwall, E. CONCISE OXFORD DICTIONARY OF ENGLISH PLACE NAMES. 4th edn. Oxford: Oxford University Press, 1974.

This gives both the derivation of individual place names and the meaning of some of the more common place name elements, such as '-ton', '-ley' and '-bury'. For each entry there is a list of alternative spellings and the dates when they first appeared, as well as the language from which the word is derived. The dictionary concentrates on place names and does not include field or street names. Ekwall, however, does not put the names in their historical context as Gelling does in *Signposts to the past: place names and the history of England*.[101] For those who want to trace field names, there is Field's *English field names: a dictionary*,[102] while for a more detailed analysis of river names Ekwall's *English river names*[103] should be consulted, both follow an alphabetical approach.

BIOGRAPHICAL INFORMATION

Biographical information is also important in local studies work, but more often it is the lesser-known people about whom information is sought. General works such as *Dictionary of national biography* cover only the most prominent people who have made their mark on the national scene, although *Modern English biography*[104] includes more people of local importance. A valuable source for local biographies is the various county biographical dictionaries, many of which were compiled at the beginning of the twentieth century. A useful introduction to this source and others is 'Some neglected sources of biographical information'.[105]

NON-BOOK MATERIAL

In addition to printed material, local studies departments include extensive collections of non-book material such as maps, illustrations and ephemera. With the exception of maps, most non-book material tends to be 'locality specific' and not to be listed either regionally or nationally.

Maps

Maps form an important and well-used part of local studies department stock, the best-known of which are those published by the Ordnance Survey, which are the most recent in a long line of maps published since the sixteenth century. When it comes to publications, Ordnance Survey maps have tended to be treated separately from non-Ordnance Survey maps. However, two recent publications have examined both types together:

Hindle, P. MAPS FOR LOCAL HISTORY. London: Batsford, 1988.

Smith, D. MAPS AND PLANS FOR THE LOCAL HISTORIAN AND COL-LECTOR. London: Batsford, 1988.

On the surface these two titles may appear to cover the same ground, but this is not the case: they are in fact complementary to each other. *Maps for local history* concentrates on county, estate, enclosure and tithe maps, town plans, transport maps and Ordnance Survey maps. *Maps and plans for local historians and collectors* covers a similar range of maps but includes an examination of more unusual ones which may be of interest to local historians, for example, military maps, marine charts and settlement plans. Both authors examine the origins of the various types of map and include bibliographies. Hindle also includes some information on special collections of maps and a list of reprinted county maps. As well as these two publications on maps and their use, a series of articles in *Local history* by Nichols entitled 'Maps and plans for local historians' is a very useful introduction to the use of maps, including such subjects as village maps and maps on communications.[106]

Until the publication of these two books, the basic introduction to non-Ordnance Survey maps was, and in many respects still is:

Harley, J. B. MAPS FOR THE LOCAL HISTORIAN: A GUIDE TO BRITISH SOURCES. London: Standing Conference for Local History, 1972.

Although the original articles on which this pamphlet is based were published over 30 years ago,[107] this book is still a useful introduction to non-Ordnance Survey maps. It examines six different types of maps and draws attention to the problems that are encountered when using them. There is also an extensive bibliography, which lists not only cartographical works but also local publications that list maps.

Until the nineteenth century, county maps were the main type of map which was published, with occasional town plans. Many county maps were reissued several times without any changes being made, except possibly in the imprint; to establish which edition is which, there are several useful bibliographies of county maps:

Chubb, T. PRINTED MAPS IN THE ATLASES OF GREAT BRITAIN AND IRELAND . . . 1579–1870. London: Dawson, 1927. Reprinted 1974.

Rogers, E. M. LARGE SCALE COUNTY MAPS OF THE BRITISH ISLES, 1596–1850: A UNION LIST. 2nd edn. Oxford: Bodleian Library, 1971.

Skelton, R. A. COUNTY ATLASES OF THE BRITISH ISLES 1579–1850. London: Carta Press, 1970.

Of these three publications, the most satisfactory from the point of view of local studies librarians is that by Rogers, who has adopted a topographcal approach, listing details of each map county by county and providing information on libraries with specific copies. Chubb and Skelton have both adopted a chronological approach, which means that it is more difficult to locate maps for a particular county quickly.

In addition to the national lists which have been published, there are important publications that list maps relating to specific counties. For example, the Bristol and Gloucester Archaeological Society published a list of Gloucester maps in 1912.[108]

An invaluable guide to Ordnance Survey maps is:

Harley, J. B. THE HISTORIAN'S GUIDE TO ORDNANCE SURVEY MAPS. London: Standing Conference for Local History, 1964.

In this pamphlet Harley outlines the history of the Ordnance Survey, after which he comments on the various editions of the small-scale Ordnance Survey maps. He also includes a section on the large-scale town plans, which are especially important for urban historians. Instead of listing these maps a series of sketch maps is used to show the areas and towns covered by them.

Photographs

Maps constitute only a small proportion of the non-book material in local studies collections. Many collections also include substantial holdings of illustrative material, often in the form of photographs. However, it should be remembered that before photographs engravings were the main form of illustration. In order to discover what collections there are, although both are now somewhat dated, it is helpful to consult:

Barley, M. W. A GUIDE TO BRITISH TOPOGRAPHICAL COLLECTIONS. London: Council for British Archaeology, 1974.

Wall, J. DIRECTORY OF BRITISH PHOTOGRAPHIC COLLECTIONS. London: Royal Photographic Society, 1977.

These two publications examine different aspects of illustrations collections. Barley tends to concentrate on prints and makes only brief references to photographic collections, whereas Wall deals specifically with photographs. Barley is arranged by county, with individual towns being listed under the county, and locations in both libraries and art galleries are given. Wall, on the other hand, has adopted a subject approach and gives little information on the full extent of collections.

Whereas engravings will tend to include 'artist's licence' in that things may be left out or added to suit the occasion, this was not so easy with photographs. The importance of photographs is that they have now been around for over 150 years and as such have a wide variety of uses, for example, to show the changes which have taken place in a locality over a period of time, as well as providing information on such subjects as costume, architectural detail, street furniture, transport, events and advertisements. Often the same photograph can provide several items of information, depending on what is being sought. Even modern photographs have their value, as things change very rapidly when redevelopment takes place. Probably the most useful way to discover the value of illustrations is to spend a short time studying individual ones, looking at the content and for detail – which, incidentally, can sometimes be used to date undated photographs.[109] Sometimes libraries try to record their town and the changes which have taken place. For an account of a modern photographic record and an assessment after 21 years there is a useful article in the *Manchester review*.[110] A useful publication for those who want to start a photographic survey or make copies of material lent to the library is:

Houlder, E. RECORDING THE PAST: A PHOTOGRAPHER'S HANDBOOK. Studley: Local History in association with K. A. F. Brewin Books, 1988.

The approach taken in this publication is a practical one aimed at helping local historians and, by implication local studies librarians, take better photographs. There are sections on equipment, storage and, from the local studies librarian's point of view, how to take clear, legible photographs of inscriptions and how to copy photographs.

On a more general level, dealing with the content of photographs, is:

Oliver, G. USING OLD PHOTOGRAPHS: A GUIDE FOR THE LOCAL HISTORIAN. London: Batsford, 1989.

This looks at the various types of photograph that exist and the use local historians make of them. Attention is drawn to the amount of information that can be gleaned by studying photographs, and this is reinforced by the use of carefully chosen examples.

As many collections of illustrations are related to a particular locality and are not by famous photographers, little attention has been paid to recording details of the scope of photographic collections in local studies departments.

Ephemera

Within any local collection there is a large body of material which is difficult to categorize as it consists chiefly of single sheets of paper. It is referred to variously as 'miscellaneous material' or 'ephemera'. It is difficult to compile a full list of the type of material that constitutes ephemera, but there is a list to be found in:

Makepeace, C. E. EPHEMERA: A BOOK ON ITS COLLECTION, CONSERVATION AND STORAGE. Aldershot: Gower, 1985.

This book defines ephemera and distinguishes it from minor publications, with which it is often confused. It also includes a detailed examination of the various types of ephemera, and how it can be collected and treated in the library situation. The appendix includes a lengthy list of various types of ephemera as well as a bibliography on the subject.

Other books which deal with ephemera are:

Clinton, A. PRINTED EPHEMERA COLLECTION, ORGANISATION AND ACCESS. London: Bingley, 1981.

Rickards, M. THIS IS EPHEMERA: COLLECTING PRINTED THROW-AWAYS. Newton Abbot: David and Charles, 1977.

After a general introduction on ephemera and its problems, Clinton examines the ephemera that has been produced in three separate areas. He deals with collecting policies as well as the uses to which the material can be put. Rickard's book, on the other hand, is intended for the private collector, but he does include a useful indication of where ephemera may be found and the wide range of material which attracts the private collector.

In addition to these books, which deal with ephemera generally, there are a number of publications that deal with specific types of ephemera. Among these are *Printed ephemera*,[111] *Collecting printed ephemera*,[112] *Ephemera of travel and transport*[113] and *Accounts rendered*,[114] which consists of billheads from shopkeepers and merchants in Pembrokeshire in the nineteenth and early twentieth centuries.

Tape recordings

Tape recordings are a significant source of oral information that has increased in importance with the advent of the cassette recorder. Some libraries have built up collections of reminiscences, sounds and eye-witness accounts. The case for oral history is put in P. Thompson's *The voice of the people: oral history*,[115] and the journal of the Oral History Society *Oral history*[116] gives an indication of the work that is currently being undertaken.

Often the amateur can be put off making recordings by the use of technical jargon, but much of the mystique is stripped away in:

Howarth, K. AN INTRODUCTION TO SOUND RECORDING FOR THE ORAL HISTORIAN AND SOUND ARCHIVIST. Radcliffe: The author, 1977.

This booklet introduces oral history for the beginner and explains, in simple terms, some of the technical details of the work, including how to make satisfactory sound recordings.

A lot of work has been done in the field of oral history, but it can be difficult to trace who has done what and where. A guide to this is:

Perks, R. ORAL HISTORY: AN ANNOTATED BIBLIOGRAPHY. London: British Library, 1900.

This bibliography comprises mainly oral history material which has either been published as complete transcripts or used to form the basis of a publication. There is a short note on the oral history content of each entry, with details of the publisher and date. There is also an extensive index of both places and subjects, so that particular places can be easily located.

A local studies department or library is a microcosm of the main library. Its subject field impinges on almost every department of the library, and hence its staff have to be familiar with a wide range of material and sources. They must be familiar not only with local material, but also with general material. Although the library may only have material on its own area in detail, the staff will need to know where to find general information on other areas and where to direct inquirers to for further information. The expansion of interest in local history has resulted in an explosion of new publishing, as well as a growth in requests for information on related subjects, such as listed buildings and archaeology.[117] Many of the items referred to in this chapter can be used by both the specialist seeking to ensure that the collection is as comprehensive as possible, and by the reference library staff seeking to answer queries or provide a guide to an area with which they are not familiar.

REFERENCES AND CITATIONS

1   Guyver, R., *A national curriculum study unit: Local history 1* and *A*

national curriculum study unit: Local history 2, Huntingdon, Elm Publications, 1994.

2 Rogers, A., *Approaches to local history*, 4.

3 Rogers, C. D. and Smith, J. H., *Local family history in England*, 4.

4 *Ibid.*, 4.

5 Library Association County Libraries Group, *Sources of local history*, 4th edn, London, Library Association, 1971.

6 Hale, A. T., *Local history handlist*, 5th edn, London, Historical Association, 1982.

7 Campbell-Kease, J., *A companion to local history research*, Sherborne, Alphabooks, 1989.

8 Library Association Local Studies Group, *Local studies librarians*, 1982– . Twice yearly.

9 Library Association Local Studies Group Scottish Branch, *Locscot*, 1984– . Twice yearly.

10 Iredale, 3.

11 Hoskins, W. G., *Fieldwork in local history*, London, Faber & Faber, 1982.

12 Dunning, ix.

13 Riden, 9.

14 Stephens, 1.

15 Campbell-Kease, 11.

16 A full account is to be found in Pugh, R. B., *The Victoria county history of the counties of England*. London, Institute of Historical Research, 1970. *See also* Pugh, R. B., 'The Victoria county histories' in *Local historian*, **13** (1), 15–22. A more recent article on the Victoria county histories by C. Cuuie is to be found in *Local history*, **38**, 12–13.

17 *Victoria county history of Essex: bibliography*, London, Institute of Historical Research, 1959.

18 Hindle, P., *Maps for local history*, London, Batsford, 1988.

19 Oliver, G., *Using old photographs: a guide for the local historian*, London, Batsford.

20 Moody, D., *Scottish local history: an introductory guide*, London, Batsford, 1988.
Moody, D., *Scottish family history*, London, Batsford, 1989.
Moody, D., *Scottish towns: a guide for local historians*, London, Batsford, 1992.
Yurdan, M., *Irish family history*, London, Batsford, 1990.

21 Stuart, D., *Manorial records: an introduction to the transcription and*

translation, Chichester, Phillimore, 1992.

Tarver, A., *Church court records: an introduction for family history and local historians*, Chichester, Phillimore, 1995.

22 Riden, P., *Probate records and the local community*, Gloucester, Sutton, 1985.

23 Doughty, M. (ed.), *Building the industrial city*, Leicester, Leicester University Press, 1986.

24 Rose, M. E. (ed.), *The poor and the city: the English poor law in its urban context, 1834–1914*, Leicester, Leicester University Press, 1985.

25 Gibson, J. and Peskett, P., *Record offices and how to find them*, 2nd edn, Plymouth, Federation of Family History Societies, 1982.

26 Pinhorn, M., *Historical, archaeological and kindred societies in the United Kingdom: a list*, Isle of Wight, Pinhorn, 1986.

27 Wyke, T. and Rudyard, N. (comp.), *Directory of local studies in north west England*, Manchester, Bibliography of North West England, 1993. A new edition is proposed for 1996.

28 Formerly *Amateur historian*.

29 The British Association for Local History is the successor to the Standing Conference for Local History.

30 *Local historian*, **1** (1), 1.

31 *Local history news*, 1982. Quarterly. Originally called *NAB: local history news*.

32 *Local history*, Issue 1, 1.

33 *Urban history yearbook*, Leicester, Leicester University Press 1974–1991. 1992– . Annual. Cambridge, Cambridge University Press. Twice yearly.

34 *Manchester region history review*, Manchester, Manchester Metropolitan University. Twice yearly 1986–1991, thereafter annually. An extensive bibliography is to be found in the Spring issue when it was published twice a year and is included in the annual volume now.

35 *Lancashire bibliography*. 16v. Manchester, Bibliography of North West England (formerly Joint Committee for the Lancashire Bibliography), 1961.

36 Douch, R., *Handbook of local history: Dorset with supplement and corrections*, Bristol, Bristol University Extra Mural Department, 1961.

37 Hodgson, H. W. A., *A bibliography of the history and topography of Cumberland and Westmorland*, Carlisle, Carlisle & Westmorland Archives Committee, 1968.

38 Leighton, M. (comp.), *Peterloo, Monday 16th August 1819: a bibliography*, Manchester, Manchester Libraries Committee, 1969.

39 Anderson, J. R., *The book of British topography*, 2nd imp., Wakefield, 1976.

40 Humphreys, A. L. A., *A handbook of county bibliographies . . . relating to the counties and towns of Great Britain*, 2nd imp., London, Dawson, 1974.

41 Library Association Eastern Branch, *East Anglian bibliography*, 1960– . Quarterly.

42 Goss, C., *Bibliography of British municipal history*, 2nd edn, Leicester, Leicester University Press, 1966.

43 *Bibliography of historical works issued in the United Kingdom*, 5v, London, Institute of Historical Research, 1957– .

44 *Writings on British history*, 25v, London, Cape, for the Institute of Historical Research, 1937– .

45 *Oxford bibliography of British history*, 6v, Oxford, Oxford University Press, 1952–77.

46 Bonser, W. A., *Romano-British bibliography*, 2v, Oxford, Blackwell, 1964.

47 Bonser, W. A., *An Anglo-Saxon and Celtic bibliography*, 2v, Oxford, Blackwell, 1957.

48 Keeler, M. F., *Bibliography of British history: Stuart period 1603–1714*, 3rd edn, Oxford, Oxford University Press, 1970.

49 Ottley, G., *A bibliography of British railway history*, London, HMSO, 1983 and *Supplement*, London, HMSO, 1988.

50 *Writings on British history*, 25v, London, Cape, for the Institute of Historical Research, 1937– .

51 Mumby, L., *How much is it worth?*, Chichester, British Association for Local History, 1989.

52 *Guide to the contents of the Public Record Office*, Rev edn, 3v, London, HMSO, 1963–8.

53 Public Record Office, *Leaflets*, 2v. Compiled from individual leaflets published by the PRO.

54 Saul, P., *Tracing your ancestors: the A–Z guide*, 5th edn, Newbury and Birmingham, Countryside Books and Federation of Family History Societies, 1995. Appendix II, 257.

55 Galbraith, V. H., *An introduction to the use of public records*, Oxford, Oxford University Press, 1963.

56 Royal Commission on Historical Manuscripts, *Guide to the reports and collections of manuscripts*, 3v, London, HMSO, 1914 and *Guide to the reports of the Royal Commission 1911–1957*, 4v, London, HMSO, 1966.

57 Storey, R. and Druker, J., *Guide to the modern records centre*, University of Warwick Occasional Papers No. 2. Coventry, Warwick University, 1977.

58 Richmond, L. and Stockford, B., *Company archives: a survey of the records of 1000 of the first registered companies in England and Wales*, Aldershot, Gower, 1986.

59 For example Cockerell, H. A. L. and Green, E., *The British insurance review: a guide to its history and records*, 2nd edn, Sheffield, Sheffield Academic Press, 1994.
Richmond, L. and Turton, A., *The brewing industry: a guide to historic records*, Manchester, Manchester University Press, 1990.
Pressnell, L. S. and Orbell, J. (eds.), *A guide to the historical records of British banking*, Aldershot, Gower, 1985.

60 Cox, R. W., *Index to sporting manuscsripts in the United Kingdom*, Frodsham, British Society of Sports History in association with Sports Historical Publications, 1995.

61 Ranger, F., 'The National Register of Archives', *Journal of the Society of Archivists*, 3, 452–62.

62 Dibben, A., *Title deeds*, London, Historical Association, new edn, 1990.
Cornwall, J., *How to read old title deeds*, Shalfleet Manor, Pinhorn, 1964.

63 Emmison, F. G. and Gray, I., *County records*, London, Historical Association, 1974.

64 Evans, E. J., *Tithes and the Tithe Commutation Act 1836*, London, Standing Conference for Local History, 1980.

65 Beckett, J. V., *Local taxation and the problems of enforcement*, London: Standing Conference for Local History, 1980.

66 Harvey, J. H., *Sources for the history of houses*, London, British Records Association, 1974.
Bushell, P., *Tracing the history of your house*, London, Pavillion Books, 1989.

67 Cheney, C. R., *Handbook of dates for students of history*, London, Royal Historical Society, 1970.

68 Gooder, E. A., *Latin for local history*, London, Longman, 1975.

69 Stuart, D., *Latin for local and family historians*, Chichester, Phillimore, 1995.

70 Emmison, F. G., *How to read local archives, 1550–1700*, London, Historical Association, 1973.

71 Mumby, L., *Reading Tudor and Stuart handwriting*, Chichester, British Association for Local History, 1988.

72 Murphy, M., *Newspapers and local history*, Chichester, British Association for Local History, 1991.

73 A useful account of this is to be found in an article by Eagle, S. and Hamilton, G., 'Preserving the perishing papers: NEWSPLAN and your local newspaper' in *Local history*, 37, Jan/Feb 1993.

74 Greenall, R. L., *The Leicester newspapers, 1850–1870: a guide for historians*, Leicester, Department of Adult Education, University of Leicester, 1980.

75 *Times index* 1785– . London, The Times.

76 *Illustrated London news*, London, 1842– .

77 *The builder* 1842–1956.

78 Harper, R. H., *Victorian architectural competitions: an index to British and Irish architectural competitions in* The builder *1843–1900*, London, Mansell, 1983.

79 *Back track*, Penryn, Cornwall: Atlantic Transport Publishers, 1986– .

80 *Industrial archaeology review*, 1976– . Vols 1–6 published by Oxford University Press. Vols 7–   published by Association for Industrial Archaeology.

81 *Archive*, Witney, Lightmoor Press, 1994– . Quarterly.

82 For London directories there is Goss, C. W. F., *The London directories 1677–1855*, London, Archer, 1932.

83 Radmore, D. F. and Radmore, S., *Guide to the directories of the West Midlands to 1850*, London, Library Association Reference, Special and Information Section, West Midlands Sections, 1971.

84 Hamilton-Edwards, G., *In search of ancestry*, Rev edn, London, Phillimore, 1974.

85 Willis, A. J. and Tachell, M., *Genealogy for beginners*, New edn, London, Phillimore, 1984.

86 Camp, A. J., *Tracing your ancestors*, Rev edn, Gifford, 1970.

87 Cole, J. A. and Armstrong, M., *Tracing your family tree*, London, Guild Publishing, 1988.

88 Smith, F. and Gardner, D. E., *Genealogical research in England and Wales*, 3v, Salt Lake City, Bookcraft, 1956–66.

89 Iredale, D. and Barrett, J., *Discovering your family tree*, 4th edn, Princes Risborough, Shire Publications, 1985.

90 Todd, A., *Basic sources for family history. 1: back to the early 1800s*, 2nd edn, Ramsbottom, Allen & Todd, 1989.

91 Bowling, R. G., *Researching family history in York Reference Library*, York, North Yorkshire County Library, 1989.
    Burgess, B. M. (comp.), *Tracing your family history in the Knowsley area at Huyton Library*, Huyton, Department of Leisure Services, Knowsley, 1989.

92 Society of Genealogists, *Parish register copies*, 2v, London, Phillimore, 1971.

93 Saul, 3.

94 Hawkins, D. T., *Railway ancestors: a guide to the staff records of the railway companies of England and Wales 1822–1947*, Stroud, Sutton and PRO, 1995.

95 For a full list of their publications, it is necessary to contact the Federation of Family History Societies, The Benson Room, Birmingham and Midland Institute, Margaret Street, Birmingham B3 3BS.

96 Finnigan, R. and Drake, M., *From family tree to family history*.
    Price, W. R., *From family history to community history*.
    Golby, J. (ed.), *Communities and families*.
    Drake, M. and Finnigan, R., *Sources and methods*.
    Cambridge University Press and Open University, 1994.

97 Gibson, J. S. W., *Census returns 1841–1891 on microfilm: a directory of local holdings*, 5th edn, Plymouth, Federation of Family History Societies, 1992.

98 Stephens, W. B., *Sources for the history of population and their uses*, Leeds, Leeds University Institute of Education, 1971.

99 Bradley, L., *A glossary for local population studies*, Matlock, Local Population Studies Society, 1978.

100 *Local population studies*, 1947– . Twice yearly.

101 Gelling, M., *Signposts to the past: place names and the history of England*, 2nd edn, Chichester, Phillimore, 1988.

102 Field, J., *English field names: a dictionary*, 2nd imp, Stroud, Sutton, 1989.

Field, J., *A history of English field names*, London, Longman, 1993.

103 Ekwall, E., *English river names*, Oxford, Oxford University Press, 1968.

104 Boase, F., *Modern English biography*, 2nd imp, 6v, London, Cass. Reprinted 1965.

105 *Bulletin of the Institute of Historical Research*, 34, 1961, 56–66.

106 *Local historian*, issues 25–31.

107 *Amateur historian*, 7, 6–8 and 8, 2, 3, 5.

108 Chubb, T., *A descriptive catalogue of the printed maps of Gloucester 1577–1911*, Gloucester, Bristol and Gloucester Archaeological Society, 1912.

109 Makepeace, C. E., 'Dating and locating unidentified photographs'; in *Proceedings and papers of 1981 symposium of the European Society for the History of Photography*, Bath.

110 Millgan, H., 'The Manchester photographic survey', in *Manchester review*, 8, 1958, 193–204.
Makepeace, C. E., 'Twenty-one years of continuous record survey', in *Manchester review*, 12, 1972, 43–8.

111 Lewis, J., *Printed ephemera*, London, Faber and Faber, 1969.

112 Lewis, J., *Collecting printed ephemera*, London, Studio Vista, 1976.

113 Anderson, J. and Swindlehurst, E., *Ephemera of travel and transport*, London, New Cavendish Books, 1981.

114 McBreaty, J. (comp.), *Accounts rendered: some Pembrokeshire merchants' and shopkeepers' billheads from the 19th and earlier 20th centuries*, Pembrokeshire, Pembrokeshire Publicity Services, 1987.

115 Thompson, P., *The voice of the people: oral history*, Oxford, Oxford University Press, 1972.

116 *Oral history*, Colchester, Oral History Society, 1972– .

117 Aston, M. and Rowsley, T., *Landscape archaeology*, Newton Abbot, David and Charles, 1974.
Brown, A., *Fieldwork for archaeologists and local historians*, London, Batsford, 1987.
Pearce, D., *Historic buildings and planning policies*, London, Council for British Archaeology, 1979.

8
Community Information

Allan Bunch

Even though community information services have been in operation in this country for over 20 years, and longer in the United States, there is, in my view, still a need to remind a new generation of librarians of just what is meant by the term.

The term 'community information' first appeared in the United States, where it was used to describe the kind of services developed during the 1960s as part of the war against poverty and urban decay. Since these services were neighbourhood-based and attempted to link the enquirer with appropriate sources of help in the community, they were called 'community information services'. The first community information service in a public library, the Public Information Center at Enoch Pratt Free Library in Baltimore, was set up in 1970 after a study conducted by a team led by Joseph C. Donohue of Maryland library school.[1]

It was Donohue who first attempted a definition of the term 'community information' and it is still one of the best. He described it as information needed to cope with 'crises in the lives of individuals and communities'.[2] Donohue expanded on this definition by identifying two types of information provided by a community information service:

1   survival information, such as that related to health, housing, income, legal protection, economic opportunity, political rights etc.

2   citizen action information, needed for effective participation as individual or as member of a group in the social, political, legal, economic process.[3]

Further experiments followed in other libraries in the United States, and by the mid-1970s reports of these began to filter through to Britain via the American professional press and as a result of a report by Ed Whalley, a Research Fellow of the Department of Library and Information Studies at Leeds Polytechnic, who visited several of these services in 1975.[4] By the end of the decade a number of libraries in Britain had set up services which, though differing from each other in some respects, could all be subsumed under the banner of 'community information'. These services showed a greater diversity than their American counterparts, where the emphasis was on the I & R (information and referral) file, with enquiries received predominantly over the telephone. In 1980 a British Library research project undertaken by the Department of Library and Information Studies at Leeds Polytechnic identified three models of community information provision in this country, which they termed 'back-up', 'direct service' and 'self-help'. A 'back-up' service was one in which librarians used their reference and bibliographical skills to produce directories, information packs and current awareness bulletins, mainly for other professionals and voluntary organizations. A 'direct service' involved the librarian in the face-to-face transfer of information with the user by actively locating local sources of information and making local contacts. The 'self-help' approach involved the librarian in collecting, compiling and arranging material in a way that made it easier for the customer to use largely unaided.[5]

1980 also saw the publication of *Community information: what libraries can do*, the result of two years' deliberation by the Library Association Working Party on Community Information. The report defined community information services as those which:

> . . . assist individuals and groups with daily problem-solving and with participation in the democratic process. The services concentrate on the needs of those who do not have ready access to other sources of assistance and on the most important problems that people have to face, problems to do with their homes, their jobs and their rights.[6]

The report also laid down practical guidelines for the development of community information in libraries and gave examples of good practice.

Today, most public library authorities would admit to providing some kind of community information service, even if no more than a collection of material (booklets, pamphlets, leaflets, packs etc.), usually arranged in broad categories and aimed at those with special needs or who experience difficulties in getting access to information that would help them with daily problem solving. Initially some of the larger authorities set up community information posts and even had community information teams to provide support to their own service points, to other professionals and to the voluntary sector. These teams were active in providing current awareness bulletins, directories, information packs, supplies of leaflets, loan collections of reference books etc. However, in the last five years, as a result of special funding drying up, budgetary pressures or restructuring, many of these specialist posts and teams have disappeared and their responsibilities have been subsumed in more general posts.

Before attempting to identify the major sources of community information there are a number of problems which this term presents both in itself and as a subject for inclusion in this book. First, *Reference information sources* is form not subject based. Community information is not a form. It exists in a wide variety of forms, from single sheets of paper and irregular newsletters produced by local groups to online databases, multivolume reference works, audiovisual material and, increasingly, other electronic forms, such as CD-ROM and the Internet.

Secondly, community information is not a single subject but, as we have seen from the definitions above, covers a range of subjects (or problem areas) and special needs. There is no agreed or official list of what those subjects should be, although a certain consensus does exist from one library authority to another, of which the following list is typical: careers, community, community (or race) relations, consumer, disability, education, employment, environment, family, government, health, housing, law, money, senior citizens, transport, unemployment, women, youth. Some libraries also include as separate categories: equal opportunities, gay rights, trade union rights, and fuel (or energy).

And thirdly, a lot of community information material is ephemeral in format, costs very little and is often free. This means that it has a short life-span in terms of currency, is rarely recorded in national or book trade bibliographies and is thus exceedingly difficult to track down. To record much of this material here would result in a long chapter with a very short life. Consequently, priority has been given to those titles which, in gardening terms, have become 'hardy perennials'. Even so, over the five years since this chapter first appeared a fair amount of material has been discontinued. I have tried to find replacements where possible. This has meant including first editions of some titles which, hopefully, have the appearance of becoming regularly updated.

Community information exists at varying levels, from neighbourhood to national and international. Although this chapter concentrates mainly on national sources, it should not be taken as implying that local publications are of lesser value. In fact, it is surprising and pleasing how often local groups, responding to the immediate needs of their community, produce excellent material which is transferable, useful and relevant in other parts of the country.

I have also included for the first time telephone numbers of organizations and publishers where I felt that these would be useful, with the caveat that over time many of these are bound to change.

GENERAL SOURCES

Bibliographies and current awareness

There is no single bibliographical service which adequately covers community information material. The *British national bibliography* provides a reasonable coverage of commercial publications and those of established organizations but is weak on the publications of smaller voluntary agencies and local groups. The time taken for items to be recorded in *BNB* is also a serious handicap to its usefulness, since up-to-dateness is a critical factor in community information. Leaflets, posters and broadsheets, audiovisual material and locally produced items deemed to be of purely local significance are simply not recorded in *BNB* as a matter of policy.

A few retrospective bibliographies have been published over the years but these are now so out of date that they cannot be recommended with any degree of assurance.

For current material, especially books and pamphlets, there has been a reduction in the sources of information since the last edition of this book. Especially sad has been the demise of the *Sunderland information exchange*, a victim of the aforementioned cuts, and *The Radical bookseller*. Even the monthly community information column contributed by the author of this chapter to *New library world*, has been moved to a bimonthly sister periodical:

LIBRARIANS' WORLD. MCB University Press Ltd. Bimonthly.

Regular column on 'Community information' covers books, pamphlets, A/V material, leaflets, and new initiatives. Extent of column allows only a small selection of the current output of community information materials to be covered.

Apart from that, there is very little else except for some limited coverage in the National Association of Citizens' Advice Bureaux's *Booklist*, part of the monthly NACAB pack and in some of the more general periodicals, such as *The Adviser, Community currents* and *Voluntary action*. These are covered in more detail below.

Leaflets

The vast number of leaflets that are available from statutory and non-statutory organizations present particular problems to librarians, both in identifying and obtaining them on a regular basis. This task has been made incomparably easier since the last edition of this book through the creation of:

FREE LEAFLETS INFORMATION SERVICE (Community Information Services, London Borough of Camden, Leisure Services Department, Crowndale Centre, 218 Eversholt Street, London NW1 1BD tel: 0171-911 1656).

Set up by Camden Libraries in 1991, with initial funding from the Public Libraries Development Incentive Scheme, this subscription service provides initially a list of all free leaflets currently available, a copy of the *FRILLS directory* (see below), and instructions on a model method of how to organize the leaflets. Each month subscribers receive a mailing containing a sample copy of new leaflet titles and new editions of existing leaflets, an instruction list detailing where to file them in the model system, and where to order bulk copies. The instructions also contain information on out-of-date titles to be withdrawn. A separate list gives details of additions and amendments to the *FRILLS Directory*. Subscriptions are £180 per annum for statutory organizations, and £150 for voluntary organizations (1995–6 rates). If you do not want to take out a subscription it is possible to purchase separately from the address above.

FRILLS (FREE INFORMATION LEAFLET SUPPLIERS).

Lists suppliers of free leaflet material in an alphabetical sequence by name of organization with subject and community language indexes. Each entry gives name, address, telephone and fax numbers of suppliers, plus in most cases a brief indication of the range of leaflets available and whether any charge is made for postage. Updated approximately every 18 months.

Another substantial listing of leaflets and suppliers comes as part of the National Association of Citizens' Advice Bureaux information packs (see below), but you would need to be a subscriber to receive this or have a friendly local bureau organizer prepared to copy it for you.

Information packs
NATIONAL ASSOCIATION OF CITIZENS' ADVICE BUREAUX INFORMA-TION SYSTEM. London: NACAB, Myddelton House, 115–123 Pentonville Road, London N1 9LZ tel: 0171-833 2181.

The information system consists of:

- information items written specially by NACAB's Information Production Department
- leaflets and booklets provided by government departments and other agencies selected because of their excellent coverage of specific topics
- reference books containing essential material and fully integrated into the system
- a comprehensive index to the whole system, with over 1200 main and 5000 subheadings
- *Update*: a magazine which provides a summary of changes in the law, current items of interest, and likely future developments
- *Booklist*: a review of new publications on topics of interest which are suitable for reference, background reading or recommendation to clients
- *Supplement*: a collection of material which is useful to advice workers, such as sources of leaflets

To maintain the Information system, an amendment pack is issued each month containing:

- amendments to the information items and leaflets to ensure that they are accurate in the light of legislative and administrative changes
- new information items and leaflets in response to major changes, or to reorganize and improve material already in the system
- new editions of the reference books as they become available
- monthly editions of *Update* and *Booklist*.

The Information System is divided into 14 categories: Communications; Travel and transport; Immigration and nationality; Administration of justice; Education; Employment; National and international; Family and personal; Social security; Health; Housing; Taxes and duties; Consumer; and Leisure. Within the broad categories there is a structure of subdivisions to make the system easy to use.

To subscribe to the Information System, a library must first obtain the approval of their local CAB and the Area Officer of the Association. They have 28 days to object to the supply of the system but would do so on very limited grounds. Approval is reviewed every year when the subscription is due. There are several conditions laid down concerning the use of the Information System: for example, a subscriber must not claim to be a Citizens' Advice Bureau or publicize that they subscribe to the service, and they may not reproduce any material prepared by NACAB.

The initial set-up costs of the system for statutory and commercial organizations are over £1000 and the annual subscription over £600. In addition, there needs to be a considerable commitment in staff time to update the system – about two days a month. That said, it is well worth the effort and expense for comprehensiveness, clarity of exposition, and up-to-dateness.

For those who do not have the space (the paper version takes up a four-drawer filing cabinet) or the staff time to update the hard copy, there is a microfiche version consisting of a single A4 binder holding approximately 340 fiches. These contain the complete Information System. Updating is simple as each month a new set of fiches is sent to replace the old one, and takes only about 10 minutes. There are some drawbacks to the fiche version as a tool for current awareness, since it is virtually impossible to identify which new or updated leaflets and information items have been added to the pack during the month. This is overcome to some extent by the provision of paper versions of *Update* and *Booklist* each month, to make it easier to use them as background reading. Another problem with the microfiche version is that it is less convenient to use when lengthy or quick consultation is required, but these are minor cavils compared with the convenience of updating and storing. The cost of the microfiche version is cheaper in the initial years because of a relatively low set-up cost compared to the paper version, but the annual subscription is some £200 more. This only pushes the total cost higher after five years.

For those who do not need the full Information System, in either hard copy or microfiche, NACAB also produces:

BASIC INFORMATION PACK. London: NACAB, Monthly updates.

This consists of three A4 customized ring binders containing information sheets on the same range of subjects as the full Information System; an alphabetical index; a current awareness bulletin highlighting significant developments in the information world; a monthly updating service; and a selection of leaflets to complement the text.

The pack is not aimed at experienced advice workers, but rather those who want to extend the range of information and advice they can offer. A useful feature is the clearly flagged warnings in the text where an experienced adviser's help is usually needed to progress further. Although it is relatively easy to use and update, library staff would benefit from training in its use. This can sometimes be arranged in conjunction with the local CAB. Libraries do not need to get the approval of their local CAB to subscribe to this pack, which is ideal for use in smaller libraries and even mobiles.

GOVERNMENT PUBLICATIONS

Official bodies in all their forms are a major source of community information, but as there is a separate chapter in this book on government publications this section deals only with ephemeral material (leaflets, posters etc.) rather than mainstream government publishing. A few items published by HMSO are mentioned in the subject categories below where these were deemed essential.

There is no consistency in the way individual government departments list their publications, or in the methods devised to enable the public and other outside bodies to obtain them. However, there has continued to be steady improvement over the last five years in arrangements for leaflet supply and in the recognition of the importance of libraries as outlets for their publicity. All departments might take note of the excellent library supply service put in place by the Benefits Agency (see below under Welfare benefits). There is a trend for some departments to employ outside agents for distributing their leaflets. Another disturbing development is the practice of some departments, mainly Quangos (Quasi Autonomous Non-Governmental Organizations), to charge for bulk supply of leaflets, e.g. Health and Safety Executive and Equal Opportunities Commission. No doubt this parsimony is budget driven, but it fails to bring important leaflets to the attention of those who may need them.

One of the best ways to keep in touch with the wide range of new and updated government leaflets is to subscribe to one of the information services available from the National Association of Citizens Advice Bureaux or to Camden Libraries' Free Leaflets Information Service (see above for details of both these services).

Another valuable source of information about government leaflets and changes or proposed changes in government legislation, is the press releases of individual departments. These can often be obtained free of charge from departments and some may even put you on a mailing list. But by far the best way for larger libraries to keep abreast of these is to take out a subscription to:

CENTRAL OFFICE OF INFORMATION PRESS RELEASE SERVICE. Daily. London: Central Office of Information, Hercules Road, London SE1 7DU tel: 0171-928 2345.

Provides subscribers with a daily list of press releases from government departments and quangos plus full text of any press release on request. The COI have also introduced a *Keyfax* service that enables users to access key facts and figures from government press releases quickly and conveniently, by fax. There is no subscription charge, the service is operated on premium rate numbers, and users are charged through their telephone bill. The essential component of the service is a twice-daily listing of press releases, which is retrieved by dialling from your fax machine; a similar arrangement exists for getting a full-text copy of any required press release. The COI has also started to use the Internet for major news items, such as the Budget announcements.

SUBJECT AREAS

Within the scope of this chapter it has only been possible to cover some key sources of information within each subject area, with the emphasis on those organizations or publications which:

- provide a current awareness service or book reviews of community information materials within each subject area
- are a source of regularly updated information on the subject
- publish handbooks or guides which are generally considered essen-

tial for any community information collection
- provide a reasonably comprehensive coverage of the subject.

There are many other organizations producing worthwhile material that it has not been possible to mention. A key source of information about these is the *Voluntary agencies directory* (see page 197) or some of the more specialized directories listed under individual subjects.

Often the best source of up-to-date information about new publications will be a periodical. Some of the most useful ones for current awareness and hard information have been covered under the subject headings below, but there is one title which does not fit neatly into any particular category, and that is:

THE ADVISER. London: National Association of Citizens' Advice Bureaux/Shelter. Bimonthly.

Provides the latest news, reviews, comments and case law on social security, housing, money advice and employment from the viewpoint of advisers. A regular feature, 'Abstracts', provides summaries of legal cases. There is also a review section of new publications.

Careers

There is so much material on careers that this section could not attempt to do justice to it. The following general titles should cover most of the basic information needed.

OCCUPATIONS. Annual. Careers & Occupational Information Centre, PO Box 348, Bristol BS99 7FE tel: 0117–977 7199.

A comprehensive reference book containing details of around 600 jobs and careers arranged by the Careers Library Classification Index (CLCI) with an alphabetical index.

JOBFILE 96: THE COMPREHENSIVE CAREERS HANDBOOK. London: Hodder & Stoughton, 1995.

A–Z reference book giving information on around 600 jobs. For each is given the required entry qualifications for young people and adults, entry and training opportunities, work details, personal qualities desirable, references to other careers publications, addresses for further information, and a list of similar jobs.

The information in *Jobfile* provides the core of various careers software packages, of which the most suitable for independent use are: *Explorer*, which allows searching of the Jobfile to find jobs that match chosen work factors, and *HEadlight*, which uses Jobfile to provide information for those considering how higher education courses relate to work. Further details of these are available from JIIG-CAL Careers Research Centre, Edinburgh EH8 9LW tel: 0131-650 4310.

WHICH SUBJECT? WHICH CAREER? 5th edn. Consumers' Association, 1994.

Assesses subject and career options available to teenagers at 14, 16 and 18. Extensive A–Z careers section outlining types of job available within each career, as well as the training and qualifications required.

For individual careers, the series published by Kogan Page can be recommended as informative, reasonably up to date and good value for money.

For those interested in video format, COIC jointly promote with the publisher a series called:

CAREERS IN FOCUS. (Edman Communications Group plc, 92 Hagley Road, Edgbaston, Birmingham B16 8LU.)

A library of video programmes designed to help all those concerned with careers to keep informed.

Children and young people

The central agency providing information, advice and curriculum development materials for young people and all those who work with them is the **National Youth Agency** (17–23 Albion Street, Leicester LE1 6GD tel: 0116-285 6789). Its publications include information packages, regularly updated briefing sheets on current issues, free leaflets, and priced publications. NYA's monthly magazine *Young people now* provides up-to-date news about young people and youth work; book reviews; current awareness; and details of conferences and courses. The magazine has an occasional supplement called 'Ad-Lib', which features some of the material added to NYA's information collection. *Young people now* is also available on audio-cassette tape.

The National Youth Agency publishes a number of useful directories:

THE NYA GUIDE TO RESIDENTIAL CENTRES. 2nd edn. Leicester: National Youth Agency, 1993.

Gives all the necessary information on over 400 establishments throughout the UK which offer residential facilities to young people and those who work with them. Useful features include a how-to section on planning and organizing a residential course, a list of useful resources on residential youth work, and information on access for people with disabilities.

DIY: DIRECTORY OF INFORMATION FOR YOUNG PEOPLE. Leicester: National Youth Agency, 1994.

Provides access to over 200 national suppliers of youth information and includes advice on different ways of presenting information to young people of all abilities, and guidelines for accessing information in languages other than English. Other features that might appeal to librarians are the NYAFAIS (National Youth Agency Focused Access Information System) – a youth information classification scheme – and a list of contacts for those who wish to find out more about The Information Shop for Young People initiative, which aims to offer high-quality high-street information provision for young people.

YOUTH SERVICE DIRECTORY 1995. Leicester: National Youth Agency, 1995.

First edition of a new regular publication giving key contacts for the statutory and voluntary youth services, together with other relevant organizations.

It is not possible to mention all the other useful publications produced by the NYA, but there is one series which especially deserves attention, namely:

THE YOUNG PERSON'S GUIDES. Leicester: National Youth Agency.

Written and designed for young people themselves, these guides provide sources of practical advice and information on each of the ten subject categories defined by the NYAFAIS classification system: education; employment and training; environment; Europe; family and relationships; health; housing; justice and equality; money; and sport, leisure and travel.

The **Children's Legal Centre** (University of Essex, Wivenhoe Park, Colchester, Essex CO4 3SQ tel: 01206 873820 or 872466: 2–5 pm) represents the interests of children and young people in matters of law and policy affecting them. It offers free advice and an information service by letter and telephone, and publishes reports, handbooks, information sheets and leaflets. CLC's periodical *Childright* (ten issues per year) contains articles, news, changes in legislation and book reviews on issues affecting children's rights.

Other guides

Ball, L. GUIDE TO TRAINING AND BENEFITS FOR YOUNG PEOPLE. London: Youthaid, 409 Brixton Road, London SW9 7DQ tel: 0171-737 8068, 1995.

Comprehensive information on the rights of young people and on the procedures of government departments and other agencies responsible for young people's training and benefits.

Database

YOUTHNET. London: YouthNet UK, Suite 502, The Chambers, Chelsea Harbour, London SW10 0XF tel: 0171-823 3333, Internet: http://www.youthnet.org.uk/youthnet.

A comprehensive computer-based information service, currently under construction, which aims to provide a signpost to all types of opportunity and help available to young people in Britain. It is already up and running (January 1996), with around 500 key national organizations and publications. It is available via the Internet but YouthNet plans to produce a CD-ROM version available on subscription. A hardcopy version is published in the annual publication *Go for it*, available by mail order from Lennard Books (tel: 01582 715866). Database entries give a brief description of the work of each organization, the number of people it helps each year, the age range, the area served, courses available, details of any costs, provision for special needs, and addresses and telephone numbers to contact. Some of the organizations listed have their own pages on the Internet and YouthNet are introducing 'hot links' to enable users to transfer across to each of those organization's own files at the click of a mouse.

Community

The major publisher on all aspects of running a voluntary organization, and of voluntary work generally, is the **National Council for Voluntary Organizations** (Regent's Wharf, 8 All Saints Street, London N1 9RL, tel: 0171-713 6161), which has an extensive range of publications. An absolute essential for any community information collection is:

THE VOLUNTARY AGENCIES DIRECTORY. Annual. London: NCVO.

An alphabetical listing of over 2200 leading voluntary organizations, ranging from small, specialist self-help groups to long-established charities. The directory also contains a list of useful addresses, including professional and public advisory bodies concerned with voluntary action.

From November 1995 *VAD* will also be available on CD-ROM, providing instant access to the listings using alphabetical look-up or word search, or by VAD organizational classifications. An interesting feature is a notepad on each listing which enables users to enter their own information, such as different contact names or details of the local branch of the organization.

NCVO's periodical *NCVO News* (ten issues per year) is a useful way of keeping informed on key issues facing the voluntary sector, as well as news, briefings, information updates and publication reviews.

The following organizations are also valuable sources of information for and about the voluntary sector:

The **Volunteer Centre UK** (Carriage Row, 183 Eversholt Street, London NW1 1BU tel: 0171-388 9888) produces a range of publications, including information sheets, resource packs, handbooks, training materials and bibliographies. Its periodical *Volunteering* (ten issues per year) combines news and views on political and practical issues. Its Update section is particularly useful as it comprises book reviews and abstracts drawn from over 100 journals and newspapers.

Community Matters – National Federation of Community Organizations (8–9 Upper Street, London N1 0PQ tel: 0171-226 0189) publishes attractively produced, practical handbooks for community organizations on topics such as community newspapers, publicity and how to start a community group. They also have a series of over 60 information sheets on specific topics concerning community groups, some of which have been translated into community languages. Their quarterly magazine *Community* carries news from community organizations around the country and updates on national matters of relevance to community groups such as legislation, campaigns and new sources of funds.

The **Charity Commissioners for England and Wales** (St Alban's House, Haymarket, London SW1Y 4QX tel: 0171-210 4477) have specific legal responsibilities to maintain a public register of charities and to investigate misconduct and abuse of charitable assets. They also publish a range of free leaflets, booklets and audio-cassettes on aspects of setting up and running charities, including political activities, campaigning, payment of trustees, investment and disposing of charitable land. A more substantial, charged publication is:

ACCOUNTING BY CHARITIES: STATEMENT OF RECOMMENDED PRACTICE. London: Charity Commissioners, 1995

Sets out recommendations on the way in which a charity should report annually on the resources entrusted to it and the activities it undertakes. Fully indexed, with a glossary and examples of financial accounts and balance sheets.

Similar bodies to the Charity Commissioners exist for other parts of the UK. For Scotland it is the **Scottish Charities Office**, Crown Office, 25 Chambers Street, Edinburgh EH1 1LA tel: 0131-226 2626 and for Northern Ireland the **Department of Health and Social Services, Charities Office**, Annexe 3, Castle Buildings, Stormont Estate, Belfast BT4 3RA tel: 01232-522595.

Fundraising

An important aspect of the work of many voluntary organizations and charities is identifying sources of funding, whether it be from trusts, commercial organizations, government or the European Community. There is no shortage of reference books, but the following are those that have proved most comprehensive, useful or up to date:

DIRECTORY OF GRANT-MAKING TRUSTS Annual. London: Charities Aid Foundation.

An expensive but essential source of reference on the location, policies and resources of grant-making bodies. Its main section is an alphabetical list of trusts, with separate geographical and subject indexes. Entries in the main sequence also note any publications issued by trusts.

FINDING FUNDS. 2nd edn. London: NCVO Publications, 1993.

Gives general information on funding for voluntary groups and summarizes current sources of money.

GRANTS FROM EUROPE: HOW TO GET MONEY AND INFLUENCE POLICY. 7th rev. edn. London: NCVO Publications, 1993.

A major publisher of guides to sources of grants and fundraising is the **Directory of Social Change** (24 Stephenson Way, London NW1 2DP tel: 0171-209 5151). The following are some of the more important titles:

A GUIDE TO THE MAJOR TRUSTS. 2v. Annual. London: Directory of Social Change.

Alphabetical sequence with subject and geographical indexes. Vol. 1 (5th edn.) covers the top 300 trusts, giving details of their backgrounds, interests and priorities, and Vol. 2 (2nd edn.) a further 700 trusts. It also includes listings of Councils of Voluntary Organizations and Charities Information Bureaux.

CENTRAL GOVERNMENT GRANTS GUIDE 1995/96. 3rd edn. London: Directory of Social Change, 1995.

Covers grants, loans and payments for services available to voluntary bodies from central government departments and other official sources.

A GUIDE TO COMPANY GIVING. 5th edn. London: Directory of Social Change, 1995.

A standard reference guide covering the charitable donations and community contributions of 1400 companies.

THE MAJOR COMPANIES GUIDE 1996/97. 4th edn. London: Directory of Social Change, 1995.

Provides details of the charitable and community support given by the UK's 400 leading corporate donors, including information on company trusts and types of grant made.

THE NATIONAL LOTTERY YEARBOOK 1995–96. London: Directory of Social Change, 1996.

Full information on all aspects of the Lottery, including listings of all grants made by distributing bodies in 1995 and how to put together a successful application.

Management

The **London Voluntary Service Council** (356 Holloway Road, London NW7 6PA tel: 0171-700 8107) produces two practical, clearly written and attractively designed guides to the law and management of voluntary organizations:

VOLUNTARY BUT NOT AMATEUR. 4th edn. London: LVSC, 1994.

A jargon-free guide to the law for voluntary organizations and community groups. Its ten chapters cover: legal structures; running an organization; recruitment; employment; health and safety; premises; insurance; financial management; 'any other business' – including street collections, lotteries and campaigning – and closing down. It is a companion volume to:

Adirondack, S. JUST ABOUT MANAGING. 2nd edn. London: LVSC, 1992.

A practical guide to good management for community groups and voluntary organizations.

A more substantial, and costly, work on the management of voluntary organization is:

CRONER'S MANAGEMENT OF VOLUNTARY ORGANIZATIONS. London: Croner Publications.

A comprehensive looseleaf reference book covering everything from setting up an organization, through to finance, fundraising, personnel and marketing. The book is kept up to date by means of a quarterly amendment service and a monthly newsletter. This is a work which is more suited to larger libraries. Set-up costs at 1995 prices are £168.55 inclusive of postage and packing for the binder, pages, four quarterly amendments and the monthly newsletter. Annual amendments and newsletter cost £74.60.

The following titles on specific aspects of the work of community organizations can be recommended:

Phillips, A. CHARITABLE STATUS. 4th edn. London: Directory of Social Change, 1994.

Popular legal guide covering charitable activities; registering; constitutional choices; limits to politics and campaigning; tax reliefs and pitfalls.

Adirondack, S. and Taylor, J. S. THE VOLUNTARY SECTOR LEGAL HANDBOOK. London: Directory of Social Change, 1996.

Comprehensive and accessible guide for all voluntary groups and their advisers, covering all relevant legal issues, not just charity law.

Stubbs, L. CHARITY PAGES. London: Directory of Social Change, 1995.

A 'yellow pages'-style directory for the charity world, listing organizations which provide services to the voluntary sector in such areas as law, accounting, computing, PR, advertising, banking etc.

Lattimer, M. CAMPAIGNING HANDBOOK. London: Directory of Social Change, 1994.

Covers campaigning techniques and the law for pressure groups and voluntary organizations.

Ali, M. THE DIY GUIDE TO PUBLIC RELATIONS FOR CHARITIES. London: Directory of Social Change, 1995.

Lively guide to every aspect of PR, from events to publications, from media relations to customer care.

Thornton, C. MANAGING TO ADVISE. London: 13 Stockwell Road, London SW9 9AU tel: 0171-274 1839. Federation of Independent Advice Centres, 1989.

Covers all the basic ingredients for running a successful advice service from conception to keeping records and resources for advice. The bibliographies will be out of date now, and new technology has moved things on, but this book is still useful for its sound advice. New edition planned for summer 1996.

Bunch, A. THE BASICS OF COMMUNITY INFORMATION WORK. 2nd edn. London: Library Association Publishing, 1993.

Covers all the basic requirements for setting up a community information service, including determining needs; type of service; furniture and equipment; staffing; collection and dissemination of information; publicity and public relations; and evaluation and monitoring.

Bibliographies and current awareness
COMMUNITY CURRENTS: THE COMMUNITY DEVELOPMENT INFOR-MATION DIGEST. Bimonthly. London: Community Development Foundation, tel: 0171-226 5378.

180 journals, books, unpublished reports and databases are scanned for articles and news items that are specially relevant to community initiatives. Items are distilled in short paragraphs and arranged under subject areas and then by subject headings. There is a term index to subject headings and, once a year, a list of periodicals regularly scanned. Mainly useful for background articles and books rather than reference material.

VOLNET UK. London: Community Development Foundation.

A package of four online databases aimed at the voluntary and community sectors. The original *Volnet* database contains over 70,000 references to newspaper and journal articles, parliamentary proceedings, books and reports on all aspects of social policy and welfare. It combines records from The Volunteer Centre UK, the Community Development Foundation, Barnardo's, the National Youth Agency, and the Joseph Rowntree Foundation. Records can be searched by many criteria including title, subject, author, date source and words in the abstract. The *Directory of voluntary action research* contains details of over 1100 current and recent social action research projects in the UK and Europe. The *UK Members of Parliament* database contains not only details of the MPs names, party and constituency, but also their interests, committee memberships, parliamentary posts and their majority at the last general election or subsequent by-election. The *International development* database contains over 100,000 references to books, journal articles and reports on all aspects of economic and social development. Can be searched by author names, title, source, subject, publication date, country, language and other fields. The current cost of accessing the database for public libraries is £211.50 including VAT.

Volnet UK is now available on CD-ROM at a cost of £600 pa (single-user) or £1000 pa (multiuser) excluding VAT from Head Software International Ltd., Croudace House, 97 Godstone Road, Caterham,

Surrey CR3 6RE Tel. 01883 343000. Subscribers receive an updated CD-ROM every quarter. Demonstration diskettes and free CD-ROM trials available.

Consumer

The most prominent organization in the field of consumer affairs is the **Consumers' Association,** publishers of the various *Which?* magazines and a range of handbooks which are essential for any community information collection. Some of these are covered under their appropriate subject. Details of their latest publications usually appear as an insert to each issue of *Which?* magazine.

Directories

CONSUMER CONGRESS DIRECTORY. Annual. London: Consumer Congress, c/o National Consumer Council, 20 Grosvenor Gardens, London SW1V 0DH tel: 0171-730 3469.

A directory of organizations in the consumer movement, giving contact address, telephone number and, in most cases, a named individual, together with a brief description of aims, objects, work and concerns.

Handbooks

First a couple of substantial free publications, which are included here because they give a user-friendly brief overview of their subject:

A BUYER'S GUIDE. London: Office of Fair Trading, 1994.

A handy little booklet giving general information on consumers' rights and advice on how to complain. Lists other useful organizations offering further help.

EUROPEAN CONSUMER GUIDE TO THE SINGLE MARKET. Luxembourg: Office for Official Publications of the European Commission, 1995.

An introduction to the consumer affairs legislation in the European Union and to other measures designed to benefit consumers. Covers cross-border shopping; protection of the consumer in general – product safety, distance selling, contracts advertising, labelling etc. – and specific sectors, e.g. toys, housing (including timeshares). Annexe lists useful addresses. Copies available in Britain from: UK Office of the European

Commission, Jean Monnet House, 8 Storey's Gate, London SW1P 3AT.

Holmes, A. 120 LETTERS THAT GET RESULTS. Rev. edn. London: Consumers' Association, 1995.

Provides model letters for a variety of situations where the consumer needs to seek redress and a summary of relevant consumer legislation, with advice on the course of action to take. Also available on two 3½ inch disks (one for Windows 3.1 and one for DOS 2.1) with explanatory booklet. The Windows program also contains the text of *350 legal problems solved* (see Legal section p. 221) and an address file of relevant trade and professional bodies, which can be added to as required.

Berry, D. THE WATCHDOG GUIDE TO GETTING A BETTER DEAL. Penguin Books/BBC Books, 1994.

Spin-off from BBC 'Watchdog' programme covering shopping, services, professionals, travel and transport, public services, money, using the law, and dealing with con and hard-sell merchants.

Disability

Information packages

DISABLED LIVING FOUNDATION HAMILTON INDEX. London: Disabled Living Foundation, 380–384 Harrow Road, London W9 2HU tel: 0171-289 6111.

A very comprehensive directory of daily living equipment comprising 23 regularly updated sections covering everything from alarms to walking frames. Each section includes full product descriptions with dimensions and suppliers' names, addresses and telephone numbers. Subscribers receive four ring binders to contain the 23 sections, quarterly mailings containing five or six updated sections, and access to the DLF Subscriber Line for professional advice or signposting. Each section has a detailed contents page, followed by an introduction and specific advice notes. There is also a separate index to the whole directory. Each quarterly mailing includes a copy of *DLF newsletter*, which gives details of courses, new DLF publications and updates to DLF's information sheets.

DISABLED LIVING FOUNDATION DATA OFFLINE.

The UK's most comprehensive database of disability equipment containing 14,000 currently available and discontinued products; names and addresses of 2000 suppliers; 700 self-help groups; help with choosing notes; and details of DLF publications. Available on CD-ROM or floppy disks. Annual subscription £500.

Periodicals

RADAR BULLETIN. Monthly. London: Royal Association for Disability and Rehabilitation (RADAR), 12 City Forum, 250 City Road, London EC1V 8AF tel: 0171-250 4119.

Provides up-to-date information on legislation, social security, housing, education and training, employment, holidays, mobility, new aids and equipment, access, sport and leisure, courses and conferences, and new publications.

Directories and other reference books

The one indispensable reference book for any community information collection is:

DISABILITY RIGHTS HANDBOOK. Annual. London: Disability Alliance ERA, 88–94 Wentworth Street, London E1 7SA tel: 0171-247 8776.

Detailed, comprehensive guide to benefits available to disabled people, how to apply for them, and how to appeal if refused. Explains other matters affecting people with disabilities, including the various services available to them. The *Handbook* also contains an extensive list of addresses and telephone numbers for disability organizations, self-help groups, advice agencies, and DSS and Benefits Agency offices throughout the UK.

The handbook is updated three times a year by *Disability rights bulletin*. Both titles are available separately or together as a Rights subscription.

Darnborough, A. and Kinrade, D. DIRECTORY FOR DISABLED PEOPLE. 7th rev. edn. London: Prentice Hall, 1995.

A substantial reference book for disabled people, their carers and those who provide services. It contains information and details of organizations and publications. Appendices include lists of publishers and stockists of items referred to in the text.

EQUIPMENT FOR DISABLED PEOPLE. Oxford: Equipment for Disabled People, Mary Marlborough Lodge, Nuffield Orthopaedic Centre, Headington, Oxford OX3 7LD tel: 01865 227592.

A series of 14 regularly updated booklets giving facts and comment on a wide range of products to make life easier for disabled people. Advice is presented in the form of points to consider before any purchase is made, and each book is fully illustrated. Most titles also contain a select bibliography. The one on 'Communication and access to computer technology' is particularly useful to librarians as it covers a variety of reading aids.

IN TOUCH 1995–96 HANDBOOK. Annual. London: British Broadcasting Corporation.

A spin-off from the BBC's 'In Touch' programme, this is an essential reference book for all concerned with sight and sight loss, covering such topics as equipment, services, rights and benefits, advice for visually impaired people, and leisure. There is also a substantial reference section.

HOLIDAYS IN THE BRITISH ISLES: A GUIDE FOR DISABLED PEOPLE. Annual. London: RADAR.

A guide to accommodation and facilities, together with advice on planning a holiday. Gives useful regional addresses and ideas for places to visit.

HOLIDAYS AND TRAVEL ABROAD: A GUIDE FOR DISABLED PEOPLE. Annual. London: RADAR.

Basic holiday details of around 100 countries, plus advice on the best organizations to contact for more details.

Education

An essential source of information about education is the **Department for Education and Employment** itself, which produces a wide range of free leaflets and booklets obtainable from: Publications Centre, PO Box 6927, London E3 3NZ tel: 0171-510 0150. There may be some changes in despatch arrangements following the autumn 1995 merger of Education and Employment.

The main consumer organization in the field of education is the **Advisory Centre for Education (ACE)**, 1b Aberdeen Studios, 22–24 Highbury Grove, London N5 2DQ tel: 0171-354 8318), which publishes a range of information sheets and handbooks aimed at parents and school governors. No community information collection would be complete without a subscription to:

ACE BULLETIN. Bimonthly. London: ACE.

Contains news, features, guidelines for governors and information sheets which reflect the parents' perspective on developments in education. In addition, the regular 'Digest' pages provide a comprehensive review of all the latest books, pamphlets, journals and Ombudsman reports on education. *ACE bulletin* carries news of all ACE publications, updates to *Education A–Z* (see below), and publishes an annual index.

Other indispensable ACE publications are:

EDUCATION A–Z: WHERE TO LOOK THINGS UP. 5th edn.. London: ACE. 1991

An alphabetically arranged reference book providing sources of information on all major educational topics. Five hundred different subject headings list over 1000 organizations, with information on a wide range of relevant publications. Fully indexed and cross-referenced. Although well overdue for a thorough revision, updated inserts are provided and *ACE bulletin* (see above) is also currently carrying updates of sections. A new edition is planned for 1996.

ACE GOVERNORS' HANDBOOK. New edn.. London: ACE. 1995

A compilation of ACE information sheets covering key aspects of governing body duties, including commentary and guidance on recent legislation affecting governors' work. New topics added to this edition are bullying, inspections, sex education and working together.

ACE SPECIAL EDUCATION HANDBOOK. 6th edn.. London: ACE. 1994

A step-by-step guide for parents and professionals to the intricacies of assessment and statementing. Includes model letters for parents and explains appeals, reviews and reassessments.

Funding directories

THE EDUCATION FUNDING GUIDE: SUPPORT FROM GOVERNMENT, TRUSTS AND COMPANIES. London: Directory of Social Change, 1996.

Information on over 200 charitable trusts, with full details of their recent educational grants, and on 100 major companies, outlining their support to schools, higher and further education, staff voluntary activities and special schemes. Also contains a full listing of TECs and Education Business Partnerships, and articles by specialist organizations, unions and leading journalists.

THE EDUCATIONAL GRANTS DIRECTORY 1994–95. 3rd edn. London: Directory of Social Change, 1994.

Comprehensive listing of educational charities which support children and students in need.

Employment

There is a substantial amount of free and priced material written for workers and employers on aspects of employment law, job-seeking, coping with redundancy, and health and safety at work. No community information collection should be without at least a reference set of free booklets from the **Department for Education and Employment** (Cambertown Ltd, Unit 8 Goldthorpe Industrial Estate, Goldthorpe, Rotherham, South Yorkshire S63 7BL tel: 01709 888688 – there may be some changes in despatch following the autumn 1995 merger of Education and Employment), **ACAS – Advisory, Conciliation and Arbitration Service** (Press Office, 27 Wilton Street, London SW1X 7AZ tel: 0171-210 3613), and the Employment Service (ES) (Head Office, Purchasing and Contracts Unit, 5th Floor, Mayfield Court, 56 West Street, Sheffield S1 4EP tel: 01742 595881/595828 – bulk supplies from Meads Ltd, Leen Gate, Lemton, Nottingham NG7 2GB).

There are several organizations which play an important role in providing information to workers and trade unionists:

The **Labour Research Department** (78 Blackfriars Road, London SE1 8HF tel: 0171-928 3649) publishes information on all aspects of employment from a trade union aspect. *Labour research* (monthly) covers news on the economy, major industries and social and political developments, as well as topics of workplace interest. Regular features include book reviews, health and safety notes, statistics and major wage deals. The latter is covered more fully in *Bargaining report* (11 issues a year) whereas statistics form a major part of LRD's *Fact service* (weekly). LRD also publishes a number of booklets of interest to trade unionists which are available either individually or on subscription (about ten titles a year). Some are on political issues, others are useful reference guides. Two that can be singled out are:

THE LAW AT WORK. London: LRD, 1994.

A brief guide to employment law.

STATE BENEFITS. Annual. London: LRD.

Guide to the full range of both means-tested and non-means tested benefits.

The **Workers' Educational Association** (Temple House, 17 Victoria Park Square, London E2 9PB tel: 0181-983 1515) is mainly concerned with providing independent adult education for workers, but some of its publications are a valuable source of information about employment, trade union and women's issues.

The **Low Pay Unit** (27–29 Amwell Street, London EC1R 1UN tel: 0171-713 7616) campaigns to improve the lot of low-paid workers. It produces leaflets, booklets, reports and a bimonthly periodical, *The new review*, which highlights interesting cases and developments in the law relating to low pay, gives in-depth analysis of rights issues, and reviews new publications. *The new review* also contains an insert called *News brief of the Employment Rights Advice Service*, which provides up-to-date information on rates of pay and benefits for low-paid workers.

The **Trades Union Congress** (Congress House, Great Russell Street, London WC1B 3LS tel: 0171-636 4030) publishes a wide range of cheap booklets, pamphlets and a few free leaflets on various aspects of employment, the economy and trade unionism.

General works

Painter, R. and Puttick, K. EMPLOYMENT RIGHTS. London: Pluto Press, 1993.

A lucid explanation of employment law in the UK as it affects individuals. Extensive use is made of examples from cases in the courts and industrial tribunals.

Kibling, T. and Lewis, T. EMPLOYMENT LAW: AN ADVISERS' HANDBOOK. 2nd edn. London: Legal Action Group, 1994.

A complete, comprehensive and practical guide to employment law, including tactical advice on case presentation in tribunals.

Equal opportunities

The **Equal Opportunities Commission** (Overseas House, Quay Street, Manchester M3 3HN tel: 0161-833 9244) has a range of free and priced leaflets on all aspects of equal opportunities, including education, employment rights, consumer rights for women and pensions for women.

Other useful publications include:

SEX DISCRIMINATION LAW. London: Labour Research Department, 1995.

LRD booklet explaining recent developments in the law and how it can be used in the fight for equality at work.

Palmer, C. MATERNITY RIGHTS. London: Legal Action Group, 1996.

Aimed at lawyers, advisers, trade unionists and employers, this new title sets out the rights of pregnant women and how these can be enforced.

Health and safety at work

ESSENTIALS OF HEALTH AND SAFETY AT WORK. 3rd edn. London: HMSO, 1995.

Produced by the Health and Safety Executive, this attractively laid-out layperson's guide to the hazards of work and the safety measures that need to be taken is essential.

OFFICE HEALTH AND SAFETY: A GUIDE FOR UNION REPS. London: Labour Research Department, 1995.

LRD booklet covering a wide range of health and safety issues in office work.

HEALTH AND SAFETY LAW: A GUIDE FOR UNION REPS. London: Labour Research Department, 1995.

LRD booklet setting out the law covering most workplaces and a look at future developments.

VDUs: AN EASY GUIDE TO THE REGULATIONS. Sudbury: Health and Safety Executive, 1995.

As using computers becomes more and more a part of everyday life, this practical guide will be helpful in identifying the legal requirements and the risks involved in using computers in the workplace.

Small businesses and self-employment

Barrow, C. THE COMPLETE SMALL BUSINESS GUIDE: SOURCES OF INFORMATION FOR NEW AND SMALL BUSINESSES. 4th edn. London: BBC Books, 1995.

Offers sources of direct help, with extensive address lists, further reading and advice on all aspects of setting up and running a small business.

Golzen, G. WORKING FOR YOURSELF. 16th edn. London: Kogan Page, 1995.

Regularly updated, standard guide to setting up and running a small business. Appendices provide sources of further information, a select bibliography and a glossary of key business terms.

LAW FOR SMALL BUSINESSES 1995/96. London: Pitman Publishing, 1995.

One of NatWest Bank's business handbooks, this clearly written practical guide has been designed for the layperson. Good use made of checklists, bullet points, specimen forms and sources of further information.

Unemployment

Finn, D. and Murray, I. UNEMPLOYMENT AND TRAINING RIGHTS HANDBOOK. 3rd edn. London: Unemployment Unit, 409 Brixton Road, London SW9 7DQ tel: 0171-737 8001, 1995.

Definitive guide to the regulations and programme rules affecting unemployment, training and benefits.

Environment

The strong and growing concern for the environment in recent years has led many larger libraries to take this subject out of community information collections in order to provide more extensive coverage. However, smaller libraries will need at least a set of leaflets from the **Department of the Environment** (Publicity Section, Room P1/163, 2 Marsham Street, London SW1P 3PY tel: 0171-276 0680; bulk copies from: Publications Despatch Centre, Blackhorse Road, London SE99 6TT).

Directories

THE GREEN INDEX: A DIRECTORY OF ENVIRONMENTAL ORGANIZA-TIONS IN BRITAIN AND IRELAND. 2nd edn. London: Cassell, 1994.

Alphabetical listing of organizations giving minimal details. Indexes to scope, keywords, geographical area and umbrella groups (by category).

NATIONAL DIRECTORY OF COMMUNITY TECHNICAL AID. ACTAC, 64 Mount Pleasant, Liverpool L3 5SD tel: 0151-708 7607, 1995.

Community Technical Aid is an independent service offering professional skills to communities who are seeking to improve the places where they live, work or play. Its directory is organized by geographical regions, then alphabetically by name of organization. There is an alphabetical index to organizations and a skill matrix at the beginning of each section.

WHO'S WHO IN THE ENVIRONMENT: ENGLAND. 3rd edn. London: The Environment Council, 21 Elizabeth Street, London SW1V 9RP tel: 0171-730 9941, 1995.

Fewer entries than in *The Green Index* but substantially more detail given, such as a description of the work of each organization, its status, publications, services provided and number of paid staff. There is a subject index, lists of useful organizations outside England, and Environment Council publications.

THE ENVIRONMENTAL GRANTS GUIDE. 2nd edn. London: Department of Social Change, 1993.

A guide to grants for environmental groups and projects from government, companies and charitable trusts.

Ethnic minorities

There are a number of specialist organizations representing the interests of ethnic minorities and race relations such as the **Institute of Race Relations** (2–6 Leeke Street, London WC1X 9HS tel: 0171-837 0041), which aims to make available information and advice on proposals concerned with race relations. Publishes books, pamphlets, bibliographies, and a periodical, *Race and class.*

The **Joint Council for the Welfare of Immigrants** (115 Old Street, London EC1V 9JR tel: 0171-251 8708) publishes priced leaflets on immigration, nationality and refugees, and an authoritative handbook on immigration legislation:

Shutter, S. IMMIGRATION AND NATIONALITY LAW HANDBOOK. London: JCWI, 1995.

Explains what UK immigration law says; what it means in practice; how to deal with immigration problems and advise asylum seekers and refugees; immigration status and benefit entitlement; the appeals system and the provisions of British nationality law. Contains details of useful contacts, a glossary of common terms, a summary of practical information, and samples of standard forms.

The **Minority Rights Group** (379 Brixton Road, London SW9 7DE tel: 0171-978 9498) aims to secure justice for minority and majority groups suffering from discrimination. Publishes reports on selected minority groups.

The **Commission for Racial Equality** (Elliott House, 10–12 Allington Street, London SW1E 5EH tel: 0171-828 7022) has free and priced leaflets on the Race Relations Act, employment and housing rights.

The **Runnymede Trust** (11 Princelet Street, London E1 6QH tel: 0171-375 1496) exists to provide information on race equality issues in Britain and the EU. Publishes reports and pamphlets.

Practical guidance on social security entitlements as they apply to anyone entering or leaving the UK is given in:

ETHNIC MINORITIES' BENEFITS HANDBOOK. London: Child Poverty Action Group, 1993.

Places particular emphasis on the provisions most likely to affect ethnic minority claimants. Fully indexed and cross-referenced to UK and EC legislation and decisions. Although not revised annually, benefits information in the *Handbook* is updated in CPAG's *Welfare rights bulletin*.

Family and personal

There is no single source of information that will cover the range of topics that might be included under this heading, but the following are some of the most useful titles on the main topic areas.

Adoption and fostering

The **British Agencies for Adoption and Fostering** (Skyline House, 200

Union Street, London SE1 0LY tel: 0171-593 2000) publish a range of booklets on aspects of adoption and fostering, including:

ADOPTING A CHILD: A GUIDE FOR PEOPLE INTERESTED IN ADOPTION. London: BAAF, 1995.

Authoritative guide to what adoption means and how to go about it. Contains details of other useful organizations and books.

Caring

THE CARERS GUIDE 1995: ESSENTIAL INFORMATION FOR PEOPLE WHO LOOK AFTER OTHERS. 2nd edn. Macmillan Magazines, 1994.

Excellent directory to all aspects of caring, from rights to residential care. Useful list of 'Helpful organizations' includes some local ones.

Death

Harris, P. WHAT TO DO WHEN SOMEONE DIES. Rev. edn. London: Consumers' Association, 1995.

A practical guide to the necessary procedures and formalities, such as registering a death and arranging a funeral, and advice on coping with grief. Includes a list of support groups.

WILLS AND PROBATE. Rev. edn. London: Consumers' Association, 1995.

Guidance on making and revising a will, plus step-by-step procedure for securing probate when someone has died.

Lesbian and gay people

Massow, I. GAY FINANCE GUIDE. Fourth Estate Ltd, 1994.

Step-by-step practical guide to tax, mortgages, pensions, savings, medical insurance, making a will and shared ownership. Index and glossary.

One-parent families

The two main national organizations representing one-parent families are: The **National Council for One-Parent Families** (255 Kentish Town Road, London NW5 1YA tel: 0171-267 1361), which publishes a variety of inexpensive welfare and legal rights guides aimed at single parents. Its occasional newsletter *One parent times* contains items of news and interest for lone parents and their children. However, NCOPF's major publication is its:

INFORMATION MANUAL.

A looseleaf file comprising 20 sections and over 200 pages of information and practical advice on such matters as benefits and tax; maintenance; single and pregnant; housing; divorce; holidays etc. Updated three times a year with access to a telephone advice line service. The set-up cost and one year's subscription to the updating service is £44.50 for libraries.

Gingerbread (16 Clerkenwell Close, London EC1R 0AA tel: 0171-336 8183) publishes a number of booklets and leaflets on welfare benefits, family law and day-care schemes. Operates an Associate Membership scheme whereby subscribers receive a monthly mailing of every new leaflet/booklet and their monthly magazine, *Ginger*.

Marriage, separation and divorce

Way, F. M. LIVING TOGETHER. London: Kogan Page, 1995.

Straightforward and practical guide to the law as it affects unmarried couples.

Gurlick, H. THE WHICH? GUIDE TO DIVORCE. 2nd edn. London: Consumers' Association, 1994.

Covers all the steps that need to be taken into account when making the legal and financial arrangements for divorce.

Van den Brink-Budgen, R. HOW TO . . . SURVIVE DIVORCE. 2nd edn. How To Books, 1995.

Sensible and helpful book providing a framework for coping with the practical and emotional problems involved. Contains lists of useful organizations and further reading.

Green, D. HOW TO COPE WITH SEPARATION AND DIVORCE: A GUIDE FOR MARRIED AND UNMARRIED COUPLES. London: Kogan Page, 1995.

Green, D. SPLITTING UP: LEGAL AND FINANCIAL GUIDE TO SEPARATION AND DIVORCE. 3rd edn. London: Kogan Page, 1995.

CHILD SUPPORT HANDBOOK 1995/96. 3rd edn. London: Child Poverty Action Group, 1995.

The definitive guide to understanding the child support scheme and coping with its implications. Includes coverage of what the key terms mean, who is affected and how to apply for maintenance; the powers of the Child Support Agency; the requirement to cooperate; and a step-by-step guide to the formula for calculating maintenance. Fully indexed and cross-referenced to law, regulations and to CPAG benefit guides.

Larger libraries might also like to consider:

Jacobs, E. and Douglas, G. CHILD SUPPORT: THE LEGISLATION. 2nd edn. London: Sweet & Maxwell, 1995.

Contains the Child Support Act and accompanying regulations and the Maintenance Enforcement Act, together with detailed annotations and cross-references.

Fuel
FUEL RIGHTS GUIDE. 10th edn. London: Child Poverty Action Group, 1996.

Well established as the standard practical guide to the rights of gas and electricity consumers, including supply; methods of payment and metering; responsibility for bills; debt and disconnection; benefits and other financial help; the work of the Regulators; and courts and legal remedies. Cross-referenced to law and regulations.

Government
Hutt, J. OPENING THE TOWN HALL DOOR. 2nd edn. London: NCVO, 1988.

A concise little guide to how local government works, what services are provided and how decisions are made, with advice on lobbying and the complaints procedure. Rather old now but the principles are still the same and it is still in print.

Lattimer, M. THE CAMPAIGNING HANDBOOK. London: Directory of Social Change, 1994.

Covers all the basic skills of modern campaigning that individuals and pressure groups can use to influence companies, local government, Whitehall, Parliament and the European institutions.

SECRET SERVICES: A HANDBOOK FOR INVESTIGATING LOCAL QUANGOS. London: Local Government Information Unit, 1–5 Bath Street, London EC1V 9QQ tel: 0171-608 1051, 1995.

Health

The government department responsible for the National Health Service and other health matters is the **Department of Health** (Skipton House, 80 London Road, Elephant and Castle, London SE1 6LW tel: 0171-972 2000). It publishes free leaflets on the NHS, National Insurance and various aspects of healthy living. A reference copy at least should be in all community information collections. Bulk supplies of these leaflets are available from Heywood Stores, Health Publications Unit, Manchester Road, Heywood, Lancashire OL10 2PZ tel: 01706 366287.

The promotion of health is the responsibility of the **Health Education Authority** (Hamilton House, Mabledon Place, London WC1H 9TX tel: 0171-383 3833), which has an extensive range of booklets, leaflets, posters and audiovisual materials, many of which are available free. It publishes two periodicals: *Healthlines* (ten issues p.a.) provides advance information, up-to-date news and views and practical advice on all aspects of health education and promotion. Each issue includes a current awareness bulletin and details of journal articles of interest to health educators. A supplement, *Healthlines plus*, features details of new health education resources, events and campaigns; *Health education journal* (quarterly) publishes original research papers and topical articles on issues of concern. Each issue includes a book review and resources digest section. Bulk orders for free publications are dealt with by local health education units. The HEA operates a quarterly mailing service on subscription, which covers a copy of the HEA's annual report; a copy of *Journal articles of interest to health educators*; and copies of recent free leaflets and posters, including its biannual complete catalogue of publications.

Directories and yearbooks

BBC FAMILY DIRECTORY. London: Health Education Authority, 1995.

A guide to organizations, agencies and support services providing, help and advice for all members of the family.

DIRECTORY OF CANCER SUPPORT AND SELF HELP. Annual. London: CancerLink, 17 Britannia Street, London WC1X 9JN tel: 0171-833 2818.

Lists 450 self-help groups, 58 sources of one-to-one support, and 51 national and regional organizations.

Indexes

POPULAR MEDICAL INDEX. Mede Publishing, 77 Norton Road, Letchworth, Herts SG6 1AD. Three issues a year plus annual cumulation.

Created by a librarian for providers of health information. It indexes medical articles, written mainly for the layperson, from over 60 journals and lists new books in the health-care field. Covers all the medical topics of popular concern. Arranged alphabetically by subject headings.

Periodicals

WHAT DOCTORS DON'T TELL YOU. Monthly. London: What Doctors Don't Tell You, 77 Grosvenor Avenue, London N5 tel: 0171-354 4592.

Regular newsletter on major health issues published since 1989. Each issue focuses on a cover story such as hypertension; dental fillings; pesticides; keyhole surgery. Back copies available and subscribers also get an annual index. Special binders available at extra cost.

WDDTY also publishes various handbooks and guides on topics such as vaccination; patients' rights; heart disease; women's screening tests; cancer etc.

Self-help

The **Help for Health Trust** (Highcroft, Romsey Road, Winchester, Hampshire SO22 5DH tel: 01962 849100) was set up as a project in 1979 to find out if consumer health information was something that was required by the community. Three years ago it was granted charitable status. The Trust provides a wide range of services, of which the most relevant to libraries will be its database services. These include:

HELPBOX.

A database of over 6500 records comprising five files of information on national and local self help groups and voluntary organizations, books, leaflets and audiovisual aids. It runs on stand alone PCs and LANs and is available on either 3.5 in. or 5.25 in. disks. A *Helpbox Plus* version is available, which includes a blank local file to enable users to edit their own data. Updates are sent on a quarterly basis. The annual cost is £200 (single-user, read-only version) and £275 (single-user, Helpbox Plus).

NHS A–Z.

First published as a 200-page manual, the *NHS A–Z* is now available as a full-text database containing information on how to complain, what services are available and how to access them, and how the NHS is funded. The database is updated annually and the fourth edition will be published early in 1996. Subscription price is £75.

Complementary medicine and therapies
Woodham, A. HEA GUIDE TO COMPLEMENTARY MEDICINE AND THERAPIES. London: Health Education Authority, 1994.

Comprehensive and objective guide to the range of alternative therapies available in the UK, from the best therapies for common ailments to how to find a reliable practitioner.

HIV and AIDS

The major national organization in the field of HIV and AIDS is **The Terrence Higgins Trust** (52–54 Grays Inn Road, London WC1X 8JU tel: 0171-831 0330) which produces leaflets on HIV and AIDS and safer sex (single copies free). It also publishes:

Nee, C. BENEFITS FOR PEOPLE WITH HIV: A HANDBOOK FOR ADVISERS 1995–96. 4th edn. London: THT, 1995.

Concentrates on those aspects of the benefits system that are most relevant to people with HIV and AIDS, including a detailed explanation of incapacity benefit.

Housing

No community information service would be complete without a set of the free housing booklets dealing with landlords' and tenants' rights published by the **Department of the Environment** (Publicity Section, 2 Marsham Street, London SW1P 3PY tel: 0171-276 0680. Bulk copies from: PO Box 151, London E15 2HF).

Also essential are several of the excellent guides produced by **SHAC**

(Kingsbourne House, 229–231 High Holborn, London WC1V 7DA tel: 0171-404 7447). This is the London arm of Shelter and from January 1996 is changing its name to **London Shelter**. Their publications are of relevance throughout the UK. Particular mention can be made of:

RIGHTS GUIDE FOR HOME OWNERS. 10th edn. London: SHAC/CPAG, 1994.

Gives practical advice on negotiating with lenders, meeting repair bills, the problems associated with relationship breakdown and the welfare benefits home owners may be entitled to claim.

THE HOUSING RIGHTS GUIDE. 6th edn. London: SHAC, 1996.

Comprehensive guide for tenants and owners without specialist knowledge, giving clear explanation of the law and practical advice on how to tackle all major housing problems. Contains lists of useful publications and addresses.

Other important organizations in the housing field are:

Shelter (88 Old Street, London EC1V 9HU tel: 0171-505 2161), the national campaign for the homeless, which publishes some useful guides to buying a home with other people, housing finance, and mobile homes. Its periodical *Roof* (bimonthly) includes feature articles, news items, reports and book reviews. Alternating with *Roof* is *Roof briefing* (bimonthly), a digest of the housing market, providing summaries of complex issues in an easy-to-read format. Shelter and SHAC are to merge in January 1996 but are keeping their separate identities for the time being.

CHAR – Housing Campaign for Single People (5–15 Cromer Street, London WC1H 8LS tel: 0171-833 2071), whose annual booklet *Benefits* is a useful guide to means-tested benefits for single people without a permanent home. Includes special sections on 16- and 17-year-olds and people from abroad.

Other guides

Wilde, P. THE WHICH? GUIDE TO RENTING AND LETTING. 2nd edn. London: Consumers' Association, 1995.

Advice to both landlords and tenants on their legal rights and how to avoid the pitfalls. Includes sample letting agreements.

Barr, A. and Barr, R. WHICH? WAY TO BUY, SELL AND MOVE HOUSE. London: Consumers' Association, 1994.

Covers the legal side of buying and selling a house; dealing with estate agents and solicitors; do-it-yourself conveyancing; expenses; insurance; and organizing the practicalities of the move. Glossary of legal terms. Separate section dealing with differences in the Scottish system.

Law

Many aspects of the law have been dealt with under other headings, so in community information collections this category is usually reserved for comprehensive, layperson guides to the law, legal aid, the justice system and civil rights.

Although its publications are aimed mainly at advisers, the **Legal Action Group** (242 Pentonville Road, London N1 9UN tel: 0171-833 2931) produces some excellent and authoritative handbooks to such topics as emergency procedures, civil legal aid, debt, employment, immigration, police powers and police misconduct etc. Its periodical *LAG bulletin* (monthly) contains articles on aspects of the law, significant cases, book reviews and lists of books received.

Civil rights are very much the province of **Liberty – the National Council for Civil Liberties** (21 Tabard Street, London SE1 4LA tel: 0171-403 3888), which publishes a wide range of guides, fact sheets, briefings and reports on particular aspects of rights. Three titles deserving of special mention are:

YOUR RIGHTS: THE LIBERTY GUIDE. 5th edn. London: Pluto Press, 1994.

Popular, jargon-free guidance to the individual's rights in law.

Randle, J. HOW TO DEFEND YOURSELF IN COURT. London: Civil Liberties Trust, 1995.

Accessible guide to the legal procedure for friends, advisers and defendants, from summons or arrest up to trial at the magistrates' or Crown courts.

PEACEFUL PROTEST. London: Civil Liberties Trust, 1995.

Liberty's guide to protest and the law, including basic checklists on organizing protest action, what the law is, and how to keep events peaceful.

The **Consumers' Association** produce a useful question-and-answer reference book on the law as it affects consumers:

Richards, K. 350 LEGAL PROBLEMS SOLVED. London: Consumers' Association, 1995.

Covers neighbour disputes, personal injury claims, faulty goods etc. and helps individuals decide whether to take appropriate action or seek professional advice. Available on computer disk as a Windows program, together with another CA book *120 letters that get results* (see p. 204 for details).

There are a number of one-volume popular reference books covering the law as it affects the citizen, but it is difficult to recommend any particular title other than the latest one published, as the law is changing daily. More useful are looseleaf, regularly updated books such as the various NACAB packs (see pages 189–91) or the slightly less user-friendly:

CITIZENS' ADVICE NOTES SERVICE (CANS): DIGEST OF SOCIAL LEGISLATION. Citizens Advice Notes Service Trust Ltd, 1 Stockwell Green, London SW9 0LJ tel: 0171-326 0356.

A comprehensive digest of social legislation in three looseleaf binders containing 16 sections on topics from administration of justice to transport: roads. Each section is divided into a series of clear notes dealing with specific aspects of the legislation. Each note states the statutory legislative authority, including the primary legislation and appropriate subordinate legislation, and is annotated and cross-referenced to other relevant sections. Initial subscription is £95 for the three binders and pages, plus ten regular updates

Money

The continued problems of debt in the first half of the 1990s, exacerbated by easy access to credit, the collapse of the housing market and unemployment, has led to further growth in debt counselling services, sometimes to the detriment of other areas of advice work. The charity **Money Management Council** (PO Box 77, Hertford SG14 2HW tel: 0992–503448), set up in the late 1980s, continues to promote education and better understanding of personal finance. It produces free fact sheets and reading lists on topics such as personal budgeting, wills, tax, pensions, savings and investments, setting up a home, mortgages and credit.

There are innumerable books giving advice to those with money on what to do with it, but rather fewer for those with money problems. For many people who find themselves in this situation, whether temporary or long-term, the welfare benefit system is intended to provide a safety net. However, the system is complicated and the rules governing entitlement are not always easy to interpret. The **Child Poverty Action Group** (1–5 Bath Street, London EC1V 9PY tel: 0171-253 3406) has produced a number of excellent and highly regarded handbooks on the benefits system which are dealt with under other headings, such as 'Welfare benefits' (p.226), 'Housing' (p.219), 'Fuel' (p.216) and 'Ethnic minorities' (p.212). Other CPAG titles more appropriate to this section are:

Wolfe, M. DEBT ADVICE HANDBOOK. 2nd edn. London: Child Poverty Action Group, 1995.

A comprehensive, one-volume guide to money advice aimed mainly at advisers. All the stages and key issues of money advice are clearly explained, accompanied by tactical advice and practical examples. The text is fully indexed and cross-referenced to the Consumer Credit Act and other legislation, and to County and High Court rules. Contains sample forms, standard letters and money advice forms.

Ward, M. COUNCIL TAX HANDBOOK. 2nd edn. London: Child Poverty Action Group, 1994.

Explains all aspects of tax, with the help of examples, tables, legal references and a comprehensive index.

The pioneer organization in the field of debt and money advice is the **Birmingham Settlement** (318 Summer Lane, Birmingham B19 3RL tel: 0121-359 3562), which has set up a **National Debtline** (tel: 0121-359 8501).

Personal income tax is covered by the hardy perennial:

WHICH? WAY TO SAVE TAX. Annual. London: Consumers' Association.

Independent, reliable, up-to-date advice in plain English on tax as it affects homes, families, pensions, inheritance and employment. From the same stable is a computer program to assist personal tax calculations called:

TAXCALC 1994–95. London: Consumers' Association, 1995.

Available in DOS 2.1 and Windows 3.1 versions. The Windows version has the facility to complete and print out a customized tax return form in place of the Inland Revenue's own. Assume that this title will also be updated annually as the previous one.

There are many charities concerned with individual poverty, and details of over 2000 of them will be found in:

A GUIDE TO GRANTS FOR INDIVIDUALS IN NEED. 4th edn. London: Directory of Social Change, 1994.

There are also numerous books on ways of making money, but the following titles from the **Consumers' Association** can usually be relied on:

Underwood, L. THE WHICH? GUIDE TO EARNING MONEY AT HOME. 2nd edn. London: Consumers' Association, 1994.

Encouraging guide to self-employment, running a small business or working from home as a company employee, illustrated with real-life case histories.

STARTING YOUR OWN BUSINESS. 5th edn. London: Consumers' Association, 1994.

Guidance on making informed decisions at every stage of setting up a business.

WHICH? WAY TO SAVE AND INVEST. 8th edn. London: Consumers' Association, 1995.

The basics of saving – where to get advice and who to complain to if things go wrong – and various areas of investment.

Having got some money, the Consumers' Association are again on hand with advice on how to give it away:

THE WHICH? GUIDE TO GIVING AND INHERITING. Rev. edn. London: Consumers' Association, 1994.

Shows how to use the tax system to increase the value of giving to charities, family and friends; how to make and renew a will and plan for inheritance.

Although pensions as a topic has already been considered in the 'Older people' section, decisions on the right pension often need to be taken at an earlier age. Again, because it is regularly updated and clearly written, the Consumers' Association guide on this subject can be highly recommended:

Lowe, J. THE WHICH? GUIDE TO PENSIONS. 2nd edn. London: Consumers' Association, 1994.

Explains the legislation, outlines possible future options, sets out what to expect from basic state pensions, SERPS, employer and personal plans, and examines the impact of EC directives on pensions.

Older people

There are numerous organizations which represent the needs of older people, but the one that is pre-eminent as a source of information is **Age Concern England** (1268 London Road, London SW16 4ER tel: 0181-679 8000). It publishes a wide range of material for those approaching retirement, and for older people and their carers, from information sheets to annual guides. The major tool for current awareness is:

AGE CONCERN INFORMATION CIRCULAR. Monthly. London: Age Concern England.

Reports developments of interest to people who work with and for older people, covering new legislation, government reports, changes in taxation and social security benefits, publications and recent journal articles, new leaflets, courses and conferences. The very full contents page on the front of the circular makes it very convenient for scanning quickly. There is an annual index.

The following are just a few of the more essential Age Concern publications:

YOUR RIGHTS. Annual. London: Age Concern England.

A clear and concise guide to money benefits for older people, including up-to-date information on pensions, incapacity and other benefits for disabled people, income support and the social fund, travel concessions, paying for residential care, and help with legal and health costs.

YOUR TAXES AND SAVINGS. Annual. London: Age Concern England.

A comprehensive explanation of the impact of taxation on the finances of older people, plus advice on managing retirement income.

THE PENSIONS HANDBOOK Annual. London: Age Concern England.

An overview of the opportunities available to people in mid-career who are keen to improve their pension arrangements. The three main types of pension schemes – state, occupational and personal – are described and guidance given on maximizing their value.

AGE CONCERN FACTSHEETS. London: Age Concern England.

Thirty-four factsheets designed for use by older people and those caring for or advising them on such topics as help with heating, money benefits and making a will. The *Factsheets* are regularly updated and are available individually or together in a folder, for an annual subscription which includes new and amended ones as they are produced.

Ashton, G. ELDERLY PEOPLE AND THE LAW. London: Age Concern England/Butterworth, 1995.

Comprehensive source of information, written for lawyers and non-lawyers, on the diverse areas of law relevant to older people. It is a more substantial work than you would usually find in a community information collection.

Directories and handbooks
GOOD RETIREMENT GUIDE. 3rd edn. London: Kogan Page, 1996

A regularly updated mine of information on all aspects of retirement, giving details of hundreds of organizations, books and other sources of information.

PENSIONERS AND CARERS: HELP FOR OLDER PEOPLE IN NEED AND ADVICE FOR THEIR CARERS. London: Directory of Social Change, 1995.

Lists national charities, grant-making trusts and agencies that can help older people, with details of how to approach them. Also contains an A–Z of statutory benefits and a special section for carers.

Welfare benefits
Essential to any community information collection is at least a reference set of all the **Benefits Agency** leaflets. In recent years the Agency has made great strides in making it easier for organizations such as libraries to find out information and obtain copies of its leaflets through the intro-

duction of the Benefits Agency Publicity Register. Membership of the Register is free by simply telephoning 0645 540 000. Members receive regular mailings of all new and updated BA leaflets, a copy of *CAT 1 Catalogue of leaflets, posters and information, GOL 1 Your guide to leaflets, posters and audio tapes in other languages*, and a quarterly newsletter, *Touchbase*, which contains updates on changes in legislation and procedures, details of new BA publications and campaigns, and changes to its catalogues of leaflets. The Benefits Agency also produces the priced publication:

BENEFITS INFORMATION GUIDE. Annual. London: HMSO.

Provides up-to-date information on UK benefits in an easy-to-use format for use by professionals and the general public. Each section gives details of qualifying conditions, the amounts payable and other factors which affect benefits.

For more detail and tactical advice on the workings of the benefits system, a community information service will need to supplement the 'official' information with guides or handbooks. The most respected and regularly updated are those produced by the **Child Poverty Action Group** (see p.223 for details of address). No collection of any size should be without the following two titles:

NATIONAL WELFARE BENEFITS HANDBOOK. Annual. London: Child Poverty Action Group.

Clear, practical guide on the whole range of means-tested benefits, with explanations of how the benefits are administered, how to claim and how to appeal. Information is fully indexed and cross-referenced to law, regulations and official guidance, and also to Court and Commissioners' decisions.

RIGHTS GUIDE TO NON-MEANS-TESTED BENEFITS. Annual. Child Poverty Action Group.

Companion volume to *National welfare benefits handbook*, with identical features.

Both the above titles are regularly updated by means of CPAG's *Welfare rights bulletin* (bimonthly), which is essential for keeping up to date with social security issues, including new regulations, guidance and procedure; Social Security Commissioners' decisions; Court decisions;

reports on benefit law and service delivery; and news from welfare rights workers.

An easy way to obtain the above titles is to take out a Rights membership subscription to CPAG, for which you receive hot off the press a copy of the latest editions of the *National welfare benefits handbook* and the *Rights guide to non-means-tested benefits*; six issues of *Welfare rights bulletin*; CPAG's *Poverty* journal, and special offers on its other welfare rights publications.

Larger libraries may also want to include in their community information or law collections the following titles, each of which collects together all the relevant statutory material on its subject, accompanied by an expert commentary:

CPAG'S HOUSING BENEFIT AND COUNCIL TAX BENEFIT LEGISLATION. Annual. London: Child Poverty Action Group, 1995. Updating *Supplement*: December 1995.

CPAG'S INCOME RELATED BENEFITS: THE LEGISLATION 1995/96. 12th edn. London: Child Poverty Action Group, 1995.

NON-MEANS-TESTED BENEFITS: THE LEGISLATION 1995/96. 10th edn. London: Child Poverty Action Group, 1995.

Women

There are many organizations and campaign groups catering for women's interests, needs and rights, but it is difficult to point to any as providing a current awareness service or range of publications that represents the whole subject adequately. The **Workers' Educational Association** (Temple House, 17 Victoria Park Square, London E2 9PB tel: 0181-983 1515) has a 'Women's studies' series of mainly booklets, apart from a substantial book published jointly with the Health Education Authority:

EVERY WOMAN'S HEALTH. HEA/WEA, 1993.

Information and activities for anyone running women's groups, covering all aspects of women's health.

The **Health Education Authority** itself has books, leaflets and videos on aspects of women's health, of which the following can be highlighted:

Tidyman, M. and Furedi, A. WOMEN'S HEALTH GUIDE. London: HEA, 1994.

Deals in depth with every topic from sexual health to juggling family and home, with the aim of helping women to help themselves to better health.

WOMEN TOGETHER: A HEALTH EDUCATION TRAINING HANDBOOK. London: HEA, 1992.

Resource for women wanting guidance on working with groups of women, or wanting to train others.

The organization **Women's Health** (52–54 Featherstone Street, London EC1Y 8RT tel: 0171-251 6580) is an independent information and resource centre for all issues involving women's health. It maintains a register of women's health groups, support groups and voluntary agencies.

Burns, A. GOING IT ALONE – RELATIONSHIP BREAKDOWN AND YOUR RIGHTS: A GUIDE FOR MARRIED WOMEN. Rev. edn. London: Shelter London Publishers, 1995.

Burns, Alison GOING IT ALONE – RELATIONSHIP BREAKDOWN AND YOUR RIGHTS: A GUIDE FOR UNMARRIED WOMEN. Rev. ed. London: Shelter London Publishers, 1995.

Aimed at individuals rather than advisers, these two complementary guides highlight the various issues, examine options and the consequences of each, and point the way to further help. Sections include emergency action, divorce, children, and how to sort out longer-term issues such as money and the home. The shelf life of this particular edition may be limited as major legislation in this field is planned for early 1996, but no doubt Shelter will be bringing out further revised editions.

REFERENCES AND CITATIONS

1 Donohue, J. C. , 'Planning for a community information center', *Library journal*, 15 October 1972, 3284.
2 Donohue, J. C., 'Community information services – a proposed definition', in Martin, S. K., *Community information politics: proceedings of 39th ASIS annual meeting*. Vol. 13. American Society for Information Science, 1976, fiche 8, frame E4.

3 *Ibid*, fiche 9, frame B12.
4 Whalley, E. D. and Davinson, D. E., *Developments in community information services in public libraries in the United States: a state of the art report and literature guide*. Leeds, Department of Librarianship, Leeds Polytechnic, 1976.
5 Watson, J. *et al.*, *The management of community information services in the public libraries*. Leeds, Public Libraries Management Research Unit, School of Librarianship, Leeds Polytechnic, 1980, 65–6.
6 *Community information – what libraries can do: a consultative document*, London, Library Association, 1980, 12.

9

Business and company information

Malcolm Stacey and Donna Shilling

The scope of this chapter is broad, but some defining is essential as a preliminary. Company information is self-explanatory, though it extends over a wide spectrum from the simple provison of a firm's telephone number to detailed financial analysis of its performance. Business information, on the other hand, has the Through the Looking Glass property of meaning what the user wants it to mean. For the purposes of this chapter (and for library purposes generally) the following is offered as a definition:

> ... information on the organizations (including firms, government departments, associations and voluntary bodies) which go to make up the economic life of the world; and information on the setting in which they operate.

For several centuries this field of interest has been served by a variety of publications, such as directories, trade journals, statistical works and manufacturers' catalogues. The scale, scope and variety of these are always expanding: as an indication, the first edition of *Current British directories* in 1953 listed 1000 titles, while its 12th edition in 1993 recorded 4127. Moreover, the transition from exclusively printed forms to electronic media has added a further very significant dimension. Traditional paper sources have yet to be superseded by computer-based services in most instances: at present the two formats complement each other well (if funds permit).

The demand for business and company information, particularly in public libraries, comes from a surprisingly wide variety of users. The public provision of appropriate material focused in the first place exclusively on the businessman [specific gender deliberate]. This emphasis is certainly the most compelling way to secure generous funding for often expensive sources, and it continues to be true that work-related enquiries dominate the business information scene. However, it is widely acknowledged that the demands of other users can help to justify this expenditure: individuals seeking employment, students at different levels and, not least, the consumer who may wish to complain about a product or invest in a company. The sources covered by this chapter thus earn a living in more ways than is sometimes recognized.

GUIDES AND BIBLIOGRAPHIES

The dominant form of material which provides business and company information is the directory, defined as a systematic listing of organizations, individuals or other categories, with details about each entry such as location, activities, personnel and so on. Although some directories appear as part of mainstream publishing, many arise from the activities of professional and trade associations or from bodies which are only incidentally publishers. As a consequence, the library's standard bibliographical tools are but a partial and erratic means of identification.

By far the most authoritative and informative guides produced in Britain are those compiled by CBD Research Ltd.

CURRENT BRITISH DIRECTORIES. 12th edn. Beckenham: CBD Research, 1993.

The three elements of the title precisely describe the contents but do not indicate the meticulous comprehensiveness of the entries, nor the remarkably specific subject index. Its presentation and accessibility betray all the signs of its regular use by the compilers themselves. There is a companion volume, *European directories*, which by 1994 had reached its third edition.

DAWSON TOP 5000 DIRECTORIES AND ANNUALS. Folkestone: Dawson UK Ltd. Annual.

This guide, appearing more frequently than *CBD* and covering a wider range of serials, is less sharply focused and less effectively indexed.

For British librarians these volumes will normally be adequate, but an American equivalent is *Guide to American directories* (13th edn, Todd Publications, 1994).

From an historical point of view the identification of titles is more problematic (and, of course, of less concern to the majority of librarians in the field).

NORTON, J. E. *Guide to the national and provincial directories of England and Wales excluding London published before 1856.* London: Royal Historical Society, 1950.

SHAW, G. AND TIPPER, A. *British directories: a bibliography and guide to directories published in England and Wales (1850–1950) and Scotland (1773–1950).* Leicester: Leicester University Press, 1988.

Many titles appear in the British Library catalogue and the *British union catalogue of periodicals* often identifies the location of permanent files.

Company information sources are very helpfully set out in three CBD Research publications:

EUROPEAN COMPANIES: GUIDE TO SOURCES OF INFORMATION. 4th edn. Beckenham: CBD Research, 1992.

For each country there are sections on company registration, forms of business enterprise, stock exchanges, credit-reporting services, printed and electronic directories, periodicals and other sources. Companion volumes cover America (50 countries) and Asia and Australasia (69 countries).

Business categories such as periodicals and statistics are within the scope of other chapters, but two guides to statistics demand mention at this point.

STATISTICS EUROPE: A GUIDE TO SOURCES OF STATISTICAL INFORMATION. 6th edn. Beckenham: CBD Research, 1995.

Over 1200 pan-European and national statistical publications are described and indexed in great detail.

INSTAT: INTERNATIONAL STATISTICS SOURCES: SUBJECT GUIDE TO SOURCES OF INTERNATIONAL COMPARATIVE STATISTICS. Routledge, 1995. 2v.

This substantial work gives access to some 400 international sources of statistical data by means of 46 broad subject groupings and a specific subject index. Titles included all cover a wide selection of countries.

Market research reports are a class of material which presents real problems of availability, but they are at least comprehensively identified on an international basis in *Marketsearch* (see below).

All these guides to the literature tend to be very inclusive and thus of most use to librarians trying to identify gaps in established collections. The needs of someone who is trying to create a core collection are perhaps best met by visits to other libraries, and by discussion with their librarians, but several studies of business information can also be consulted with profit.[1] It must always be remembered that this is a field where currency is critical. Both printed and electronic sources change constantly to reflect this and no detailed guide can be wholly reliable.

TELECOMMUNICATIONS DIRECTORIES

Telephone directories are perhaps the class of directory most familiar to the general public. Indeed, the *Concise Oxford dictionary* somewhat surprisingly puts them in first place in its definition of directory. Yet they are often undervalued and overlooked when an enquirer is seeking information. The ubiquity of the telephone directory in both private and business locations, at least in the west, makes the listing of subscribers an outstandingly valuable asset, even with the increasing popularity of ex-directory numbers for individuals. In most countries the alphabetical listing of subscribers is paralleled, often in a separate publication, by a classified arrangement of businesses (the almost universal *Yellow pages*).

The United Kingdom provision is in many ways typical, though possibly presented in a more baffling way than some countries', both to domestic and overseas users. The numerous volumes appear at regular intervals, although only the *Yellow pages* as frequently as annual. The cost of a complete set is considerable, but happily British Telecommunications recognizes the particular contribution which public libraries make to its business by supplying them without charge. The whole set is available on microfilm, which is appropriate in some circumstances. Telephone directories are ideally suited to the medium of CD-ROM. The BT Phonedisc covers all UK business and residential entries and appears quarterly. In addition, online access to the BT Phonebase system is available via Prestel. Newer products include Teledisc, with business names, addresses and numbers, and Probase, which produces a British version of the US Phonedisc from BT data.

Telephone directories from most overseas countries are in practice only obtainable through BT (International Directories, Longridge Road, Preston PR2 5AY), which provides an effective and well-organized source of supply of hardcopy versions. Commercial sources need to be investigated for electronic equivalents: for example, DDA (Digital Directory Associates) produces US Phonedisc, a quarterly three-disc set of business listings and residential listings (eastern and western states).

Although the telephone is the dominant medium, fax is expanding very rapidly, largely at the expense of telex. Many countries issue directories uniform with their telephone directories (although the United Kingdom has ceased to issue a fax directory). An expensive, selective but very convenient single source for all countries is available:

JAEGER & WALDMANN INTERNATIONAL FAX DIRECTORY and JAEGER & WALDMANN INTERNATIONAL TELEX AND TELETEX DIRECTORY. Darmstadt: Jaeger & Waldmann. Annual.

In each set of volumes subscribers are listed alphabetically within each country. In addition to the primary purpose of providing numbers, *J & W* also acts as an invaluable worldwide listing of organizations and their postal addresses. A companion set of volumes offers a yellow-pages facility, each classified heading being subdivided by country. A CD-ROM version is available.

GENERAL BUSINESS DIRECTORIES

The most frequent kind of enquiry in the business information field centres round the identification and location of enterprises. Often more detailed data are requested in addition. In the United Kingdom, as in most other countries, the sheer volume of businesses precludes the production of a single, all-embracing source, even if only a telephone number is required (although computers make this aim more achievable, as BT Phonedisc demonstrates). Nonetheless, British enquirers benefit from a very impressive range of business directories. At first sight many appear to be duplicating each other, but in practice they offer distinctive options to the discriminating searcher.

The UK markeet is dominated by the three Ks:

KELLY'S BUSINESS DIRECTORY. East Grinstead: Kelly's Directories. Annual.

First published in 1877, Kelly's has both the longest pedigree and possibly the most familiar name in directory publishing. In one volume some 82,000 companies are listed alphabetically, with address, telephone and fax numbers and line of business. The same companies are also listed under more than 15,000 product headings, although in this section telephone numbers are lacking unless the firm has paid for a display entry. Kelly's remains a reliable, substantial and easy-to-use work, especially in libraries which cannot afford a selection of such tools. It is especially useful if a representative list of firms in a particular product or trade category is required with minimum effort.

KEY BRITISH ENTERPRISES. Britain's top 50,000 companies. High Wycombe: Dun and Bradstreet. 6 vols. Annual.

KBE attempts, with much success, a great deal more than Kelly's, but in its printed version is a multivolume production. Although rather fewer companies are included, each entry contains a useful extra array of data, including names of directors, trade names, turnover, profit, number of employees and parent company (if any). All this is presented in one alphabetical sequence and is enough to satisfy a high proportion of enquirers in many libraries. The remaining volumes are likely to be less used but much valued when appropriate: broad product categories, geographical listings, rankings by size of workforce or turnover, and trade names. *KBE* is available on CD-ROM in two versions. One covers the top 50,000 companies and offers roughly the same content as the hardcopy version, with a very flexible search engine. The second, the top 200,000, is similar, again with a good search engine and extremely good print and download facilities.

KOMPASS UK REGISTER. East Grinstead: Kompass Publications. Annual.

Kompass provides information on about 41,000 companies, many of course identical to *KBE*, but the primary arrangement is by county and town, which sometimes meets a need. A two-stage search is therefore required when a particular company is sought; each entry resembles that in *KBE*, though usually less informative. Kompass's distinctive feature is the sophisticated product listings, in which company names and very specific product headings provide the coordinates for a grid with symbols representing manufacturers, wholesalers and so on. This is a daunting system which requires more than one pair of hands, but with practice it offers an impressive retrieval method. Other Kompass volumes contain financial data, trade names (see below) and affiliations.

Kompass is available in various electronic formats. *Kompass CD-Book* contains information from the two principal volumes; access includes Kompass product code and postcode. *Kompass UK on CD* contains 190,000 companies. Online access can be direct from Reedbase Online, which also embraces the same 190,000 companies, or through DIALOG. The latter also includes electronic versions of *Dial industry, Kelly's, UK trade names* and *Directory of directors.*

Two other sources are essential in any library attempting a basic business information service:

COMPANIES HOUSE DIRECTORY. Cardiff: Companies Registration Office. Quarterly, with weekly updates.

More commonly identified as the *CRO directory*, this source is available only in microform and online. It provides a single alphabetical listing of all companies registered in the United Kingdom (about 1,000,000) and appears to be the answer to many enquiries. Although it is less helpful than some users expect, it is in fact indispensable in a number of ways. The entries comprise registered address, registration number, date of registration, year-end date and dates of filing of the latest annual returns and accounts. It is possible to squeeze from these bald facts some vital evidence on companies which cannot be found elsewhere: possible geographical location, age, availability of records, and simply a company's existence or otherwise. The quarterly publication is supplemented by (optional) weekly updates. A companion product lists dates for all dissolutions and name changes over the past 20 years. By definition, *CRO directory* cannot provide information on the equally large number of partnerships and sole traders that exist, nor can it usually answer an enquiry in itself, but it offers a vital link in the search process.

Companies House online can be accessed via Mercury Business Intelligence and, via a menu-driven system, provides an alternative which is not only more up to date, but allows searches for directors and disqualified directors, accounts and other company documents. Orders can be placed for microfiche copies of company files.

WHO OWNS WHOM UK AND REPUBLIC OF IRELAND. High Wycombe: Dun and Bradstreet. Annual.

The main source of information on company affiliations appears in two volumes: one lists some 6500 holding companies, with their family trees of about 100,000 subsidiaries, while the second records the subsidiaries with their parents. This is precisely what some enquirers need, but more often the volumes will be consulted, like *CRO directory*, as a step in the enquiry chain. It is particularly effective in identifying familiar names which have been submerged by absorption into a larger group. Companion volumes provide a similar function for Europe, North America, and Australasia and the Far East.

Many enquiries relate to businesses beyond Britain. Although few libraries in this country can begin to offer the same depth of service in this respect as for domestic enterprises, there are extensive resources to be found, most of them geared to English-speaking users.

Kompass provides the most familiar and easily identified source on individual overseas countries, and produces volumes for more than 40 states which substantially mirror the UK version. In practice, smaller counries are afforded greater depth of coverage but the outward conformity encourages exploration and assists retrieval. There are electronic versions on CD-ROM and online via DIALOG and *Kompass Online*.

Dun and Bradstreet likewise cater for foreign enquiries:

DUNS EUROPA. High Wycombe: Dun and Bradstreet. Annual.

This multivolume work is particularly useful in providing, similar to *KBE*, for some 35,000 companies in 26 countries data. A single pan-European index is invaluable when the company's nationality is unknown. Some 2.5 million firms are included in Duns Market Identifiers via DIALOG.

The United States poses special problems in the directory field by reason of its size. A country such as Belgium may receive comprehensive treatment in a two-volume work, but a similar production for America would be too vast and expensive to market. Nonetheless, for use overseas three directories will often produce essential data:

THOMAS REGISTER OF AMERICAN MANUFACTURERS. New York: Thomas. Annual.

The many volumes of this work are mainly devoted to 52,000 product listings. Under these headings 145,000 firms are listed by state, which is more relevant to domestic than overseas users. The most-used volumes are likely to be the single alphabetical listing of companies, broadly along the lines of *Kelly's*, and also an index of 100,000 trade names. The online version via DIALOG and the *Knight-Ridder CD-ROM* also include 44,000 companies from *Thomas food register* and entries for Canadian companies.

STANDARD & POOR'S REGISTER OF CORPORATIONS, DIRECTORS AND EXECUTIVES. New York: Standard & Poor's. Annual.

Although containing only one-third of the number of companies in *Thomas*, the depth of detail is correspondingly greater, especially in the corporate, financial and personnel fields. The online databases reflect these features, and *Standard & Poor's Corporations* is the CD-ROM version.

NATIONAL DIRECTORY OF ADDRESSES AND TELEPHONE NUMBERS. Detroit: Omnigraphics. Annual.

This compact volume manages to provide an alphabetical listing of 125,000 firms, public bodies and other organizations, with full postal address, telephone and fax numbers, and a classified arrangement in 18 broad subject areas backed by a very good index. It is a model for other countries to emulate.

A British source for American companies should be mentioned:

ANGLO-AMERICAN DIRECTORY: AMERICAN CHAMBER OF COMMERCE (UK). Kogan Page. Annual.

A single alphabetical sequence lists both American and British firms, with their agents or distributors in the other country. Addresses, telephone numbers and lines of business appear against each entry.

SECTORAL DIRECTORIES

The sources outlined in the previous section provide any library with a respectable core collection in business information. They may well be the most appropriate place to turn for many enquiries, and offer greater detail than some ostensibly more specialized directories. Most of them, however, are better equipped to answer queries about manufacturers than other kinds of enterprise; as a result, alternative sources may be preferred for categories such as retailers, services, the voluntary sector and the professions. Happily there is no shortage of suitable sectoral directories, at least in Britain, and almost every trade, profession or activity is covered by a directory of some kind, collectively exhibiting a fascinating diversity of currency, accuracy and usefulness.

There are around 4000 such titles currently published in the United Kingdom alone, and it may be helpful to attempt some broad categorization. Under each type a few titles are identified as models: they must stand as representatives of hosts of similar volumes.

Directories produced as commercial ventures

Publishers long ago realized that directories could be profitable, especially those aimed at the business community. The results of this awareness have been varied in the extreme. One sentence must be adequate to dismiss into outer darkness those directories based exclusively on paid entries, which in some cases never actually appear, although gullible businesses have paid for inclusion. Quite different are titles of long standing compiled by reputable publishers (many of them members of the Directory Publishers Association) which succeed in making a profit and meeting a public need at one and the same time. A handful of British examples effectively illustrate the astonishing scope of what is on the market. Most are revised annually, all regularly.

DIRECTORY TO THE FURNITURE AND FURNISHING INDUSTRY. Tonbridge: M-G Information Services. Annual.

This contains all the essential ingredients of a trade directory: manufacturers' names and addresses, product listings, trade name index, list of relevant associations. Interestingly, it also covers the retail sector and gives alphabetical and geographical listings of shops.

IRON AND STEEL WORKS OF THE WORLD. Metal Bulletin Books. Every four years.

Although produced in Britain, this treats the industry in all parts of the world on an equal footing, unlike some 'international' directories whose bias towards their native country is all too apparent. Its leisurely publishing cycle is a reflection of the very large scale of the establishments and the great detail given on each one.

DIRECTORY OF BRITISH ASSOCIATIONS AND ASSOCIATIONS IN IRE-LAND. Beckenham: CBD Research. Biennial.

Another of CBD's exemplary compilations, *DBA* presents a wealth of data on associations in the minimum space, all indexed in great depth. It not only answers enquiries about particular bodies, but is also a means of identifying referral points, since associations are often prime contacts by reason of their libraries, publications and general expertise. In advance of most sectoral directories, *DBA* is available on CD-ROM.

Publications of trade associations and professional bodies

The usefulness of this category is uneven. A trade association's list of members has its uses, but by definition will not list firms which are not in membership. Membership lists of professions may give no more than an address against each name, but many are more valuable.

ROYAL INSTITUTE OF BRITISH ARCHITECTS. DIRECTORY OF PRACTICES and DIRECTORY OF MEMBERS. RIBA. Annual.

Although the entries for individual members are brief, each practice is described in terms of its partners and recent commissions, in addition to all the essential locational data.

BTHA HANDBOOK AND GUIDE TO THE BRITISH INTERNATIONAL TOY AND HOBBY FAIR. British Toy and Hobby Association. Annual.

This combination of a trade-fair catalogue with a trade directory results in a useful volume which contains all the essential sections: members' names and addresses, trade name index and classified product list.

Official publications

Central and local government are in some instances the sources of directories, either because there is a statutory obligation or because the data are readily available to meet an expressed need.

LONDON DIPLOMATIC LIST. HMSO. Biennial.

This official listing of all foreign diplomats posted to London must be in regular use in embassies, and also identifies each country's establishment in the United Kingdom.

DTI QA REGISTER: THE UNITED KINGDOM REGISTER OF QUALITY ASSURED COMPANIES. HMSO. Annual with amendments.

A multivolume work which gives essential information on the quality assessment of individual companies. Enquirers are frequently directed to it, but its scale and cost restricts its availability to larger libraries.

LOCALITY DIRECTORIES

In the past a substantial proportion of the directory stock of reference libraries consisted of volumes on individual British localities, often identified in a generic way as Kelly's. This extensive range of titles, including many produced by firms other than Kelly's, is all but extinct, though from a historical standpoint back-runs are highly prized and heavily consulted. So, this category of directory is nowadays somewhat depleted, and as a result there remains a gap which has yet to be filled in the availability of information on, for example, an area's topography, local government, magistrates, churches and organizations. The much-consulted lists of private residents have been only partially replaced by the vast expansion of the telephone directory.

Selective coverage of local information is sometimes offered by annual publications issued by local newspapers, with titles such as 'Citizen's guide'. The quality of such compilations is very uneven and their existence outside their circulation area little known. More widespread and ambitious is the Thomson series of some 140 volumes.

Postcode directories for the United Kingdom appear in a series of regional volumes and offer a useful source, not just for postcodes but for establishing the existence of addresses and, increasingly, for the very large lists of businesses and other organizations.

As a means of locating individuals the register of electors is always available at the appropriate local library. Despite the reduction in comprehensiveness which has been observed in recent years, the register remains an effective way of verifying the occupants of a particular property.

Many local authorities see the economic value of producing directories of firms in their areas. The best of these can be informative about both individual enterprises and their products and services. Similar publications arise from chambers of commerce or trade, but these do not list non-members.

Most British local authorities sponsor guidebooks, the best of which can be helpful sources of information on all aspects of a community. Bibliographically they are elusive, and there is a regrettable tendency for them to become promotional rather than informative.

COMPANY INFORMATION

Within the broad classification of business information companies are perhaps the most visible category. Company information encompasses a firm's location and activities, its structure and performance. It is obvious that many of the sources already cited are ideally suited to provide company information: *CRO directory*, the three Ks, any trade directory, to name just a few. This section seeks to identify sources which reveal company data in depth, and especially the all-important financial aspects.

An unusual starting point may sound more like an economic history text:

INTERNATIONAL DIRECTORY OF COMPANY HISTORIES. St James Press. In progress.

This multivolume and expanding survey of business histories allocates several pages to the historical development of each company, and by so doing illuminates the present-day operations in a way that few other sources attempt. A cumulative index picks up contributions which update articles in earlier volumes. There is a noticeable American bias, but in an age of multinationals this can be seen as an advantage.

More obvious titles focus on the current situation:

HAMBRO'S COMPANY GUIDE. Hemmington Scott Publishing. Quarterly.

Essential financial data on British public limited companies is presented in a standard tabulated format. This is a concise source for enquirers needing a little more than the general business directories can offer.

HOOVER'S HANDBOOK OF AMERICAN BUSINESS. Austin, Texas: Reference Press. Annual.

This covers 500 American corporations – very much the tip of the iceberg – and is broadly comparable to *Hambro*.

A long-established format for company information has been cards or, more accurately, folded sheets of paper:

EXTEL FINANCIAL UK QUOTED COMPANIES SERVICE. Extel Financial. Cards updated daily.

This is just one of numerous parallel services covering British and foreign companies in great depth. Prominent aspects are time series of profit-and-loss accounts, balance sheets, dividends, extracts from the latest annual report and news items on new issues, takeover bids and personnel changes.

Such a format was crying out for computerization and Extel is available on CD-ROM and through a number of online hosts, including DataStar and DIALOG. The flexibility of electronic access is irresistible in contrast to the version on cards, with the risk of loss and staff-intensive filing that they entailed.

McCARTHY CARDS UK. Warminster: McCarthy Information. Cards updated daily.

This card service also features UK companies, but presents its data in the form of press cuttings. It also offers sector reports. As with Extel, its potential is vastly enhanced by electronic access, online direct or via FT PROFILE, on CD-ROM, featuring extracts from about 80 British and foreign newspapers and updated monthly.

Many electronic business sources derive from established paper products, but the specialized company finance field has seen the birth of valuable services which lack printed equivalents.

JORDANWATCH. Jordan and Sons. Database.

Accessible via DataStar, this service offers information on almost 100,000 UK companies, including some small ones. Five-year series of data are given in addition to other Extel-type facts. It is updated weekly.

FAME. BVD. CD-ROM.

This disc's claim is 'financial analysis made easy', with some justification, and is in effect the CD version of JordanWatch. It can be searched by a number of criteria and data can be displayed graphically.

ICC. ICC. Database.

This is another source of company information, accessed via DIALOG, which gives the full text of major UK companies' accounts and much information on over 200,000 other companies. It can also be used o obtain credit ratings, a field to which public libraries formerly had no access. Once again, the use of computerized sources has thrown open this sensitive area and there are many competing suppliers.

NFOCHECK. Infocheck. Database.

Company reports on most British businesses, including credit rating and industrial performance.

CCN. Nottingham: CCN. Database.

One of the largest firms of its kind in Europe provides credit scoring and business information on several million UK businesses, and is venturing on to the Internet with BIGnet, which offers fee-based access to data.

D & B ACCESS. Dun and Bradstreet. Database.

On the international scene Dun and Bradstreet offer direct access via Dunsnet to vast databases relating to all parts of the world. The compact report is straightforward credit checking based on the D & B rating, whereas the comprehensive report is a full service along the lines described above.

Company annual reports may appear somewhat homegrown sources of intelligence after the instant data of the electronic world. They are certainly uneven in quality. Some do not aspire to be more than promotional, once they have met their statutory obligation, but many are worth consulting both for what they reveal and what they conceal about a company. Although they are normally available on demand, they form a tiresome category of material for many libraries, especially for those who need to cover all sectors. Public libraries will at least attempt to file reports from their own locality.

PRODUCT DATA AND TRADE NAMES

One further aspect of enquiries about firms remains to be noted. In many libraries the demand for product and service data will be apparent, but on a smaller scale than that for locational, financial and other details. Many directories are geared to meet this demand: the respective means adopted by *KBE* and *Kompass* have already been noted, although the exclusion by *Kompass UK trade names* of the pharmaceutical, food, drink and tobacco sectors is a serious deficiency. A few specialized directories are more ambitious on the product front.

BARBOUR INDEX: BUILDING PRODUCTS COMPENDIUM. Barbour Index. Annual.

This handsomely presented volume consists mostly of well-illustrated surveys of product groups which give detailed specifications of manufacturers' goods. The attraction to the librarian is the very precise indexing coupled with company names and addresses and trade names. Few sectors are as well served in this way as the construction industry.

ELECTRONIC ENGINEERING INDEX. Bracknell: Technical Indexes. Biennial.

Less ample than Barbour in presentation, this and similar TI indexes are immensely useful guides to their fields. Products are specified in great detail and the company listings are especially good on importers and distributors. These directories are simply byproducts of a system of presenting manufacturers' catalogues in microform, but they earn a place on the shelves in their own right.

Trade literature originates as glossy brochures in one form or another. Such material can only be collected by general libraries with difficulty, but more worthwhile results can be obtained where a sectoral or regional focus is possible, or where microform versions are obtainable. Local studies libraries may attempt to acquire at least a representative range from their own area.

A specific aspect of product data is the trade name, brand, trade mark or service mark. The baffling tendency for producers to disguise their identity and location on their goods and to oblige prospective customers to undertake time-consuming searches generates the opportunity for librarians to impress with minimum effort. Many trade directories contain lists of trade names, though it must be admitted that imported brands may be difficult or impossible to trace in some sectors since their existence may nowhere be registered.

KOMPASS UK TRADE NAMES. East Grinstead: Kompass Publications. Annual.

Around 100,000 trade names current in Britain are listed alphabetically, with a description of the kind of product and details of owner's name. Company names and addresses are listed in a parallel index; this also brings together all the brands of each firm. This is the best single printed list, but has the major disadvantage that as a matter of policy it excludes the major sectors of food, drink, tobacco and pharmaceuticals. It is necessary to turn to individual trade directories in these fields.

SOFTWARE USERS' YEARBOOK. VNU Business Publications. Annual.

An industry which abounds in elusive brands and acronyms is computer software. This directory very often succeeds in identifying a name which has been seen or overhead by the enquirer.

Electronic access to trade names has furtherc enhanced librarians' facility in this field. The Kompass source just described can be accessed via DIALOG and there are other online alternatives.

TRADEMARKSCAN UK. Thomson and Thomson. Database.

This allows 700,000 registrations and applications to be accessed via DIALOG, including lapses since 1983; CD-ROM is not yet available. The United States equivalent is also on DIALOG and has appeared on CD-ROM. Federal registrations date from 1884 and updates occur twice weekly. A benefit of computer-based access to trade names is the ability to cope with corrupted spellings and unusual presentations of words.

MARKET RESEARCH

A thorough investigation of the potential market is rightly regarded as a high priority, both by aspiring entrepreneurs and by business students. A few expect to find all the answers in a single source, but equally few realize the diversity of the sources and the cost of acquiring some of them. The price levels of many market research tools put them way beyond the budgets of publicly funded libraries, yet their inevitable absence can lead to underselling of a library's more run-of-the-mill means of supporting the market researcher. Most of the areas covered by this chapter have a bearing on filling out the picture of a particular sector: trade statistics offer very precise data on many products; directories can identify the presence or absence of competition; financial information on companies is publicly available; journals contain up-to-date indications of market trends.

Nonetheless, many enquirers seek some kind of synthesis of this mass of facts, and market research reports are produced in stupendous numbers to meet this need, from a brief feature in a trade paper to a weighty international survey. Much of this material has to be classed as grey literature, with potential hindrances to identification and acquisition, but a magisterial bibliography is at hand:

MARKETSEARCH: INTERNATIONAL DIRECTORY OF PUBLISHED MARKET RESEARCH. Arlington Management Publications. Annual with updates.

It is a surprise to find that this record of published research actually exists and is revised annually. More than 20,000 reports worldwide are described in terms of scope, geographical coverage, size, price, date and publisher. Access is by way of a very specific subject index to broad SIC headings. Not all enquirers are deterred by the typical price of several hundred pounds; in any case, it is instructive to know what has been published.

At the opposite end of the spectrum there is a useful monthly index of market intelligence items in journals:

STATISTICS AND MARKET INTELLIGENCE. Birmingham Public Libraries. Monthly.

Some 60 British periodicals are scanned for suitable features and indexed under broad market headings. It has the advantages of being current and of leading to sources that are fairly widely available.

A similarly down-to-earth index of long standing retains an unambitious paper version, but also appears on CD-ROM and on the Internet:

RESEARCH INDEX. Dorchester: Business Surveys. Fortnightly.

This appears in two sequences, one of companies and the other of subjects, including commodities and countries. More than 60 British newspapers and trade papers are indexed under about 225 subject headings. Publication is very prompt, and again there is the advantage that most of the sources are widely available.

More valuable, but naturally far more expensive, are services which provide the full text of such references. McCarthy, the best example, has already been described in relation to company information.

A few popular series of market research reports have been supplied in paper versions in the larger public and academic libraries. Names such as *Key notes* and *Mintel* are frequently quoted and therefore requested. Their cost and liability to theft has restricted their wider circulation, but newer formats are making them more accessible.

KEY NOTES. ICC. Database.

Reports on some 170 sectors, many with a consumer bias, appear regularly and present a detailed market overview, including data on major countries. Free-text searching allows the retrieval of specific tables or items of interest. Online access is via FT PROFILE, and the CD-ROM version can be received at a range of intervals to suit the pocket, from monthly to three-yearly.

Economist Intelligence Unit, with its Country Reports and 'Business International' via DIALOG, is another high-quality product which now offers the CD-ROM alternative.

Throughout this chapter there has been a constant refrain between examples in the form of non-print media. The online solutions of a few years ago have been rivalled, and to some extent put in the shade, by the more manageable attractions of CD-ROM. The speed with which one medium develops into another renders many descriptions of formats of almost academic interest after a few years. The scene is now being transformed again as business information workers, along with most of their colleagues, contemplate, investigate and exploit the largely unexplored possibilities of the Internet. Businesses are finding that it promises to provide an expanding route into the market place, and librarians and information scientists will wish to follow their lead. Firms such as CCN will see a gateway into their services through the Internet, and the same is likely to apply to the old-established hosts.

Business information provision has already benefited immeasurably from the expansion of paperless sources. Access to all US telephone numbers on three insignificant discs is a typical example of how the facilities of a library have been transformed. These benefits are accompanied by challenges. One is the increasing invisibility of information sources. A large collection of US telephone directories was hard to ignore as one entered a library: its CD-ROM version will never catch the eye in the same way, even if producers do try to compensate with elaborate promotional literature.[2] There is also the perception that failure to produce a desired result at the first keystroke can lead unwary enquirers to assume that the information is not available. In contrast, the more laborious and time-consuming manual search may allow more time for alternative search strategies to evolve. In a field where small items of information can be of great value, it will be necessary to devise ways to ensure that the exponential growth arising from the Internet will be matched by equally enhanced quality of retrieval.

REFERENCES AND CITATIONS

1 See works by Bakewell, Haythornthwaite and Kaye below.
2 A view expressed by Sir Charles Chadwyck-Healey in a *Financial Times* interview quoted in *Business information review*, **11** (4), 1995, 71.

SUGGESTIONS FOR FURTHER READING

Bakewell, K. G. B., *Business information and the public library*, Aldershot, Gower, 1987.
  Although now dated in many ways, this still succeeds in relating information provision to real libraries.
Business information review
  Essential quarterly reading with a good balance of expansive surveys and brief updating items.
Haythornthwaite, J. (ed.), *The business information maze: an essential guide*, London, Aslib, 1990.
Kaye, D., *Information and business: an introduction*, London, Library Association Publishing, 1991.
  The best recent survey of the field.
Online/CD-ROM business information
  Regular newsletter featuring individual providers, complemented by Foster, P. (ed.), *Online/CD-ROM business sourcebook 1995–96*, East Grinstead, Bowker-Saur, 1995.

10
News and Current Affairs

Christine D. Reid

News and current information have become an important part of all our daily lives. We have, in fact, become a society which cannot get enough news: turn on the radio and you will get hourly news updates. There are now television channels devoted solely to 24-hour news. The UK is virtually unique in having a highly developed national newspaper market, with 85% of the population reading a newspaper on a regular basis.

The amount of information being produced in the world is enormous and still growing. However, unlike conventional publishing, speed is of the essence in dealing with the news. This became very evident, perhaps for the first time, during the Gulf War, when broadcasts by CNN were bringing reports to television screens more or less as they were happening. To be 'news', information needs to be transmitted to the world at large in the shortest possible time. This urgency for fast information is one of the strengths of news items as sources of information. However, this can also lead to difficulties in tracing relevant items of news.

Newspapers are instant history, whatever they may seem on the day of publication. They will be consulted for years as authoritative accounts of contemporary events. Frequently items reported in the press will never appear in print in any other source. Reports of crimes, gossip, fashion, sport, social issues, science, the arts and passing references to individuals can all be equally important to researchers, and may never appear in any other source. This therefore means that newspapers are an important source of primary information, in particular as a record of events as they happened. Newspapers are also important, as the power of the press in forming public opinion and in influencing decisions is undeniable. More major events of historical, political and economic importance usually find their way into more formal printed sources – initially news digests, then annual surveys and yearbooks, chronologies and, years later, they may be covered by academic research studies or other publications considering a particular subject or time period. Until recently newspapers were an unwieldy source of information with few indexes and almost insurmountable problems of storage – hence back files were difficult to locate if they existed at all. However, major developments have been brought about by the speed, power and sophistication of information technology and communications systems. The development of internationally accessible online databases has made news information accessible as never before.

Most news never appears anywhere other than in the newspapers of the following day. Therefore, unless it is available online, it is 'lost' forever except to those few organizations who have the need, the time and the money to maintain large libraries of press cuttings. However, there are limitations to retrieval accuracy, both in print and online. In both cuttings files and printed indexes, retrieval is possible only through fairly broad subject headings and selected biographical files, but almost the opposite occurs in retrieval from an online full-text database. Very specific pieces of information can be easily obtained here, whereas broad subject searches tend not to be very effective.

If there is no online file or index of a particular newspaper, the only way to find the information needed is to identify the date of an event from a chronology or year review, then to trace titles likely to have reported the event, and finally to locate a file of the original in a local library or in the British Library.

This chapter concentrates on news as a source of current information. However, for tracing historical events, chronologies, year reviews, yearbooks, indexes and locations of back files are also discussed. No attempt is made to chart in detail the several name changes of some of the titles referred to. Consequently, the date given for the first edition indicates that the current publication can be traced back continuously to that date, although there may have been several name changes over the years.

ELECTRONIC SOURCES

Information technology has had a significant impact on the newspaper industry. More important, however, than the change to being compiled and printed electronically is the fact that the information in the newspaper can be made more easily accessible. Transferred into an online database, today's news can be searched electronically before the printed version is available. The most important national newspapers, newswire services, weekly specialist trade journals, newsletters and many other magazines and periodicals are available full-text electronically.

The major database hosts supplying news information are:

FT PROFILE, part of the Financial Times Group, based in Sunbury-on-Thames, Middlesex

NEXIS, from Mead Data Central of Dayton, Ohio

DIALOG, part of Knight-Ridder Information, based in Palo Alto, California.

The most important source for UK newspapers is FT PROFILE. It currently hosts individual files providing full-text access to 14 UK newspapers, including the *Daily Mail*, *Financial Times*, *The Independent* and *The Times*. These can be searched individually or as part of the *News* grouping. FT PROFILE is, in addition, an excellent starting point for news of an international nature. The grouping *European News* collects together continental English-language news sources including *The Irish Times* and *The European*, while the *International News* grouping provides access to international newspapers, including *The International Herald Tribune*, *Washington Post* and *Dow Jones News*. With the increasing importance of access to original news in the major European languages, FT PROFILE has groupings accessing French, German, Italian and Spanish news. These provide full-text access to *Frankfürter Allgemeine Zeitung*, *Les Echos*, *Le Monde* and *Il Sole 24 Ore*.

FT PROFILE also provides access to *Reuter Textline* and *FT McCarthy*. *Reuter Textline* is one of the leading sources of business information. It contains news and comment, most in full-text format, from approximately 600 international sources including the world's leading newspapers, magazines, trade journals and newswires. In addition, *Textline*'s coverage of UK regional news makes it a particularly useful source. The data from many of the sources date back to 1980 and are currently updated seven times a day.

FT McCarthy, developed from the *McCarthy Card Service*, provides international business and company coverage from over 70 key sources. All major UK newspapers are covered and a strong coverage of European titles is also provided, frequently in their original language.

Particular care needs to be taken when using an electronic database to ensure exactly what is covered. Although publishers and hosts will claim that a particular database is 'full text', the assumption that all articles and features from a paper have been included can frequently be false. Frequently certain categories of material are deliberately omitted for a variety of reasons, such as copyright restrictions. These can include complete sections of a newspaper, such as the arts or sports pages, commissioned articles, letters to the editor, editorials, obituaries and advertisements. No online file reproduces long tabular material such as the pages of stock market prices. Other major omissions from online databases include photographs, diagrams and tables, all of which can make a valuable contribution to the understanding of an article. Where these prove to be important, the only recourse is to the original printed version.

Increasingly newspapers are appearing in compact disc format, which can include more information than the online version. *The Times and the Sunday Times CD edition* contains selected graphics and photographs from 1991 onwards. *The Guardian on CD-ROM* has included maps and tables from 1992. Most of the newspaper CDs are updated quarterly, and although this delay can be frustrating for those who wish to be completely up to date, newspapers on CD are an increasingly important resource as they open up a whole world of information never before possible. Particular articles can be retrieved and coverage of a topic can be traced over several months or even years, all in a matter of a few minutes. CD-ROMs provide improved access to the news. They are, however, not a substitute for archival storage as they do not contain the complete newspaper.

The Internet is increasingly becoming a useful source from which to access newspapers and other news. American news may currently dominate, but increasingly news from countries traditionally difficult to trace is becoming available, for example *Bulgaria News Archive, Croatian Radio News, China News Digest, Taiwan Daily Times. Newslink* (Internet address http://www.newslink.org/) currently provides links to approximately 1000 newspapers and magazines across the Internet.

UK newspapers with Internet addresses include the following:

The Electronic Telegraph	http://www.telegraph.co.uk/
The Financial Times	http://www.ft.com/
The Herald	http://www.cims.co.uk/cims/

News on the Internet can be updated frequently and can be read at any time of the day anywhere in the world. Sites spring up in response to special events such as sports tournaments, and disasters like the Kobe earthquake. These provide up-to-the-minute reporting.

NEWSWIRES

Newswires are valuable for their immediacy, for on-the-spot updating and commentary. They provide direct access to original news material, which forms the basis of many media reports. They are therefore extremely useful for researching the facts as they were first reported. Much of the material is also not included in newspapers or radio and television broadcasts. The following are among the most useful:

The Press Association – available online from FT PROFILE. April 1995– . Updated four times a day.

Reuter News – available online from FT PROFILE. January 1992– . Updated daily. Also available on DIALOG. January 1987– . Updated continuously.

Agence France Presse – available online from DIALOG. June 1991– . Updated continuously.

AP (Associated Press) News – available online from FT PROFILE. September 1983– . Updated daily. Also available online from DIALOG. January 1984– . Updated continuously.

The Press Association is the national news agency for the UK providing information to the national press, regional press and broadcasters. Reuters News covers all news stories with the reliability and objectivity Reuters journalists are renowned for. Associated Press is biased towards American news and interests.

Reuter Business Briefing combines the news as it is happening from Reuter's wire services with the Regulatory News Service from the International Stock Exchange and five years' archive information from *Textline*. This is one of a new breed of information products which is aimed at delivering information directly to the end-user.

Newswires have the advantage over newspapers in that they do not just cover topical events but continue to monitor events even when the story has long been out of the international spotlight.

NEWSLETTERS

Newsletters are another important source of very valuable information. They can provide timely, very focused and detailed information frequently not found anywhere else. They can also provide a specialized slant on the news. Companies, banks, government departments, trade and industry associations all publish a variety of newsletters, many of which are too specific and too expensive to find their way into many libraries. Therefore the most effective and cost-effective way to access them is via an online database. The best places to start are:

Predicasts Newsletters, available online from FT PROFILE, DIALOG and DataStar. This provides access to the full text of more than 600 specialist newsletters.

NewsNet is an online system based in Bryn Mawr, Pennsylvania, which is devoted entirely to newsletter coverage. It carries over 800 full-text newsletters.

Of specific interest to the business researcher are the *Financial Times Business Reports* series of newsletters. These provide current market and industry news covering the areas of business and finance, energy, media and technology. These again are accessible online via FT PROFILE and DataStar.

With more and more sources becoming available electronically, it becomes important to know what is available where. The most useful sources here are:

NEWSPAPERS ONLINE. Needham Heights, MA: BiblioData. Biannual.

FULLTEXT SOURCES ONLINE. Needham Heights, MA: BiblioData. Biannual.

Allcock, S. and Osborne, J. THE ONLINE MANUAL. 3rd edn. Oxford: Learned Information, 1994.

NEWS BROADCASTS

None of the broadcast news transmitted in the UK on either radio or television is available in any published form. In the United States, however, things are very different. The *ABC News Transcripts and Index* have been published on microfiche since 1970 by Research Publications, Woodbridge, Connecticut.

Among the various electronic products are:

Broadcast News on CD-ROM. Reading: Research Publications International, 1993– .

This provides the full text of news, documentaries and interviews taken from CNN, ABC News, National Public Radio and PBS networks.

CBS News Transcripts Ondisc. Ann Arbor, Michigan: UMI.

NBC News Transcripts Ondisc. Ann Arbor, Michigan: UMI.

Both of the above carry complete transcripts on television news programmes broadcast by CBS and NBC respectively.

For purposes of monitoring broadcast news around the world the British and American governments have divided the world between them, exchanging all information received. BBC linguists listen in to broadcasts and news agency reports from around 140 countries in 70 different languages. These are then translated into English and published as:

BBC SUMMARY OF WORLD BROADCASTS. Reading: BBC, 1939– .

Published six days a week, the *Summary of World Broadcasts* provides the latest in-depth political news, complemented by a weekly economic report. It is available in five separate sections covering the different regions of the former Soviet Union, central Europe and the Balkans, Asia-Pacific, Middle East and Africa, Latin America and the Caribbean. This is a particularly valuable source as a record of events, speeches and policy statements from countries which are not normally covered in any depth by the international media. The data are also available online via FT PROFILE from January 1987 and from NEXIS.

NEWS DIGESTS

A news digest service can provide in a concise, factual way background information about world affairs, current events or political changes in another country. The two best known publications of this type are:

KEESING'S RECORD OF WORLD EVENTS. Cambridge: Cartermill Publishing, 1931– .
Available online from FT PROFILE, January 1983– .

FACTS ON FILE WORLD NEWS DIGEST WITH INDEX. New York: Facts on File, 1940– .
Available online from DIALOG, January 1982– .

Published monthly, *Keesing's* is an extremely useful reference source on world politics and economics, international events and defence. Each issue begins with full coverage of the major world news stories from the previous month, followed by a news digest section containing concise, factual articles. A reference section provides background briefings on countries, political systems and principal international organizations. These will all be updated at least once in the course of a year. The indexing has been greatly improved and contains entries for countries, subjects and names in one sequence. *Keesing's* has a much stronger coverage of international affairs than its main rival *Facts on File*. It is also recognized as being unbiased and authoritative. There is also a bimonthly publication called *Keesing's UK Record*, which concentrates on UK current affairs.

Facts on File is a US-published news digest service, and although it claims world coverage it has a definite American bias. It does, however, now carry both a European and a developing countries section. It is published weekly and is therefore much more current than *Keesing's*. The two services do, however, complement rather than compete with one another.

News digests are becoming increasingly accessible via the Internet. This is particularly the case for those from developing countries. However, these are mostly out to attract business to a country, so beware: you may not be being presented with a whole story. They are, however, useful sources and most are freely available, e.g. *China News Digest Global News, Bosnet*, which covers news briefs about Bosnia, and *Central Europe Today News Service*.

NEWSPAPER INDEXES

There are two main categories of indexes to newspapers, those which index a specific paper and those which cover a range of newspapers. Unfortunately, as publication is usually several months behind, these published indexes are of little use for current issues. One additional difficulty with newspapers is that they follow a continuous publishing process with new editions appearing throughout the day: for example, *The Times* produces six editions a day. However, it is only the last edition of the day that is indexed. Therefore, stories which are ousted during the course of a day can be extremely difficult to trace.

Only three British national newspapers produce their own indexes:

THE TIMES INDEX. Reading: Research Publications, 1785– .

THE GUARDIAN INDEX. Ann Arbor, Michigan: UMI, 1986– .

MONTHLY INDEX TO THE FINANCIAL TIMES. Reading: Research Publications, 1981– .

Of these, *The Times Index* is the most well known and most generally available in reference collections. In addition to indexing itself, it also indexes *The Sunday Times* and its magazine, *The Times Literary Supplement*, *The Times Educational Supplement*, *The Times Educational Supplement Scotland* and *The Times Higher Educational Supplement*. The indexing in *The Times* is very detailed and consistent. Items are indexed under personal name, subject, country or locality. It is published monthly with annual cumulations. *The Times Index* is an extremely useful tool for researching dates, which can then be checked in other newspapers of the time for alternative accounts of an event.

The Monthly Index to the Financial Times has, naturally, quite a substantial overlap with *The Times Index*. However, as *The Financial Times* is a business-based daily paper, its strength lies in its worldwide coverage of company, financial and industrial news. It is, however, an excellent source of general news and of arts reviews. It is also an extremely useful source for information about people, frequently proving to be the only source of biographical data on business people.

Two services which index several of the national newspapers are worthy of mention:

THE CLOVER NEWSPAPER INDEX AND COMPANY DATA SUPPLEMENT. Biggleswade, Clover Publications, 1986– .

This appears almost weekly, with 46 issues a year, and aims to appear within eight days of the last issue indexed. It indexes *The Daily Telegraph, The Guardian, The Times, The Financial Times, The Independent, The Observer, The Sunday Times* and their respective colour supplements, and *The Economist.* It is arranged under very broad subject headings, which can be unhelpful, and there is a distinct lack of cross-referencing. It is, however, produced quickly and cheaply and represents good value for money. It has recently been produced on CD-ROM.

RESEARCH INDEX. Broadmayne, Dorset: Business Surveys Ltd, 1965– .

This is published fortnightly and indexes articles of business and financial interest appearing in approximately 70 newspapers, trade journals and magazines. It is an invaluable tool for the business researcher as it appears within two to three weeks of the news appearing in print. However, like *The Clover Index*, it is produced cheaply and the indexing takes getting used to.

Published indexes to newspapers come and go as compilers are defeated by the high costs and such a labour-intensive task, particularly where local newspapers are concerned. The British Library Newspaper Library has a record of over 1000 indexes, most of them unpublished and transitory, and often dependent on the resources of the local public library. One of the rare published indexes is the *Glasgow Herald Index.* It began life in 1906 and was updated in the mid-1980s to 1987. Current access is, however, only available via CD-ROM or online.

There are a number of published indexes to American newspapers:

THE NEW YORK TIMES INDEX. Ann Arbor, Michigan: UMI, 1851– .

THE WASHINGTON POST INDEX. Ann Arbor, Michigan: UMI, 1971– .

CHRISTIAN SCIENCE MONITOR INDEX. Ann Arbor, Michigan: UMI, 1945– .

THE WALL STREET JOURNAL INDEX. Ann Arbor, Michigan: UMI, 1955– .

The New York Times Index is published semimonthly with an annual cumulative volume. It is a very good, detailed index for American business news in particular, but it does have international coverage. *The Wall Street Journal Index* is published monthly with an annual cumulative volume. It is a valuable source of business information, particularly on American business and companies.

Most of the printed indexes to American newspapers can be consulted in the UK only at the British Library Newspaper Library. DIALOG does, however, provide online access to all of the above-mentioned indexes, through either *National Newspaper Index* or *Newspaper Abstracts*, which is the online newspaper and abstracting service of UMI.

In this era of online access to information, printed indexes do still have a valuable role to play in that they allow you to browse much more easily than is possible with an online database.

Although not a specialized index to newspapers, the Public Affairs Information Service, New York, is also worthy of mention in this section. Its two monthly publications, *PAIS Bulletin* 1914 – and *Foreign Language Index* 1968 – provide exceptional international coverage of social conditions, international relations, government, business and economics. Although they both index journals, books, reports and government documents published anywhere in the world, in various languages, the indexes are published and annotated in English. In addition to a printed version, *PAIS* is available online on DIALOG and on CD-ROM.

CHRONOLOGIES

A chronology is a useful method of identifying dates which can then be used to refer back to the printed copies of newspapers, although it may be that a brief entry in a chronology is sufficient in itself. Annual chronologies are frequently included in yearbooks and almanacs, but more comprehensive, separately published historical chronologies with good indexes often provide a better, faster answer. Most chronologies include not only major political, economic and social events but also cover events in the arts and sciences. With an overall arrangement by date, they are frequently subdivided into subject sections. It is, however, unfortunate that they do not always give the specific dates of events, often preferring a general reference to the month. Owing to the vast volume of information these volumes attempt to cover, errors do occasionally creep in, and it is often necessary to check several sources to be certain of a correct date.

Some examples of comprehensive chronologies include:

Storey, R. L. CHRONOLOGY OF THE MEDIEVAL WORLD, 800–1491. Oxford: Helicon, 1994.

Williams, N. CHRONOLOGY OF THE EXPANDING WORLD, 1492–1762. Oxford: Helicon, 1994.

Williams, N. and Waller, P. CHRONOLOGY OF THE MODERN WORLD, 1763–1992. 2nd ed. Oxford: Helicon, 1994.

Waller, P. CHRONOLOGY OF THE 20TH CENTURY. Oxford: Helicon, 1995.

Events for each year are given a double-page spread showing two parallel sets of information: first, a listing of political, military and international events; and secondly, achievements are listed across a broad range of themes, such as science, arts, music, literature, births and deaths. It is therefore an easy task to identify events and the background against which they occurred.

Other, less comprehensive, contributions to this field include:

CHRONICLE OF THE 20TH CENTURY. London: Dorling Kindersley, 1995.

CHRONICLE OF THE YEAR. Farnborough: JL International Publishing, 1988– .

These mix newspaper-style reporting, academic scholarship and numerous illustrations to bring to life the events they describe, seemingly as they happen.

Newspapers should also be remembered as an excellent and inexpensive source of year chronologies well worth retaining. At the end of a year or in early January most publish reviews of the year's events, often well illustrated. Specialist articles are also frequently published, reviewing the year in a particular area such as the arts or sports, in addition to political and international developments.

YEAR REVIEWS

With a longer look and more time at their disposal, annual reviews can present a better perspective, summarizing trends in various fields. Provided the year of search is known, a check through several of the year reviews makes a strong reference source for events, although for contextual purposes reference to preceding and subsequent years is needed, and some year reviews provide a cumulative index in each volume. Frequently the year on the spine of these publications can be the year of publication, and not the year being dealt with in the contents.

Four major general reviews can be singled out:

THE ANNUAL REGISTER: A RECORD OF WORLD EVENTS. London: Longman, 1758– .

THE AMERICANA ANNUAL. Danbury, Connecticut: Grolier, 1923– .

BRITANNICA BOOK OF THE YEAR. Chicago: Encyclopaedia Britannica, 1938– .

UNIVERSALIA. Paris: Encyclopedia Universalis, 1973– .

Although all of these volumes contain brief chronologies of the year, their main function is to provide a general review of events, either by country or by subject or both.

The Annual Register is the doyen of the group, and its feature articles are perhaps better for catching the flavour of a year than for factual reference. The main part of each annual volume consists of surveys by specialist contributors, with a major chapter on the UK and shorter general articles on every other country. It also includes articles on broad issues such as international organizations, defence, the sciences, the arts, sport, economic and social affairs. It also reprints some documents and speeches of international importance, and has a six-year economic and social statistical survey of the UK and the USA with international comparisons, and an obituary section.

Other year reviews are linked with encyclopedias. Most are well illustrated, wide ranging and detailed. The *Americana, Britannica* and *Universalia* (in French) are fairly typical, taking the form of a large number of articles on the affairs of the year arranged by subject, a section of biographies and obituaries, and a detailed ten-year index. Since 1985 about a third of the *Britannica* annual volume has been headed 'Britannica world data' and provides a country-by-country statistical portrait of the world by major thematic subjects, enabling easy comparison between countries, and listing the national statistical sources used.

Year reviews are also frequently included in yearbooks, for example the *Europa regional surveys* series. Other annual regional and national surveys include *L'Année politique, économique et sociale en France* (Paris: Editions de Moniteur, 1876–), and *Africa contemporary record: annual survey and documents* (New York and London: Africana, 1968–).

YEARBOOKS

Yearbooks are excellent and convenient sources of general background information on overseas countries. They can also quickly provide facts on history, geography, population, politics and trade. As with many reference works, care needs to be taken to check the currency of the data contained in an annually produced yearbook. However many now do include the editorial cut-off date.

The most important titles here include:

THE STATESMAN'S YEAR BOOK. London: Macmillan, 1864– .

This compact volume provides basic information on all countries of the world. This includes history, geography, climate, population, government, defence, international relations, economy, energy and natural resources, trade and industry, and communications. It is an extremely useful source of current facts and statistics.

THE EUROPA WORLD YEAR BOOK. London: Europa, 1926– .

This directory provides profiles of international organizations and countries. For each major international organization it gives the address, membership, finance, organization and activities, principal historical events and specialized agencies. The majority of *Europa* contains individual country profiles, with each country being dealt with in three sections: an introductory survey which describes location, climate, recent history, language and government; a statistical summary which covers population, major industries, agriculture and finance; and finally a directory giving names and addresses of government officials, national organizations, the judicial system and major trade and industrial companies. It also includes a listing of the major national newspapers and periodicals which can be consulted for more detailed information about specific events in a country.

Europa also publish a very useful series of *Regional surveys of the world* whose titles are:

Africa South of the Sahara. 1971–
Eastern Europe and the Commonwealth of Independent States. 1992–
The Far East and Australasia. 1969–
The Middle East and North Africa. 1948–
South America, Central America and the Caribbean. 1986–
USA and Canada. 1990–
Western Europe. 1990– .

These volumes follow the format and content of the *Europa world year book*, although each begins with review essays providing a general overview of the region and a discussion of topical issues. These volumes provide an authoritative, accurate and convenient source of country data.

Another useful series of annual regional reviews is published by the World of Information. Titles here are *The Africa Review, The Americas Review, The Asia & Pacific Review, The Europe Review,* and *The Middle East Review.* All are published together under the title *The World Business and Economic Review* (Walden Publishing and Kogan Page). These concentrate on providing business and economic information, and after discussing the main social, economic and political events of the previous year, together with other key facts, the country entries provide details of official languages, currency, time zones and climate, visa and passport regulations, transport details, plus a directory of hotels, banks and chambers of commerce. World of Information also make all this available online via FT PROFILE.

Space does not allow mention of all national yearbooks which earn their keep on the shelves of reference libraries. Not every country publishes an official yearbook but many do so, either as an official government publication which can occasionally be available gratis from an embassy or compiled by a commercial publisher.

Britain: an official handbook (London: HMSO), compiled by the Central Office of Information since 1946, is the official handbook of the UK. This provides a factual overview of government policy and other important developments, describing the workings of government and other major institutions; the various sections of the economy; social, cultural and environmental matters; international affairs; and British achievements in many fields. It also includes some statistics.

The many foreign national yearbooks, all similar to *Britain,* include *Hong Kong: a review of the year; Year Book Australia; Pakistan Year Book;*

Israel Yearbook & Almanac; New Zealand Official Yearbook.

ALMANACS

These indispensable and handy annual volumes have a fascinating history going back to Roger Bacon and Rabelais, but the main purpose today of the English-language almanacs is not so much for calendar and astronomical data as for the compendia of current facts of all kinds relating to the minutiae of modern living and officialdom. Two worthy of special mention, very similar in approach, which are frequently to be found side-by-side in any reference collection, are:

WHITAKER'S ALMANAC. London: Whitaker's, 1868– .

THE WORLD ALMANAC AND BOOK OF FACTS. New York: Pharos, 1868– .

Whitaker's is virtually a mini-encyclopedia – perhaps the archetypal form – still quaintly describing itself on the title page as 'an almanac for the year of our Lord . . . '. The range of information is a remarkable triumph of compression and comprehensiveness and so, if baffled by an enquiry, try *Whitaker's* first. Back issues should be retained for the sake of non-repeated items, and for the chronologies. The index at the front is good but not without fault, and the user has to be prepared to think laterally.

The principal US almanac, *The World Almanac,* is equally venerable and naturally better on American aspects, although its scope is worldwide. It is especially good for US national and local politics and statistics and for chronologies, including disasters, storms, volcanic eruptions, kidnappings, oil spills and assassinations. Other miscellaneous items include a noted personalities section, movies, bestsellers, heights of tall buildings, and notable bridges in the USA.

NEWSPAPER DIRECTORIES

Several sources exist to identify newspapers published for a particular region or at a particular time. The most frequently consulted guides to newspapers and periodicals published in the UK are:

BENN'S MEDIA DIRECTORY. Tonbridge: Benn Information Services, 1846– .

BRAD (BRITISH RATE AND DATA). Barnet: Maclean Hunter, 1954– .

WILLING'S PRESS GUIDE. East Grinstead: Reed Information Services, 1871– .

Unfortunately none of these titles is completely comprehensive, and therefore it is frequently necessary to consult more than one. Both *Benn's* and *Willing's* have changed publishers and titles over the years: *Benn's*, known for many years as the *Newspaper press directory*, was started by Charles Mitchell, an advertising agent, and *Willing's* was *May's* until 1890. Both have sections on UK newspapers, arranged by location and region, while foreign newspapers are listed under the country of publication. *Benn's*, in addition, includes material on broadcasting and electronic publishing. *BRAD* is published monthly and is aimed more at the advertising industry, as it includes the cost of placing advertisements and the copy requirements of particular newspapers. An interesting historical survey of these and other newspapers directories of the Victorian era appears in the *Journal of newspaper and periodical history*, 3 (2), 1986, 20–8.

The best-known American periodical directory is:

GALE'S DIRECTORY OF PUBLICATIONS AND BROADCAST MEDIA. Detroit: Gale Research, 1869– .

Formerly known as *Ayer's*, this directory identifies newspapers, periodicals and broadcast stations across North America. In 1989, the *Gale international directory of publications* was introduced. This biennial provides geographical access to international newspapers and periodicals.

The Editor & Publisher international year book, published annually since 1924, describes daily newspapers from around the world and covers the major weeklies, foreign-language papers and speciality publications published in the USA. In France, the *Annuaire de la presse et de la publicité* has been published annually since 1878. *Ulrich's international periodicals directory* can be another extremely useful source.

With the increasing growth in newsletters, several specialized directories have been appearing to aid with their identification. The best known is probably *Gale's newsletters in print* (Detroit: Gale Research). Published biennially, this directory primarily covers newsletters published in the USA and Canada. *Business newsletters directory* (Headland: Headland Press, 1993) is one of the better sources to locate UK published newsletters.

LOCATING NEWSPAPERS

Locating recent copies of the principal national newspapers has never been too much of a problem, as some will be held in the local public reference library. Most large libraries hold a file of *The Times*, probably on microfilm, and *The Times index*. Back files of the 'popular' and local press are, unfortunately, very rare.

The only comprehensive library of newspapers in the UK is the British Library, which has an outstanding collection. Photocopies can be provided if the exact bibliographic details of an article are known. However, the library is not staffed to undertake detailed research, and so a personal visit to the Reading Room is normally necessary to trace vague references or to make subject searches. Information in newspapers is more or less inaccessible unless a date is known, and sources referred to earlier in this chapter have to be used to provide the key to the extraordinary and fascinating treasury of information otherwise kept locked in a newspaper. The Newspaper Library has a good collection of the comparatively few indexes which are published, and back sets of *Benn's* and *Willing's* press guides, which will guide an enquirer to the relevant national, local and foreign titles published at the time of an event.

The main collection of newspapers in the British Library is in the Newspaper Library at Colindale in North London, which houses daily and weekly newspapers and periodicals, including London newspapers from 1801 onwards, English provincial, Welsh, Scottish and Irish newspapers from about 1700 onwards and a large collection of Commonwealth and foreign newspapers in western and Slavonic languages from all countries. British national newspapers for the last six months, and other UK papers for the last two to three years, are not usually available as access to them is not permitted until they have been bound or microfilmed. *The catalogue of the Newspaper Library, Colindale* (London: British Library, 1975), in eight volumes, lists UK papers held up to the end of 1970 and overseas titles to the end of 1971, arranged by place and title.

Pre–1801 London newspapers are housed in the British Library in central London together with some other remarkable historical collections. The Burney Collection of 700 volumes of newspapers from 1603 to 1800 is particularly valuable for research as, most unusually, the papers are arranged by date, so that different titles of the same date are bound together. The British Library's Oriental and India Office Collections, also in London, hold newspapers printed in oriental scripts in the countries of the Near East, the Indian subcontinent, and the Far East, and also South Asian newspapers printed in English.

For other locations, *The world list of national newspapers*, compiled by R. Weber (London: Butterworths, 1976) reports holdings of over 1500 newspapers in major British libraries, with the exception of the British Library Newspaper Library. It is updated by *The world list of national newspapers: revised entries: March 1984*, published as *British Library Newspaper Library newsletter. Supplement no.1, 1984*. There also exist a few union lists for identifying the locations of specific types of newspapers in British libraries. For American newspapers, *The American newspaper holdings in British and Irish libraries* (British Association for American Studies, 1974) is a good starting point and Hewitt's *Union list of Commonwealth newspapers in London, Oxford and Cambridge* was published in 1960 by Athlone Press.

The difficulty of identifying and locating UK local newspapers, apart from those held at Colindale, is being addressed by the British Library's Newsplan project. This is a major cooperative programme between local and national libraries which aims to survey, microfilm and preserve local newspapers. Regional surveys have been carried out for the whole of the UK and Ireland which provide comprehensive inventories of newspaper collections and specific recommendations for their preservation. The published Newsplan reports extend to ten volumes. Back files of several newspapers on microfilm can be purchased from the Newspaper Library, and a detailed catalogue of those which can be purchased is available on request. Other major suppliers of newspapers on microfilm are Research Publications, Reading, and University Microfilms International, Ann Arbor, Michigan.

There are also a number of regional union lists of UK newspapers, which are usually compiled and published by a local public library. Examples here include *The bibliography of British newspapers*, whose volumes cover *Wiltshire*, 1975, *Kent*, 1982, *Durham and Northumberland*, 1982, *Derbyshire*, 1987, *Nottinghamshire*, 1987; *Directory of Scottish newspapers*, 1984; *Northern Irish newspapers*, 1737–1987. The best starting point for help in locating a local or regional newspaper is without doubt the public library in the area.

The offices of newspapers themselves can occasionally supply back copies, but probably only the most recent. An enquiry to a newspaper's library may or may not produce a helpful response: it must be remembered that newspaper libraries exist first and foremost to serve their own journalists, and little time is available to assist an outside enquirer, however important the request. Several commercial information services exist based on press cuttings libraries. The BBC, *Financial Times*, Press Association and *Daily Telegraph* will all provide information from their cuttings libraries and other sources, for a fee. Press cuttings agencies which provide a tailor-made service are listed in *Willing's* and *Benn's* press directories. However, these companies do not usually supply a retrospective service.

NEWSPAPER HISTORY

To follow up any aspect of British newspaper history there are three excellent, comprehensive volumes:

Linton, D. THE NEWSPAPER PRESS IN BRITAIN: AN ANNOTATED BIBLIOGRAPHY. London: Mansell, 1987.

Linton, D. THE TWENTIETH-CENTURY NEWSPAPER PRESS IN BRITAIN: AN ANNOTATED BIBLIOGRAPHY. London: Mansell, 1994.

Griffiths, D. (ed.) THE ENCYCLOPEDIA OF THE BRITISH PRESS. London: Macmillan, 1992.

The newspaper press in Britain was the first significant bibliography of the British newspaper press. It contains over 2900 critically annotated references on all aspects of the subject, from individual local and national newspaper histories to journalists', cartoonists' and proprietors' biographies and autobiographies, to the politics, sociology, industrial relations and management of newspapers. It includes an appendix on the chronology of British newspaper history 1476–1986 and an archival source for approximately 150 individual newspapers. *The twentieth-century newspaper press in Britain* builds on the earlier volume. It takes the entries for twentieth-century newspaper history and adds to them, producing a bibliography documenting the press from 1900 to 1994. The entries include a large number of articles from periodicals, but books and theses are also included. The histories of individual newspapers include the special issues that papers tend to produce for their own centenaries.

There are many histories of individual newspapers, of which the most detailed is the six-volume *The history of The Times* (London: The Times, 1935–93). Other histories are listed in Linton's bibliographies and are usually published to coincide with a significant anniversary of a newspaper. For current work in the field of newspaper history the *Journal of newspaper and periodical history*, Volume 1, 1984– publishes well-researched articles on the topic, book reviews, abstracts of theses and an annual review of research work.

Of several books on the international history of newspapers, a particularly well illustrated and detailed one is Anthony Smith's *The newspaper: an international history* (London: Thames and Hudson, 1979). Smith charts the history of newspapers from before the first daily publication in the world, *Einkommende Zeitung* (Incoming News), in 1650 to the late 1970s when the old press barons had mostly surrendered their empires, and before the publishing and technological upheavals of the 1980s led to the demise of 'Fleet Street', for so long a world-renowned name in daily newspapers.

Newspapers and news are extremely important sources of current and historical information. They can, however, be frustrating owing to the difficulty of locating the exact information among the vast plethora of information which is being added to with every passing second. Searching through newspapers can be an arduous and time-consuming task. It is also an absorbing and fascinating area of research where much long-forgotten and irrelevant information is scanned before the required information is successfully located.

SUGGESTIONS FOR FURTHER READING

Eagle, S. (ed.), *Information sources for the press and broadcast media*, London: Bowker Saur, 1991.

Lupham, L., *Newspapers in the library: new approaches to management and reference work*. New York, Haworth, 1988.

Nicholas, D. and Erbach, G., *Online information sources for business and current affairs: an evaluation of Textline, NEXIS, Profile and DIALOG*, London, Mansell, 1989.

Whatmore, G., *The modern news library*, London, Library Association, 1978.
   This is the key British work, and although it is now out of date it is still essential reading for basic principles.

11
Periodicals

Hazel Woodward

DEFINITIONS

Harrod's librarians' glossary (8th edn. Aldershot: Gower, 1995) defines a periodical as 'A publication with a distinctive title which appears at stated or regular intervals, without prior decision as to when the last issue shall appear. It contains articles, stories or other writings, by several contributors'. In current usage the terms periodical and journal are synonymous, whereas the term magazine is reserved (in UK usage) for more popular, mass-circulation titles.

Periodicals are subsumed within the wider category of serials. The British Standard *Code for bibliographic identification (biblid) of contributions in serials and books* (BS 7187: 1989) defines a serial as 'a publication in printed form or not, issued in successive parts, usually having numerical or chronological designations, intended to be continued indefinitely'. If this definition is strictly interpreted, the term serial encompasses an extremely wide range of publications, including periodicals, journals, newspapers, society transactions, conference proceedings, newsletters, technical and research reports, yearbooks and annuals, and national and international government publications. Such coverage in one chapter would clearly not do justice to this complex area; this chapter will therefore concentrate upon reference material specifically relating to periodicals and their associated indexes, in both printed and electronic formats.

REFERENCE USE

Periodicals are an important element of the reference collection, especially in academic, commercial, industrial and research libraries. Current issues of periodicals are of particular importance in those areas of scholarly communication relating to science, technology, business and politics, where the latest up-to-date information is essential for research and development. Furthermore, articles within periodicals frequently discuss highly specialized topics and include information which is not yet (and may never be) available in monographs. In those libraries which retain back-runs of periodicals, the older volumes may have relevance to historical research and furnish contemporary opinion on a given topic or person.

PROBLEMS OF ACCESS

Many of the problems associated with access to periodical titles stem from the massive international growth of published literature. The first periodicals appeared in the latter half of the seventeenth century (a well-known example is the *Philosophical transactions of the Royal Society*, which began in 1665), and the publication format flourished throughout the eighteenth and nineteenth centuries. Thomas[1] states that 27 periodicals were being published in the USA by 1810. By the twentieth century the increasing flow of new titles had turned into a flood, creating the so-called 'information explosion', with increasing numbers of periodicals, in ever-more specialized subject areas, being published. This is well illustrated by examining the first edition (1932) of *Ulrich's international periodicals directory* (New York: Bowker), which listed 6000 titles, and comparing it to the 34th edition (1996) which lists 165,000 titles. Such proliferation of information has had a major impact upon print-based periodical collections. Even major national libraries can no longer hope to acquire, maintain and retain comprehensive periodical collections.

The other significant factor which has affected the size and scope of collections during the last decade is the escalation of subscription prices. A detailed statistical survey of periodical prices is published annually by Blackwell in the *Library Association record* (London: Library Association); figures show that the average price of a periodical rose from £100.81 in 1985 to £277.91 in 1995. Over this same period library budgets have at best remained static, and at worst decreased in real terms. An initial response to the problem was to buy fewer monographs, but eventually most libraries have been forced into cancelling significant numbers of periodical subscriptions.

It is ironical that whereas academics, researchers and librarians have increasing access to published information via online databases,

CD-ROM databases and networked library online public access catalogues (OPACs), escalating subscription prices and shrinking library budgets mean that fewer and fewer titles are purchased from the ever-growing range available. This has resulted in two significant changes in the way in which journal literature is disseminated and accessed. The first is the explosive growth in the past five years of electronic journals (e-journals). The 1995 edition of the ARL *Directory of electronic publications* (Washington, DC: Association of Research Libraries)[2] – commonly referred to as the *ARL Directory* – lists over 700 titles, of which it is estimated that over 100 are refereed e-journals.[3] The *ARL Directory* is updated on a daily basis by an electronic mailing list *NewJour,*[4] which delivers details of new e-journals to subscribers' electronic mail (e-mail) boxes.

The second important change is the increasing reliance being placed upon document delivery. In the UK this has traditionally involved obtaining photocopies of articles from the British Library Document Supply Centre (BLDSC). A list of *Current serials received* (Boston Spa: BLDSC, 1995), which comprises the titles and shelf numbers of all current serials received by the BLDSC and the Science Reference and Information Service (SRIS), is a useful listing for libraries. Companion publications include *Serials in the British Library* (London: British Library, 1995), which contains data derived from three MARC files back to 1950; and *Keyword index to serial titles* (Boston Spa: BLDSC, 1996) a quarterly microfiche publication providing access to over 500,000 serial titles. BLDSC also produces *Boston Spa serials on CD-ROM,* containing the serial holdings of five major UK libraries, including BLDSC, Cambridge University Library and the Science Museum Library. A more recent initiative from BLDSC is an electronic contents page and document delivery service, *Inside information,* which provides details of the contents of over 10,000 of the most frequently requested journals held at BLDSC. The service is available on CD-ROM and via the Bath Information Data Service (BIDS). Further details relating to BLDSC publications and services can be found on the British Library's World Wide Web (WWW) service *Portico.*[5] BIDS also provides access to another electronic contents page and document delivery service – *UnCover* – which provides contents page information on some 17,000 journals.[6]

TYPES OF PERIODICAL

Periodical publications exist to satisfy a variety of different needs and interests, ranging from current affairs and hobbies magazines through to learned academic and scientific journals. They can be broadly grouped into the following categories.

Commercially produced periodicals

Periodicals published as a commercial venture comprise the largest category. Once subscriptions are established, magazines and journals can provide a lucrative source of revenue for publishing houses. At one end of the spectrum are the low-cost mass-circulation titles such as *Practical photography* (Peterborough: EMAP) and *Country life* (London: IPC Magazines). At the other end of the spectrum are the high-cost low-subscription titles from academic journal publishers. Major international publishers such as Elsevier, Blackwell and Academic Press currently publish several hundred different titles, mainly aimed at the academic library market. Their titles cover very specialized areas of academic interest, for example *Journal of paleolimnology* (Dordrecht: Kluwer Academic Publishers) and *Sociology of health and illness* (Oxford: Blackwell).

During 1995 a number of commercial publishers (for example, Carfax, Chapman & Hall and Elsevier) announced that they would be making the electronic version of many of their printed journals available to libraries. Individual publishers' catalogues are a useful source of information in the fast-moving area of electronic publishing, and many of these can be accessed on the WWW from the *Publishers' catalogs home page*.[7] The most comprehensive source of information relating to individual e-journal titles is the previously mentioned *ARL directory*.

A wide variety of printed publishers' directories are available to libraries, including *International literary market place: the directory of the international book publishing industry* (New York: Bowker, 1996) which – despite its title – does include journal publishers; and *Directory of publishing: United Kingdom, Commonwealth and overseas* and *Directory of publishing: Continental Europe* (London: Cassell, 1995). A useful Internet sources for publisher information is *AcqWeb's directory of publishers and vendors*.[8]

Learned society journals

Journals emanating from academic and professional organizations and institutions constitute an important segment of the journal market, although there has been a trend in recent years for the production and distribution of learned society journals to pass to commercial publishers. For example, the Royal Meteorological Society's *International journal of climatology* is actually published by Wiley. Nevertheless, large numbers are still published by professional organizations, and many of these journals are regarded as core titles within their academic discipline, for example the range of *IEE proceedings* published by the Institution of Electrical Engineers, Stevenage, and the various journals published by the American Chemical Society.

Learned society publishers are also moving into the electronic publishing arena alongside commercial publishers. For example, the Institute of Physics was recently involved in the ELVYN e-journal project[9] and has subsequently announced that the electronic versions of several of its print-based titles will be made available to libraries. Further information about learned societies and e-journals can be obtained from the *Electronic journals and learned society web site* at Queens University, Belfast.[10]

Letters journals

Letters journals, such as *Tetrahedron letters* (Oxford: Pergamon), may also fall within the category of journals published as a commercial venture. However, unlike traditional journals they do not contain full-length articles, only short preliminary communications on new developments and initiatives in research, frequently in the areas of science and technology. The aim of such titles is to speed up the publication and distribution of scholarly information. Publications with a similar aim frequently include the word 'communications' in their title, for example *Synthetic communications* (New York: Marcel Dekker).

Speed of publication is one of the major reasons for the proliferation of e-journals, as electronic information can be made available to the academic and research communities far more quickly than can printed information. Thus, letters journals may well migrate to the electronic environment more rapidly than other types of journals. *Electronics letters online* (Stevenage: Institution of Electrical Engineers) is but one example.

House journals

A house journal is a publication produced by a company primarily to communicate information to its staff and shareholders. Some house journals are little more than ephemeral newsletters, but others do contain important contributions to knowledge. Bank reviews, for example *Lloyds bank news* (London: Lloyds Bank), frequently contain useful information and articles on a variety of economic issues, and the house journals of major companies, for example *Taywood news* (Southall: Taylor Woodrow), can provide useful trade and business information. House journals are often available free of charge, although there is an increasing tendency for companies to levy a subscription charge to libraries. P. M. Dunning and D. M. Sawyer's *House journals held by the Science Reference Library* (2nd edn. London: British Library Science Reference Library, 1985) is a useful retrospective checklist. Further titles may be traced through Adeline M. Smith's *Free magazines for libraries* (4th edn. McFarland and Co., 1994).

Newsletters

The printed newsletter is a brief publication conveying up-to-date news and information, usually relating to a specific society or business organization. Such newsletters are normally free or low-cost, low-circulation publications. Newsletters are frequently omitted from the standard periodical directories; however, they can be traced through *Newsletters in print* (7th ed. Detroit: Gale, 1994), which provides detailed entries for over 11,000 sources of information on a wide range of topics under 33 subject headings. The *Oxbridge directory of newsletters* (New York: Oxbridge, 1994) is a similar publication covering North American newsletters.

Although many thousands of printed newsletters are currently published, this type of publication is one which is well suited to the electronic environment. The *ARL Directory* provides bibliographic details of over 200 electronic newsletters, for example, *Newsletter on serials pricing issues*.[11] In addition, many organizations which in the past published printed newsletters now make information about their organization and its activities available on the WWW.

Translation journals

International scholarly and research literature is published in many different languages, and translation journals are a major source of information on foreign-language journal articles. A translation journal may be either a cover-to-cover translation of a periodical title into another language (usually English), or a journal which offers selected articles in translation. A useful guide is *Journals in translation* (5th edn. Boston Spa: BLDSC and the International Translation Centre, 1991), which includes a titles listing and a keyword index; titles available from the BLDSC are indicated, as are other sources from which copies may be ordered.

Progress in . . .

This category of periodical appears in a variety of guises and includes titles beginning *Progress in . . . , Developments in . . . Advances in . . .* and *Year's work in . . . .* The majority of these titles began publication as annual or irregular reviews of the literature in a particular subject area, for example *Year's work in English studies* (London: John Murray). Some, however, now appear on a more frequent basis: for example *Progress in solid state chemistry* (Oxford: Elsevier) which is published four times a year.

PERIODICAL FORMATS

Although the printed periodical is still dominant, there is an increasing number of alternative formats available to libraries.

Microforms

Journals on microfilm and microfiche still have an important role to play in library collections. Microforms are normally acquired either as a space-saving device or because older and rarer journal titles are no longer available in printed format. UMI is one of the largest microform publishers, and their annual catalogue *Serials in microform* (Ann Arbor, Michigan: UMI, 1995) gives details of a wide range of publications; the 1995 catalogue includes over 19,000 serials titles and 7000 newspapers. *Guide to microforms in print* (München: Saur, 1995) is also an annual listing of microform titles, comprising books, journals, newspapers and other serial publications, and including a directory of publishers and distributors.

Full-text journals online

An increasing number of full-text journals are available via a variety of online host systems, including STN International DIALOG, and Data-Star. As far back as 1983 the American Chemical Society mounted 18

ournals, initially on BRS, as a full-text file. Many journals are now acces-
ible from a variety of host systems. Some are included in collections of
ull-text materials, such as *World financial markets*, available via NEXIS,
vhich contains the full text of a range of economics journals and newslet-
ers; others are available online as individual titles, for example *Food engi-
eering international* (Rednor, Pennsylvania: Chilton) and *Planning
eview* (Oxford: International Society for Strategic Management and
lanning). Lists of online full-text journals are incorporated in the docu-
nentation of individual host systems; alternatively, for a more compre-
ensive list consult *Full-text sources online* (Oxford: Learned
nformation), which claims to be the definitive reference source on the
ubject. It is published twice a year and is available on a subscription
asis.

Full-text journals on CD-ROM

D-ROMs are the major growth area in journal publishing. In 1987 the
econd edition of the *CD-ROM directory* (London: TFPL) listed only a
andful of full-text journals, including – predictably – such titles as
D-ROM librarian (Westport, Connecticut: Meckler). By 1995 the direc-
ory listed over 8000 titles! CD-ROM journals fall into two categories.
irst, individual titles such as *The Economist* (Chadwyck-Healey) and
ournal of bacteriology (American Society for Microbiology). It is interest-
ng to note that a number of publishers are beginning to use CD-ROMs
o archive back issues of their journals, and some are including the
rchive CD-ROM as part of the subscription to the printed journal. The
econd category is collections of full-text journals on CD-ROM. UMI is
major publishers of such collections and their output includes *Proquest
usiness periodicals global* (the full text of 450 business journals) and
roquest IEEE/IEE publications* (the full-text of all IEEE and IEE pub-
cations). Owing to the upsurge in popularity of this format new titles
re constantly being published, making directories out of date even
efore publication. Nevertheless, the annual *CD-ROMs in print*
Westport, Connecticut: Meckler, 1995) is a useful source of information,
onsisting of a CD-ROM title directory, a companies directory and sup-
orting indexes.

E-Journals

letworked e-journals represent a very fast growing area of journal publishing. E-journals may be the electronic versions of existing printed journals or, increasingly, exist only in electronic format. Many are currently available free of charge on the Internet; a smaller number are subscription based. Many e-journals are based on mailing-list software (for example, listproc, majordomo, and mailbase); some of these deliver full text to subscriber e-mail boxes, others deliver contents pages and abstracts. Other client/server applications are also being used in the publishing of e-journals: these include gopher and WWW.[12]

Reference has already been made to the e-journals listings *ARL Directory* and *NewJour* bulletin board. In addition there are a number of very useful e-journal sites accessible via the WWW. These include the following sites: *WWW Virtual library*; *ARL directory of electronic publications;* University of Houston Libraries; CICNet- E-serial archive gopher and North Carolina State University.[13]

PERIODICALS DIRECTORIES, BIBLIOGRAPHIES AND DATABASES

For reference purposes libraries require a range of directories, bibliographies and databases in order to make the best use of, and provide access to, information about journals. In addition to the library's own list or database of periodical holdings, the following types of reference tool should be available:

- bibliographies or databases of journals which provide information on their correct titles, frequencies, title changes, publisher, history, editors, prices etc.
- union lists of periodicals which supply information about the location of titles. Union lists will normally be either geographical (for example, local and regional lists) or of a subject nature.

Current general directories and databases

Owing to the vast and diffuse worldwide journal publishing output, no single directory or database can claim to be comprehensive. Thus, each library will need to make available a range of sources most suited to its users needs. An extremely large number of periodical directories are published both in printed format and electronically.

General national and international listings of titles should be available in most libraries. Although press guides are covered in more detail in another chapter, passing reference must be made to *Willing's press guide* (121st edn. East Grinstead: Reed Information Services, 1995) and its US equivalent the *Standard periodicals directory* (18th edn. New York: Oxbridge Communications, 1994). Other useful information is contained within media guides such as the annual *Benn's media* (Tonbridge: M-G Information Services, 1995) published in two volumes covering the UK and Europe and the World, and the monthly publication *BRAD: British rate and data* (Barnet, Hertfordshire: MacLean Hunter).

Two major listings vie for supremacy of coverage in this general category. The first (because it has been established longer) is *Ulrich's international periodicals directory* (34th ed. New York: R.R. Bowker, 1996). Published annually in three volumes with quarterly supplements, *Ulrich's* currently lists over 165,000 titles. Up until 1987 *Irregular serials and annuals* was published as a sister volume, but all data are now included in one sequence. The main sequence is a classified list of titles, accessed by a title index and an ISSN index. Other listings include an index to publications of international organizations, cessations and serials available electronically. Detailed information about individual titles includes year first published, ISSN, publisher and address, price, language, editor, title changes, format and circulation. A particularly useful feature is the inclusion of the indexing and abstracting services that cover the title. *Ulrich's* is also available both online and on CD-ROM.

The serials directory (Birmingham, Alabama: Ebsco Publishing, 1995), published in five volumes, claims 'to provide easy access to more information on more serials titles than any other printed source available'. It is based upon Ebsco's (subscription agents) internal database and the Library of Congress CONSER file. Like Ulrich, it is arranged by subject category with a title and ISSN index, and it provides a similar range of detail about each title, including indexing and abstracting information. Publication of *The serials directory* (which is also available on CD-ROM) coincides with a growing awareness in the serials industry that subscription agents' databases contain a wealth of bibliographical data which can be an extremely useful information source to both librarians and publishers. Many of the major international agents produce extensive printed catalogues of serial titles, which are available to customers free of charge (for example Blackwell, Swets, Dawsons) and increasingly agents are also providing online access to their databases (for example *DataSwets* and Blackwell's *Connect* service).

Another extremely valuable reference source is the CD-ROM *ISSN compact* (Paris: ISSN International Centre) which is distributed by Chadwyck-Healey. It contains ISSN and bibliographic information on over 600,000 periodicals from 193 countries.

General serial directories can be a useful tool for librarians in terms of selection of new titles and overall collection development decisions. However, apart from the rather general *Magazines for libraries* (8th edn. New York: R. R. Bowker, 1995), bibliographies do not normally attempt to evaluate the relative merits of individual titles within their subject areas. Some guidance may be obtained from directories which list the abstracting and indexing services that cover individual titles, as important core journals will be included in the coverage of the major abstracting services relating to that subject area. For evaluation purposes many librarians utilize the ranked lists of journal titles, arranged in broad subject groups, published annually on microfiche in *Journal citation reports* (Philadelphia: Institute for Scientific Information [ISI], 1995).

Current subject bibliographies

A vast number of bibliographies of periodicals covering specific subject areas are available. Librarians working in special or departmental libraries might identify bibliographies relating to their subject of interest by checking general bibliographical tools such as the *British national bibliography* (London: British Library National Bibliographic Service), which has a separate section in its classified sequence for serial bibliographies. *Journal citation reports* (Philadelphia: ISI, 1995) can also be used to identify core lists of titles in specific subject areas. It is worth noting that several publishers specialize in current bibliographical material: R.R. Bowker, for example, publish a range of titles such as *Law books and serials in print*; *Scientific and technical books in print* and *Medical and health care books and serials in print*. These publications are subsets of Bowker's *Books in print* database and the Bowker International Serials Database (from which is produced *Ulrich's international periodicals directory*). Another prolific publisher in the field of serials bibliography is Greenwood Press in London. Their current catalogue lists numerous titles such as *Labor and industrial relations journals and serials: an analytical guide*; and *Cancer journals and serials: an analytical guide*.

Retrospective bibliographies

Various attempts have been made over the years to produce historical bibliographies of periodicals. Bibliographies covering the very early years of journal publishing include W. S. Ward's *Index and finding list of serials published in the British Isles 1789–1832* (Lexington: University of Kentucky Press, 1953) which lists over 5000 items, and H. C. Bolton's *Catalogue of scientific and technical periodicals, 1665–1895* (2nd edn. Washington, DC: Smithsonian Institution, 1897). Two other publications which now act as important general bibliographies, but which started life as union lists, are R. S. Crane and F. B. Kaye's *Census of British newspapers and periodicals, 1620–1800* (Reprinted. London: Holland, 1966) and *British union catalogue of periodicals* (London: Butterworths, 1955–80), frequently referred to as *BUCOP*. This latter title is an extremely important source for historical bibliography and is normally available in most medium-sized to large libraries. BUCOP claimed to be 'a record of the periodicals of the world, from the seventeenth century to the present day, in British libraries'; it ceased publication in 1980 and is succeeded by *Serials in the British Library*, discussed previously.

Other important sources include the *New Cambridge bibliography of English literature* (5v. Cambridge: Cambridge University Press, 1969–77) and *Tercentenary handlist of English and Welsh newspapers, magazines and reviews* (London: The Times, 1920. Reprinted. London: Dawsons, 1966). A detailed analysis of the history and development of scientific and technical periodicals from 1665 to 1790 is provided by Kronick.[14] Major directories covering more recent periods of history are Michael Wolff's *The Waterloo directory of Victorian periodicals, 1824–1900* (Oxford: Pergamon, 1980) and *World list of scientific periodicals published in the years 1900–1960* (4th edn. London: Butterworths, 1963–5). Containing more than 60,000 titles in the natural sciences, the *World list* ceased publication after the fourth edition and was incorporated into *BUCOP*.

Retrospective bibliographies dealing with specific types or subject groups of periodicals can also be very important to historical research. Examples include *Women's magazines, 1693–1968* (London: Michael Joseph, 1970); *The little magazine: a history and a bibliography* (New Jersey: Princeton University Press, 1946); and *Serial publications in the British parliamentary papers, 1900–1968: a bibliography* (Chicago: American Library Association, 1971).

Union lists

Because of the existence of the BLDSC, and the resulting centralization of the UK interlibrary loan network, current union lists of periodical titles are not such a major and prolific feature of serials librarianship as in North America, where the interlibrary loan system is organized on a regional basis. The main aim of union lists of periodicals is to provide locational information about the holdings of a group of libraries. Mention has already been made of *BUCOP*, which ceased publication in 1980: this was the only publication that attempted to provide locational information for periodicals in UK libraries. Yet other countries still maintain thriving union lists or databases. For example, the OCLC database holds about 800,000 records for serial titles in major US libraries. This is available in the UK via the OCLC FirstSearch service, which is offered to UK higher education libraries via a Combined Higher Education Software Team (CHEST) deal. The Scandinavian union catalogue, *Nordisk samtkatalog over periodika (NOSP)*, incorporates the holdings of about 500 libraries and is also available on the Internet. Details of other national union lists and databases are given by Mullis.[15]

In a large library system spread out over a wide geographical area, a union list is essential if college and departmental libraries are to be informed of periodical holdings in other parts of the system. The *University of London union list of serials* (London: The University Library), for example, has been in operation since 1979 and is updated twice yearly on microfiche. Other extensive library systems, such as Essex County Library and Cambridge University, have also produced similar union listings.

Union lists are extremely expensive – in terms of staff time – to set up and maintain, and they are difficult to compile if participating libraries operate a range of differing manual systems or incompatible automated systems. These factors, combined with the reluctance of library users to travel to other libraries, and the findings of research by MacDougall[16] which demonstrate that it is cheaper to obtain a photocopied article from the BLDSC than from other local libraries, probably explain the scarcity of current, general, regional union lists. Moreover, in recent years more and more libraries have made their OPACs available on the Internet. These are further discussed in the following section on library catalogues.

However, in specialized subject areas compilation of union lists has thrived. This may be due to the fact that provision within BLDSC of highly specialized journal literature is incomplete, particularly in relation to foreign titles and obscure back-runs. It is therefore useful to have additional bibliographical and locational information in the form of union lists. Examples include C. Travis and M. Alman's *Periodicals from Africa: a bibliography and union list of periodicals published in Africa* (Boston: G. K. Hall, 1977. Supplement, 1985), and the ongoing *Union list of periodicals held in institute and school of education libraries* and *The British union catalogue of music periodicals*.

Library catalogues

Printed library catalogues are becoming somewhat of a rarity as more and more libraries computerize their holdings and provide access via an OPAC. Nevertheless, some major national libraries do still publish their catalogues in printed format or on microfiche. Some, such as the Oxford University's *Catalogue of English newspapers and periodicals in the Bodleian Library, 1622–1800* (Oxford: Bibliographical Society, 1936) are useful for historical bibliography. Other, such as the *Cambridge union list of serials* (Cambridge: Cambridge University Library) – which publishes semi-annual cumulations on microfiche – aim to be a current listing.

The most important development in access to library catalogues has been growth in the availability of library OPACs on the Internet. Almost all UK higher education and research library OPACs can be accessed through the *NISS Information Gateway*.[17] For access to over 1000 library OPACs throughout the world, consult the *WWW Library Directory*.[18]

GUIDES TO THE CONTENTS OF PERIODICALS

With the increasing number of periodical titles being published and the inability of libraries to keep abreast of this output, two major problems face scholars and researchers. The first is keeping up to date with the periodical literature in a particular subject discipline. The second is conducting a comprehensive, retrospective search of the literature over a given period of time. In order to assist the researcher in these tasks, an enormous range of secondary services or abstracting and indexes services has proliferated. Examples of some of the major services will now be examined.

Current awareness services

A popular but basic method of current awareness which is practised by many library users is browsing through the current issues of journals on the library shelves; however, it must be recognized that this is not a particularly efficient or effective method of keeping up to date with the bulk of the literature. In addition to internal current awareness initiatives operating within individual libraries and current awareness services offered by online hosts, an extremely useful group of publications entitled *Current contents* (Philadelphia: Institute for Scientific Information) are published in the following subject areas: *Agriculture, biology and environmental sciences*; *Arts and humanities*; *Life sciences*; *Physical, chemical and earth sciences*; *Clinical medicine*; and *Engineering, technology and applied science*. The printed versions of *Current contents* are published on a weekly basis and simply comprise copies of contents pages of journals. Their importance lies in the fact that they do not undergo sophisticated editing procedures, and therefore the information they contain is up to date. ISI also publish *Current contents* on disc.

Similar types of publications, also based on the speedy reproduction and dissemination of contents pages, exist across a variety of subject areas. These include the weekly *Contents of recent economic journals* (London: HMSO), which covers English-language journals in the field of economics, and the fortnightly *Contents pages in management* (Manchester: Manchester Business School).

A wide variety of electronic current awareness services are also available. The previously mentioned BIDS *UnCover* service provides contents page information for over 17,000 journals. *UnCover* also offers a service called *Reveal*, which delivers contents pages directly to users' personal e-mail boxes. The majority of commercial online databases offer current awareness services known as *Alerts*. Results from these searches can be delivered in printed or electronic format, but they are relatively expensive. In addition, both commercial and learned society publishers are beginning to offer table of contents services (TOCs) over the Internet: for example, Elsevier Science provides TOCs for over 100 of their journals[19] and the IEEE Computer Society has TOCs for 18 IEEE titles.[20]

Indexing and abstracting services

Most periodicals of any reference value produce indexes of their own, usually at annual intervals. Occasionally cumulative indexes will be compiled covering five or ten years; remarkably, *The engineer* (London: Morgan-Grampian) produced a 100-year index in 1956. However, when breadth of coverage is essential, indexes to individual journals are not particularly useful and researchers should consult one, or several, of the printed indexing and abstracting services and/or electronic databases.

Indexes and abstracts (whether print or electronic) are continuing bibliographic publications which aim to provide coverage of the literature in a given field of knowledge. They may be discipline oriented, i.e. covering a particular subject discipline such as psychology, biology or chemistry, or they may be mission oriented, i.e. covering an interdisciplinary area of interest such as the oil industry. The basic difference between an abstracting service and an indexing service is that abstracting journals provide an abstract (or résumé) of the cited article, whereas indexing journals provide only a citation. There are even examples of hybrid publications, such as the recent Butterworth publication *ASSIA – Applied social sciences index and abstracts*.

In order to guide the user to the most appropriate index or abstract, a useful publication is *The index and abstract directory* (3rd edn. Birmingham, Alabama: Ebsco Publishing, 1993). Section 1 of this publication lists some 56,000 serial titles which are covered by one or more indexing or abstracting services, by subject. Section 2 is arranged alphabetically by the name of the indexing or abstracting service, and lists all serial titles covered by that service.

Indexing services

Probably the best known of early periodical indexes is W. F. Poole's *An index to periodical literature 1801–1881* (4th edn. Boston, Massachusetts: Houghton, 1891). The original two-volume work was extended by the publication of five supplements up to 1907. The index included 479 US and British periodicals, with entries mainly by subject. A more recent attempt to provide a key to the nineteenth-century journal literature is Walter E. Houghton's impressive work, *Wellesley index to Victorian periodicals 1824–1900* (5v. London: Routledge & Kegan Paul, 1966–89). Each of the first four volumes takes a selection of important titles, gives a brief introduction to that title and then provides the contents list of each individual issue. The recently published index in Volume 5 consists mainly of a bibliography of contributors, plus an index of initials and pseudonyms.

Another early attempt to harness the growing literature was the *Readers' guide to periodical literature* (New York: H. W. Wilson, 1900–). The cumulated volumes (Vol. 1 covering 1900–4) are still available from

H. W. Wilson, and the early volumes make fascinating study, covering such diverse titles as *Century magazine, Engineering magazine, Music, Harper's bazaar* and *Popular science monthly.* From this humble beginning the H. W. Wilson Company has gone on to become one of the leading publishers of periodical indexes, and their catalogue now lists over 20 important indexing services, including *Applied science and technology index, Business periodicals index, Education index, Index to legal periodicals, Social sciences index,* and the still-extant *Readers' guide to periodical literature!* Printed Wilson indexes normally appear either monthly or quarterly, with annual cumulations; only English-language material is covered and there is a definite bias towards North American coverage. All Wilson indexes are available online and on CD-ROM, and nearly all titles are accessible electronically via the *OCLC FirstSearch* service, which is available to UK higher education libraries through a Combined Higher Education Software Team (CHEST) deal.

The UK has no comparable publisher, but there exists a multitude of periodical indexes from a wide variety of publishers. *British humanities index* (East Grinstead: Bowker-Saur) is a useful quarterly publication, with annual cumulations, covering articles appearing in newspapers and journals published in Britain. 'Humanities' is interpreted broadly to include the arts, economics, history, philosophy, politics and society. The index grew out of *Subject index to periodicals* (London: Library Association, 1915-61) which split into three parts, all of which are still published. The other titles resulting from the split are the bimonthly *Current technology index* (East Grinstead: Bowker-Saur) – formerly *British technology index* and the quarterly *British education index* (Leeds: Leeds University Press). All three printed indexes are simple to use; they contain specific headings with subheadings and 'see' references; all are also available on CD-ROM.

Other major indexing services include *Index medicus* (Washington, DC: US National Library of Medicine), which is the principal medical indexing service, covering some 3000 biomedical journals. Monthly author and subject indexes are issued, with multivolume cumulations. Supplements include *Medical subjects headings* (MeSH) and *List of journals indexed in index medicus.* For smaller libraries *Abridged index medicus is* available, covering approximately 100 journal titles. The database is widely available online, several different publishers have produced a CD-ROM version, and it is accessible via the *OCLC FirstSearch* service.

Current index to journals in education (Phoenix, Arizona: Oryx Press) is a monthly guide to the current periodical literature in education, covering articles published in approximately 740 major educational and education-related journals. It is part of the ERIC database, sponsored by the Educational Resources Information Center (ERIC), US Department of Education. A sister publication, *Resources in education,* also forms part of the ERIC database and covers current research findings, projects and technical reports, speeches, unpublished manuscripts and books. The ERIC database can also be accessed online, on CD-ROM and via *OCLC FirstSearch.*

Mention should be made in this section of citation indexes. Citation indexes are published by the Institute for Scientific Information (ISI), Philadelphia, and comprise the following titles: *Science citation index (SCI)*; *Social science citation index (SSCI)*; *Arts and humanities citation index (AHCI)* and *Compumath citation index.* Whereas most periodical indexes use some form of subject approach to tracing information, in a citation index the subject of a search is a reference, rather than a word or subject heading. In the printed version, the search begins with the author of a reference identified through a book, bibliography, footnote, encyclopedia etc., and this is then checked in the *Citation index* section. When the author's name and appropriate reference is located, the entry will then list all the current citations to that work. Having noted this list of citations, the searcher then turns to the *Source index* section to obtain the complete bibliographical data for the citations. An additional search strategy is offered by the *Permuterm subject index* which, as the name suggests, is a permuted title-word index to the article titles. Every significant word is paired with every other significant word in the same title, thus producing a 'natural language' indexing system. Thus, if a relevant starting title is not already known, one can be found through the keyword index.

The three citation indexes were the first electronic databases to be offered to the UK higher education community at a discounted rate over the Internet. They are mounted at Bath University, and the resulting service, known as BIDS (Bath Information Data Service), has since expanded considerably. Other databases offered via BIDS include Embase *(Excerpta medica)* and Compendex *(Engineering index).* A recent feature of printed indexes which have migrated to the electronic environment has been the addition of abstracts in the electronic version, thus blurring the distinction still further between indexing and abstracting services.

There have been a number of attempts to catch up retrospectively with journal material which is inadequately covered in existing services. Such publications require an enormous amount of research, and consequently cover very specific subject areas. Titles include Barry Bloomfield's *An author index to British 'little magazines' 1930–1939* (London: Mansell, 1976); K. I. MacDonald's *The Essex reference index: British journals on politics and sociology* (London: Macmillan, 1975); and L. Batty's *Retrospective index to film periodicals* (New York: Bowker, 1975). A more recent attempt to provide access to older journal articles is *Periodicals contents index (PCI)* (Cambridge: Chadwyck-Healey). Available on CD-ROM, and more recently on the Internet through a CHEST deal, *PCI* provides article-level access to the contents of more than 2000 scholarly journals in the humanities and social sciences, from their beginnings to 1980.

Abstracting services

The advantage that abstracting services have over indexing services is that they can save the researcher considerable time locating and scanning unsuitable references. Borko states that 'at best, abstracts can save about nine-tenths of the time needed to read the original documents'.[21]

One of the earliest abstracting services was *Science abstracts* (London: Institution of Electrical Engineers), which began publication in 1898. It was not long (1903), however, before the growth of published information demanded that the title split into two series: Series A *Physics abstracts,* and Series B *Electrical and electronics abstracts*. In 1966 Series C *Control abstracts* was added. For 90 years *Science abstracts* has been recognized as the premier English-language information service in the fields of physics, electrotechnology and, more recently, computing. In 1967 INSPEC (Information Service for the Physics and Engineering Communities) was formed as the Information Division of the Institution of Electrical Engineers. To maintain its position and to deal with the ever-increasing growth in published information, INSPEC developed a computer-based information retrieval system for its abstracting services. Important INSPEC titles include *Physics abstracts*; *Electrical and electronics abstracts*; and *Computer and control abstracts*. They are available in printed format, online and on CD-ROM, and journal articles comprise about 80% of the total items.

Chemical abstracts (Columbus, Ohio: American Chemical Society) is another major abstracting service which has its origins at the beginning of the twentieth century, starting in 1907. The official statement of *Chemical abstracts* is as follows: 'It is the careful endeavour of Chemical Abstracts to publish adequate and accurate abstracts of all scientific and technical papers containing new information of chemical and chemical engineering interest and to report new chemical information revealed in the patent literature'. The abstracts are selected from more than 12,000 scientific journals from more than 150 countries, and about 75% of references are to journal articles. *Chemical abstracts,* which is available both in printed form and online, contains informative abstracts of the original documents, i.e. the intention is to provide the user with enough information on the contents to establish whether the original is worth consultation.

Despite its title, *Engineering index* (New York: Engineering Information Inc.) is actually an abstracting journal. Claiming to be 'the index to the world's engineering developments' the printed service is published monthly with annual cumulations; three-year cumulations are also available. Citations and abstracts are arranged under main subject headings selected from the SHE (Subject Headings for Engineering) authority list. Users can search for information by subject heading in the abstracts section, by subject in the accompanying subject index, or by author in the author index. *Engineering index* is available online, on CD-ROM and more recently via BIDS. The BIDS service provides access to the Compendex databases comprising *Engineering index* and the contents page service *Page one.*

In the biological and life sciences *Biological abstracts* (Philadelphia: BIOSIS) is the major abstracting service. Published fortnightly, the printed work contains an abstract section which can be browsed by concept headings (listed at the front of each issue), an author index and a subject index. The subject index appears quite daunting, owing to the fact that the typeface is extremely small and the layout is in narrow columns. Keywords are printed in bold face in the centre of the column and subject context words are located to the right and left of each keyword. Other indexes to this work include the *Biosystemic index,* used to find entries by taxonomic category, and the *Generic index,* used to find entries according to genus or genus-species name. *Biological abstracts* is also available on CD-ROM, and in 1995 it was offered to UK higher education libraries via the Internet as a CHEST deal, the service provider being the newly established Edinburgh Data and Information Access (EDINA).

The social sciences, management and economics are all served by a variety of abstracting services, although few can claim to be as comprehensive as their counterparts in the sciences and technology. The *Anbar* abstracting service (Bradford: MCB University Press) commenced in 1961 to cover the field of management. It has expanded to cover six major fields of management science, and all titles are available individually both in printed copy and on CD-ROM – *Electronic anbar.*

Psychological abstracts (Arlington, Virginia: American Psychological Society) began publication in 1927 and is now an established core abstracting title, providing access to the world's literature in psychology and related behavioural and social sciences. Published monthly, the abstracts are listed under 16 major classification categories with an author and brief subject index. An expanded cumulation is published at the end of each volume. *Psychological abstracts* is available on a CD-ROM entitled *PsychLit*, which also provides access to psychological book contents information.

Although a large proportion of abstracting services cover the sciences, social sciences and technology, the arts and humanities are not entirely neglected. A major service covering historical literature is *Historical abstracts. a bibliography of the world 's historical literature* (Santa Barbara, California: ABC-Clio). The abstracts are published quarterly in two parts: Part A modern-history abstracts, and Part B twentieth-century abstracts; 2100 major history journals of the world are scanned, and geographical coverage is worldwide, with the exception of the US and Canada, which are covered by *America: history and life* (Santa Barbara, California: ABC-Clio).

CONCLUSION

Traditional printed periodicals present a range of problems to the library manager. New titles are constantly being published, current titles change or split into several parts, unannounced supplements appear and prices spiral at an alarming rate. Such constant momentum and change also means that they are very difficult to control bibliographically, posing problems for librarians and users alike. Concern about the amount of space occupied and the low use of many journal titles within library collections has also prompted many librarians to question the cost-effectiveness of current provision.

A potential solution to the problem is the electronic publication of journal information and literature. As is evident from this chapter, a high proportion of indexing and abstracting services, bibliographies and directories have already migrated to the electronic environment and are available online, on CD-ROM and, more recently, via the Internet. Many libraries are now acquiring a growing proportion of these types of publication in electronic format, and many publishers are becoming concerned about the viability of their print-based publications, particularly abstracting and indexing titles.

Full-text e-journals are also beginning to appear on CD-ROM and via online hosts and the Internet. Currently only about 100 refereed e-journals are available via the Internet but this number is set to escalate as many of the major commercial journal publishers – and many learned society publishers – make the electronic versions of their printed titles available on the networks.

It would appear that scholarly communication – which is facilitated primarily by journal literature – is in a period of transition. Publishers and librarians are beginning to integrate electronic publishing formats into their range of services, but little is known, as yet, about end-user acceptance and reaction. The next five years will probably see a phase of parallel provision. Which will triumph – printed or electronic formats – remains to be seen.

REFERENCES AND NOTES

1   Thomas, I., *History of printing in America*, New York, The author, 1874, Vol. 2, 292.
2   *ARL directory of electronic publications,* 5th edn, 1995.
    URL: gopher://arl.cni.org:70/00/scomm/edir/edir95/jz
    URL: http://www.gold.ac.uk/history/hyperjournal/arl.htm
3   Woodward, H., 'Electronic journals in libraries', in *Project ELVYN: an experiment in electronic journal delivery. Facts, figures and findings,* edited by F. Rowland and others, London, Bowker-Saur, 1995, 49–63.
4   *NewJour* mailing list. To subscribe send message to:
    majordomo@ccat.sas.upenn.edu
    In body of message type: subscribe NewJour
5   The British Library's WWW service *Portico* can be accessed at:

ttp://portico.bl.uk

6 BIDS WWW pages can be accessed at: http://wwwbids.ac.uk

7 *Publishers' catalogs home page* can be accessed at:
   http://www.lights.com/publisher/

8 *AcqWeb's directory of publishers and vendors* can be accessed at:
   http://www.library.vanderbilt.edu/law/acqs/pubr.html

9 Rowland, F. *et al.*, *Project ELVYN: an experiment in electronic journal delivery. Facts, figures and findings*, East Grinstead, Bowker-Saur, 1995.

10 The *Electronic journals and learned society web site* can be accessed at:
   http://Journals.eecs.qub.ac.uk/ElectronicJournals.html

11 *Newsletter on serials pricing issues.* To subscribe send message to:
   listproc@unc.edu.
   In body of message type: subscribe prices [your name]

12 Woodward, H. and McKnight, C., 'Electronic journals: issues of access and bibliographical control', *Serials review*, **21** (2), Summer 1995, 71–8.

13 Hitchcock, S., A survey of STM online journals 1990–95: the calm before the storm. A WWW document.
   URL: http://journals.ecs.soton.ac.uk/survey.html

14 Kronick, D.A., *A history of scientific and technical periodicals: the origin and development of the scientific and technical press, 1665–1790*. 2nd edn. New Jersey, Scarecrow Press, 1976.

15 Mullis, A., 'Access to serials: national and international cooperation', in Woodward, H. and Pilling, S., *The international serials industry*, Aldershot, Gower, 1993, 233–58.

16 MacDougall, A. F., Wheelhouse, H. and Wilson, J., *A study of various aspects of cooperation between East Midlands university and polytechnic libraries.* BLRDD Report 5989. British Library, 1989.

17 The *NISS Information Gateway* can be accessed at:
   http://www.niss.ac.uk/

18 The *WWW Library Directory* can be accessed at:
   http://www.albany.net/~ms0669/cra/libs.html

19 Elsevier Science TOCs can be accessed at: http://www.elsevier.nl

20 IEEE Computer Society TOCs can be accessed at:
   gopher://info.computer.org:70/11/Abstracts

21 Borko, H. and Bernier, C. L., *Abstracting concepts and methods*, London, Academic Press, 1975.

SUGGESTIONS FOR FURTHER READING

Buettel, F. and Graham, M. (eds.), *Serials management: a practical handbook*, London, Aslib and the UK Serials Group, 1990.

Cook, B. (ed.), *The electronic journal: the future of serials based information*, New York, Haworth Press, 1993.

Norstedt, M.L. (ed.), *New scholarship – new serials: proceedings of the North American Serials Interest Group*, 8th annual conference, June 10–13, 1993, Brown University, Providence, RI, New York, Haworth Press, 1994.

Page, G., *Journal publishing: principles and practice*, London, Butterworths, 1987.

Tuttle, M. and Cook, J. (eds.), *Advances in serials management*. Vol. I, Greenwich, Connecticut, Jai Press, 1986.

Palm, M. and Dunn, P. S. (eds.), *If we build it: scholarly communications and networking technologies: proceedings of the North American Serials Interest Group*, 7th annual conference, June 18–21, 1992, University of Illinois at Chicago, New York, Haworth Press, 1993.

Serials: the journal of the United Kingdom Serials Group, Vol. 1, 1998– . Oxford, UKSG.

Serials Review, Vol. 1– , 1975– . Greenwich Connecticut, Jai Press.

Tuttle, M. (ed.), *Advances in serials management*, Vol. 1, 1986– . Greenwich, Connecticut, Jai Press.

United Kingdom Serials Group, *Serial publication: guidelines for good practice in publishing printed journals and other serial publications*, Oxford, UKSG, 1994.

Woodward, H. M. and Pilling, S. (eds.), *The international serials industry*, Aldershot, Gower, 1993.

12
Government publications

Valerie J. Nurcombe

Mention 'government publications' in Britain and most librarians and others immediately assume *British* official publications. Few have any extensive knowledge of the great body of official publications generated by every country during the daily work of the executive and administrative bureaucracy. The depth of the coverage of British official publications in this chapter reflects the orientation of this book. The pattern of publishing in most countries is similar, reflecting the machinery of government. It is virtually impossible to understand most countries' official publications without an up-to-date working knowledge of, or good current reference guide to, the structure of their administrative machinery.

Official publishing in most countries generally follows one of two models:

1 A central publishing agency is responsible for the majority of official publishing, particularly in relation to the legislative assembly. It controls and documents its output, thus reflecting the activities of the government.

2 Laws, papers and proceedings of the administrative and executive bodies, including any representative assembly, are recorded in an 'official journal' publication. This is usually published regularly and frequently. Relevant information must be sought in order of occurrence through any indexes which may exist. Any other documents are published by the department responsible. The departments are left to organize their own publishing activities and may or may not keep adequate bibliographic records.

Whichever model is encountered the trend in the 1980s towards an increasing number of publications has changed in the 1990s to an increased emphasis on economy. Cost recovery requirements have meant that more publications are priced which were formerly available freely, and fewer in total have been published. Pricing encourages marketing, which is assisted by listing or cataloguing. Hence there is an increase in the number of individual catalogues and lists available. The degree of detail and the comprehensiveness of the content may be variable. However, bibliographic control of official publications has rarely been a strong point in any country and, although the British complain about their problems, many countries look towards the British model as one of the ideals, envying the level of information available on the existence and availability of official publications.

In Britain since the Second World War there has been a growth in major collections of official publications, with increased demand outside the immediate vicinity of Whitehall and Westminster, partly because of the large-scale development of universities and polytechnics, but also because there is no national repository scheme such as in the United States. In Britain official publications are subject to copyright deposit, thus ensuring that there are major collections in the British Library, the National Libraries of Scotland and Wales, at Trinity College Dublin, and at the Universities of Oxford and Cambridge. The depository system in the United States ensures that all States have at least one major collection of official publications receiving deposit copies of most publications. This encourages the development of specialist librarians to service and exploit them, but the system is currently threatened by the changes from print publishing to other media and the lessening of deposits in alternative media, or when publications are available in full text on the Internet. Other countries have a greater or lesser degree of depository regulation.

British collections of official publications from other countries include those mentioned above, the libraries of the larger universities and colleges and the larger public libraries. The British Library of Political and Economic Science at the London School of Economics deserves special mention. Many academic institutions with courses relating to particular countries will have good official publications collections in those areas, e.g. the various University of London Institutes. Alternatively, some embassies will have a limited current collection but know the where-abouts of resources. The most useful guides are mentioned below.

In terms of official publications no collection or listing can ever be regarded as comprehensive. Most give brief warnings that they contain reference to as many publications as have been brought to the attention of the listing body, or deposited with the library. In the days of swift photocopying and laser-printers producing word-processed documents quickly and easily in sufficient numbers for a level of distribution that would constitute publication, many 'publishers' do not realize that their department is publishing at all and do not comply with deposit requirements. This is due either to the cost of the number of copies required, to ignorance, or to a desire to ensure that only a few selected eyes see the item. This lack of deposit, even with the local libraries and information units within government departments and related bodies, frequently contributes to the factors that transform official publications into 'grey literature', difficult to identify or locate.

No government's publications reveal all the information about its activities which the public may wish to have. In the UK unpublished information of historical interest is made public, selectively, under the 30-year rule, by the deposit of documents at the Public Record Office. But whether the information released is new or old, the provisions of the Official Secrets Acts must be observed. It should be remembered on both sides of the Atlantic that much unpublished official information has not been withheld because it is 'classified' but only because it was not regarded as published or worth publishing. Such information may frequently be obtainable on request to the appropriate department, particularly since the 'open government' initiative requires the disclosure of certain types of information within certain time limits.

BRITISH GOVERNMENT PUBLICATIONS
The term 'British government publications' is not synonymous with 'HMSO'. Today, so many documents are published directly by government departments and institutions that only about 20–30% of official publications are actually published, or even stocked, by Her Majesty's Stationery Office.

It should be pointed out that the Patent Office and the Ordnance Survey are massive publishers in their own right. Nor are the following available from HMSO, although some HMSO bookshops stock them for counter sales: Geological Survey maps, Admiralty charts, British Standards Institution and BBC publications. The Health and Safety Executive contracted out both their publishing and distribution to HSE

Books in 1993, initially without any specific commercial outlets other than Dillons, to which group the company belonged. Later other outlets were able to become distributors, including HMSO Books. Similar situations may arise as publishing arrangements for the government continue to change in the late 1990s and become more commercial.

Every government department, agency, institution or advisory board and (in the past) nationalized industry acts, to some extent, as its own publisher. Many departments publish both through HMSO and independently, according to the type and market of the publication concerned. The sheer number and the potential value of non-HMSO official publications have caused such concern that steps have been taken to list them and improve their availability.

Guides to government publications, where they exist, are usually unofficial and rarely updated. David Butcher's *Official publications in Britain* (2nd edn. London: Library Association Publishing, 1991) is the only current guide in existence offering clear and broad coverage of local and central government, the former not being covered elsewhere. Frank Rodgers', *A guide to British Government publications* (New York: H. W. Wilson, 1980) is rapidly becoming dated. Rodgers explains, with considerable administrative and bibliographical details, the present pattern of our government publications. John Pemberton's *British official publications* (2nd ed. Oxford: Pergamon Press, 1973) is in need of revision, but remains useful for its thorough coverage of Parliamentary publications.

Written from the USA viewpoint, Barbara E. Smith's, 'British official publications: 1. Scope and substance' (*Government publications review*, 4 (3), 1977, 201–7); '2. Publication and distribution' (*Government publications review*, 5 (1), 1978, 1–12); '3. Accessibility and use' (*Government publications review*, 6 (1), 1979, 11–18), although now dated, contain information not readily available elsewhere.

Governments themselves rarely explain their publications. As agents for the legislature and the government departments, the central government publishers, such as HMSO, feel it is not their responsibility.

Official publishers

HMSO

HMSO is vitally important because HMSO alone has the authority to publish on behalf of Parliament. Initial publication remains its own privilege and responsibility, and since the creation of Parliamentary Copyright in the 1988 Copyright Act the Houses also delegate the administration of Parliamentary Copyright to HMSO.

The singular importance of HMSO publications, coupled with their large number, is reason enough for studying them. In 1994 about 8500 titles were published, of which around 5400 were Parliamentary, statutory and regulatory, and nearly 3200 agency items were stocked. The scope and importance of HMSO's publications may be appreciated by visiting one of the HMSO Bookshops, where the display of HMSO and agency publications is more elaborate than in a library. Alternatively, try browsing through HMSO's *Monthly catalogue*.

The coverage of HMSO publications by the *British national bibliography*, although not arbitrary, is selective. For economic reasons it cannot be otherwise. Many libraries therefore acquire HMSO's official lists and catalogues: the *Daily list,* the *Monthly catalogue* and *Annual catalogue*, and the *Sectional lists*. In the *Daily list* the main divisions are 'Parliamentary publications' and 'Non-parliamentary publications', called the 'Classified list' in the *Monthly catalogue* and *Annual catalogue*. The latter brings together Parliamentary and Non-parliamentary reports of each department, e.g. Command Papers are entered under 'Command Papers' in the Parliamentary section and again under the name of the relevant department in the Non-parliamentary section. The *Daily list* is available on Prestel and publications may be ordered directly. Experiments are currently in progress mounting current publications' information on the Internet (http://www.hmsoinfo.gov.uk/).

The production of the *Monthly catalogue* and the *Annual catalogue* is now computerized and publication is usually within six weeks of the end of the month. The annual volume usually appears within three months. HMSO's full database has been on BLAISE since 1989. The CD-ROM publication *UKOP* (see below) should be consulted for a general database of 'all' official publications.

The *Sectional lists* detail HMSO publications, and those of selected international organizations' publications for which HMSO is the British agent, currently in print. Most lists are departmental, e.g. Employment, Transport, Home Office, but there are an increasing number of topic-related ones such as *Housing and construction, Environment*. They are obtained from the Norwich headquarters of HMSO. All addresses are given in every copy of the catalogues.

In a rather casual way ministers sometimes announce that a White Paper, or the report of some investigating committee, is due to be published 'shortly', 'next week' or whatever. Other items are published to coincide with speeches or debates, e.g. the text of the budget speech each November (formerly in March). There are very few ways of checking when these are actually published other than scanning the *Daily list* or using the Internet pages.

HMSO's sales service

The average bookseller is little concerned with HMSO publications, but in most of the larger cities of the UK one bookseller has been appointed as official agent for HMSO. In London, Birmingham, Bristol, Manchester, Cardiff, Edinburgh and Belfast HMSO has its own HMSO Bookshop selling HMSO publications and others, supplementing the postal service of the Publications Centre in London.

For an advance annual subscription a library can obtain all HMSO's major publications automatically as published. This Selected Subscription Service (SSS) may seem rather expensive, but it saves time and labour in ordering. It is possible to subscribe to Parliamentary or Non-parliamentary publications or Statutory Instruments separately. Thus a subscribing library may have only a partial collection of documents relating to a particular topic. The diversification of publishing media means that some are now excluded from the SSS: agency publications, electronic and microfiche publications, Customs Tariffs, forms and posters, House of Commons *Votes & proceedings* and House of Lords *Minutes of proceedings*, periodicals on subscription, *Hansard, London gazette,* Services regulations, manuals, licences and amendments (including Department of Trade and Industry ones relating to Civil aviation), separately published maps and charts, art reproductions, defence specifications, *Statutes in force,* nationalized industry reports not published by HMSO, all reprints, and Northern Ireland publications with ISBN prefix 0337. These can be obtained on standing order or subscription services. A list of subscribing libraries is published and makes a useful guide to the more comprehensive collections.

A useful background to HMSO's services is found in the bicentennial book by Hugh Barty-King, *Her Majesty's Stationery Office: the story of the first 200 years 1786 to 1986* (London: HMSO, 1986).

Non-HMSO publications

Since World War II there has been a massive growth in the number of non-HMSO official publications. In addition to the many published directly by government departments, there are many others published by agencies and the extraordinary number of Councils, Committees and Boards in the public sector which are in some way linked with the central government, e.g. the British Council. Thus the publications of some departments and agencies are listed both by HMSO and elsewhere. The libraries of many departments and sections such as Trade and Industry, Education, Health, Building Research Establishment, have published their own lists of publications including those not published by HMSO and some published by HMSO, but most are willing to admit that they know they do not see everything published.

Publishing patterns are changing. The Property Services Agency was privatized in 1992 and the few of its publications which continue are now published commercially. The Health and Safety Executive is mentioned above. All its publications are now non-HMSO, and even free ones are distributed by HSE Books. The contract is due for renegotiation in 1996. HMSO continues to publish the full text of many HSE titles on *OSH-CD* (Offshore Safety and Health). In 1995 Building Research Establishment (BRE) announced that it was setting up a joint venture commercial company with EMAP to undertake all its publishing: Construction Research Communications Ltd. Their catalogue lists in-print titles from BRE, Centre for Accessible Environments, Department of the Environment and a few others. The BRE continues to list its titles published each year in the *Annual review*. Other commercial joint ventures exist where departments and agencies have a good range of marketable publications, e.g. the British Museum and English Heritage.

With the cooperation of most of the departments, agencies and institutions acting partly or entirely as their own publishers (with the obvious exceptions of the Patent Office and the Ordnance Survey), Chadwyck-Healey began in 1980 to publish a comprehensive list of non-HMSO publications, and also to provide microfiche copies of most of those items listed in *Catalogue of British official publications not published by HMSO* (Cambridge: Chadwyck-Healey, 1980–). This has bimonthly and annual cumulations and a keyword index.

Chadwyck-Healey cover as many as possible of the official departments and bodies issuing publications. Each issue lists all publications sent to them during that period, not necessarily those issued during that period. For example, if a division joins the list of contributors at a certain date it will often deposit its back file of publications at one time, and these will appear over several issues, although they may date back to the 1970s, the previous year and so on. There is good subject indexing and a detailed directory of addresses and contacts.

The *Catalogue* has developed in conjunction with HMSO's database to form the joint basis for *UKOP*, alias *Catalogue of United Kingdom official publications on CD-ROM* (London: HMSO/Chadwyck-Healey). Initially this database was updated quarterly, now bimonthly. *UKOP* represents the complete set of HMSO's catalogues and of the Chadwyck-Healey catalogues since 1980. Launched in September 1989 it is a cooperative venture, available from HMSO or Chadwyck-Healey on subscription. This purports to cover 'all' the publication output of the British government, but there are inevitable lapses which can be shown when tracing annual and other series, particularly of some of the utility companies.

Stephen Richard's *Directory of British official publications: a guide to sources* (2nd edn. London: Mansell Publishing, 1984) was useful in locating sources of these publications but unfortunately the third edition was never completed and no revision is in view. The changes in the government and the development of myriad agencies in the last six to eight years mean that its use has declined. However, it still shows the scope of non-HMSO publications, in subject and form, including a surprising number of serials, some very useful ones distributed free. Particularly important are the reports and papers not issued by HMSO. There are also advisory booklets on subjects as various as education, food and nutrition, construction research and the prevention of accidents. Most major departments were covered and many smaller advisory and research bodies, some of which did not use HMSO then or now.

Machinery of government

The government's interests, which are linked with its responsibilities, and the vast amount of expert knowledge and experience it can draw upon to administer them, produce a remarkable range of publications, varied both in form and subject. Government publications cannot be divorced from the departments etc. that produce them. The machinery of government is not constant. Serials and series change their names and departments; reports that were Parliamentary may become Non-parliamentary; publications which were HMSO may become non-HMSO. Catalogues announce or list publications but do little to explain them.

Departmental changes have been frequent over the past 40 years. Since 1970, HMSO has noted them briefly in its catalogues. Otherwise it is essential to consult either a regular list such as the *Civil Service yearbook* (also now available as *Civil Service directory on CD-ROM*) or Dod's quarterly *Parliamentary companion*. For example, the Ministry of Transport was absorbed into a new superministry called the Department of the Environment, but later emerged as the present Department of Transport. More recently the Department of Health and Social Services has split into the Department of Health and Department of Social Security, and in 1995 the Department of Education merged with Department of Employment.

To help with understanding the working of the government in relation to its publishing, scan Butcher or Pemberton (the working of Parliament changes little) and the texts by Englefield mentioned below. The standard text on the working of Parliament is *Erskine May's Treatise on the laws, privileges and proceedings and usage of Parliament* (21st edn. C. B. Boulton (ed.), London: Butterworths, 1989). The House of Commons Information Office issues a series of leaflets on the working of Parliament which are updated when the major changes occur. These should soon be available on the Internet. Useful in tracing these patterns of organization in all countries are the Chadwyck-Healey microfiches *Government organization manuals, 1900–1980*, available by region and country; 526 microfiches relate to Britain.

Parliamentary publications

A point which soon becomes evident when one uses HMSO's lists and catalogues is that British government publications have an official classification, unrelated to subjects, based on their administrative history. These are Parliamentary publications and Non-parliamentary publications. Parliamentary publications are directly related to the activities of Parliament: many are either series or serials and all are HMSO publications. Table 12.1 lists all the major series and serials which make up the Parliamentary publications. To explain them it is more convenient to divide them into two groups: House of Commons, House of Lords, including papers, Journals and *Hansard*; Bills, Acts and measures.

Table 12.1 Parliamentary publications

PARLIAMENT

HOUSE OF LORDS
PUBLICATIONS
Minutes
Journal

HOUSE OF COMMONS
PUBLICATIONS
Votes and proceedings
Journal

Official reports of the Parliamentary debates (Hansard)
Official reports of the Parliamentary debates: Standing Committee debates
Papers and bills

Bills
Papers
Weekly information bulletin

PAPERS PRESENTED TO PARLIAMENT BY COMMAND
Command papers

ACTS AND MEASURES
Public general acts
Local and personal acts
Measures of the General Synod of the Church of England

House of Commons, House of Lords

Votes and proceedings (Commons) and *Minutes* (Lords) equate with the agendas and minutes of most committees elsewhere. The are published daily, mainly for members of the two Houses. The *Journals* of the two Houses are the official and permanent annual record of their proceedings. As their main use outside Westminster is for historical research, they are seldom found except in academic libraries.

The *Official reports of the parliamentary debates,* commonly known as *Hansard* (in honour of their first publisher, Luke Hansard), are a complete and reliable record of what is said in Parliament. They are far more informative than the parliamentary reports in the press. There are two series, one for each House. Both are published daily while Parliament is in session. Later they are cumulated into bound volumes which incorporate any corrections deemed necessary. There are weekly, volume and sessional indexes.

The section of the Commons *Hansard* devoted to its daily ritual called 'Question Time' is worth remembering, as it includes useful information, some of it statistical. A good deal of trouble and expense is devoted to providing answers to Members' questions. Note that *Hansard* includes written as well as oral answers, and that the numerical column numbering is in two sequences, proceedings and written questions. It can be unnerving to discover that column 239 reverts to 63, and some time later, perhaps after column 98, column 240 may follow.

Reports of the debates of Standing Committees of both Houses are published separately by HMSO and listed in the catalogues. These are the important committees which consider the details of Bills. The demand by historians for back-runs of *Hansard* and the *Journals* has led to the publication of complete sets of them in microform (see below). There is neither a *Journal* nor a *Hansard* for the meetings of the Cabinet and its Committees.

The *House of Commons papers* are a numerous and important series, including returns printed by direction of the House; reports and accounts required under the provisions of certain Acts; the Minutes of Proceedings of Standing Committees; and the reports of the Select Committees of the House. The number of Select Committees has increased over the past decade. They now include Committees on Expenditure, Environment, European Community Legislation, Science and Technology and Public Accounts. Designed to strengthen the influence of Parliament over the executive, the Select Committees have no powers and are expected to report and gather the information they need to do that effectively. Their reports are increasingly being given publicity by the media. Check with *House of Commons weekly information bulletin* or *Parliamentary companion* for current Select Committees in any session.

The *House of Lords papers* form one series and are fewer. Both *House of Commons papers* and *House of Lords papers* are numbered serially within the parliamentary session. Formerly the numbering was by regnal years but this was dropped during the 1970s after a period of dual numbering.

A Command Paper is presented to Parliament by a minister, by command of the sovereign. It may be a treaty, a statement of government policy or a report. If the latter, it could be a serial report or the *ad hoc* report of a Royal Commission or departmental committee. Many treaties and exchanges of notes emanate from the Foreign Office as Command Papers. Reports of investigating commissions and committees are often headline news. Such reports of commissions, committees, working parties and tribunals are commonly referred to by the names of the respective chairmen. For example, the Department of Trade *Report of the Committee to consider the law on copyright and designs* (Cmnd 6732, 1977) is known as 'The Whitford Report', after Mr Justice Whitford, the chairman of the Committee. In addition occasional reports from individuals are known by the names of their authors. A quick way of identifying such reports is to refer to the various series of indexes: Stephen Richard, *British Government publications: an index to Chairmen of Committees and Commissions of Inquiry* (London: Library Association. Vol. I: 1800–99, 1982; Vol. II: 1900–40, 1974; reprinted 1982; Vol. III: 1941–78; Vol. IV: 1979–82, 1984); and *Index to Chairmen of Committees: Committee reports published by HMSO indexed by Chairman* (London: HMSO, 1983) quarterly with annual cumulations.

Although the reports of Royal Commissions are always published as Command papers, the evidence submitted to them appears among the Non-parliamentary publications. For peculiar administrative reasons, the reports of departmental committees may be published either in the Command Papers series or as Non-parliamentary publications.

Command Papers are numbered in series of indefinite length, one series being distinguished from another by a prefix taken from the letters of the Command. The present Cm series, which is the sixth, began towards the end of the 1986–7 session. Abbreviations have been:

	1 – 4222	1833 – 69	Cmd.	1 – 9889	1919 – 56
C.	1 – 9550	1870 – 99	Cmnd.	1 – 9927	1956– 85/6
Cd.	1 – 9239	1900 – 18	Cm.	1 – –	1986/7 –

The *House of Commons weekly information bulletin* (London: HMSO, 1978–) is compiled by the House of Commons Library and provides information on the progress of new legislation and the composition of Commons' committees. It also lists the latest White Papers and Green Papers. From 1978 to 1981 there was also a *House of Lords weekly information bulletin*.

Bills, Acts and measures

A Bill is a draft of a proposed Act of Parliament. It may be public, local, or personal. Local Bills, which were numerous, are promoted by local authorities, nationalized industries and other corporate bodies and were often concerned with transport matters, e.g. the *Merseyside Metropolitan*

Railway Bill, which became the *Merseyside Metropolitan Railway Act 1975.* They have decreased in number in 1994–5 and since the *Transport and Works Act 1992* are no longer required in transport matters. They are not necessarily published but the House of Lords Library usually has a copy and maintains an index. Personal Bills, now rare, are published by their promoters

Public Bills are published by HMSO. A public Bill, if is it not thrown out, is likely to be reprinted several times, with amendments, on its way through Parliament. A public Bill which has passed both Houses and received the Royal Assent becomes a Public General Act (sometimes called a Statute). Public General Acts are first published separately and then in annual bound volumes called *Public General Acts and Measures,* as they include the measures passed by the General Synod of the Church of England. (Up to 1971, 'Measures' meant the 'Measures of the National Assembly of the Church of England'.)

HMSO published an annual *Index to the Statutes covering legislation in force on 31st December 19*** and an annual *Chronological table of the Statutes,* indicating which were in force until 1993. These are now suspended pending the availability of the SPO database (see below). In 1972 the Statutory Publications Office inaugurated a loose-leaf edition of current Public General Acts called *Statutes in force.* For this edition the Acts were reprinted in their latest amended form as booklets, which are filed in looseleaf binders in subject groups, e.g. agriculture, road traffic. This has now ceased revision (see below). Both were compiled by the Statutory Publications Office (SPO). Local and Personal Acts, unlike the original Bill, are also published by HMSO, but not in collected volumes. Those volumes published are listed by HMSO as Non-parliamentary publications. Up to 1962 Acts of Parliament were cited by the years of the sovereign's reign covered by the relevant parliamentary session, but since 1963 the numbering has been within the calendar year, e.g. the *New Towns Act 1975* c42. (c., sometimes written as ch., meaning 'chapter' within the Statute Book, the bound volumes).

Many of the above publications may shortly be superseded by the new database being compiled by the SPO, *Statute law database.* Currently in preparation, it is envisaged that it will be available as an online database and on CD-ROM. Published volumes should be created from it. Unfortunately, some publications have been suspended 1993–6 during its preparation.

Parliamentary Online Information System (POLIS), compiled by the House of Commons Library's Indexing Unit, is now available from Context Ltd either as three disks and an online update service, or as the current session online only by subscription. Some libraries must have up-to-date information on parliamentary activities. Obvious examples are the two parliamentary libraries, the libraries of the national newspapers and broadcasting organizations. Since October 1980 the House of Commons Library's Indexing Unit has operated POLIS through various third-party computer services. Although it was created primarily for the benefit of the members and staffs of the two Houses of Parliament, POLIS is also more widely available on a subscription basis. It includes subject-indexed references to the parliamentary debates; parliamentary questions and answers; the debates of the House of Commons Standing Committees; the Papers and Bills of both Houses; the Command papers series; references to EC legislative material, UK and foreign official publications; and the book catalogue of the House of Commons Library. Like most computerized information sources POLIS is a database, not a databank, i.e. it provides references to published sources of information – in this case to Parliamentary publications.

Non-parliamentary publications

This term was first used by HMSO in 1923. Previously, these documents had been referred to either as 'Official publications' or as 'Stationery office publications'. Non-parliamentary publications may be published by HMSO and are listed in their catalogue and Chadwyck-Healey's according to the departments, institutions, boards etc. from which they emanate.

Non-parliamentary publications may be conveniently reviewed in four groups, as follows:

- Statutory Instruments which, like the Statutes, are primary sources of the law
- the reports of those investigating committees which are *not* published as Command papers
- most of the numerous statistical series
- a miscellany of advisory and information publications by experts (not all of them in the government's employ) on many aspects of science, technology, medicine, education and the fine arts.

Statutory Instruments

Statutory Instruments are the best-known part of that complicated body of legal source literature called subordinate legislation. A Statutory Instrument is made by a minister under the authority of a specific Act of Parliament, to which it is a vital, although sometimes only a temporary, appendage. SIs, like Acts, can be of national or local application. The latter may not be published by HMSO. SIs frequently deal with aspects of legislation too detailed to be incorporated in Acts, such as the *Building regulations*. As they can be amended or revoked at short notice, SIs can be applied to emergencies more conveniently than can Acts, and will typically implement a temporary water restriction, for example. In such a situation the regulation may run for a number of days before being reconfirmed or submitted to Parliament. A typical example is SI 1989 No. 1212 *The Copyright (Librarians and Archivists) (Copying of Copyright Material) Regulations 1989*, made by the Secretary of State, Department of Trade and Industry, in accordance with the sections 37 (1), (2) and (4) and 38–43 of the *Copyright, Designs and Patents Act 1988*, c. 48.

SIs are first published separately and listed in HMSO's *Daily list*. They are later collected into the monthly and annual *List of Statutory Instruments*. These used to exclude local instruments, and some which were revoked during the year in which they were promulgated, or which are listed as 'unpublished'. No SIs are listed in the HMSO monthly and annual catalogues. The appropriate department usually keeps copies and the relevant local authorities are sent copies. HMSO publishes a CD-ROM containing the full text of all SIs published since 1 January 1987. It is available on subscription and updated quarterly. This is a joint venture with Context Ltd and updated monthly on their *JUSTIS Online* service (subscription).

Reports

Since World War I a number of reports of departmental investigative committees and working parties which formerly would have been issued as Command Papers have been issued as departmental Non-parliamentary publications. To research workers, whose happy hunting ground is the bound volumes of the Sessional Papers, the alienation of some reports from the Command Papers series is a nuisance. Over the past 50 years most of the famous reports on educational matters have been Non-parliamentary. Not all reports on matters of public interest are government reports. *The structure and reform of direct taxation* (the Meade Report) was published by Allen and Unwin for the Institute of Fiscal Studies in 1978.

Statistical publications

Government departments are assiduous in the collection of statistics. The government itself needs them, and has both the authority and the resources to compile them. In the publicity brochures distributed by the Central Statistical Office there are references to 'the Government Statistical Service', a term not to be found in HMSO's catalogues. This refers to the Central Statistical Office itself and the statistics divisions of all the major government departments, including the Office of Population Censuses and Surveys, which is responsible, among other things, for the decennial census in England and Wales; and the Business Statistics Office, formerly of the Department of Industry but transferred to the Central Statistical Office in 1989, which used to compile an extensive series of *Business monitors* (monthly and quarterly), providing statistics of production within a wide range of industries. These have now been privatized to Taylor Nelson and the range changed, *UK markets* and *UK household expenditure* being the two main series, with price rises and wider availability of computer-readable data and data by fax.

The Central Statistical Office (CSO) collects statistics from all the statistical divisions of the departments, and digests them in convenient form for general use. It also draws the attention of commerce, industry and the general public to the existence and value of government statistics, through exhibitions, press announcements and the widespread distribution of free pamphlets. The CSO's principal HMSO publications are the *Monthly digest of statistics, Annual abstract of statistics, Social trends* (annual), *Regional trends* (annual) and *Economic trends* (monthly). There is also *Population trends* (quarterly) from OPCS.

The major source of information on the government's statistical series, of which there are many, is the detailed CSO *Guide to official statistics* (6th edn. London: HMSO, 1990; a new edition will be available in paper and CD-ROM versions during 1996), but the more important are listed in a free pamphlet, revised annually, called *Government statistics: a brief guide to sources* and obtainable from Central Statistical Office, Information Services Division (Cabinet Office, Great George Street, London SW1P 3AL). This is particularly valuable as it lists not only publications but departments with telephone numbers and extensions for statistical enquiries. Worthy of note is the Chadwyck-Healey microfiche set of *British government publications containing statistics, 1801–1977*, available in 17 subject sets.

Miscellaneous

In a short space it is impossible to do justice to the variety of HMSO publications which fall under this heading. They include important reference works, such as *Britain: an official handbook, including bibliographies*, the *Aspects of Britain* series and periodicals such as the *London gazette*, the medium for official notices. Many of the figures formerly available in *British business* (now ceased) are available either in Central Statistical Office Press Notices (subscriptions are available from the Information Division) or in the Association of British Chambers of Commerce serial *Business briefing*, using information provided by the Department of Trade and Industry.

A random sample of subjects dealt with by HMSO Non-parliamentary publications in any year gives some support to HMSO's claim that its publications deal with almost every subject under the sun: industrial air pollution, information technology, adult literacy, safety in nuclear power stations, early musical instruments as works of art, and the history of Kew Gardens, for example.

A White Paper is a statement of government policy. It may indicate the broad lines of a particular future legislation. It may or may not have a white cover. A Green Paper is a statement of proposed action by the government, which is published for discussion. HMSO normally (but not always) provides the document with a green cover and usually adds (Green Paper) to the catalogue entry. Confusingly, some consultative documents (Green Papers) are non-HMSO publications and the department may publish only a few duplicated and stapled sheets.

Relevant official departmental publications are now cited in the many online databases, particularly those from government departments, such as HSELINE, DHSSDATA, BRIX/FLAIR, the input from Transport and Road Research Laboratory to IRRD, the international ICONDA, initially developed with the Property Services Agency. Many publications are reproduced in CD-ROM products such as *OSH-CD* and *Food safety plus*. These assist greatly with information retrieval where indexing may be limited in the original publication.

Developments in 1994–5 are increasing the possibility that by the time this appears in print a significant amount of information about the British government, if not the actual text of official publications, will be available on the Internet via the CCTA site xxx@gov.uk, http://www.open.gov.uk. For two years the budget speech has been available within five minutes and its use in 1995 was purported to be high. Details of HMSO titles on the net have been mentioned above. The need to recoup the costs of print publication may limit full publishing on the net for some time to come, but the proceedings of the recent SCOOP seminar covering official publishing on the net will be published in early 1996, providing useful details of addresses. Developments will be locatable via the net indexing tools and the scene will have changed radically by 1997–8.

Standing Committee on Official Publications

The Standing Committee on Official Publications (SCOOP), a subcommittee of the Information Services Group of the Library Association, was formed in 1981 to provide helpful liaison between HMSO and its major customers. The committee has worked towards improvements in HMSO's services, including some changes in its catalogue and sales services. SCOOP regularly reports developments in official publishing in *Refer*, the journal of the Information Services Group, which has also published the proceedings of most SCOOP seminars. These reflect the latest information on official publishing, particularly examining the departmental publications and changes.

Retrospective bibliographies and reprints

The demand for these has risen steeply since World War II, partly because many people have cultivated a taste for historical research, but more specifically because there is now boundless interest in the political, social and economic life of the nineteenth century. HMSO keeps some publications in print and maintains stocks of others available on demand, for example Statutory Instruments. HMSO will supply photocopies of out-of-print Parliamentary publications and Statutory Instruments through the British Library Document Supply Centre.

Research libraries which need complete or extensive runs of Parliamentary publications have access to reprint and microtext series, thanks to the diligence of scholars, the initiative of reprint publishers, and the cooperation of HMSO. Access to government publications was not the only problem: their bibliographical control was imperfect and confusing. Some research libraries have sets (original or microtexts) of the House of Commons Sessional Papers. At the beginning of the nineteenth century, a Speaker of the House of Commons devised a scheme for binding the Bills, Papers and Command Papers published each session in four classes: Bills; Reports from Committees; Reports from Commissioners; Accounts and Papers. Within each class arrangement was alphabetically by subject. This system survives, but has been modified since 1969–70 to two classes: Bills, Reports, Accounts; and Papers. There is no obligation to use this system, with its own contents lists and indexes. Many libraries arrange Parliamentary Papers numerically within their respective series. The House of Commons Sessional Papers have their own indexes, including decennial cumulations, and an excellent half-century cumulation: House of Commons, *General index to the bills, reports and papers printed by order of the House of Commons and to the reports and papers Presented by Command, 1900 to 1949* (London: HMSO, 1960) is important for retrieval. The Readex Microprint Corporation, New York, has reissued, by its unique method of microreproduction called Microprint, almost complete sets of the *Journals, Hansard* and the *House of Commons Sessional Papers.* The former Irish University Press published between 1967 and 1972, in about 1000 volumes, handsomely bound in half leather, facsimile reprints of many important nineteenth-century government reports, selected with the help of Professor and Mrs P. G. Ford. For full details of this series see the classified *Catalogue of British Parliamentary Papers in the Irish University Press 1000 volume series and area studies series 1801–1900* (Dublin: Irish Academic Press, 1977). This includes an abstract of every Paper in the series. *House of Commons sessional papers of the eighteenth century*, compiled and edited by Sheila Lambers in 147 volumes (Wilmington, Delaware: Scholarly Resources, 1975–6) includes all eighteenth-century Bills and Papers known to be extant, reproduced in facsimile. Volume I includes a long introduction by the editor and a list of Papers for 1715–60. Volume II lists Papers for 1761–1800.

Chadwyck-Healey's microfilm editions cover a wide range of papers and reports, including *Reports from Committees of the House of Commons 1715 – 1801 printed but not inserted in the Journals of the House*, with a *General index*. There is also *House of Commons Parliamentary papers, 1801–1900*, edited by P. Cockburn, in 46,196 microfiches with a subject catalogue separately and a guide. During the 1980s they have published microfiche sets of *Hansard, House of Commons Journal,* House of Lords Parliamentary papers and a monthly COM index to Commons papers from 1989–90. The list expands and the medium is now CD-ROM, adding many more full-text titles to the range.

There are too many shorter catalogues and indexes to list here. Most can be found with the good Parliamentary Papers collections. Most important are the Ford indexes and breviates which list parliamentary papers from 1833 to 1983. These well-known bibliographies, compiled by Professor P. G. Ford and Mrs G. Ford, with their associates at Southampton University, are systematically arranged under subjects, and are well indexed. The bibliographies called breviates include abstracts of the reports listed. The selection was based upon the known needs of students. They are supplemented by *A guide to parliamentary papers: what they are, how to find them, how to use them* (3rd edn. Shannon: Irish University Press, 1972). Their work is continued into the modern age with the project at the Ford collection at Southampton University during 1995–6 to develop Internet catalogues of official publications.

HMSO sale catalogues are also reprinted: *Annual catalogues of British Government publications 1894–1970* in seven volumes (Cambridge: Chadwyck-Healey, 1974–5). This microfiche reprint includes quinquennial indexes from 1936 to 1970.

The United States Historical Documents Institute has published a complete microfiche collection of HMSO publications which is accompanied by *Cumulative index to the annual catalogues of Her Majesty's Stationery Office publications, 1922–1972,* compiled by Ruth Matteson Blackmore in two volumes (Washington, DC: Carrollton Press, 1976).

NORTHERN IRELAND

From 1921 to 1972 the province of Northern Ireland had its own Parliament, commonly referred to as Stormont. During that period there was a pattern of Parliamentary and Non-parliamentary publications for Northern Ireland similar to that for the United Kingdom, although the number of publications was, of course, very much smaller. However, in 1972 the Northern Ireland Parliament was abolished. Since then the province has had direct rule from Westminster except for the short duration of the elected Assembly January–May 1974, whose function was monitorial and consultative.

The official publications emanating from Northern Ireland have always been published and distributed by HMSO Belfast, which until 1987 issued monthly and annual lists. The main HMSO lists and catalogues now include these. The retrospective bibliography of the Parliamentary publications of Northern Ireland is on similar lines to the Ford breviates: Maltby, A., *The government of Northern Ireland 1922–1972: a catalogue and breviate of parliamentary papers* (Dublin: Irish University Press, 1974) and Maltby, A. and Maltby, J., *Ireland in the nineteenth century: a breviate of official publications* (London: Pergamon, 1979).

COPYRIGHT

The enacting of the Copyright Designs and Patents Act 1988 has created a new category of 'Parliamentary copyright'. This includes Bills (but not Acts), *Hansard, Votes and proceedings,* Lords *Minutes* and House *Papers* and Parliamentary material not published by HMSO. 'Crown copyright' is defined as covering words 'made by Her Majesty or by an officer or servant of the Crown in the course of his duties'. It covers a wide range of publications, whether published by HMSO or not, including all Acts of Parliament, Statutory Instruments, maps and charts, MOD and Ordnance Survey.

HMSO have been asked to administer Parliamentary copyright in those titles which they publish. All librarians should be aware of HMSO's advisory letter, 'Dear Librarian' of 21 April 1995, on copying from any of these publications. If in doubt, consult the Crown Copyright office at HMSO in Norwich on any matter of reproduction.

Of particular note is the wide permission to copy Statutory Instruments three months after publication and Acts six months afterwards. Care should always be exercised in the non-commercial use of such copies. Commercial arrangements must be made specifically with HMSO. Librarians should also be aware of the Statutory Instrument *1989/1212 Copyright (Librarians and Archivists) (Copying of Copyright Material) Regulations 1989.* HMSO's Copyright Unit has issued a helpful *Copyright: a brief guide for Government departments* and *Copyright and libraries,* both of which are obtainable from the Unit at Norwich,

UNITED STATES GOVERNMENT PUBLICATIONS

In terms of variety, number of titles and sales, HMSO claims to be the largest publisher in the British Commonwealth. By the same token, the

Office of the Superintendent of Documents (SUDOCS), Washington, DC, can claim to be the largest publisher in the world. The printing of Congressional and departmental documents is the special responsibility of the Government Printing Office (GPO). In 1895 the Office of Superintendent of Documents was created, within the GPO, to handle efficiently their cataloguing, sale and distribution. All official federal documents are allocated a number, which is often used for cataloguing and retrieval, from its own classification system: its SUDOC number. James Bennett Childs has called the USA 'the classical land for government publications'. The production of government publications in the USA is enormous. This provides a great challenge for American librarians which they cannot ignore, owing to the elaborate depository system for federal documents. The Freedom of Information legislation also means that much is readily and freely available which is priced or unavailable in other countries.

The federal depository library system is administered by SUDOCS, and through it nearly 1200 American libraries receive free copies of publications, excluding those intended specifically for official use. The depository system was strengthened in the 1960s by the establishment of a small number of regional depository libraries, which are obliged to receive and retain one copy of all the publications nominated for deposit. The other depository libraries are allowed to select the classes of publications they require. The increased volume of microfiche and CD-ROM publications in the 1980s reflects the space problems now being encountered by these libraries. However, the increasing use of the Internet for publication in the USA is threatening the basis of these depository collections, as the publications which no longer appear in print are naturally no longer deposited. Concern has been expressed in the pages of the *Government publications review*, now renamed *Government information quarterly*.

Interest in US government publications in Britain is concentrated in comparatively few libraries, among them the British Library, Official Publications and Social Sciences section, renamed at the end of 1995 Social Policy Information Service, London; the British Library of Political and Economic Science, London School of Economics; and the libraries of the provincial universities which support related research. The acquisition of US government publications by British libraries is a perennial source of difficulty. There is no official British agent but several booksellers specialize and even have a Washington office, and online ordering through the various databases facilitates purchase. The Internet can also be widely used.

Official catalogues of US government publications

The major source of information on US government publications is the Superintendent of Documents' *Monthly catalog of United States government publications* (Washington, DC: Government Printing Office, (GPO) January 1985– .) (The title has changed several times since it was established in 1895.) Although a substantial publication, this does not list all federal publications. Like the HMSO catalogues it has block exclusions, notably patent specifications and maps, but some items are excluded only because there are many non-GPO documents which have not been reported to SUDOCS.

Since July 1976 the production of the *Monthly catalog* has been computerized and compiled according to the Anglo-American code. It is arranged under the names of federal departments and independent agencies alphabetically. Each issue is indexed in four separate sequences: author, title, subject and series/report, which cumulate half-yearly and annually. Index references are to the serial entry numbers, not to the pages of the *Catalog*. It is also available on DIALOG and the net. There is an annual *Serials supplement*.

GPO sales publications reference file (PRF) catalogues all in-print items and is available in microfiche. The six yearly cumulations give access to out-of-print publications. DIALOG also includes an order service. Various subject bibliographies of US government publications are available from SUDOCS on request.

Among the unofficial, selective sources of information on new US government publications are 'Views and over-views on/of US documents' in *Government publications review*. Many reports and similar types of publications are included by National Technical Information Service (NTIS) in its abstract services and online databases, which includes an order service through DIALOG and is available on CD-ROM.

The major reference works on US government publications are listed in the *Guide to reference books* by Eugene P. Sheehy (10th edn. Chicago: American Library Association, 1987. Supplement 1992), which also includes a comprehensive list of retrospective bibliographies of US government publications.

The range of US government publications

US government publications have a comparable structure to that of British government publications, but this is not readily apparent in the arrangement of the *Monthly catalog*. The writers on US government publications define their basic structure in various ways. Most simply, it consists of: Congressional publications; publications of the Presidency; departmental and agency publications; and publications of the judiciary. The first is comparable to British Parliamentary publications, and the third to British Non-parliamentary publications. There have been many indexes to and reprints or microfiche editions of each series, mainly by companies such as Congressional Information Service Inc., Carrollton Press and United States Historical Documents Institute Inc. These are best located in one of the guides. Joe Morehead and M. Fetzer's *Introduction to United States documents* (4th edn. Littleton, Colorado: Libraries Unlimited, 1992) presents the titles in lists according to the type of document.

Congressional publications

The daily *Congressional record* includes a transcript of the activities of Congress, the edited reports of the debates of the Senate and the House of Representatives. It is issued daily with cumulated volumes for each session. The *Journals* of the Senate and the House are published at the end of each session. 'Papers' are published in four series, *Senate reports, House reports, Senate Documents, House documents*, collectively known as 'The serial set'. Each is designated by the session and by number. Congressional committee *Hearings* is the transcripts of testimony given to various types of congressional committee.

Congressional Bills and Laws are otherwise known as Statutes. Many Bills are introduced to Congress; few become Laws. Those that do are first published separately ('slip laws'), and later in sessional volumes called *Statutes at large*. As in the UK there are public laws and private laws, and in addition there is secondary legislation, i.e. Presidential proclamations and executive orders. Congressional reference works include the *Official Congressional directory*. The Congressional Information Service publishes a number of lists including an *Index to publications of the United States Congress,* 1 (1), 1970– . This is monthly with a quarterly cumulated index and annual volume. There are detailed subject and document number indexes. It is available online on DIA-

LOG, who are putting many of their databases on to CD-ROM.

Publications of the Presidency

Orders, proclamations and other Presidential documents emanate from the White House Office, the Executive Office of the President and other sources. This is not a clear-cut group but a large one. The Office of the Federal Register has since 1965 published a *Weekly compilation of presidential documents*, which is distributed by GPO. It also publishes a number of other series both currently and retrospectively covering presidential papers. All aspects of the State Department are part of the Presidency, including the budgetary process. It has been well publicized that the Office of the President can be contacted on the Internet. The *Federal register* on DIALOG is a full-text database of US federal agency regulations, proposed rules, legal notices, meeting and hearing notices, including compliance requirements.

Departmental and agency publications

This range of publications issued by the 12 departments: Agriculture; Commerce; Defense; Health; Education and Welfare; Housing and Urban Development; Interior; Justice; Labor; Transportation; the Treasury; the Department of State and the numerous agencies, defies summary. The departmental publications include periodicals, reference works, subject series and a wealth of statistics. The frequent changes in the machinery of the government in the USA are reflected in the official *United States Government manual,* published annually.

Publications of the judiciary

This group, normally of interest only to law librarians, includes the publications of the Supreme Court and other federal courts. Their reports and notations are well covered in guides to legal resources. Much is available online through LEXIS. LEXIS also covers the legislation of the USA.

OTHER COUNTRIES

As interest in Europe increases so does the interest in official publications of European countries in particular. The EU is covered elsewhere in this volume. In Europe, although some countries follow the British model, many have an official gazette covering all legislation, debates, papers and so on. This is the model for the European Commission *Official journal.* As it is impossible to discuss the publications of other countries in this brief space this is best done using Eve Johansson's (ed.) *Official publications of Western Europe.* Vol. 1: Denmark, Finland, France, Ireland, Italy, Luxembourg, Netherlands, Spain and Turkey; Vol. 2: Austria, Belgium, Federal Republic of Germany, Greece, Norway, Portugal, Sweden, Switzerland and United Kingdom (London: Mansell, 1984, 1988). Each country is covered in a similar pattern, written by a specialist from the country or with long experience in their publications. The pattern of government is outlined, with an indication of the publications ensuing and a section on bibliographic control.

The first volume to cover official publications over the whole world was published in 1990 by CIS for the Government Documents Round Table of the American Library Association. Edited by Gloria Westfall, the *Guide to official publications of foreign countries* is a country-by-country list of the major official publications of each country as selected by the editor for that country. The abstract for each indicates content and coverage. A second edition is in preparation for publication in 1996. Also due for publication in 1996 is a complementary volume: *Information sources in official publishing* (edited by Valerie J Nurcombe for Bowker Saur). This volume aims to cover the world region by region, sometimes country by country, according to the homogeneity of the region and the discretion of the chapter author, providing a background to the range of official publishing. It is discursive with emphasis on other more detailed descriptions, whereas the former lists specific titles only with no background on the publishing practices and lists available.

SUGGESTIONS FOR FURTHER READING

Government publications in general

Cherns, J. J., *Official publishing: an overview: an international survey and review of the role, organization and principles of official publishing,* Oxford and New York, Pergamon, 1979.

For recent developments in government publishing at large, and informed articles on all aspects of government publications, see the file of the former *Government publications review* now *Journal of government information.* (New York and Oxford: Pergamon Press, 1974– . Bimonthly). The emphasis is on American official publications, but there are useful articles on British and other countries' official publications.

British government publications

There is a considerable literature on British Parliamentary procedure – no specific text is mentioned. However, the former Deputy Librarian of the House of Commons Library has published a number of texts which clarify the relationship between publications, Parliamentary procedures and Whitehall.

Englefield, D. J. T., *Parliament and information: the Westminster scene*, London, Library Association, 1981.

Englefield, D. J. T., *Whitehall and Westminster: government informs Parliament: the changing scene*, Harlow, Longman, 1985.

Government publications of the USA

Bailey, W. G., *Guide to popular US government publications*, 3rd edn. Littleton, Colorado, Libraries Unlimited, 1993.

Downey, J. A., *US Federal official publications: the international dimension*, Oxford and New York, Pergamon, 1978.

Morehead, J. and Fetzer, M., *Introduction to United States public documents*, 4th edn. Littleton, Colorado, Libraries Unlimited, 1992.

Sears, J. L. and Moody, M., *Using government information sources: print and electronic*, 2nd edn. Oryx Press, 1994.

Government publications of other countries

Although government publications exist the world over, not many countries have authoritative manuals on their official publications. This is being remedied slowly.

Bishop, O., *Canadian official publications*, Oxford and New York, Pergamon, 1981.

Coxon, H., *Australian official publications*, Oxford and New York, Pergamon, 1980.

Fry, B. M. and Hernon, P., *Government publications: key papers*, Oxford and New York, Pergamon, 1981

Kuroki, T., *An introduction to Japanese government publication,*. Oxford and New York, Pergamon, 1981.

Maltby, A. and Mckenna, B., *Irish official publications: a guide to Republic of Ireland papers*, Oxford and New York, Pergamon, 1980.

Pemberton, J. E., *The bibliographic control of official publications*, Oxford and New York, Pergamon, 1982.

Westfall, G., *Bibliography of official statistical yearbooks and bulletins*, Cambridge, Chadwyck-Healey, 1986.

Westfall, G., *French official publications*, Oxford and New York: Pergamon, 1980.

Zink, Steven D. (series ed.), *Government documents bibliographies*, Cambridge, Chadwyck-Healey.

Ongoing, with the first two being general and the next two relating to the USA.

13

Official publications of international organizations

Elizabeth Anker

Official publications of international organizations are a vital primary reference resource. They include the legislative texts on which the organizations are founded and they also contain the core materials for major decision-making processes.

Fifty years have elapsed since the signing of the United Nations Charter and it will soon be the 39th anniversary of the signing of the Treaty of Rome, which established the European Economic Community (EEC) and the European Atomic Energy Authority (EURATOM). These two events may seem insignificant as mere dates on paper, but the developments that have taken place since their implementation clearly show how world events are related to official documentation.

In many cases the making of a treaty provides the foundations for great political building processes, which may face either demolition or extension, depending on the strength of the foundations. Currently preparations are being made for the 1996 Intergovernmental Conference to debate and amend the Treaty on European Union, and official publications have been appearing in readiness for this major event since the signing of the Treaty at Maastricht, in 1992. This continuous process of development and refurbishment of the international political fabric of our existence shows that official documentation is an endless product providing materials for current debate and historical facts for future generations to acknowledge.

The prolific output of official publications from international orgnaizations now makes it hard for us to believe that at the time of the

UN Charter, and even a decade later with the Treaty of Rome, very few people had access to officially published materials. Even those who were fortunate enough to have knowledge of and access to them generally regarded them as 'difficult'; and bibliographical sources were even more obscure than the publications.

Why is the situation so different today? Indeed, there are now so many bibliographic aids that the choice is as overwhelming as the varied means of access to international official publications. In the past the whole concept of official publishing seemed of little consequence other than to the organizations themselves. Consequently, there was little desire to write bibliographical works on the subject. However, today there is a vital need to be informed and to remain informed.

The developments and discussions now taking place affect us all profoundly. Whether the subject is the environment or an important treaty, the decisions that are made will have global significance. For example, the Global Forum held at the Earth Summit in Rio de Janeiro, Brazil, in 1992, was followed two years later by the Global Forum held in Manchester in 1994. These two meetings generated substantial texts.

United Nations AGENDA 21: PROGRAMME FOR ACTION FOR SUS-TAINABLE DEVELOPMENT, Rio Declaration on Environment and Development, Statement of Forest Principles. The final text of agreements negotiated by Governments at the United Nations Conference on the Environment and Development (UNCED) 3–4 June 1992, Rio de Janeiro, Brazil. United Nations Department of Public Information, DPI/1344, 1993 Sales No. E.93. I.II. ISBN 92 1 100509 4

Manchester City Council FIRST STEPS. LOCAL AGENDA 21 IN PRAC-TICE. Municipal Strategies for Sustainability as presented at Global Forum '94 in Manchester. London: HMSO, 1995. ISBN 0 11 701871 6

These will no doubt stimulate further discussion at the 1996 UN 'Cities Summit' (HABITAT II) Conference in Istanbul.

There are similar instances where the publications of one international body are closely linked with those of another, in both subject and scope. This endorses the fact that matters to be addressed are now of global significance. Subjects such as integration, sustainability and world trade now feature prominently in the publications of international organizations. With the same problems to be solved in different parts of the world, there is a growing need for cooperation – which is yet another subject.

The sheer volume of literature generated in the process of addressing international issues is formidable. An idea of the vast range of international official publishing can be acquired by consulting a very reliable and comprehensive reference work which currently covers over 32,000 international organizations in approximately 225 countries:

Union of International Associations (Brussels) YEARBOOK OF INTERNATIONAL ORGANIZATIONS 1995/96.
VOL.1: Organization descriptions and cross-references, July 1995. ISBN 3 598 22225 4.

VOL.2: International organization and participation: country directory of secretariats and membership (geographic volume), August 1995. ISBN 3 598 22222 X.

VOL.3: Global action networks: subject guide and index, September 1995. ISBN 3 598 22223 8.

This is a well-recommended reference tool. Each volume can be purchased as a separate item, but there is a saving of 13% if they are purchased as a complete set. Another very good work is:

Schiavone, G. INTERNATIONAL ORGANIZATIONS: a dictionary and directory. 3rd edn. London: Macmillan, 1992. ISBN 0 333 56464 2.

A single A–Z comprehensive factual volume. The 22-page introduction provides an excellent historical overview of international affairs.

TREATIES

The *Vienna convention on the law of treaties* gave consideration to 'the fundamental role or treaties in the history of international relations'. Article 5 relates to 'treaties constituting international organizations and treaties adopted within an international organization'. These thoughts are reiterated in the preamble to the *Convention on the law of treaties between states and international organizations or between international organizations.* Much more evidence can be found to show the importance of treaties to the foundation and development of international organizations. Indeed, a number of enquirers find that they need to consult treaties as a primary part of their research into international organizations. This need has shown that there is often some measure of doubt concerning the location of these legal instruments, therefore some guidance on sources might be useful. Confusion can arise because the word 'treaty' does not always feature in the title or because insufficient detail is known, e.g. there has been more than one 'Vienna Convention'. In this case one needs to be sure of either the full title or some other unique feature by which to identify the document, e.g. correct date of publication, command number or treaty series number.

There is often more than one source of location for treaties, e.g. the Treaty of Rome has appeared in a number of texts, and so too has the Treaty of European Union. Currently, there is a very attractive and compact edition of the European treaties (in three small volumes), with thumb index and silk bookmarks.

European Commission. EUROPEAN UNION – SELECTED INSTRU-MENTS TAKEN FROM THE TREATIES. Book 1, Volume 1, ISBN 92 824 1240 7; Volume 2, ISBN 92 824 1180 X; Book 2 (in preparation). Luxembourg: Office for Official Publications of the European Communities, 1995– .

The first volume of Book 1 contains the texts of the Treaty of European Union and the Treaty establishing the European Community, the Accession Treaty and other treaty materials in frequent use. The second volume of Book 1 includes the texts of the European Coal and Steel Community (ECSC) and the European Atomic Energy Authority (EURATOM). Book 2 will contain the whole set of basic Treaties.

Treaty materials can also appear as Agreements (including Exchange of Notes) and Protocols. Examples are:

Agreement: GENERAL FRAMEWORK AGREEMENT FOR PEACE IN BOSNIA AND HERZEGOVINA, signed at Paris on 14 December, 1995. Cm.2951. London: HMSO, 1996. ISBN 0 10 131542 2.

Exchange of Notes: EXCHANGE OF NOTES . . . CONCERNING THE DIS-POSAL OF THE 'BRENT SPAR' OFFSHORE INSTALLATION, OSLO, 7 July, 1995. Cm.2951. London: HMSO. ISBN 0 10 129512 X.

Protocol: EUROPEAN UNION, THE TREATY . . . P.2, 27. Cm.3151. London: HMSO, 1996. ISBN 0 10 131512 0.

Reference sources

A good source for treaty materials is the Command Paper sequence of the British Parliamentary Papers (i.e. European Communities Series, Miscellaneous Series or Treaty Series categories).

Bowman, M. J. and Harris, D. J. MULTILATERAL TREATIES. Index and current status. London: Butterworths, 1984. ISBN 0 406 24277 7.

This compact reference tool was compiled at the University of Nottingham Treaty Centre. In addition to the adequate references to treaty locations there are also comprehensive notes. Part A contains full entries for treaties concluded during the period from 30 June 1983 to 1 January 1994 (or, in some cases, earlier). Part B provides new status and other information for treaties in the main volume of the index. *The 11th cumulative supplement* is the latest that is currently available. (The cumulative supplements from issue 4 onwards are published by the University of Nottingham Treaty Centre and it is possible to place a standing order with the Centre to receive later supplements as they become available.)

The University of Nottingham Treaty Centre responded to an invitation from the Foreign and Commonwealth Office to prepare a fourth volume to update the previous work of Professor Clive Parry, *Index of British Treaties 1101–1968*, Vols. 1–III, by Clive Parry and Charity Hopkins (London: HMSO, 1971). The project was funded by grants from the Leverhulme Trust and researched by Miss J. Shepherd (retired head of the Foreign and Commonwealth Office):

G. B. Foreign and Commonwealth Office AN INDEX OF BRITISH TREATIES – Vol. 4: covering the period 1969–1988 with information updating the entries in volumes 2 and 3. Shepherd, J. A. and Harris, D. J. (London: HMSO, 1992, ISBN 0 11 591681).

United Nations MULTILATERAL TREATIES DEPOSITED WITH THE SECRETARY-GENERAL. Status as at 31 December 1994. New York: UN, 1995. (ST/LEG/SER.E/13) (UN pub. Sales No. E.95 V5). ISBN 9 21 133484 5.

This index facilitates the use of the United Nations Treaty Series.

The expansion of world trade, with increasing emphasis on globalization and innovation, has significant implications for intellectual property. Provision for information on treaties in this area is provided by:

INDUSTRIAL PROPERTY AND COPYRIGHT. Monthly Review of the World Intellectual Property Organization.

The *Review* and two sets of treaties (i.e. Industrial Property Laws and Treaties, and Copyright and Neighboring Rights, Laws and Treaties) are supplied as a complete set with a single subscription. An alternative for those needing only the texts of treaties is the fairly new CD-ROM product, IPLEX, issued by the International Bureau. Information for the *Review* and treaties set, and also the IPLEX CD-ROM, may be obtained from WIPO Publications, Sales and Distributions Unit, 34 chemin des Colombettes, 1211 Geneva 20, Switzerland.

There are two series provided by Simmonds & Hill Publishing Ltd which contain authoritative editions of important international instruments. The International Legal Editions are text only and the Soft-Text Editions contain a disk or disks (as ASCII files), a binder and slipcase along with printed materials and notes. There is a soft-text edition of *The World Trade Organization*, ISBN 1 898029 13 X, approx 30pp + disk. Available from: Simmonds & Hill Publishing Ltd, 49 Woodstock Road, London E17 4BH. Tel: 0181 923 4380; Fax: 0181 523 5926.

TREATIES AND ALLIANCES OF THE WORLD

Now offered on CD-ROM. It comprises an analysis of treaties and alliances in world politics; a listing of international organizations with agreements; *Cold War treaties and alliances; Regional Agreements as well as Trans-regional alliances.* This sixth edition has been reviewed and completely updated to provide a major reference work. The CD-ROM is available from October 1995. Contact: Microinfo Ltd. Tel: 01420 86848.

Access to treaty materials is important. Therefore a variety of different forms have been covered to provide a choice from which the most appropriate product may be selected.

COUNCIL OF EUROPE (CE)

The Statute of the Council of Europe was signed on 5 May 1949, by the ten founding member states: Belgium, Denmark, France, Ireland, Italy, Luxembourg, The Netherlands, Norway, Sweden and the United

Kingdom. It now comprises 34 members. The common aims which these countries have are: 'to work for greater democracy and human rights; to improve living conditions and promote human values'.

The work of the Council is channelled through two main organs, the Committee of Ministers and the Parliamentary Assembly. These are served by an international secretariat headed by the Secretary-General, who is elected for a five-year period.

The publications reflect the principles of Article 1 of the Statute of the Council of Europe. The following are good examples of part of the aims to be achieved:

Council of Europe. Parliamentary Assembly. Debates. BRIDGING THE GAP. THE SOCIAL DIMENSION OF THE NEW DEMOCRACIES. Strasbourg: Council of Europe Publishing, 1995. ISBN 92 871 2739 5.

Council of Europe HUMAN RIGHTS – A CONTINUING CHALLENGE FOR THE COUNCIL OF EUROPE. An overview of Council of Europe human rights activities from 1949 to the beginning of 1995.

Other useful publications that are available are:

A EUROPEAN STORY. The Council of Europe and the European Parliament in Strasbourg. Liège: Editions du Perron, 77 bd. E. de Laveleye, B-4020 Liège (1986); Council of Europe, Report on the activities of the Council of Europe (the year); Council of Europe, Catalogue of publications (the year).

There is an excellent yearbook which is published under the auspices of the Council of Europe. Presented in bilingual format (i.e. French and English, the official languages of the Council of Europe) it contains a wealth of information about European organizations and the OECD (but excludes European organs or Commissions of the United Nations and specialized agencies):

ANNUAIRE EUROPEEN/EUROPEAN YEARBOOK. DORDRECHT/ BOSTON/LONDON: Nijhoff, 1948.

The latest edition: Vol.XLI – 1993 (published 1995) ISSN 0167 6717; ISBN 0 7923 3305 5 comprises a section on articles, a very comprehensive documentary section and an extensive bibliography (139 pages) arranged by subject. There is also a cumulative list of the articles of preceding volumes.

In 1990 a partial agreement of the Council of Europe established the European Commission for Democracy through Law (popularly known as the 'Venice Commission'). This is a consultative body which cooperates with member states of the Council of Europe and also with non-member states in promoting basic principles of democracy. A bulletin of information from the Commission is issued:

Council of Europe. Secretariat of the Venice Commission. BULLETIN ON CONSTITUTIONAL CASE-LAW 1993 – 1 – . Strasbourg: Council of Europe F-67075 Strasbourg CEDEX. Tel: (33) 88.41.20.00; Fax: (33) 88.41.27.94/64.

There are three issues of this publication per year. Each issue contains summaries of the most significant decisions of constitutional courts as well as North American and European courts with similar jurisdiction, including the European Court of Human Rights. The bulletin provides a very useful reference tool for constitutional lawyers, researchers and students.

A large number of Council of Europe publications are available from HMSO: Agency Section, 51 Nine Elms Lane, London SW8 5DR. In addition to the priced publications there is also a vast collection of documents which can be accessed via the relevant departments.

ADDRESS: Council of Europe, F-67075 Strasbourg Cedex, France.

EC/EUROPEAN UNION

The organization known as the European Community evolved from the signing of two well-known treaties. The Treaty of Paris, signed in 1951, established the European Coal and Steel Community (ECSC); The Treaty of Rome, signed in 1957, established the European Economic Community (EEC) and the European Atomic Energy Community (EURATOM). The joining together of these three separate communities comprising the countries of Belgium, France, the Federal Republic of Germany, Italy, Luxembourg and The Netherlands, formed the original organization. The Single European Act, signed in 1986, amended the earlier treaties and provided for a more integrated and therefore more effective Europe. The number of member states has gradually increased from the original six to the present 15 members.

The Treaty of European Unions, signed in Maastricht on 7 February 1992 (consistently referred to as 'the Maastricht Treaty') has established the present European Union, which contains the European Community as one of its three main divisions.

In view of the major changes that are currently taking place in Europe, care should be taken to make sure that only up-to-date documentation is used as the main source of information. This can be difficult to achieve when even annual reports of organizations are usually issued up to 12 months after the date of the year which they are covering. However, there are two annual reports from the European Commission which deserve a mention as they provide a very good overview of events:

European Commission GENERAL REPORT ON THE ACTIVITIES OF THE EUROPEAN UNION. Luxembourg: OOPEC, 1995. ISBN 92-827-5897-4.

The introduction of this report is 'the European Union in (the year)'. There are chapters on Community finance and Community law and other major areas. There is also a diary format of the year under month and date headings, highlighting the most significant events (e.g. 1 January 1995 – Austria, Finland and Sweden join European Union).

European Commission THE COMMUNITY INTERNAL MARKET. Luxembourg: OOPEC, 1995.

This report provides an assessment of the achievements of the internal market and also records any shortcomings to date. It is in fact a record of recent progress and an indication of future intentions.

There are a few excellent secondary sources available which, if it is acknowledged that some of the detail will be dated, do provide very good basic guidance. Comprehensive coverage of the Community institutions and their documentation can be found in:

Thomson, I. THE DOCUMENTATION OF THE EUROPEAN COMMUNI-TIES: a guide. London: Mansell, 1989. ISBN 0 7201 2022.

A further reference guide for which there is now a fifth edition:

Jones, A. and Budd, S. THE EUROPEAN COMMUNITY: a guide through the maze. 5th edn. London: Kogan Page, 1994. ISBN 0 7494 1201 1.

This excellent work provides guidance on how to set up a good basic library of European official materials without cost; how to keep up to date; advice on the use of the *Official journal*, and many other extremely useful pieces of information relating to sources. Basic facts of the European Community and the transition from the single market are also covered, as well as the individual policies in Europe (e.g. energy, environment, science and technology etc.) Despite the excellence of this publication, two points must be made as an updating measure: (1) the number and titles of Directorates-General of the European Commission are liable to change, as are our own government departments; (2) there is now an extra *Official journal* series (i.e. from the Office for Harmonization in the Internal Market) covering Community trade marks (and eventually designs). Issue No. 1 in this series appeared in September 1995. This series will not, however, be supplied under the usual terms to European Documentation Centres and may therefore be difficult to access in many libraries.

Most directories are informative and there is usually a wide choice available. Europe is no exception. The two directories mentioned here have been chosen for their extensive coverage of important areas and for their economical price.

European Commission EUROPE INFO – Directory of important information sources on the European Union. Luxembourg: Office for Official Publications of the European Communities, 1995. ISBN 92-827-4950-9.

This is a trilingual (English, French and German) directory containing five sections of information on networks and other European Union information sources. Section 1 explains the status of the different categories of information outlets (e.g. European Documentation Centres etc.) and provides locations (with telephone and fax numbers); Section 2 covers the various Community Programmes (e.g. IMPACT, for the promotion of electronic information services in Europe); Section 3 contains detail of the Office for Official Publications and includes EU and European law information on CD-ROM and tenders online daily (TED-ALERT); Section 4 provides a description of EU information on the Internet and interchange of data between administrations (IDA) online. Information on most structures and communications techniques is also included; Section 5 covers Representation Offices of the Community institutions.

European Commission INTERINSTITUTIONAL DIRECTORY – European Union – September 1995. Luxembourg: Office for Official Publications of the European Communities. ISBN 92 827 5130 9.

This is a supplementary volume to the electronic database of the same title. However, the printed source, being updated periodically, is an excellent reference tool in its own right. The structure of the Community institutions is described as well as other related bodies, e.g. the European Parliament: this section contains membership details under political and pressure groups, commissions etc. Points of contact (i.e. names, addresses, telephone numbers) are given throughout this volume. Instructions are also given on how to use the electronic directory via ECHO and OVIDE/Epistel.

For those who have in the past hunted endlessly for information on topics such as the 'Cockfield' paper, the 'Kangaroo Group' or the 'Schengen Agreement', or indeed more recently for information on the 'Social Chapter', there is now a compact volume which is very helpful. it does not contain bibliographic details, but at least it provides a reasonably adequate secondary source. The arrangement is alphabetical, with keywords appearing in bold type throughout the text. There is also a very usful 16-page bibliography of historical and current materials relating to Europe:

Bainbridge, T. with Teasdale, A. THE PENGUIN COMPANION TO EURO-PEAN UNION. London: Penguin, 1995. ISBN 0 14 016510 X.

The Commission issues a number of different serial publications. Two examples are: (1) *Europe on the move* (previously known as *European file*) includes the following titles: *European Union*; *The Single Market*; and *The institutions of the European Union*. The titles in this series are updated fairly regularly; (2) *Eurobarometer. Public opinion surveys* (Standard Series) has been issued during spring and autumn since 1973. The spring 1995 issue No. 42 provides figures, opinions and charts on 'The first year of the new European Union'. Issued by Directorate-General X, Survey Research Unit, T120-1/107, Rue de la Loi 200/Wetstraat 200, B/1049 Bruxelles; Tel: (32.2) 299.94.39. E-mail: K reif@mhsg.cec.rtt.be; Internet: Europa Server: http:/www.cec.lu

Keeping currently aware of all the official business that is taking place around the world can be an exacting task. However, some institutions provide timely information either free or at a very modest fee for documentation. A number of free documents issued by the Information Office of the European Parliament are:

Press release – provides a summary of the agenda before the beginning of the session.

The briefing – published in advance of a session, it provides a summary of the reports for debate.

EP news – covers major events of each session.

The week – a more detailed summary of events; issued about two weeks after each session.

A commercially produced current awareness guide is:

EUROPEAN ACCESS. Cambridge: Chadwyck-Healey, 1980– . Bimonthly.

The first issue for 1996 will include a separate index volume covering the period 1988–95 (i.e. since Chadwyck-Healey have been the publishers).

Providing information for business-related enquiries is not always easy, especially if available resources are limited. A substantial reference work is:

European Commission. DG I I I. Directorate A. Unit III/A/3/. PANORAMA OF EU INDUSTRY 95/96. ISBN 92-827-4703-4.

This gives an intensive review of the situation and outlook of the manufacturing and service industries in the European Union. As with 'Europe in figures', there is a comparison of Community figures with those of the USA and Japan. To supplement the main volume, which is produced annually, there is a bimonthly issue: PANORAMA OF EU INDUSTRY, SHORT-TERM supplement, latest information on the EU industry.

A comprehensive reference work on acronyms etc. is:

Ramsay, A. EUROJARGON. 3rd edn. London: Capital Planning Information, 1995. ISBN 89886 906 5.

UNITED NATIONS

The fundamental aim of the United Nations is to promote international peace and security, but other factors are also important and are therefore part of the ultimate aim. These include a basis of respect for human rights and the need for cooperation in both economic and social affairs.

The major governing body is the General Assembly, comprising all member states (currently 185). In addition to the General Assembly there are three Councils: the Security Council, the Economic and Social Council and the Trusteeship Council. The principal judicial body of the UN is the International Court of Justice. The Secretariat is the administrative body of the UN.

Each session, the General Assembly and the three Councils produce the accounts of their proceedings, resolutions and reports (including annual reports). The International Court of Justice also produces reports in addition to judgments, advisory opinions and orders.

The principal reference work of the UN is:

United Nations, Department of Public Information YEARBOOK OF THE UNITED NATIONS. Vol. 47. New York: UN, 1993. E.94.I.1. ISBN 0-7923-3077-3.

Beginning with a report of the Secretary-General on the work of the United Nations for the year, this extensive reference annual includes various activities involving a multitude of issues. Part 2 covers the intergovernmental organizations related to the United Nations and appendices. An historical introduction to the UN can be found in Volume 1 which covers the year 1946/7. The yearbook of the UN is not available as an agency publication from HMSO. It can be obtained either from Kluwer Law International, P. O. Box 85889, 2508 CN The Hague, The Netherlands, or as a standing order item from UN Publications, Palais des Nations, Office C-115, 1211 Geneva 10, Switzerland, or a local distributor. Back issues are available on microfiche. To mark the 50th anniversary of the United Nations a special edition of the *Yearbook* has been published:

United Nations, Department of Public Information YEARBOOK OF THE UNITED NATIONS, special edition – UN Fiftieth Anniversary. The Hague/Boston/London: Martinus Nijhoff, UN, 1995. ISBN 0 7923 3122 5. Sales No. E.95.1.50.

This volume presents an invaluable overview of five decades of peace-keeping and international cooperation and includes many important historical texts. The introductory chapter traces the origins of the UN and includes 'Dumbarton Oaks' conversations and proposals. The volume is an excellent reference resource of the UN. It is equally valuable either as a single volume or as a complement to a set of UN *Yearbooks*.

United Nations material falls basically into four groups:

1   Official records: the accounts of proceedings and published documents of the official bodies of the UN. Official records are given a document symbol (e.g. GA.OR = General Assembly, Official Records).

2   Working documents: agendas, draft resolutions etc. in mimeographed form.

3   Periodicals: there are many titles which can be classified as UN serials. Apart from the statistical items, one of the most popular and perhaps one of the most widely consulted serials is: *UN chronicle* (published quarterly). This gives coverage to each session of the Security Council and the General Assembly, and reports on a wide range of activities of the entire UN system.

4   Sales publications: these are publications which are not included in any of the other three groups. Items in this group are issued in a more commercial format. Two examples of sales items are:

United Nations, Department of Public Information BASIC FACTS ABOUT THE UNITED NATIONS. New York: UN, 1992. E93.1.2. ISBN 92 1 100299 9.

This provides a general introduction to the role and functions of the UN and its related agencies.

United Nations, Department of Public Information ONCE UPON A TIME: the United Nations: 50 years for peace [video + booklet] directed by Catherine Charbon. New York: UN, 1995; GV. E.95.0.13. ISBN 92 1 100701 1.

United Nations (the year): publications catalogue is available free of charge from HMSO Books, Publicity Dept., Duke Street, St Crispins, Norwich NR3 1PD. Tel: 01603 695907. Fax: 01603 696784.

A standing order service is available for categories of publications and these may be subscribed to singly or with one or more of the other categories. The subjects covered by this service are:

I	General information and references
II	Economics
III	Affiliated bodies
IV	Social questions
V	International law
VII	Political and Security Council affairts
VIII	Transport and communication
IX	Disarmament and atomic energy
X	International administration
XI	Narcotic drugs
XIII	Demography
XIV	Human rights
XVI	Public finance and fiscal questions
XVII	International statistics
XX	UNICEF publications.

Standing orders for official records may also be added to these categories.

Indexes and guides

The United Nations Bibliographic Information System (UNBIS) is the name given to the online bibliographic and factual information systems developed by the Dag Hammarskjold Library. The operation of this system provides comprehensive bibliographical control of United Nations publications. The system also provides a wide range of information and reference services relating to the many activities of the UN.

The United Nations Documents Index (UNDOC) is a product of UNBIS. *UNDOC* gives a comprehensive coverage of United Nations documentation, including full bibliographic description and subject, author and title indexes. It also produces a checklist of UN documents received at headquarters (issued ten times a year). The production of a cumulative edition of UNDOC has proved to be unmanageable, and therefore all cumulative volumes of *UNDOC: Current index* are now issued in microfiche form. Since 1987 UNDOC has been produced at quarterly intervals.

There is a new publication which provides a really efficient way to access United Nations publications:

UNBIS plus on CD-ROM. ISSN 1075-3877; Chadwyck-Healey for and on behalf of the United Nations.

This comprises bibliographic detail of UN documents and publications and also many thousands of non-UN publications acquired by UN Libraries. There is also full text of the documentation relating to the major UN organs. Two files currently exist: Retrospective file: all files to 1992 on 2 CD-ROMs, and Current file: all files from 1993 on 1 CD-ROM. Networking is permitted for non-profit organizations on one site. An explanatory folder with precise details of hardware and software requirements and cost is available from Chadwyck-Healey Ltd, The Quorum, Barnwell Road, Cambridge CB5 8SW. Tel: 01223 215512; Fax: 01223 215514. E-mail: mail@chadwyck.co.uk.

Within the United Nations system of organizations there are a number of specialized agencies. For the purpose of this chapter four of these have been chosen.

Food and Agriculture Organization (FAO)

The Food and Agriculture Organization, established in 1945, aims to raise the levels of nutrition and living standards of the populations of the member states; to improve the efficiency of the production and distribution of all food and agricultural products; to improve the conditions of rural populations; and by contributing to a growing world economy thus ensuring humanity's freedom from hunger.

The head of the Food and Agriculture Organization is the Conference, and the Council is the governing body. There is also a consultative framework made up of a number of Commissions and subsidiary groups.

As the fundamental aims of the FAO are related to food, agriculture and the world economy, the publications of this organization are of necessity based upon these and related subjects.

Various series of studies and technical papers are issued throughout the year, each of them has some relevance to the basic aims. Agriculture is represented by FAO in *FAO agriculture* series, e.g. no.28, *The state of food and agriculture 1995* contains a special chapter: Agricultural trade: entering a new era (with diskette). Rome: FAO, 1995. ISSN 0081 4539.

A general statistical overview is provided by:

FAO YEARBOOK: TRADE. Vol.19. Rome: FAO 199 – . ISSN 0071 7126.

Bibliographical access can be achieved by consulting *FAO books in print* or *FAO documentation: current bibliography*. For those requiring historical bibliographical detail, the catalogue of FAO publications is a useful reference tool.

The IT resources of FAO are probably the most advanced of all the UN agencies. The database of the International Information System for Agricultural Sciences and Technology (known as AGRIS) contains the details of AGRINDEX, which is also accessible in DIALOG File 203.

The United Nations Bookshops, in both New York and Geneva, carry a full range of 'specialized agency' material. The appropriate address for FAO is: Food and Agricultural Organization of the United Nations, Via delle Terme di Caracalla, 00100 Rome, Italy. HMSO also supply a number of FAO publications as Agency items.

International Labour Organization (ILO)

The International Labour Organization is the longest-established organization of the UN system. The constitution of the ILO was included in the League of Nations Peace Settlement, 1919. During the period 1945–46, the constitution was amended, and subsequently the ILO became a 'special agency' of the UN. It now comprises 173 member states. The ILO is mainly concerned with the creation of programmes which will not only help to secure full employment, but help to promote higher living standards. Further to these aims is the ILO's commitment towards establishing job satisfaction and training as well as fair play and working conditions.

The principal organ of the ILO structure is the International Labour Conference. The International Labour Office, headed by a Director-General, is also part of the ILO. This body serves as a secretariat to the ILO and provides publishing facilities for the organization.

Being a long-established organization, the ILO has developed an extensive publishing programme. Minutes of the ILO Governing Body contain the Official records. From the beginning the ILO has also provided information on international and national law relating to labour and social security. This information is used by governments and major policy makers as well as many institutions and individuals.

Law and regulations have been recorded in the Legislative series, 1920–89; Labour law documents: treaties and legislation on labour and social security from 1990–5. The final issue 1995/3 contains an index of international agreements, laws and regulations since 1990. From 1996 the printed format will cease. It is to be replaced by computerized information available electronically via LABORLEX, which consists of two separate computerized databases. ILOLEX contains international labour standards. Available on CD-ROM, it is a very sophisticated but also user-friendly research tool. It will eventually be available on the Internet. NATLEX is a bibliographic database featuring national laws on labour and social security. It was created in 1984 and contains 20,000 references. The information contained in these databases will be available on CD-ROM. Enquiries to: ILO Publications, International Labour Office, Ch-1211, Geneva 22, Switzerland.

A reference volume containing international labour standards is now available:

INTERNATIONAL LABOUR CONVENTIONS AND RECOMMENDATIONS 1919–1994. 2v. ISBN 92 2 109192 9.

A forward look is presented in:

VISIONS OF THE FUTURE OF SOCIAL JUSTICE: Essays on the occasion of the ILO's 75th anniversary. 1994. ISBN 92 2 108011 0.

The WORLD LABOUR REPORT 1995, ILO, 1995. ISBN 92 2 109447 2; ISSN 0255 5514.

Volume 8 in the series includes a statistical annexe on diskette, presenting a world view of social and labour conditions. Topics in this edition include ageing, societies, privatization and retraining.

The world of work is published five times a year. Although it is not an official publication of the ILO it nevertheless includes some worthwhile articles, e.g. No. 14 1995, a historical, current and prospective overview of the workplace which covers in particular the subject of teleworking, with special references to European enterprises. Issued by the Bureau of Public Information, ILO. Tel: +4122/7997912.

The 83rd Session of the International Labour Conference to be held in Geneva in June 1996 has, as item V on the agenda: 'Employment policies in a global context'. This item is set for general discussion.

Researchers requiring a comprehensive historical record of the ILO will probably be interested in the microfilm editions of the *Reports and record of proceedings of the ILO Conferences from 1919–* produced by World Microfilms Publications, London.

International Monetary Fund (IMF)

The International Monetary Fund, established in 1945, aims to promote international monetary cooperation and to stabilize international currencies. It also seeks to aid the balanced development of world trade and provides funds to assist member states in temporary financial difficulties.

The IMF is headed by a Board of Governors, currently 181, representing all member states. The official business of the IMF is recorded in the *Summary of proceedings of the annual meeting of the Board of Governors* held during September of each year. This report has been produced since 1946. An annual report is also issued containing sections on the world economy and 'the Fund' (in the year of the report), and appendices. The appendices to the *Annual report* contain various financial statements and articles. Especially useful is the list of publications issued for the year, e.g. in the *Annual report* for 1988/9 the list of publications appears on pp.82–3.

The information produced by the IMF as a result of research provides the international community with vital sources. The IMF produces a number of other informative publications. These include a series of occasional papers and a number of surveys on world economic issues:

The WORLD ECONOMIC OUTLOOK is published twice yearly to present an official global analysis of economic developments. ISSN 0256 6877.

Another useful publication is the *IMF survey*, published since August 1972. It contains a digest of news concerning the 'Fund' presented as sections on selected topics, national economies and fund activities (in varying order). It is produced 23 times per year (on alternative Mondays). An index to this serial and the supplements is produced annually.

Woods, J. INTERNATIONAL MONETARY COOPERATION SINCE BRETTON WOODS provides an insight into the working of the organization since the Bretton Woods Conference.

This unofficial history has been compiled with the full cooperation of the IMF and is based on archival records belonging to the organization. IMF Publications Services, 19th Street, 700 New York 10-540.

World Health Organization (WHO)

The World Health Organization was established in 1948. Its main aim is

rade agreement as the second part of the work of a Preparatory Committee of the United Nations Conference on Trade and Employment. The original concept of the GATT was intended to be part of a two-stage development, the first stage being the Charter that was supposed to create an International Trade Organization (ITO). However, the negotiations at the World Conference in Havana failed to lead to this conclusion, although the GATT continued and during its existence it presided over eight rounds of multilateral trade negotiations. During the final round (i.e. the Uruguay Round) the GATT was transformed from an institution based on a multilateral treaty to an international organization with permanent status, known as the World Trade Organization, which came into force on 1 January 1995. There is a White Paper presented to Parliament by the President of the Board of Trade: *The Uruguay Round of multilateral trade negotiations*. Cm. 2599. London: HMSO, 1994. ISBN 0 10 125792 9.

A trilingual brochure (in English, French and Spanish), published in 1995, fully describes the World Trade Organization's role and function.

GATT activities was published for the last time in February 1996. It covers the period 1994–5 and the preparation for the new World Trade Organization. *GATT activities 1994–95,* ISBN 92 870 1142 7.

GATT focus (the official newsletter) No. 113 final issue, Dec. 1994 and *WTO focus* (newsletter) January/February No. 1 – 1995 cover the implementation Conference and the opening of WTO. Page 4 of this issue of *WTO focus* contains a useful Fact file concerning the WTO. There are many more publications available – too many to mention. *WTO publications* (catalogue) can be obtained from: World Trade Organization, Information and Media Relations Division, Centre William Rappard, rue de Lausanne 154, CH-1211, Geneva 21, Switzerland. Tel: (022) 739 50 19; Fax: (022) 739 54 58.

There is also a facility on the Internet for accessing an order form to print out or to order by e-mail. Internet (World Wide Web server): http://www.unicc.org/wto. Internet enquiries: webmaster@wto.org.

HMSO – BIBLIOGRAPHIC CONTROL

HMSO provides an agency service for a number of bodies, including European and international organizations. Full bibliographical details of the international official publications supplied by HMSO's agency service are printed in the *Daily list* (published on weekdays except for Bank

Holidays). This list is available on subscription from HMSO, either on a daily or a weekly basis. The weekly subscription is just over half of the price of that quoted for lists that are posted daily.

A monthly cumulation of HMSO daily lists is issued as HMSO *Monthly catalogue*. In addition to a list of the agency publications there is also an annual cumulation of agency titles issued under the title *HMSO agency catalogue* for the year.

In addition to the printed catalogue services, HMSO, in partnership with Chadwyck-Healey, produces a combined catalogue of UK official publications and publications of European and international organizations on CD-ROM. *The catalogue of United Kingdom official publications (UKOP)* (unfortunately, the title does not indicate that agency publications are included) contains records from 1980 to date. From April 1996 UKOP will be issued bimonthly instead of quarterly, thereby improving the currency of the information provided.

The new UKOP is available for free trial (also new software). Contact: Chadwyck-Healey Ltd, The Quorum, Barnwell Road, Cambridge CB5 8SW. Tel: 01223 215512; Fax: 01223 215513; e-mail: marketing@chadwyck.co.uk. Price £990 plus VAT (NB: Public libraries are allowed discount.)

HMSO Books, 51 Nine Elms Lane, London SW8 5DR. *Enquiries*: Tel: 0171 873 8401 (phone for 30-day free trial of UKOP); Fax: 0171 873 8463. *Subscriptions*: Tel: 0171 873 8499; Fax: 0171 873 8222; e-mail: bibliographics@hmso.gov.uk.

Informative brochure available from HMSO Books. UKOP may be networked under a Licence Agreement.

LIBRARY PROVISION FOR OFFICIAL PUBLICATIONS

The collection needs suitable treatment (i.e. the best acquisition policy and classification scheme) in accordance with budgetary limits, type of user, size of collection, availability of space and staff time.

It is not enough to acquire as many official publications as an individual budget will allow: quantity is not always an important factor. A smaller collection that is well chosen and well kept can be a greater asset than a collection that is larger and inefficiently run.

Prospective users need to be aware of the location and arrangement of the material. Accessibility can be improved if the material is shelved in one area. A display of the more significant recent acquisitions can provide good current awareness service, and one which any hard-pressed user might be grateful for. However, whereas a display of material can be regarded as optional, the provision of adequate shelf signs is essential; especially if the collection is arranged within a larger area of social science materials. A handout explaining the scope of the collection and the principles of arrangement is a useful tool. Alternatively, if automated facilities are available, a 'help screen' on the main library terminals will serve a useful purpose.

Catalogues, indexes and any other bibliographical aids should be easily accessible and their use fully explained. If there are online facilities or CD-ROM, these should also be available near to the collection. Facilities for access to the Internet should also be publicized if they are available.

14
Statistical sources

David Mort and Lynne Clitheroe

Published statistical data are an important information resource of value to all sections of the community. Regularly published statistical time series cover a range of subjects, including national economic and financial trends, demographic trends and characteristics, business conditions, economic activity and industrial structures, production and markets for specific products and services, labour market data, and social areas such as education, crime, health, and sports and leisure.

The vast majority of statistics in most countries are produced by national governments and their agents. These are usually known as official statistics, and in the UK Sir John Boreham has traced them back to major statistical exercises such as the Augustan census in Roman Britain and the *Domesday Book* (Boreham 1984).[1] The first modern population census was carried out in 1801, records of foreign trade go back to the 17th century, and the first census of earnings was in 1886. Although UK statistics have a long history, there can be no doubt that some of the major changes in the collection, publication and use of statistics have taken place in the last decade.

In the 1980s the resources devoted to official statistical activities were reduced at a time when measuring economic and social activity became more complicated. In business sectors, for example, statistics had historically concentrated on traditional manufacturing sectors but the 1980s were characterized by the rapid growth of the service sector and official statistics failed to respond to this change. Privatization of various public services also created problems, as sectors previously measured as a matter of course became less easy to quantify. Emerging employment trends, such as self-employment, working from home, part-time work, and the rowth of small businesses, also required a new approach.

At the same time as the above socioeconomic changes were taking place, the increasing influence of the news media gave many statistics a more prominent role. Almost every day a new economic or social statistic is announced in the UK and digested and commented upon by TV newsreaders, journalists, city analysts and various experts. Politicians regularly throw statistics at each other across the House of Commons, usually putting their own interpretation on a particular set of figures.

UK OFFICIAL STATISTICS

This period of considerable economic and social change, coupled with a higher profile for statistical data, has inevitably led to more public scrutiny of statistical data and, in the late 1980s in particular, the accuracy and reliability of some official series were increasingly questioned. The Pickford Report,[2] published in 1989, made recommendations for improvements in official statistics and, in 1990, concern among users was reflected in a Royal Statistical Society report, *Official statistics: counting with confidence*.[3] In the same year a government statistician, writing in the *Treasury bulletin*,[4] began his article with the statement: 'there is no doubt that the quality of UK economic statistics has deteriorated over the last few years', and the then Chancellor of the Exchequer, John Major, indicated his concern to the Treasury and Civil Service Committee[5] about the statistical base for economic statistics.

In the 1990s improving the quality of official statistics has been a central aim, beginning with a series of measures announced in May 1990 known as the Chancellor's Initiative,[6] concentrating on statistics relating to services, companies and the balance of payments. This was followed by a second package of measures known as the Chancellor's Initiative Phase II,[7] which looked at areas such as retail sales, output of goods and services, and the balance of payments. Other improvements have taken place since then and these, along with some future plans for UK official statistics, are described in 'You can count on us – with confidence', an article in a 1995 issue of the *Journal of the Royal Statistical Society*, by Bill McLennan.[8]

Other changes taking place to UK official statistics include a reduction in the amount of data available in traditional hardcopy formats, the 'privatization' of some major official series, and the emergence of more electronic sources. Many regular hardcopy statistical sources only provide a tiny percentage of the data that are actually collected from governmen surveys. However, more detailed data, often packaged to meet a particu lar client's demands, can be obtained on demand from the relevan department, usually for a fee. For particularly popular surveys, where demand for the data is relatively high and where the major users are busi nesses, the government has appointed various private-sector agents t market and sell – and perhaps add value to – the data, and some of these are described later in the chapter. Rather belatedly, more UK official sta tistics are also appearing in electronic formats, primarily CD-ROM, and some of the key titles are mentioned in the appropriate sections.

The organization of UK official statistics

The Government Statistical Service (GSS) is the collective name given t all the statistical activities carried out by central government. In Octobe 1995 the GSS published its second annual report[9] highlighting the main developments during the year, including the establishment of the *Officia statistics code of practice*.[10] The Code of Practice was designed to meet two main aims: to promote uniformly high standards across producers of offi cial statistics, and to maintain public confidence in official statistics. Firs published in April 1995, the code will be reviewed regularly, probably for the first time after two years.

Statistical collection and production by the UK government is essen tially decentralized, with individual departments having their own statis tical teams. There is also some geographical decentralization, with the Welsh Office, Scottish Office and the Northern Ireland Office responsi ble for various publications relating to their own areas. This geographi cal split can cause problems for the user of statistics. For example obtaining detailed population estimates for all the above areas, plu England, requires a reading of separate publications for England and Wales, Scotland and Northern Ireland. There may also be confusion sur rounding the exact geographical coverage of a particular publication some official publications cover the United Kingdom, others Grea Britain, others England and Wales, and some just England, Scotland Wales or Northern Ireland.

Until recently two specialist statistical units, the Central Statistica Office (CSO) and the Office for Population Censuses and Survey (OPCS), covered topics of particular importance and the CSO wa responsible for coordinating the statistical output of the GSS. Two devel opments in recent years have strengthened the role of the CSO and placed more emphasis on the compatibility and coherence of government statistics. In November 1991 the CSO was launched as an executive agency, under the government's 'Next Steps' initiative,[11] reporting directly to the Chancellor of the Exchequer. At the same time, many key economic and business statistics, previously the responsibility of individual departments, were transferred to the CSO, and others have been transferred since. For example, as well as economic and industry sector statistics, the CSO became responsible for labour market data when the Employment Department merged with the Department of Education in 1995. The first review of the CSO's agency status began in November 1994, with the results contained in *the Agency review report.*[12] As an executive agency the CSO also produces a regular annual report and a corporate plan.

Another major step in the move towards a greater coherence in UK government statistics came in April 1996 with the formation of a new Office for National Statistics (ONS). This resulted from a merger of the CSO and OPCS, and the launch document[13] noted that 'the purpose of the merger is to meet a widely perceived need for greater coherence and compatibility in Government statistics, for improved presentation, and for easier public access'.

Guides

One of the first publications to appear from the new ONS was the latest edition of the *Guide to official statistics.*[14] Its first edition in 1976 won a Besterman Medal as an outstanding bibliography, and since then new editions have been published at approximately five- or six-year intervals. The 1996 edition comprises a general introduction to the work of the GSS followed by specific chapters on: population; education; labour market; health and social care; income and living standards; crime and justice; housing; environment; transport; social statistics; the economy; agriculture, forestry, fisheries, food; production and manufacturing; distribution and other services; and public services. It is an essential guide to UK official statistics, but a major weakness is that it is only published every few years. The many changes in titles and statistical sources that took place in the early 1990s, for example, made the edition published in 1990 look out of date after a relatively short period.

Another useful guide is the annual *Government statistics – a brief guide to sources,*[15] available free of charge from the ONS. The guide provides basic details of the main statistical publications and services from central government and also includes a list of contact points, with telephone numbers, for specific statistical series. The statisticians at the end of these telephone lines are usually very helpful and the best source of information on specific statistics and subject areas. The guide provides a useful basic introduction to official statistics and gives specific addresses for statistical publications which are not usually available through HMSO, such as certain Scottish, Welsh and Northern Ireland titles, and some specific departmental publications. *Statistical news – developments in official statistics*[16] is a quarterly bulletin with articles and news items on statistical issues. In an attempt to broaden the market for official statistics, the ONS has also produced a glossy catalogue of its core publications, including hardcopy and electronic sources. The *ONS Catalogue*[17] has brief details of each publication, a photograph of the cover, and price and order information.

The *Reviews of United Kingdom statistical sources (RUKSS)*[18] series began in 1969, and by the beginning of the 1990s there were 29 volumes, all of which, except Volume 5, titled *General sources of statistics,*[19] are subject based and provide a detailed guide and a critical appraisal of the published data in a specific subject area. Sadly, Volume XXIX (number 29) is the last in the series. Published in 1992 , it covers the distribution sector.[20]

Key sources

A basic collection of UK official statistics would at least include the *Annual abstract of statistics, Monthly digest of statistics,* the monthly *Economic trends,* and the annual publications *Social trends* and *Regional trends.* Other standard statistical publications include *Financial statistics,* published monthly, and the yearbooks *UK national accounts blue book* and *UK balance of payments pink book.* All these titles are now produced by ONS and distributed through HMSO. Statistical compendia are published by the regional statistical offices, and these include *Digest of Welsh statistics, Focus on Northern Ireland,* and *Scottish abstract of statistics.*

For the most up-to-date information on economic and financial trends, *ONS first releases* are press releases circulated on the day that a particular statistic is published. *ONS first releases* on specific subjects, such as retail prices or the balance of payments, can be purchased on subscription and there is also a fax-back service, *ONS Statfax*, which can fax relevant data to inquirers on demand on the morning of the statistical release. Headline figures are available within a couple of minutes of the official release time of 9.30 am, and soon afterwards the entire *First Release* is available.

Major sectors of the economy, such as construction, transport and agriculture, are covered by specific annual and more frequent publications. Examples include *Housing and construction statistics*, published annually and quarterly, the annual *Transport statistics Great Britain* plus regular *Transport bulletins*; and *Agricultural statistics UK*, published annually. The results of the *Annual census of production (ACOP)* are published in a series of *ACOP business monitors*, usually two years after the census year to which they relate. Information on the sales, exports and imports of specific products is contained in *UK markets,* a series of 125 separate reports comprising 91 annual titles and 34 quarterly titles covering 4800 products. *UK markets,* launched in 1994 to replace the *Business monitor statistics of manufacturers sales* series, is published by the market research company Taylor Nelson AGB, but it is based entirely on data collected by the ONS.

The traditional preoccupation of official statistics with manufacturing industries means that the coverage of the service sector is still patchy and considerably less exhaustive, although the situation has improved a little in recent years. A series of *Business monitors* includes the general *Service trades business monitor* and specific titles on retailing, wholesaling, catering and allied trades, and the motor trade.

Central government departments are responsible for some of the largest regular social and consumer surveys carried out in the UK. These include the *Family expenditure survey (FES)* with basic results published annually in the *Family spending* report; the *General household survey (GHS)*, with an annual report of the same name; and the *National food survey (NFS)*, with key results published annually in the *Household food consumption and expenditure* report. More detailed analysis of the results of all these surveys are available from the relevant statistical contact point.

The largest survey of all is the *Population census,* currently carried out every ten years, with the published output comprising a range of national, regional, county and other local area reports. However, the published output is just the tip of the iceberg and more detailed statistics from the population census are available from the Census Office. A comprehensive guide to the range of data produced from the census is the *Census users' handbook* published by GeoInformation International[21] (1995).

Population trends, published quarterly, provides up-to-date information on demographic trends and includes articles on population issues, while various *OPCS monitors* are designed for the quick release of population data. The demise of the Employment Department has led to some changes in labour market publications. The well-established monthly *Employment gazette* has been replaced by a slimmer volume, *Labour market trends,* concentrating on key labour market issues. Other important titles in this area are the annual *New earnings survey* and the regular *Labour force survey.* Specific annual publications examining social trends include *Education statistics for the UK, Criminal statistics England and Wales,* and *Health and personal social services statistics.*

Electronic sources

The development of electronic services based around UK official statistics has been a relatively slow process, but the pace began to quicken in 1995 and 1996. The spread of CD-ROM technology has been one factor encouraging the transfer of more series into electronic formats, and user demands for more easily manipulated data have also been a major influence. The CSO's first CD-ROM product, *Social trends 1970–1995,* brought together 25 years of data from one of the CSO's flagship publications, and this has been followed by *Social trends 26 CD-ROM.* Other CD-ROM products include *Regional trends on CD-ROM, Family spending CD-ROM,* and the *Guide to official statistics on CD-ROM.* All these products, available direct from HMSO, have been priced at a relatively low level to encourage use by a wide range of organizations and individuals. Other CD-ROM products have resulted from cooperation between the GSS and private-sector organizations. These include the CD-ROM version of *UK markets* and various census-based packages available on CD-ROM and on diskette.

The *CSO databank,* originally developed as an online facility for government departments and research users, is currently available to a wider audience as a series of 'datasets' on diskette and other electronic formats. These datasets correspond approximately to the core economic and financial publications produced by ONS: *Economic trends, Financial sta-*

tistics, Monthly digest of statistics, Producer prices, Retail price index, Consumers expenditure, UK economic accounts, UK balance of payments pink book and *UK national accounts blue book*. The ONS has also created a piece of software, *Navidata*, for use with the datasets.

The *ESRC data archive*, based at the University of Essex, has the largest collection in the UK of computer-readable data on social and economic topics. The archive holds over 5000 datasets and most relate to postwar Britain, although an increasing number of historical studies covering earlier periods are also available. Data can be made available in a variety of ways, including on CD-ROM, through a network, or on diskette. Major data holdings include: UK Census data; General household surveys; Family expenditure surveys; ONS databank; Labour force survey; British crime surveys; and British social attitudes surveys.

Large statistical databases have been passed to the private sector and academic institutions to market on behalf of the GSS. One of the first such arrangements involved detailed product import and export data available via various agents listed at the front of the monthly publication *Overseas trade statistics of the United Kingdom*. Other agreements include *NOMIS*, an online database of labour market data accessible via the University of Durham, *Labour force survey* data from 1984 onwards available from the computer bureau *Quantime,* and detailed analysis of the *International passenger survey (IPS)* from three main agents, Information Research Network (IRN), IPS Sales and MDS Transmodal.

The ONS now has a World Wide Web (WWW) site on the Internet, although at the time of writing the information on this site was confined to details of publications rather than any hard data. The web site address is http://www.emap.co.uk/cso/. Other web sites of interest to users of official statistics include the Treasury site, http://www.hm.treasury.gov.uk and http://www.open.gov.uk/index/fistats.htm. The latter site is an index giving leads to government departments producing statistics.

NATIONAL STATISTICS OUTSIDE THE UK

The range of subjects covered by UK official statistics is replicated in most of the major countries of the world. What may differ is the organization of official statistics and the amount of detail available on specific subjects in particular countries. The organization of official statistics in the UK is essentially decentralized, but in other countries a more centralized approach may be taken. In The Netherlands, for example, all the official statistical activity is centralized in an independent unit, the Central Bureau of Statistics. Sweden has a similar agency, Statistics Sweden (SCB). In France, where considerable resources are devoted to official statistical activities, the central statistical office's headquarters known as INSEE are in Paris, but every French region also has its own statistical information point. Germany has a central federal statistical office known as the Statistisches Bundesamt, and statistical offices in most of the individual states, or Länder. A general description of the organization of official statistics in various European countries can be found in the *Journal of the Royal Statistical Society, Volume 154, 1991*[22] and a more detailed review is found in *Organization of statistics in the member countries of the European Community*, a 1992 report from Eurostat.[23]

Basic statistical reference sources for virtually all countries include some form of annual abstract of statistics and a monthly or quarterly digest of statistics. Population censuses, industry surveys and labour force surveys are also found in most countries. Some harmonization has taken place in the content and presentation of these surveys across national boundaries, but at a detailed level there are still difficulties in making meaningful comparisons between countries. In other areas, such as product sales information and specific social sectors, differences between definitions and survey methods make international comparisons even more difficult.

Most national statistical offices produce an annual catalogue or guide to their statistical publications and services. Examples include INSEE's *Catalogue Général des produits et services*[24] and the annual *Verzeichnis der Veroffentlichungen*[25] from the German statistical office. Every few years the German statistical office produces an English-language guide, *Survey of German federal statistics*, while the French statistical office, INSEE, has a special service for English-speaking users where regular details of new publications and new statistical surveys and methodologies are sent automatically.

Mention should also be made of the *American statistics index (ASI)*,[26] from the Congressional Information Service (CIS). This is a detailed guide which includes not only general information on a publication but specific information on individual tables and time series within a publication. Another useful country-specific guide is the *DIR guide to Japanese economic* statistics,[27] with detailed descriptions of published statistics and survey and compilation methods.

INTERNATIONAL STATISTICS

The major international organizations, such as the European Union, United Nations (UN), Organization for Economic Cooperation and Development (OECD), International Monetary Fund (IMF) and the World Bank, have an established role as collectors of statistics from various countries and producers of international statistical compilations and reports. In an ideal world, the classification schemes and definitions which provide the basis for statistics in one country would be the same as in another, but this is rarely the case. In an effort to produce some level of consistency across countries, the European Union's statistical office, Eurostat, and the UN have led international attempts to produce common classifications and statistical methodologies and, when successful, the results are so-called 'harmonized statistics' across countries. The success stories have been overseas trade data, population census data, labour force surveys, consumer opinion surveys and industrial trends surveys, and some economic indicators. Areas where progress has been much slower include industrial structure data, data on services, and many areas of social statistics.

The *Harmonized system (HS)* is an overseas trade classification established in 1988 and now used by all the major trading countries of the world. It covers around 5000 product headings, and in Europe the *Combined nomenclature* (CN) extends the HS to cover approximately 9500 headings. Another classification used in international trade is the *Standard industrial trade classification (SITC)*, a well-established classification scheme developed by the UN. Reaching an international consensus on an acceptable classification of national economic activity has been much more problematic largely because most countries have their own well-established and unique industrial classification schemes, such as the *Standard industrial classification (SIC)* in the UK, the *NAP* classification in France, and the *Systematisches Guterverzeichnis für Produktionsstatistiken (GP)* in Germany. The USA also has a *Standard Industrial Classification (SIC)* but this is quite different from the UK version. International attempts to produce a common classification, such as the *International Standard Industrial Classification (ISIC)* from the UN and the *NACE* classification from Eurostat, have so far failed to become accepted by many countries. One area where some progress is being made is product sales data. In the 1990s Eurostat has devised a product classification known as *PRODucts of the European COMmunity, or*

PRODCOM. All EU member states are obliged to use the PRODCOM product list for their product sales statistics.

Selected titles

Core statistical titles from the international organizations are predominantly economic or general statistical compilations. The main examples are the UN's *Monthly digest of statistics* and *Statistical yearbook*, OECD's *Main economic indicators* and *Economic outlooks* for specific countries, the monthly *Eurostatistics* and *Eurostat yearbook*, *Basic statistics of the EU*, and *Europe in figures* from Eurostat, and *International financial statistics* published monthly by the IMF. Unesco publishes the *Unesco statistical yearbook*, concentrating on social statistics, and demographic trends are well covered by the UN's *Demographic yearbook* and the annual *Demographic statistics* from Eurostat. World Bank publications concentrate on developing economies, with annual publications such as *World tables* and *Social indicators of development*.

Information on specific sectors from the international organizations has improved in recent years, although it is still not as comprehensive or as up to date as the national statistics. Some good examples of international publications include the *Panorama of EU industry* from the European Commission with commentary and data on key sectors, and the *OECD STAN database for industrial analysis*, with information on 46 manufacturing sectors in 12 OECD countries. *Enterprises in Europe* is a two-volume report from the European Commission with detailed statistics by country on the number of enterprises and establishments in various manufacturing and service sectors. A key strategy of Eurostat is to improve its coverage of the services sector, and *Business services in Europe*, published in 1995, is part of a pilot survey with two main aims: to provide basic statistical information on the business services sector within member states, and to test and develop a methodology for the regular collection of statistical data on business services to be provided on a harmonized basis by all member states.

Guides

All the international bodies produce regular statistical guides and catalogues. Eurostat, for example, publishes a regular *Eurostat catalogue*,[28] and *Sigma, bulletin of European* statistics,[29] which contains feature articles and news items on developments in European statistics.

A recent initiative is *INSTAT – International statistics sources subject guide to sources of international comparative statistics*.[30] Published in 1995, *INSTAT* is a guide to specific subjects covered by international publications rather than just the publications themselves. It has references to around 400 published sources based on a survey of these sources between 1991 and 1994. Now in its fifth edition is *Statistics Europe*[31] from CBD Research Ltd. This is a guide to the major official statistical publications in Europe and some non-official sources. Other volumes in this series, including *Statistics Australasia*, *Statistics Africa*, *Statistics Asia*, and *Statistics America* are no longer published.

There are also guides to specific subject areas within the statistical field, and recent examples include *Sources of transport* statistics,[32] a brief guide to sources in the UK and elsewhere, and *Population statistics*,[33] a comprehensive review of population surveys.

Electronic sources

The major international organizations have been actively developing electronic versions of many of their core publications in recent years. Examples include the *Eurostat yearbook* CD-ROM, *UN statistical yearbook CD-ROM*, and *World data* from the World Bank. The OECD has concentrated on diskette versions of many of its time series. A selection of electronic sources of international statistical data is described by Mort in *Electronic sources of European economic information and business statistics*[34] (1996).

Countries such as the USA and Canada have also been at the forefront of statistical developments on the Internet. For example, many USA official statistics are accessible via the Internet. Internet addresses include http://www.census.gov/, providing population census data, and http://stats.bls.gov/, containing Bureau of Labor Statistics. Both these sites are accessible free of charge, while a fee-paying site is http://www.stat-usa.gov/. Further details of relevant web sites containing statistical information are available from *Useful statistical addresses on the Internet*,[35] a regularly updated pamphlet from the Information Research Network.

NON-OFFICIAL STATISTICS

Whereas central governments and international organizations are responsible for the majority of published statistics, other important producers are 'non-official' or 'non-governmental' organizations, such as trade associations, banks, chambers of commerce and other local agencies, research companies, academic institutions, trade journal publishers, media organizations and others. Publications from these sources can often provide more detailed information than official statistics, information on sectors and topics not covered by official statistics, or different types of data such as forecasts, opinion surveys, salary surveys, end-user statistics, local area data or price information. Examples of leading statistical publishers outside central government in the UK would include the Bank of England, the Confederation of British Industry (CBI), the Chartered Institute of Public Finance and Accountancy (CIPFA), British Tourist Authority (BTA), and trade and professional associations such as the Society of Motor Manufacturers and Traders (SMMT), the Advertising Association, the British Insurance Association, the Association of Manufacturers of Domestic Electrical Appliances (AMDEA), and the Biscuit, Cake, Chocolate and Confectionery Alliance (BCCCA).

A problem for the user of this material is that the quality and reliability of data from non-official sources can vary considerably, and tracking down relevant publications can sometimes be difficult. In the UK, the *Guide to official statistics*14 provides some details of the major non-official sources. The *Directory of British associations*36 from CBD can also provide a starting point for information on trade association statistics. A more specific guide, containing references to around 900 UK non-official statistical sources, is *Sources of unofficial UK statistics*,37 published by Gower. The third edition of the guide was published in 1996.

Details of trade associations outside the UK compiling statistics can be found in various directories, including the *Directory of European industrial and trade associations*38 from CBD and the *Encylopedia of associations*39 from Gale Research Inc. Euromonitor's *World directory of non-official statistical sources*,40 first published in 1996, contains details of approximately 2000 statistical titles worldwide and is the result of a merger between two previously published titles: *European directory of non-official statistics* and *International directory of non-official statistics*. In the USA a detailed guide to non-official sources is the *Statistical reference index (SRI)*,41 with details of specific tables in publications from trade associations, trade journals, research institutes, and state agencies and institutions.

LIBRARIES AND INFORMATION SERVICES

A number of libraries in the UK have extensive statistics collections and most of these are open for general use. A selection of these are briefly described here.

The Export and Marketing Intelligence Centre (EMIC) at the Department of Trade and Industry in London houses a collection of international economic and business statistics aimed primarily at UK exporters. The collection is restricted to material covering the last few years, but its country coverage is comprehensive. Other international collections of statistics are held at the LSE library in London and the University of Warwick library in Coventry, and both these collections have historical holdings of many titles. Access to both libraries is restricted to bona-fide researchers and a prior appointment is desirable.

The library of the ONS at Newport has a good collection of UK business statistics, including both official and non-official sources, while the OPCS library in London is an important source for UK and international demographic data.

EMIRS is a fee-based telephone inquiry service offered by EMIC and *INTERSTAT* is a specialist statistical information brokerage service operated by the Information Research Network (IRN) from London.

USER GROUPS AND USER TRAINING

Various user groups and consultative committees advise the GSS on its statistical activities: members of these groups are drawn from industry, the public sector, academia and other areas of economic activity. A description of these groups and committees is available from the ONS.[42] The Royal Statistical Society has a number of groups monitoring developments in official statistics and the *Journal of the Royal Statistical Society* has regular news items and feature articles on developments in UK statistics. A general group of users is the Statistics Users Council (SUC), which runs an annual conference and has various subgroups on specific subject areas. A recent initiative has been the Business Statistics Users' Group, established in 1995.

Practical training sessions and seminars on statistical sources are organized by various organizations, including The Library Association, Aslib and the Market Research Society. The private training organization TFPL runs a regular introductory course on business information with a statistical element, and also has a specific course on understanding economic statistics. The Information Research Network specializes in public seminars and in-house training packages covering statistical issues, and a popular event is *Unravelling the mysteries of statistics and market data,* a one-day course on understanding statistical terminology and concepts.

REFERENCES AND CITATIONS

1 Boreham, J., 'Official statistics', *Journal of the Royal Statistical Society A,* **147,** 1984, 174–85.
2 Cabinet Office, *Government economic statistics: a scrutiny report,* London, Cabinet Office, 1989.
3 Royal Statistical Society, *Official statistics: counting with confidence,* London, Royal Statistical Society, 1990.
4 Hibberd J., 'Official statistics in the late 1980s', *Treasury bulletin,* **1,** 1990, 2–13.
5 Major J., *Minutes of evidence,* London, HMSO, 1990
6 Economic Trends, 'Improving economic statistics – the Chancellor's initiative, *Economic trends,* **448,** 1991, 84–97.
7 Caplan D. and Daniel, D., 'Improving economic statistics', *Economic trends,* **460,** 1992, February, 87–8.
8 McLennan B., 'You can count on us – with confidence, *Journal of the Royal Statistical Society A,* **158,** 1995, 467–89.
9 Government Statistical Service, *Annual report,* London, ONS, 1995.
10 Government Statistical Service, *Official statistics code of practice,* London, ONS, 1995.
11 Central Statistical Office, *Agency framework document,* London, CSO, 1991.
12 *Central Statistical Office, Programme strategies 1994–95 to 1996–97,* London, CSO, 1994.
13 Office for National Statistics, *Office for National Statistics,* London, ONS, 1996.
14 Office for National Statistics, *Guide to official statistics No 6,* London, HMS0, 1996.
15 Office for National Statistics, *Government statistics – a brief guide to sources,* London, ONS (annual),
16 Office for National Statistics, *Statistical news,* London, HMSO, quarterly.
17 Office for National Statistics, *The ONS catalogue 199– ,* London, ONS (annual).

18 Various authors, *Reviews of UK statistical sources*, London, Chapman & Hall (regular).

19 Lock G. F., *General sources of statistics, Volume V reviews of UK statistical sources*, London, Heinemann, 1976.

20 Moir, C. and Dawson J. A., *Distribution: volume XXIX reviews of UK statistical sources*, London, Chapman & Hall, 1992.

21 Openshaw, S. (ed.), *Census users' handbook*, London, GeoInformation International, 1995.

22 Royal Statistical Society, 'Appendix 2: summary of the administrative frameworks within which national statistical offices operate in other countries, *Journal of the Royal Statistical Society A*, **154**, 1991, 38–41.

23 Arl, G., *Organization of statistics in the member countries of the European Community, volume 1 – essays on the 12 national statistical institutes: comparative study*, Luxembourg, Office for Official Publications of the European Communities, 1992.

24 Insee, *Catalogue general des produits et services, Paris*, INSEE (annual).

25 Statistisches Bundesamt, *Verzeichnis der Veroffentlichungen*, Wiesbaden, Germany (regular).

26 Congressional Information Service, *American statistics index*, Washington, CIS (annual plus updates).

27 Matsuoka, M., and Rose, B., *The DIR guide to Japanese economic statistics*, Oxford, Oxford University Press, 1994.

28 Eurostat, *Eurostat catalogue*, Luxembourg, Eurostat (annual).

29 Eurostat, *Sigma – bulletin of European statistics*, Luxembourg, Eurostat (quarterly).

30 Fleming M. C. and Nellis, J. G., *INSTAT – International statistics sources: subject guide to sources of international comparative statistics*, London, Routledge, 1995.

31 CBD Research Ltd, *Statistics Europe*, 5th edn, Beckenham, CBD Research Ltd, 1996.

32 Transport Statistics Users Group, *Sources of transport statistics*, London, TSUG, 1995.

33 Benjamin, B., *Population statistics*, Aldershot, Gower Publishing, 1989.

34 Mort, D., 'Electronic sources of European economic and business statistics – part 1', *European business intelligence briefing*, February, 1996.

35 Clitheroe, L., *Useful statistics addresses on the Internet*, London, Information Research Network, 1996.

36 CBD Research Ltd, *Directory of British associations*, Beckenham, CBD Research Ltd, 1995.

37 Information Research Network, *Sources of unofficial UK statistics*, 3rd edn, Aldershot, Gower Publishing, 1996.

38 CBD Research Ltd, *Directory of European industrial and trade associations*, Beckenham, CBD Research, 1991.

39 Gale Research Company, *Encylopedia of associations*, Detroit, Gale Publishing, 1995.

40 Euromonitor, *World directory of non-official statistical sources*, London, Euromonitor Publications, 1996.

41 Congressional Information Service, *Statistical reference index*, Washington, GIS (annual plus updates).

42 Office for National Statistics, *The GSS consulting users: statistical advisory and consultative committees and user groups*, London, ONS, 1994.

15

Grey literature, standards and patents

C. Peter Auger

DEFINITIONS

Reference material relating to grey literature (especially reports, theses, conference papers and symposia proceedings), to standards and to patents places an extra degree of responsibility on the librarian. The reason for this is that when readers with queries about these materials have been correctly introduced to the appropriate sources, they are nevertheless frequently unable or unwilling to pursue their enquiries with quite the same facility they show when directed to more conventional and certainly more familiar works such as dictionaries, directories or encyclopedias. Difficulties for readers arise partly because in these areas publications are genuinely not easy to use, and partly because they are unfamiliar. In addition, the reference material embodies to a greater or lesser degree information and documents which may be subject to various obstacles, restrictions and constraints not encountered elsewhere, such as the frequent use of amendments and updates (standards specifications), the requirement to demonstrate a 'need to know' (research reports), the non-availability of listed publications (conference papers withdrawn before presentation), authors' rights to be consulted (theses), and publications in the form of legal documents (patents). Yet such sources, especially in the fields of science and technology, often provide information not obtainable elsewhere, sometimes because it is too detailed or specialized to warrant the expense and delay of formal editing and assessment. Thus the librarian is more likely to be asked for extra guidance and in consequence needs to have a good understanding of the material in question.

Many libraries, even when they have a definite acquisition policy towards such materials, have tended to shy away from the task of cataloguing, indexing and arranging them and have instead established special collections arranged on some broad fundamental characteristic, with a heavy emphasis and reliance on externally produced indexes and guides. In some areas bibliographic control is indifferent or inconsistent; documents may as a result appear under more than one identity. Added to this are the problems of considerable variety in physical format, which prevents collections from being shelved alongside other printed material because, for example, they are issued as pamphlets (conference papers), microfiche (research reports), typescripts (theses), or as flimsies with a limited life (draft standards).

Despite this heterogeneity, however, such publications justify their juxtaposition in the present chapter by virtue of one important common feature: they are all amenable to treatment as series, wherein each individual item has its own unique and sometimes widely recognized identifier, most often in the form of an alphanumeric code.

In recent years attempts have been made to place as much as possible of the material under consideration under the broad heading 'grey literature', which is usually defined as material which is difficult to acquire and not normally available through the book trade. The tangible outcome of these attempts at coordination has been the database SIGLE, which was set up following a conference in York in 1978, and became operational in 1981: SIGLE (System for Information on Grey Literature in Europe). Den Haag, The Netherlands: EAGLE (European Association for Great Literature Exploitation).

SIGLE contains over 290,000 records from research teams focusing on the pure and applied sciences, technology, economics, social sciences and the humanities. The database represents a comprehensive source for information which may never become available through commercial channels. SIGLE is available online through BLAISE, STN International and SUNIST; the database can also be obtained as a CD-ROM from SilverPlatter. SIGLE is regularly supplied with brief bibliographical entries of appropriate items contributed by various national centres in Europe. In the United Kingdom this responsibility falls to the British Library Document Supply Centre, which has an announcement journal devoted solely to grey literature (see below).

The concept of grey literature is a useful one which is gradually gaining acceptance (and indeed now features as an entry in many everyday desk dictionaries such as *Chambers dictionary*), but most authorities exclude standards and patents which, for the reasons noted above, feature in this chapter. There is also an increasing tendency to count as part of the grey literature certain categories of central and local government publications, which are discussed elsewhere in this book.

REPORTS

The term 'report' in its everyday sense is well understood as indicating an account given, or an opinion formally expressed, after an investigation or an appraisal. However, when reports are looked at collectively as a form of literature, the question of definition becomes a little more difficult. In the context of reference material, reports may be regarded as accounts from government establishments, scientific institutions and industrial laboratories about work performed and results achieved, rendered to their client and sponsors. This is certainly the case with reports in the fields of science and technology, where they are frequently known as research and development (R&D) reports. In recent years the format has increasingly spread to other areas, especially education and economics.

Reports often contain extensive descriptions of experiments, investigations, studies and evaluations, fully supported by figures, graphs and tables, and more recently by computer printouts. Normally reports do not remain silent about unsuccessful projects, and since they are written during or immediately after the activities they describe, they contain results and data on the very latest stages of research in a particular area. They are therefore of great importance as a communication medium in those regions of science and technology where changes are being made at a very rapid rate, as for example electronics and aerospace. It is no coincidence that such fast-moving subject areas are also of great importance to governments, for reasons of defence and military strength. Consequently many reports start life as documents issued by the agencies of the armed services, or by government departments. Indeed, the origins of many series of reports, still being issued today, can be traced back to the massive research programmes conducted during World War II. Much of the world's report literature originates in the United States and, owing to the fact that the greater part of this literature is issued on the authority of various government establishments and agencies, i.e. with the support of public funds, as many as possible of the resulting reports are sooner or later made available to the public, always subject to the overriding factor of national security. When a report is considered unsuitable for public release it is usually described as being 'classified', and as a result not available to readers who are unable to demonstrate a 'need to know'.

Even when entirely free from security and distribution restrictions, reports are still regarded by journal editors and commercial publishers alike as unpublished documents which have not been subjected to the rigours of refereeing or editorial control. Consequently, reports have tended to be ignored in the majority of conventional abstracting services and national bibliographies. Instead, it has for a good many years been the custom to publish details of newly issued reports in specialized announcement journals, the presentation and content of which are quite different from those of other current awareness services.

Reports constitute the largest category of documents within grey literature, and a major announcement medium covering a very wide range of disciplines, and embracing foreign as well as United States documents, is:

GOVERNMENT REPORTS ANNOUNCEMENTS AND INDEX (GRA&I). Springfield, Virginia: US Department of Commerce, National Technical Information Service (NTIS). 26 issues per annum.

GRA&I is a highly structured abstracting publication, the format of which has been designed with librarians and technical information specialists in mind. NTIS is the central source for the public sale of US government-sponsored research, development and engineering reports, and for sales of foreign technical reports and other analyses prepared by national and local government agencies and their contractors or grantees.

Each entry in *GRA&I* usually records a document's accession number, corporate author, title, personal author, date, pagination, contract number, report number, availability and cost. Also included is an abstract, supplemented by a note of the indexing terms applied. Abstracts are arranged by the NTIS subject classification scheme, which uses some 40 broad subject categories which are further separated into over 350 subcategories.

In addition to the twice-monthly issues of *GRA&I*, NTIS uses other means to announce the availability of new publications, notably a series of newsletters:

NTIS ALERTS (formerly called ABSTRACT NEWSLETTERS). Springfield, Virginia: US Department of Commerce, NTIS.

NTIS alerts are intended to focus on 190 highly specialized subjects, ranging from agribusiness to physics, from engineering to manufacturing, and from the environment to health and urban planning.

Online access to the NTIS *Bibliographical database* is available through a number of hosts, and information available covers the period from 1964 to the present. Data are also available in CD-ROM format from 1980 to the present.

Whereas *GRA&I* and its associated services are extremely wide in their subject coverage, there are also several announcement journals that concentrate on a narrower, albeit still broad, area of activity. Inevitably there is a fair degree of overlap between *GRA&I* and the more specialized announcement services. First there is:

SCIENTIFIC AND TECHNICAL AEROSPACE REPORTS (STAR). Washington, DC: US Government Printing Office. Twice monthly.

Publications abstracted in *STAR* cover a large section of grey literature documents and include reports issued by the National Aeronautics and Space Administration (NASA) and its contractors, other US government agencies, corporations, universities and research organizations throughout the world. Pertinent theses, translations, NASA-owned patents and patent applications are also abstracted. The value of *STAR* lies in its thoroughness of coverage and its subject scope, which includes all aspects of aeronautics and space research, supporting basic and applied research, and applications. Aerospace aspects of earth resources, energy conservation, oceanography, environmental protection, urban transportation and other topics of high national priority also receive attention. NASA information is available online through the NASA Scientific and Technical Information (STI) Program, which has established a partnership with the European Space Agency (ESA).

Secondly, the increasingly important energy field is covered by:

ENERGY RESEARCH ABSTRACTS (ERA). Washington, DC: US Government Printing Office. 24 issues per annum.

ERA began publication in 1977 and is compiled by the Office of Scientific and Technical Information of the US Department of Energy

(DoE). *ERA* may be regarded as the successor to *Nuclear science abstracts (NSA)*, an announcement journal published between 1948 and 1976 and still regarded as a reference work of the highest value. *ERA* continues to devote a large amount of its coverage to nuclear energy, but nowadays its contents reflect DoE's broader charter for energy systems, conservation, safety, environmental protection, physics research, biology and medicine. For reports in the field of nuclear energy proper, there is still:

INIS ATOMINDEX. Vienna: International Atomic Energy Agency. 26 issues per annum.

INIS atomindex is prepared as part of the Agency's International Nuclear Information System (INIS) and its purpose is to construct a database identifying publications relating to nuclear science and its peaceful applications. INIS uses the term 'non-conventional literature' rather than grey literature, and defines it as 'all literature other than journal articles or commercially produced books'. INIS information is available online as the *INIS database*, which dates from 1976. A CD-ROM version is also available.

Away from the realms of science and technology, a noteworthy reports announcements service is:

RESOURCES IN EDUCATION (RIE). Washington, DC: US Government Printing Office. 12 issues per annum.

RIE, once known as *Research in education*, is sponsored by the Educational Resources Information Center (ERIC), part of the US Department of Education. ERIC is a nationwide information network for acquiring, selecting, abstracting, indexing, storing, retrieving and disseminating reports on all aspects of education. It consists of a coordinating staff in Washington and 16 clearing-houses at universities or professional bodies across the country. ERIC acts as both a document provision agency and a bibliographic service, with a heavy emphasis on reports and projects. *RIE* calls its abstracts résumés and highlights publications of special significance to educators. All résumés are numbered sequentially by accession number, beginning with the prefix ED for ERIC Document. *RIE* is available online from 1966 to date, along with *Current index to journals in education (CIJE)*; both publications can also be obtained in CD-ROM format.

Research workers in the United Kingdom tend to rely heavily on the

United States announcement journals, but can, when the occasion demands, turn to a key source of information about British reports and other documents available to all without restriction, namely:

BRITISH REPORTS TRANSLATIONS AND THESES (BRTT). Boston Spa: British Library Document Supply Centre (BLDSC). 12 issues per annum.

BRTT has developed from its predecessor *BLL announcement bulletin* to become a comprehensive bibliography of material falling within the category of grey literature, which is defined as semi-published documents such as reports, theses and translations – in fact, items which can be difficult to identify and locate. *BRTT*'s aim is to help increase the awareness of such material and so promote its wider use, and it does this by listing British reports literature and translations produced by United Kingdom government organizations, local government bodies, universities and learned institutions, all of which are available from BLDSC. *BRTT* also lists most doctoral theses accepted at British universities, plus selected British official publications of a report nature which are not available through HMSO.

The BLDSC is a major contributor to SIGLE (noted above) and all the material listed in *BRTT*, except translations, appears in the SIGLE database. BLDSC also publishes:

JOURNALS IN TRANSLATION. Boston Spa: BLDSC. Irregular.

Journals in translation lists those journals which are translated cover-to-cover or selectively, together with journals which consist of translations of articles collected from multiple sources. The publication also includes the multisource translation serials issued by various government sources in the United States. Translations of individual articles are reported to the International Translations Centre, Delft, which provides access to its records through *World translations index*, issued both as a database and as a printed periodical.

Although reports can be catalogued in the same way as published literature, using personal authors and corporate authors for the main entries, they are normally identified and filed by report numbers of one sort or another. Considerable efforts have been devoted by librarians to imparting some measure of bibliographical control to reports literature, and in some areas well-known report number series present few difficulties to regular users. A good example is the series of AD reports issued by the US Department of Defense. The initials AD derive from Astia Document, and Astia itself stood for the Armed Services Technical Information Agency, a body formed in 1951. There are several reference guides to report numbering schemes, among which is:

Aaronson, E. J. REPORT SERIES CODES DICTIONARY. 3rd edn. Detroit: Gale Research, 1986.

The *Dictionary*, which updates the compilation originally produced by members of the Special Libraries Association in New York, provides details of over 20,000 report series codes used by nearly 10,000 corporate authors.

Another important source is:

ALPHANUMERIC REPORTS PUBLICATIONS INDEX (ARPI). 3rd edn. Boston Spa: BLDSC, 1996. Issued every two years.

ARPI allows access by the report code to the British Library's collection at Boston Spa of over four million reports held in 11,600 different series. In March 1995, to mark its standing as a corporate and national resource, this collection was named the National Reports Collection.

THESES

A thesis may be regarded as a statement of investigation or research, presenting the author's findings and any conclusions in support of his or her candidature for a higher degree, professional qualification or other award. On the basis of this definition it becomes apparent that a thesis has several features in common with a report of the kind noted above: both present details of investigations and research, both offer findings and conclusions, both are submitted to an overseeing body (the university or college in the case of a thesis, the sponsoring agency in the case of a report), and both are unpublished documents. The thesis often describes investigations of an advanced nature, reflecting the writer's attempt to extend the limits of knowledge in his or her chosen subject. As such, a thesis can be an important document for other research workers, since it will contain results not available elsewhere, even though such results must be regarded primarily as intended to show a candidate's grasp of a given subject and the research methodology involved. Many theses eventually appear in an amended form as journal articles or monographs, and are frequently cited as individual items in the literature.

Since 1950 the standard reference work on information about current British theses has been:

INDEX TO THESES WITH ABSTRACTS ACCEPTED FOR HIGHER DEGREES BY THE UNIVERSITIES OF GREAT BRITAIN AND IRELAND. London: Aslib. 4 issues per annum.

The *Index* covers approximately 10,000 theses each year, and since 1953 has been produced by Aslib with the active collaboration of the academic bodies concerned. From Volume 35 onwards Aslib undertook an expanded and improved version of the *Index* to include the full text of abstracts and a greatly enhanced subject index. A CD-ROM version incorporates details of British theses going back to 1716, a date which coincides with another important reference source:

Bilboul, R. RETROSPECTIVE INDEX TO THESES OF GREAT BRITAIN AND IRELAND 1716–1950. Santa Barbara, California: Clio Press, 1976.

The printed version of Bilboul is a comprehensive, five-volume work. In the United States, where the preferred term is dissertation rather than thesis, the principal source of reference is:

DISSERTATION ABSTRACTS INTERNATIONAL (DAI). Ann Arbor, Michigan: University Microfilms International. Monthly or quarterly.

DAI began publication in 1938 as *Microfilm abstracts*, became *Dissertation abstracts* in 1952, and assumed its present title in 1969. In 1966 the publication was split into two sections, Section A (*The humanities and social sciences*, monthly) and Section B (*The sciences and engineering*, monthly). In 1976 a third section, Section C (*Europe*, quarterly) was started and initially it represented European institutions only, but in 1989 the title was changed to Section C (*Worldwide*) to cover institutions in all parts of the globe.

Each entry in *DAI* comprises the following information: title of the dissertation, author's name, year, awarding institution, and the order number allocated by the publishers of *DAI*. This number acts as a unique identifier in a manner similar to that of a research report accession number. A strong feature of *DAI* is the comprehensiveness of the abstracts, each of which is usually half a page in length. *DAI* is available online and also in CD-ROM format.

An aid to the retrospective searching of dissertation material is to be found in:

COMPREHENSIVE DISSERTATION INDEX (CDI). Ann Arbor, Michigan: University Microfilms International.

CDI is made up of 37 volumes covering the years 1861–1972, and lists more than 417,000 dissertations accepted by institutions in North America. The *CDI ten-year cumulation 1973–1982* cites over 350,000 dissertations; the *CDI five-year cumulation (1983–1987)* brings together in 22 volumes over 175,000 dissertations; and annual supplements complete the picture. In the United Kingdom it has long been the practice for candidates to submit their work in typescript form, with just a handful of bound copies being prepared. On the continent, however, it has long been a common convention to have theses issued as printed documents, sometimes with as many as 200 copies of a title. This procedure enhances availability and greatly simplifies the establishment of library collections on an exchange basis. Each European country keeps its own national record of theses, as for example:

GESAMTVERZEICHNIS DEUTSCHSPRACHIGER HOCHSCHUL-SCHRIFTEN (GVH), 1966–1980. Munich: K. G. Saur.

GVH was published in 24 volumes during the years 1982–7, and is complemented by an index and further supplementary volumes. The main section of *GVH* covers dissertations, postdoctoral theses and university publications from the principal German-speaking nations, namely Germany, Austria and Switzerland.

CONFERENCES AND SYMPOSIA

Papers in a preliminary form made available prior to or actually at meetings and conferences, where they are presented by their authors in person, are commonly termed preprints or meetings papers. The practice of preparing such papers is especially common in the United States, and many large American technical societies issue preprints, often in large quantities, in advance of their meetings. Each paper is identified by a serial code not unlike a research report number. After the meeting or conference has taken place the papers are often reviewed for content, and all or a certain proportion are selected for inclusion in a society's permanent records, or in a conference organization's official transactions. The items ot selected for such archival treatment are simply listed, sometimes bstracted by announcement journals, quite often cited in bibliographies, nd of course requested by readers. A peculiar feature of meetings papers s that not all the titles promised to a conference organizer (and so ssigned preprint numbers in advance) are actually submitted in written orm; some may be presented orally, some may never be presented at all. Nevertheless, because they have been announced and numbered they end to be quoted in lists and bibliographies as though they really were btainable.

The physical forms which conference literature can take include the preprint noted above; the bound conference volume, available either during or shortly after the event; a conference record as part of or as a supplement to an established journal; and a conference record which features extended abstracts only.

Generally the library will want to have access to two main types of information about conferences and meetings: first, what events are due to take place? and secondly, what form will the official record take? On the first count it is possible to consult various sources, such as:

FORTHCOMING INTERNATIONAL SCIENTIFIC AND TECHNICAL CONFERENCES. London: Aslib. 4 times per annum.

However, given the transitory nature of the information concerned it s probably more effective to ignore printed sources, at least when conducting a comprehensive search, and instead rely on online databases. Two such useful sources are:

MEETINGS AGENDA. Gif-sur-Yvette: Service de Documentation, Commissariat a l'Energie Atomique.

Meetings agenda is available through Questel and contains announcements of congresses, conferences, meetings, workshops, exhibitions and fairs due to take place around the world.

FAIRBASE. Hanover: Fairbase Database Limited.

Fairbase is accessible through a number of hosts and provides details of fairs, exhibitions and meetings due to take place in over 100 countries.

Once meetings and conferences have taken place the problem becomes one of identifying the permanent form in which the proceedings are subsequently published. In the United Kingdom the National Lending

Library (as it then was) began in 1965 to publish the *Index of conference proceedings received by the NLL*. Today the British Library Document Supply Centre compiles and issues:

INDEX OF CONFERENCE PROCEEDINGS. Boston Spa: BLDSC, monthly.

This lists 16,000 new conferences annually. A cumulation covering the period 1964–88 is available on microfiche. The *Index* also appears in a CD-ROM version called *Inside conferences*, and forms a database with details of 500,000 papers each year.

In the United States a number of publications offer information on conferences and meetings, including:

CONFERENCE PAPER INDEX. Bethesda, Maryland: Cambridge Scientific Abstracts. 7 issues per annum.

This *Index* covers the life sciences, the physical sciences and engineering on a worldwide basis, and cites around 50,000 conference papers annually. There is also:

INDEX TO SCIENTIFIC AND TECHNICAL PROCEEDINGS (ISTP) Philadelphia, Pennsylvania: Institute for Scientific Information (ISI). 12 issues per annum.

The compilers of this publication estimate that about 10,000 scientific meetings take place each year, and that three-quarters of them (conferences, seminars, symposia, coloquia, conventions and workshops) result in a published record. ISTP indexes published proceedings from around the world and from a range of scientific disciplines.

STANDARDS

Standards are officially approved specifications applicable in various sectors of trade and industry, and cover such topics as methods of testing, terminology, performance and construction requirements, and codes of practice. Usually they are prepared by agreement and cooperation between interested parties, and are subsequently used to simplify and rationalize production and distribution, to ensure uniformity, reliability and safety, and to eliminate wasteful variety. Standards can also be considered as constraints which may hinder the development of new and improved ideas, and so act as a brake on scientific and technical progress

On balance, however, standards must be regarded as vital to the success of any advanced industrial society, and the various collections of standards available at national and international level are ample evidence of the vital contribution they make to the manufacturing and commercial aspects of everyday life.

The average standard specification is not a lengthy document – usually a pamphlet of a few pages, typically with details of methods, measurements, definitions, properties and processes. A standard invariably has an identifying alphanumeric code, which in many cases can acquire international recognition and significance. Many different bodies – national and international standards organizations, trade associations, technical societies, and government departments – issue standards. In the United Kingdom the official body with responsibility for preparing and issuing standards, and for encouraging their use, is the British Standards Institution (BSI). The key to BSI activities lies in:

BSI STANDARDS CATALOGUE (Previously known as the *British Standards yearbook*). London: BSI, annually.

The *Catalogue* lists over 13,000 BSI publications and each year more than 1200 new or revised standards are issued. Standards are drawn up by all those who have a particular interest in a subject: manufacturers, users, research organizations, government departments and consumer bodies. All are available for public comment before they are published in their final form. In order to keep interested parties up to date, BSI issues:

BSI STANDARDS CATALOGUE SUPPLEMENT. London: BSI, monthly.

Most other industrialized countries have their own national standards organizations, and their publications are widely quoted in the literature. In Germany the Deutsches Institut für Normung (DIN) issues:

DIN KATALOG FÜR TECHNISCHE REGELN. Berlin: Beuth Verlag, annually.

The *Katalog* contains the bibliographical data for all DIN standards and draft standards, as well as data for more than 200 other collections of technical rules. In all, it provides references to more than 100,000 German, foreign and technical rules. Supplements are issued regularly throughout the year.

France too is active in standardization, and the official body responsible for issuing standards is Association Française de Normalisation (AFNOR), which produces:

AFNOR CATALOGUE DES NORMES FRANÇAISES. Paris: AFNOR, annually.

AFNOR administers some 19,000 national and international standards currently in force.

In the United States there are very many bodies active in the preparation of standards, and although there is a central organization, the American National Standards Institute (ANSI), its main function is to coordinate and approve the publication of standards developed by qualified technical and professional societies, trade associations and other groups, which voluntarily submit their specifications to ANSI for approval. Details are to be found in:

CATALOG OF AMERICAN NATIONAL STANDARDS. New York: ANSI, annually.

The *Catalog* is supplemented by the monthly *ANSI reporter*.

The United States Department of Commerce, through the National Institute of Standards and Technology (NIST), formerly the National Bureau of Standards (NBS), publishes the compilation:

STANDARDS ACTIVITIES OF ORGANIZATIONS IN THE UNITED STATES (Special Publication no 681). Washington, DC: US Government Printing Office. Revised periodically.

Although the advantages of national standardization programmes are considerable, the ultimate benefits are derived when standards are issued on a regional or an international basis. In the case of the European Union, a comprehensive guide is:

COMMON STANDARDS FOR ENTERPRISES. Luxembourg: EU, 1994.

The publication gives a complete listing of the technical harmonization laws and specifications affecting conformity assessment procedures. At the international level two major bodies are active, the International Organization for Standardization (ISO – from the Greek word *isos,* meaning equal) and the International Electrotechnical Commission (IEC). A list of all ISO standards is given in:

ISO CATALOGUE. Geneva: ISO, annually.

Technical information on standards is coordinated through ISONET, an organization of 63 national standards information centres providing rapid access to half a million standards.

The work of the IEC concerns matters relating specifically to the development of standardization in the electrical and electronic engineering fields; all other subject areas fall within the remit of ISO. The publications which are available from IEC are listed in:

IEC CATALOGUE. Geneva: IEC. Annually.

IEC also prepares the *IEC bulletin* and the *Technical guide* series.

PATENTS

A patent is an official document setting out in considerable detail an inventor's solution to a particular problem; the patent document embodies a grant to the inventor of the sole right for a specific period of years (usually 20) to make, use or sell the invention disclosed. All such inventions must meet certain criteria of novelty and must be capable of industrial application. Normally the librarian is not concerned with the drafting, filing, exploitation and contesting of patents, since these tasks are the province of the inventor himself, the organization for which he works, the patent agent and the official examiner. Nevertheless librarians are frequently the recipients of questions on many aspects of patents, and in the United Kingdom a Patent Information Network has been established to facilitate the inspection of published patent specifications and other patent publications. The Network consists of a mixture of national, public and university libraries in Aberdeen, Belfast, Birmingham, Bristol, Coventry, Glasgow, Leeds, Liverpool, London, Manchester, Newcastle, Plymouth, Portsmouth and Sheffield.

Patent specifications often reveal technical information at a much earlier date than other literature, and frequently they review and examine the prior art which led up to a particular invention. When taken collectively patents can be indicative of trends in a specific subject area, and so cannot be ignored when conducting a literature search on any scale.

All major industrial countries have a national patents system, because it has long been recognized that the protection obtained in return for the disclosure of ideas acts as a stimulus to the inventive spirit, and so benefits technical progress in a most positive manner. The value of patents as a source of information, particularly in libraries, has been discussed by:

Eisenschitz, T. S. PATENTS, TRADE MARKS AND DESIGNS IN INFOR-MATION WORK. London: Croom Helm, 1987.

Countries which are signatories to the 1883 Paris Convention for the Protection of Industrial Property are obliged to publish what is termed 'an information journal' providing details of granted patents and registered trade marks. In Great Britain the publications in question are the *Official journal (patents)* and the *Official journal (trade marks)*; in the United States the title is the *Official gazette of the United States patent and trademark office*; and in Germany it is *Patentblatt*. A great deal of information on the contents of patent documents can be obtained from specialist abstracting and indexing organizations, as for example:

WORLD PATENT ABSTRACTS (WPA). London: Derwent Information Limited.

WPA constitutes a series of weekly publications devoted to single countries and for a given country, where the output is large, the title is divided into a number of editions based on subject categories. The abstracts in WPA are also used to create the online databasefile *World patents index (WPI)*.

It is customary for companies and organizations which employ people to invent to file patent applications in leading industrial countries throughout the world, each of which (as has been noted) has its own patents system. In the course of time an application for a patent made in Great Britain can also result in granted patents in countries such as the United States, Germany and Japan. Equally many overseas countries file applications with the British Patent Office in Newport, Gwent, and more and more with the European Patent Office in Munich. Thus there is a strong international aspect to patents, one manifestation of which is the system of International Classification Marks, the principles of which are given in:

INTERNATIONAL PATENT CLASSIFICATION (IPC) and its companion volume OFFICIAL CATCHWORD INDEX. Geneva: World Intellectual Property Organization (WIPO). Updated regularly.

The *IPC* has become an internationally recognized classification sysem which is controlled by WIPO and assigned to patent documents by ndividual patent offices. The *Catchword index* is intended to indicate the part or parts of the *IPC* in which matter relating to any given subject is ikely to be found, with explanations where confusion might arise as for nstance Lighters (barges) and Lighters (devices for igniting).

Details of the activities of the European Patent Office (EPO) can be ound in:

OFFICIAL JOURNAL OF THE EUROPEAN PATENT OFFICE. Munich, EPO. Monthly.

The first issue of the *Journal* appeared in 1977, and the publication is mainly devoted to the announcement of decisions of the Board of Appeal of the EPO. Details of published applications, arranged according to the *PC* schedules are disclosed in:

EUROPEAN PATENT BULLETIN. Munich: EPO. Weekly.

Finally, WIPO itself publishes an announcement journal, namely:

PCI GAZETTE: GAZETTE OF INTERNATIONAL PATENT APPLICA-TIONS. Geneva: WIPO. Two issues per month.

The *Gazette* is an official publication under the Patent Cooperation Treaty (PCI), and the bulk of the contents is devoted to abstracts of PCI applications, presented in a compact format allowing two applications per page.

CONCLUSION

All the categories of reference material described above demand a considerable amount of study and application if the user is to make full and effective use of the resources which the categories have to offer individually and collectively. Research reports call for an understanding of the world of research and development establishments and laboratories; theses and dissertations require an insight into the procedures for the award of higher degrees; conference proceedings and meetings papers necessitate an appreciation of the eagerness of scientists, engineers and other workers to enhance their public reputations; standard specifications depend on a grasp of the diversity of standards issuing bodies; and with patents some knowledge of the concepts of intellectual property is essential.

The observations made and the examples quoted are but small indications of the scope and nature of what in part is grey literature and in part well-established highly specialized forms of reference material.

SUGGESTIONS FOR FURTHER READING

Auger, C. P., *Information sources in grey literature*, 3rd edn, London, Bowker Saur, 1994.

Auger, C. P. (ed.), *Information sources in patents*, London, Bowker-Saur, 1992.

Mildren, K. (ed.), *Information sources in engineering*, 3rd edn, London, Bowker-Saur, 1996.

Wherry, T. L., *Patent searching for librarians and inventors*, Chicago, American Library Association, 1995.

16
Audiovisual materials

Anthony Hugh Thompson

ARRIVING AT DEFINITIONS

Everything we learn in our lives is conducted to our brains through our five senses, whether we are print-literate or print-illiterate. According to the Industrial Audiovisual Association in the United States, the learning process involves these senses in the following proportions: taste 1%; touch 1.5%; smell 3.5%; hearing 11%; and sight 83%.[1] When we increase our knowledge by using recorded learning materials, whether they be print, magnetic recordings on tape or disc, images on film or whatever, we use two of our senses, sight and hearing, to absorb the information. Print is a collection of encoded images or symbols, the meanings of which has to be taught, but it is absorbed through sight. There have been attempts to use the other senses – 'smelly' books, tactile objects, films with associated smells and even movement of the viewer's seat or environment – but these are either 'gimmicks' or unsuitable for recording for mass use. Thus, currently available learning materials use sounds and images, either separately or together. For example, print or photographs are visual, a recording of music is audio, and video is both.

A generic term for these diverse learning materials is 'audiovisual'. Thus all forms of recorded information are audiovisual in that they are audio, visual or both. The main types are books, journal, newspapers, maps, charts and posters; slides, cinefilm, microforms, overhead transparencies; audio, video and computer tapes, cassettes, discs and other digital formats, and real objects. Essentially, all the records of man's achievement are audiovisual materials.

Reinforcement for this generic term comes from outside the profession. Tom Hope, an American statistician, stated that 'audiovisual' embraces all technologies, whether past, present or yet to be dreamed. AV is a concept of prepared programme communications. It is not just one medium. When and if scientists perfect a recording system that stores information in a one inch steel cube, it too will become an AV medium. Any process that accomplishes a unique communications function at an affordable cost can become an AV tool.[2]

Evidence that our profession uses the term 'audiovisual' in this way is easy to find. The periodical *Audiovisual librarian: multimedia information*, for example, has from its beginning 22 years ago, dealt with all information formats available at the time, including books. Many libraries have 'audiovisual librarians' who look after all formats except books, but even they cannot manage without print in their collections in some form.

Using the generic term 'audiovisual' gives all forms of recorded information equality and overcomes negative barriers created by format.[3] 'Audiovisual' is a term for now *and* the future, as recorded information for the foreseeable future is going to continue to consist of sounds and images. With the continuing development of digital recording techniques, all new formats to come will be capable of recording data to recreate both sounds and images on the same medium (though they may not all do so). And we will continue to 'read' these sounds and images.[4]

The history of audiovisual materials has been bedevilled by terminology and the 'bandwagon syndrome'. Librarians have often called audiovisual materials 'non-book materials', or 'non-print'. Apart from being negative and divisive, neither description is accurate today. Is an audiocassette recording of Dylan Thomas reading his own book still a book? Are the *Editions and adaptations of Shakespeare* on CD-ROM no longer print? Does it matter? Such descriptions are unhelpful to the development of a forward-looking profession. Those that still use them show that they have failed to realize that our work is concerned primarily with information and not the format in which it is packaged.[5]

The 'bandwagon syndrome' is also unhelpful. Audiovisuals got 'left behind' by the seemingly more exciting computer technology. Some outside librarianship, and to a lesser degree some within it, have now decided that 'audiovisual' is 'old hat' and that 'multimedia' is the current jargon phrase. But there is no conflict between 'audiovisual' and 'multimedia'. 'Multimedia' describes a situation where information is presented in a variety of audiovisual formats, each contributing its own unique learning experience. However, publishers and computer professionals are using 'multimedia' in a narrower sense to describe a single information carrier – a videodisc or a CD-ROM – which contains information such as sound, text, pictures and computer programs that would previously have required several audiovisual formats. 'Multimedia' is also used to describe the computer on which these formats are used. There is no more need to change the word 'audiovisual' to 'multimedia' than there is to upgrade the word 'library'.

Following on from the broad definition of 'multimedia', a 'multimedia library' is one that has developed to provide appropriate audiovisual materials in an integrated approach to the communication of information. At present, true multimedia libraries are very few. A large collection of books and a few separate collections of the other audiovisual materials, often in separate departments and managed by separate staff, does not constitute a multimedia library.

There are other forms of audiovisuals, but unless an effort to record them is made they remain transient. Television, the various forms of teletext, images on a computer screen and cinema are all transient images to the information professional. Increasingly some of them are becoming available in recorded form, but particularly in the case of cinema the copies may not be exactly the same as the original. There have also been other audiovisual formats that have outlived their usefulness, including filmstrip, film-loop, 8 and 9.5 mm cinefilm and 78 and 33 1/3 rpm audio recordings.

THE BOOK IS DEAD?

'The book is dead' is a phrase being bandied around by multimedia producers, and the writer uses it in lectures to encourage library school students and professionals into thinking about the future of the services they provide. But is the book dead? After a long period of technological development, its situation is analogous to that of the steam railway locomotive in the UK in the 1950s. After more than a century of supremacy the steam locomotive was joined by diesel, and then electric locomotives. Its fate was sealed and it was surprisingly quickly replaced by these new and more efficient forms of motive power. Yet 40 years later there are still steam railways operating in the hands of enthusiastic 'believers', and the steam engine still has many followers. After 500 years of supremacy the book, which is limited to communicating print and still pictures, is now being joined by rapidly developing formats such as CD-ROM which can communicate far more to the user. The combination of laser disc technology and digital recording techniques enables us to store together on one disc any form of print, sound, pictures (both still and moving) and computer data. And having observed the speed with which audio and videocassettes, CDs and now CD-ROMs have become internationally used, who can any longer guarantee that the book – or many of the other audiovisual formats we have become used to – will not go the way of the steam engine? The book and print are two different things, however. Print has a major role for the foreseeable future; the book is simply a method of packaging that information.

This chapter, then, will concentrate on the more recent forms of audio-visual material which are available for use in information services.

THE VALUE OF AUDIOVISUAL MATERIALS

In the United Kingdom and elsewhere, our profession has not been wholehearted in its acceptance of the more recent audiovisual materials as resources. Sadly, this situation is also found in many developing countries with low levels of print literacy, but whose populations are becoming increasingly aurally and visually literate through exposure to television, radio and audiocassettes. There are outstanding exceptions to this situation around the world, but information services which have achieved undoubted success in multimedia development continue to go virtually unnoticed in the United Kingdom, although some of the best are just across the Channel in France.

The development of photography, cinematography and sound-recording took place during the latter half of the nineteenth century, whereas video recording is a comparative newcomer, having been developed after the Second World War. The digital revolution followed, leading to the development of the compact disc family, of which CD audio and CD-ROM are now firmly established. One day it will be generally recognized that the development of digital recording was of the same magnitude in the history of technology as was the invention of movable type. Surely it must be obvious even to the most committed bibliophile that the vast range of information recorded by these technologies has value as an information service resource? How will they cope when their favourite reference books appear only in CD-ROM format, offering users enhanced searching and learning facilities, as is already happening? It should also be apparent that a significant proportion of our users, and probably nearly all the people who could but choose not to use our services, now prefer to obtain their information from these resources and not from the printed word.

The Industrial Audiovisual Association also suggested that the book was the least effective means of communicating information. Their research showed that people remember only 10% of what they read, while remembering 50% of what they saw and heard.[6] Obviously, more research needs to be undertaken on this topic, but increasingly people's responses, especially those of younger people, would suggest that there is some validity to these statistics. Can we any longer deny the power of sound and vision to communicate information? Such media satisfy the needs of many who can see and hear, without their wanting to turn to printed or other resources to complement the information; others will investigate further, using other resources, including print. Is this not how it should be in a multimedia age?

Nor do the more recent audiovisual materials constitute a small and insignificant group of media related primarily to entertainment. By 1986, it was suggested that between 700,000 and 800,000 'non-book' items had been published over the preceding 20 years, compared to between 800,000 and 1 million monographs in the same period.[7] These cover a wide range of formats dealing with a similar range of subjects to those dealt with by books. A proportion of these 'non-book' items do relate to entertainment, but then so do a proportion of books published.

RECENT AUDIOVISUAL MATERIALS AS REFERENCE MATERIALS

Consider the momentous events of the past century – how much of your knowledge do you owe to print and how much to sounds and pictures? The horrors of the First and Second World Wars – trench warfare, concentration camps, sea and air battles; man's first landings and steps on the moon; the destruction of Challenger; the devastation caused by the recent San Francisco and Armenian earthquakes; the breaking-down of the Berlin Wall and the movement to democracy in eastern Europe; the recurrent famines in Ethiopia and other African countries; the Gulf War and the crisis in the former Yugoslavia; and our perceptions of the famous and infamous, the good and the evil, the sane and insane who have found a place in the history of the century? And where did your knowledge of other 'happenings' – perhaps less momentous but equally important and fascinating – come from? The lifestyles of a multitude of birds, animals and insects that you have never encountered in 'real' life; the extermination of elephants and rhinos and other animals for greed; art, paintings, music, sculpture, film, theatre, ballet, opera; the list is endless.

Virtually all people's perceptions of the world are created by the sounds they hear and the visual images they see. For nearly all of us, our understanding of the world we live in is increased by audio and visual images on the radio and cinema and television screen. For some of us, reading also enhances this understanding – but only approximately one-third of the population of the world is print-literate in the true sense of the word, and even here the degree of literacy and the desire to learn from print varies enormously.

Yet for the most part our profession internationally still gives the impression that it believes that the only primary sources of information are print-based. Many information services stock only these materials, and in many others print-based materials still form by far the largest proportion of the stock. Could the belief that the 'book is best' be actively hindering many peoples' access to the information that they require (but cannot read [or understand] for themselves)?

Not all print-based resources are primary source materials. For most people, the primary source material for a Shakespeare play would be a live performance. Shakespeare wrote plays to be seen, not books to be read. Failing the holding of a troupe of actors, a library should have the second-best, and that is now a video recording of the play, not the book of the play, which is at best third-best. The definitive version of a Dylan Thomas story is a sound recording of Dylan reading it. The primary source of Kennedy's Cuba speech is the film of that speech, not the printed version, and the same can be said of the words of Hitler and many, many others. These primary sources contain not only the words themselves, but much more information to help us understand better: the emotion, the accent, the histrionics, the actuality (or as close to it as we can get). Indeed, the moving images and sounds of most of the events covered in the last few paragraphs form the primary source material for a study of those subjects.

Yet how many libraries and information services, other than those dedicated to specific formats or specialist organizations, have adequate, let alone good collections of these records of man's achievement? And how many information services include the more recent audiovisual records in their reference collections? Our users must have access to primary source materials if they are to understand any subject properly; print-based resources alone cannot provide all the information and the experiences necessary. Indeed, our profession is failing in our stated duty if we fail to make such primary sources available.

Which sources would our users prefer? How much longer can we go on ignoring the needs and preferences of our actual and potential users, and our responsibilities to them? How much longer can we ignore the experience of those members of our profession who have become multimedia in their approach, and to whom relevance rather than format is the selection criterion? Nowadays, any organization that does not fulfil its responsibilities has a short future indeed.

BARRIERS TO MULTIMEDIA DEVELOPMENT

One of the barriers to developing a multimedia information collection, (where primary source material is held regardless of its format), is the lack of an infrastructure related to the acquisition and bibliographic control of the more recent audiovisual materials. In some countries, such as the United States, where the Library of Congress has taken responsibility for books and other audiovisual formats, an infrastructure for all audiovisual formats has been developed. In the United Kingdom, and many other countries where the national library has not yet taken full responsibility for all audiovisual materials, such an infrastructure has not had the opportunity to develop in anything other than a piecemeal and incomplete way.[8] Yet this will change – the introduction of audiovisual formats such as CD-ROM containing large collections of printed materials has caused national libraries to realize that they cannot obtain these materials under copyright or legal deposit without extending the law to include them.

Another barrier to developing a multimedia collection is that of developing technology. Whereas the book has had a long, distinguished lifetime as a container of information, the same cannot be said of some of the more recently developed audiovisual materials, which appear today and are gone tomorrow. This is true of all technology today: change happens much more quickly than it did in the past, and the information profession is no more immune than any other. Like them we have to learn to adapt, otherwise there will be greater gaps in our preservation of the records of man's achievement than at present.

Therefore, a brief examination of the more recent audiovisual formats, their value and their likely future is pertinent if we are to create balanced multimedia collections in appropriate formats. Only some of the audio-visual formats that currently exist are of value to library collections. Techniques for the storage and handling of these materials are not dealt with in this chapter, but can be found elsewhere.[9]

MICROFORMS

Space-saving microforms consist of two main types: 16 mm and 35 mm wide roll microfilm carries a reduced image of print, illustrations or com-puter-generated information. Microfiche consists of sheets of film 15 × 10 cm, each containing approximately 100 pages of information. Microforms should have a lifetime of 150 years or more, but they are eas-ily damaged in use.

The uses of microforms include the preservation of the information content of deteriorating paper-based formats such as manuscripts, books and newspapers; accessing information in rare or single-copy documents without handling the document itself; publishing periodicals with lim-ited circulations or replacing bound copies of back numbers; and for reg-ular updating of library catalogues and periodicals holdings.

Reasonable publication costs, easy in-house production and the ability of some computer peripherals to generate microforms cheaply, may extend the life of microforms for a while. They are, however, being replaced by recordable optical discs and CD-ROMs in many areas.

AUDIO RECORDINGS

Audio recordings encompass music, the spoken word, natural and man-made sounds, and in-house produced recordings such as oral histories and talking newspapers. Older analogue recording technology is being replaced by digital technology, giving higher-quality sound and no loss of quality when duplication or copying takes place.

At present only two audio formats are worth acquiring for library col-lections, although for a time many collections will have a dwindling col-lection of long-playing records in their stock. The CD is a development of the original optical analogue video disc, although on the CD the infor-mation is recorded digitally. Manufactured and handled properly, it does not deteriorate in use and has a considerable lifetime. As such it is an ideal library medium.

Less effective than the CD, the audiocassette is more susceptible to damage, although less so than the long-playing record. It still uses analogue recording technology, and has proved to be a popular format as most users internationally have playback equipment.

Open-reel audiotapes are normally only used and found in information services where in-house production is undertaken. Recorders use either analogue or digital technology. Open-reel tape is not suitable for library users.

The future of these formats is uncertain. CDs and audiocassettes can be expected to be available for the foreseeable future, although 1996 sees the introduction of CDs with double the present storage capacity, with the possibility of vastly increased capacities to come. There is a movement by industry to build equipment that will record and/or playback either audio or video, and to develop the CD family to include both audio and video material on the same disc. It is logical, and beneficial to users, that these two areas of audiovisual media should combine in the future.

OVERHEAD TRANSPARENCIES

The OHT is widely used in education and training as a teaching and learning aid. OHTs can be produced on plastic sheets by computer graphics/word-processing programs, or by freehand lettering. They are projected using an overhead projector. They can also be projected by a projection unit connected to a computer; however, this equipment still needs further development to be really effective. Paper copies of OHTs are perfectly acceptable as library holdings and originators should be persuaded to deposit paper rather than plastic copies. Overhead transparencies will continue to be used for some time, as there is no other format that is more efficient or economical for this task.

SLIDES

Many information services hold 35 mm photographic slide collections which are valuable in building up visual collections economically. As well as purchasing commercially published slides, it is not difficult for information professionals to create slides, provided copyright is not infringed. However, slides are fragile and need careful storage and handling. Because of the nature of colour film, slides have a comparatively limited lifetime, which may be from 10 to 20 years in normal use.

The future of the slide is limited – huge collections of visual images are now being published on optical video discs, PhotoCDs and CD-ROMs, some of which are being produced by libraries. Filmless cameras, which record still images on magnetic discs which can be viewed on a video screen, combined with the increasing costs of photographic film, may hasten the demise of slides for all but professional or dedicated photographers.

REAL OBJECTS

Real objects, such as stuffed birds and crocodiles, model railway engines, skeletons, bricks and building materials, and a wide range of other objects, are usually found only in school resource centres, or libraries of organizations specializing in specific areas, such as building or architecture. There is no 'national' bibliographic control of such materials.

CINE FILM

Cine films are now rarely acquired or held outside the libraries of broadcasting and film/video production services, because their high price makes purchase unrealistic. Much film material is now available on videocassette, which is an inexpensive and robust format for use in information services. Today, professional film and television production companies are gradually changing over to digital recording on videocassette, and increasingly disc.

VIDEO RECORDINGS

In addition to the large number of cinema productions on video, a rapidly increasing range of original video productions of value to information services is being published.

As with audio recording, the move has been towards the packaging of videotape into cassettes, and the VHS videocassette format is now the most commonly used format, internationally and in libraries. Constantly being improved, with equipment prices decreasing in real terms, this system is likely to be in use for the next ten years or more, because of its extensive international take-up. Virtually every published programme is available in this format, and the equipment also allows the information service to undertake its own in-house original and off-air recording, copyright permitting.

If an information service wishes to acquire analogue videocassette recordings produced only in the United Kingdom (or from other countries using the PAL system), the purchase of a PAL VHS videocassette

recorder or player is perfectly satisfactory. If the service purchases programmes from other countries which use the NTSC or SECAM systems,
then it must have a multistandard VHS recorder or player. Recent multistandard VCRs available in the UK convert their output to PAL, so the
purchase of an additional multistandard television receiver is no longer
necessary. Videocassette recording is beginning to be replaced by record-
able/erasable video disc systems.

COMPACT DISC FAMILY

This group of related formats (and any future digital formats developed
from them) are of immense value to information services and have the
potential to become the main media format used by them. The CD family began with the analogue and later the digital video disc. It is the only
format so far developed that has the recording abilities of all the other
audiovisual formats put together. The CD family has now developed to
comprise 30 cm, 20 cm and 12 cm discs (including CD audio, CD-ROM,
CD-V, CD-i, PhotoCD and the still developing recordable or record-
able/erasable discs).[10]

CD audio has virtually replaced the long-playing record, and over
10,000 CD-ROM titles had been published internationally by the end of
1994. The various CD formats are making vast databanks available to
information services which would previously have been impractical to
publish by conventional means. Some libraries, notably the Library of
Congress, the Bibliothèque Publique d'Informations and the
Mediathèque of the City of Science and Industry in Paris, are producing
their own video and compact discs, some of which will hopefully be available for purchase. Already a number of previously book-based reference
materials are now being published as CD-ROMs, including encyclopedias and dictionaries, trade directories, timetables and bibliographies.
Some of them are no longer being published in a paper format. Other reference materials will follow suit where and when necessary.

Using some of the CD formats requires the connection of the player to
a computer to enable the publication to be used interactively. Here the
computer contains a program which responds to the instructions and
answers of the user, and controls the way in which the contents of the
discs are accessed. It is in this convergence of compact disc and computer
technology that the most exciting developments in information provision
in the future will lie.

COMPUTER PROGRAMS

Having moved beyond housekeeping systems, it is now common for libraries to provide computers for users for word-processing or to experience a range of computer programs. Computer technology is bedevilled with problems of standardization and rapid developments in technology. It is logical for information services to use computer equipment either from the IBM PC-compatible or the Apple Macintosh range. Unfortunately, even within a range of compatible computers some lack of standardization is created by new developments, for example in improved chips or controlling programs such as Windows. This is a problem that information professionals with large collections of computer software must be aware of when selecting new equipment and software, as older programs may not run on new computers or vice versa. There is no effective 'bibliographic control' of computer software, which is issued either in the form of floppy disks or increasingly on CD-ROM.

THE INEVITABILITY OF CHANGE

Should these developments cause us to worry? Could not an encyclopedia published on CD-ROM give us far more valuable information than the traditional book-based encyclopedia? If we look up 'Mahler' in a book-based encyclopedia, we can only read about him and perhaps see a photograph. If we look up 'Mahler' in a CD-ROM encyclopedia we can not only read about him and see relevant photographs, but also hear examples of his music, see a historic sequence of film of him conducting a concert, and hear his voice. It can be updated much more regularly than the paper version, as well as taking up far less space. Controlled by the computer, it can be far quicker and easier to access the information than ever before, as well as being far more attractive to most of our younger [and older?] users.

Change will bring many advantages. Librarians who have converted from card catalogues to computerized catalogues with online terminals have survived, and have learned new professional skills in the process.

ARRANGEMENT OF MULTIMEDIA COLLECTIONS

Total separation of the more recent audiovisual materials from the book and earlier formats is both illogical and retrograde in the light of the success of subject arrangement. What we should *not* do is to treat the more recent audiovisuals as something different, creating separate departments to deal with them and placing them under the control of an 'audiovisual librarian' or its equivalent. Unfortunately, many libraries who do adopt this method of dealing with the more recent materials go one stage further and 'hide' the audiovisual department in the basement or some other inaccessible area, ensuring that few users will be aware of its existence and guaranteeing minimal usage of these materials.

Equally, the total integration of all audiovisual materials including books into one sequence, although it may solve some problems of user awareness in some smaller information services, is a practical impossibility in a large information service. Such services will already have had to create several sequences of book materials, for a variety of reasons, including economy of space, subject departmentalization etc. It would be unrealistic to think that one could take a step backwards when adding additional formats to the collection. The best solution is one of partial integration, shelving the various materials on the same subjects in separate sequences but as close to each other as possible, and always in the same area. The necessary playback equipment should be on open display in the same area, and preferably switched on and working during opening hours, as it advertises the presence of the new media. Videocassettes filed in the same sequence as books look like books; videocassettes, shelved separately but next to the books on the same subject look like videocassettes and as such self-advertise their presence in the collection. Staff should be responsible for the selection and use of *all* audiovisual formats in their subject area, thus ensuring that the user receives the best possible integrated multimedia service.

THE BIBLIOGRAPHY OF THE MORE RECENT AUDIOVISUAL MATERIALS

Despite the considerable numbers of the more recent audiovisual materials that have been published over the years, Antony Croghan[11] showed that disproportionally small numbers of these items have found their way into some information services. He rightly dismissed the old excuse for small or non-existent collections of the new media – 'you can't find out about the media!' with the response 'you can if you look hard enough!' He also stated that there is an urgent 'need for the central archival collection – the British Library – to take the provision of NBM much more seriously than it does'. There are now signs that it is doing so.

Logically, in a country with well organized national bibliographies for print materials it should not be any harder to search for the more recent audiovisual materials than it is for print. Yet this is often the case. Although the situation is improving, information professionals still have to conduct lengthy searches over a wide range of potential sources. The major cause of these problems is the lack of legal deposit and a central archive of all information materials. The implications of this situation for future generations of information professionals, users and researchers are appalling.

CURRENT AND RETROSPECTIVE BIBLIOGRAPHY

General bibliographies

The ideal for many information professionals would be one source to which they could refer for details of all audiovisual materials. In the United States, *CDMARC bibliographic* (seven CD-ROM discs updated quarterly) already contains 4.8 million USMARC records of printed, music and visual materials and computer files notified to the Library of Congress for copyright purposes.

Legal deposit in the United Kingdom does not yet extend beyond print-on-paper, with the result that a central source of bibliographic information about *all* audiovisual materials does not, and probably could not, exist. A major and developing problem for the British Library and the other legal deposit libraries is that they are not able to request on deposit many significant print-based items that are now being published in the newer formats, especially CD-ROM. There are ongoing discussions concerning the extension of legal deposit to all published audiovisual materials. If this can be enacted, as is logical, the *British national bibliography* could be extended to include all new publications regardless of format.

Despite this lack of legal deposit, the situation in the UK is slowly improving. The National Sound Archive, part of the British Library, now has an online catalogue. The British Library is now publishing the *British national film and video guide*, based on data supplied by the British Film Institute. This still leaves significant areas to be covered, including those publications in the rapidly developing compact disc formats. Although comprehensiveness of bibliographic control and collections cannot be achieved without the legal deposit of all audiovisual materials, these are steps in the right direction.

Please note that the bibliographies of audiovisual materials that follow do not normally include print-on-paper publications.

The British Library did experiment in 1979 with the publication of a separate catalogue of audiovisual materials of interest to education in the widest sense. It excluded most 16 mm film and videocassettes, as these were already covered by the *British national film catalogue*, and music, which was covered by commercial catalogues such as those published by the *Gramophone*. The tragedy is that, despite the success of the catalogue, the experiment was suspended in 1983. However, the work done was of considerable value and this catalogue is valuable as a retrospective bibliography.

BRITISH CATALOGUE OF AUDIOVISUAL MATERIALS. 1st edn. London: British Library, 1979. First supplement, 1980. Second supplement, 1983.

This began as an experimental catalogue based on the audiovisual materials processed by the British Library/Inner London Education Authority Learning Materials Recording Study. As well as being published in paper form, the catalogue and supplements can be accessed online via BLAISE-LINE as AVMARC.

AVMARC. British Library via BLAISE-LINE. (Information about BLAISE-LINE on Internet: http://portico.bl.uk/nbs/blaise/overview.html and on accessing BLAISE-LINE http://portico.bl.uk/nbs/blaise/access.html#access).

The AVMARC file includes records on all subjects and of all types of audiovisual materials (except music and films). In 1989 a further 16,000 records of new items received by the ILEA were added, and AVMARC now contains nearly 23,000 records.

The British Library is currently planning to open negotiations with the Library of Congress and the National Library of Canada on harmonizing their respective MARC formats. If negotiations are successful, this will inevitably result in an extension of provisions for handling audiovisual material.

AUDIOVISUAL MATERIALS FOR HIGHER EDUCATION. London: British Universities Film and Video Council, 1995– .

The CD-ROM version of the BUFVC's AVANCE database contains

details of 14,000 titles of film, video, multimedia and other AV formats suitable for higher education and research; 2000 records are added annually. The disc is updated every six months. It also contains the catalogue of books in the BUFVC Information Service Library. This continues and replaces the 1990 *BUFVC catalogue* published on paper and microfiche.

INTERNATIONAL DIRECTORY OF EDUCATIONAL AUDIOVISUALS [IDEA]. Caterham: Oxmill Publishing (Head Software International Ltd, Croudace House, 97 Godstone Road, Caterham, CR3 6RE), 1995– .

This CD-ROM, cumulated quarterly, contains details of over 400,000 audiovisuals (including British) indexed by NICEM (National Information Center for Educational Media) in New Mexico.

NATIONAL AUDIOVISUAL LIBRARY FILM AND VIDEO CATALOGUE. National Audiovisual Library (Freepost CS141A, Bangor, Gywnedd, Wales), 1994– .

Issued in looseleaf and updated every two years, this catalogue of educational audiovisual materials now contains more than 5000 items. Copies of the catalogue are available from the above address or enquiries can be made by telephone: 01248 370144.

Audio recordings

NATIONAL DISCOGRAPHY. London: Mechanical Copyright Protection Society Ltd.

Claimed to be the most comprehensive database of musical works and recordings in the world, this database is used by the MCPS for licensing sound recordings and by the British Library as its catalogue of recent releases for the National Sound Archive. It contains details of 2 million musical works, 1.2 million recordings, performer and copyright information, and can be searched in many ways. Currently a range of services are available online, or from the National Discography Information Service by telephone or fax (tel. 0181 677 9110 or fax 7251). It is planned that the *National discography* will be made available on CD-ROM.

THE GRAMOPHONE CLASSICAL CATALOGUE. London: Retail Entertainment Data Publishing Ltd. (Paulton House, 8 Shepherdess Walk, London N1 7LB), 1951– .

The *Gramophone classical catalogue master edition* is published twice a year and claims to be the most comprehensive catalogue of currently available classical recordings in the UK. It covers recordings in all available formats. It is available in print-on-paper and CD-ROM formats (see RED CD-ROM below). As part of the subscription, each month there is an update to the *Classical catalogue* entitled the *New release information service*.

RED CD-ROM (MusicMaster and Gramophone databases). London: Retail Entertainment Data Publishing Ltd. (Paulton House, 8 Shepherdess Walk, London N1 7LB), 1995– . Updated every two months.

Cumulations of the entire *Gramophone* and *Music master* databases, it gives details of nearly 1 million commercially available recordings of music of all types by more than 100,000 classical and popular artists, track listings, release and deletion dates, catalogue numbers and distribution details. Both databases are available separately, also on CD-ROM from the same publisher.

ROCKBASE PLUS [CD-ROM]. Llandysul: Record Research Publications (Terry Hounsome, Ewyn y Don, Sarnau, Llandysul, Dyfed SA44 6QA), 1995– .

A CD-ROM containing 400,000 tracks on 120,000 albums, 100,000 singles by 40,000 artists and 320,000 musician cross-references.

ROCKnROM. Melton Mowbray: ROCKnROM (PO Box 25, Melton Mowbray LE13 0BR), 1995– .

A quarterly updated CD-ROM published by Penguin Electronic, contains details of 800,000 recordings, 400,000 works and of the rock recording industry, with cross-references and links.

LASERLOG. Stamford: Trade Services Information Ltd. (Cherrybolt Road, Stamford, Lincs. PE9 2HT), 1995?– .

Over 130,000 currently available popular and classical music titles, with cross-referenced indexes. Updated weekly.

BIBLIOLOG. Stamford: Trade Services Information Ltd. (Cherryholt Road, Stamford PE9 2HT), 1995– .

Currently available spoken-word titles on cassette or CD, with cross-referenced indexes. Updated monthly.

RED SPOKEN WORD CATALOGUE. London: Retail Entertainment Data Publishing Ltd, 1995.

Lists 11,000 currently available titles in all areas, with indexes and cross-references in this first edition.

NIPPER. London: National Sound Archive, 1995–.

The NSA's online catalogue Nipper came into operation in October 1995, and can be accessed at the NSA or by telephone 0171 412 7440 or fax 7441. Its coverage is not yet complete: data are still being added.

CD-ROMs

CD-ROM DIRECTORY. 15th edn. LONDON: TFPL (17–18 Britton Street, London EC1M 5NQ). Updated every six months.

This CD-ROM contains details of approximately 9000 CD-ROM and multimedia CD titles published worldwide, plus a list of publishers.

CD-ROMS IN PRINT. Detroit: Gale Research. Annual.

A successor to the Mecklermedia publication, the 1996 edition of this print-on-paper directory contains details of more than 8000 CD-ROM titles and 3800 publishing and distribution companies.

MICROINFO CD-ROM CATALOGUE. Alton: Microinfo Ltd, 1995.

A catalogue of over a thousand Microinfo, and another 130 publishers' CD-ROMs and floppy disks. Updated as required – some new publications are given in Microinfo *CD-ROM newsletter*.

CD-ROM TITLES REVIEW. Coventry: National Council for Educational Technology, 1995.

A catalogue with reviews of some 500 CD-ROM titles suitable for primary schools.

SWETS CD-ROM CATALOGUE. Lisse, The Netherlands: Swets and Zeitlinger BV. Annual.

Contains details of over 1000 CD-ROMs available through Swets subscription service.

Computer software

SOFTWARE USER'S YEAR BOOK. London: VNU Business Publications Ltd, (VNU House, 32–34 Broadwick Street, London W1A 2HG. Tel 0171 316 9638). Annual.

This CD-ROM contains details of over 15,000 software products and 5000 companies producing them. Hypertext-type links, cross-references. A print-on-paper version in two volumes (suppliers/products) but containing less information is also available.

EDUCATIONAL SOFTWARE, DATABASE OF. in: NCET DIRECTORY ON CD-ROM. Coventry: National Council of Educational Technology [NCET], 1996.

Publication is expected in 1996. Until published contact NCET, tel. 01203 416994 or fax 411418.

DIALOG. Information on DIALOG database catalog on Internet: http://www.dialog.com/dialog/databases/database-1-18.html#8

BUYER'S GUIDE TO MICRO SOFTWARE (SOFT). File 237
DATAPRO SOFTWARE DIRECTORY. File 751
MICROCOMPUTER SOFTWARE AND HARDWARE GUIDE. File 278.
SOFTBASE: REVIEWS, COMPANIES AND PRODUCTS. File 256.

Film and videogram bibliographies

BRITISH NATIONAL FILM AND VIDEO CATALOGUE. London: British Film Institute, 1963–1991.

Published quarterly, with annual cumulations, BNFVC contained records of 72,000 films and videocassettes that may be screened to non-theatrical, that is, non-fee-paying audiences, in the United Kingdom. It covered non-fiction, short fiction and full-length feature films and videograms, including some interactive video discs. Arranged by UDC, there was an additional alphabetical listing of fiction films and videocassettes with brief annotations. It contained subject, title and production (sponsors, production companies, distributors, technicians, artists and others associated) indexes. Prior to 1984 the catalogue was known as the *British national film catalogue*.

BRITISH NATIONAL FILM AND VIDEO GUIDE. Boston Spa: British Library NBS, 1995– .

Quarterly with annual cumulations. This continues the work of the BNFVC above, with the addition of some multimedia programmes, and is based on current BNFVC records from the SIFT (Summary of Information on Film and Television) database compiled by the BFI. There are now BNFVC records for some 82,000 productions to the end of 1995 and approximately 500 are added each quarter.

VIDEOLOG. Stamford: Trade Services Information Ltd. (Cherryholt Road, Stamford, Lincs. PE9 2HT), 1984?– .

Over 21,000 currently available entertainment video titles, cross-referenced indexes. Paper version updated fortnightly. CD-ROM version updated monthly.

FILM INDEX INTERNATIONAL. Cambridge: Chadwyck Healey, 1994– . Annual.

Published jointly by the BFI and Chadwyck-Healey, this CD-ROM now contains data on over 90,000 films of all types, countries and languages, based on the SIFT (Summary of Information on Film and Television) database compiled by the BFI. It also contains biographical details of more than 30,000 people and 330,000 periodical references up to the end 1994. Comprehensively indexed and cross referenced.

THE INTERNET MOVIE DATABASE.
Internet: http://www.cm.cf.ac.uk/Movies

This developing database contains 750,000 entries, including 59,000 international film titles. Searching is by title, members of the cast or production team, characters in the film and other categories. Associated with each film are reviews, plots, locations used, bibliographies and links to other areas of the database.

GIFFORD, Denis, THE BRITISH FILM CATALOGUE: A REFERENCE GUIDE. 3rd edn. London: British Film Institute, 1996.

Sets out to be the complete catalogue of every British fiction film produced for public entertainment since the invention of cinematography.

The first edition of an equivalent volume for British non-fiction films produced for public entertainment is also planned for publication in 1996.

INTERNATIONAL FILM ARCHIVE CD-ROM. London: FIAF, 1995– .

Updated regularly, this CD-ROM contains, among other useful material, *Treasures of the archives: silent films in archive collections*, consisting of over 22,000 records comprehensively indexed.

Internet
OFFICIAL 'INTERNET WORLD' INTERNET YELLOW PAGES. London: McGraw-Hill, 1996.

This new annual publication (by Gregory B. Newby) is expected during 1996, (replacing Mecklermedia's *On Internet 94*). Published on paper, it is accompanied by a CD-ROM which is an electronic version of the book with an extra 15,000 entries, and the Quarterdeck Browser.

MAXWELL, C., NEW RIDERS' OFFICIAL INTERNET YELLOW PAGES. Indianapolis: New Riders Publishing (201 West 103rd Street, Indianapolis, IN46290), 1994.

A directory of Internet resource listings, arranged like a classified telephone directory. Subject indexes, glossary and an introduction to the Internet.

Visuals
GODFREY, J. AND MCKEOWN, R. (eds.) VISUAL RESOURCES FOR DESIGN. Art Libraries Society UK and Ireland, Visual Resources Committee, 1995.

Contains a section on such general sources of information on visual resources as exist, plus a directory of suppliers of visual resources for design and the fine arts.

CASHMAN, N. D. (ed.) SLIDE BUYERS' GUIDE: AN INTERNATIONAL DIRECTORY OF SLIDE SOURCES FOR ART AND ARCHITECTURE. Englewood, Colorado: Libraries Unlimited Inc., 1990.

International coverage of information on slide buying. Updated by regular additions in the Visual Resources Association's VRA Bulletin.

NATIONAL ART SLIDE LIBRARY CATALOGUE. Leicester, De Montfort University.

The library's catalogue contains over 40,000 records. It can also be accessed through three local access points (Finsbury Public Library, the

University of the West of England, Bristol, and the College of Art, Leeds). It is hoped that access will be increased by mid-1996, possibly through the Internet.

VISUAL RESOURCES ASSOCIATION WEB SITE. Internet: http://www. vra.oberlin.edu

VRA are developing this web site to serve as a source of information to anyone interested in visual resources. It contains links to the VRA Bulletin ('. . . a gold mine of materials for the VR manager') and other publications and to 'Additional resources', including other organizations in the field such as the Art Libraries Society of North America, the Clearinghouse of Image Databases and the Getty Information Institute.

ART ON SCREEN ON CD-ROM. New York: G. K. Hall & Co. (c/o Library Reference Order Processing, Simon and Schuster, 200 Old Tappan Road, Old Tappan, NJ 07675), 1995.

A CD-ROM covering more than 22,000 films and videos on the visual arts.

MAYER INTERNATIONAL ART AUCTION RECORDS ON CD-ROM. Cambridge: Chadwyck-Healey, 1994– .

400,00 records covering 1988–93 relating to paintings, prints, drawings and sculpture. Searching by artist, title, school, among others.

Microforms

GUIDE TO MICROFORMS IN PRINT. 2v. Munich: K. G. Saur. Annual.

SUBJECT GUIDE TO MICROFORMS IN PRINT. Munich: K. G. Saur. Annual.

SUPPLEMENT TO THE GUIDE TO MICROFORMS IN PRINT. Munich: K. G. Saur.

A supplement issued six months after the *Guide* and the *Subject guide*. Author, title and subject arrangement.

INTERNATIONAL GUIDE TO MICROFORM MASTERS. Munich: K. G. Saur. Annual.

Available on CD-ROM only.

REFERENCES AND CITATIONS

1 Patterson, O. (ed.), 'Special tools for communication', USA: Industrial Audiovisual Association, 1962. Quoted in Rigg, Robinson P., *Audiovisual aids and techniques*, London, Hamish Hamilton, 1969.

2 Hope, T., Comment in *Audiovisual*, September 1984, 19.

3 Thompson, A. H., 'Knowledge or format?', *Audiovisual librarian*, 12 (4), November 1986.

4 Thompson, A. H., 'Editorial', *Audiovisual librarian*, 20 (3), August 1994.

5 Thompson, A. H., 'Knowledge or format?', *Audiovisual librarian*, 12 (4), November 1986.

6 Patterson, O. *ibid.*

7 Croghan, A., 'Non-book media in general collections', *Audiovisual librarian*, 12 (3), August 1986.

8 Croghan, A., 'Half of one per cent: the British Library and non-book media', *Audiovisual librarian*, 12 (2), May 1986.

9 Thompson, A. H., *Storage, handling and preservation of audiovisual materials*, Holland, Nederlands Bibliotheek En Lektuur Centrum, 1983. (IFLA AV in action, no. 3.)

10 Stokell, A., 'The future is disc-shaped'. Part 1, *Audiovisual librarian*, 21 (3), August 1995; Part 2, *Audiovisual librarian*, 21 (4), November 1995.

11 Croghan, A., 'Non-book media in general collections', *Audiovisual librarian*, 12 (3), August 1986.

Index

Scope: there are index entries under:
- titles of works named in the text;
- author/title of works named in the text. 'Author' includes editors and compilers, and, in appropriate cases, corporate bodies;
- authors (only) of works listed in end-of-chapter references and reading lists;
- subjects and forms of presentation of named works, and of topics discussed in the text.

Limitations
- works mentioned only as instances of a type of reference material are indexed selectively;
- forms of presentation are indexed selectively. Physical formats (principally electronic formats and microforms) are indexed only when the format itself is discussed in the text;
- British government departments and agencies are entered directly under their names. *Great Britain and United Kingdom* are not used as topical index terms: works or topics with a UK limitation are indexed under their subjects;
- only first named authors have entries. Forenames are reduced to initials.

Filing
- filing is word-by-word. Initial articles are omitted. Internal prepositions, articles and conjunctions are ignored.

Index

Index

British technology index 288
British Telecom, telephone directories 234–5
British Toy and Hobby Association 241
British union catalogue of music periodicals 285
British union catalogue of periodicals 283–4
British Universities Film and Video Council 398
broadcast news 257
Broadcast news on CD-ROM 257
Brockhaus Enzyklopädie 80
Brown, A. 183
BRTT *(British reports, translations and theses)* 371
Bryan's dictionary of painters and engravers 108
Bryant, H.B. *Robert Graves: an annotated bibliography* 37
BSI (British Standards Institution) 377
BSI standards catalogue 377
BT (British Telecom), telephone directories 234–5
BT Phonebase 235
BT Phonedisc 234
BTHA Handbook and guide to the British International Toy and Hobby Fair 241
BUCOP *(British union catalogue of periodicals)* 283–4
Buettel, F. 295
BUFVC (British Universities Film and Video Council) 397–8
Builder 163
Building products compendium (Barbour index) 246
Buildings of England series 151
Bulletin on constitutional case-law 331
Bulletin of the Society of Cartographers 123
Bunch, A. *The basics of community work* 201
Burchfield, R. 71
Bureau of Labour Statistics 359
Burgess, B.M. 182
Burke's ... peerage, baronetage and knightage 112
Burke's royal families of the world 112
Burnet, J. *et al. The autobiography of the working class* 116
Burns, A. *Going it alone* 229
Bushell, P. 180

Business briefing 312
business directories 235–41
  international 237–9
business information 231–250
  European Union 335
  from newspaper indexes 260
  guides and bibliographies 232–4
  statistical sources 358
Business information review 250
Business monitor series 353
Business newsletters directory 267
business periodicals, CD-ROM 279
business records 159
Business services in Europe 358
Business Statistics Office 311
Business Statistics User Council 361
Butcher, D. *Official publications in Britain* 299
Butler, A. *Lives of the saints* (1756–9) 107
Buyers guide (Office of Fair Trading) 203
Buyer's guide to micro software 401

calendars, archives 161
Cambridge biographical encyclopedia 97
Cambridge encyclopedia 78
Cambridge encyclopedia of Australia 89
Cambridge encyclopedia of language 84
Cambridge guide to literature in English 87
Cambridge international dictionary of English 54
Cambridge medieval history 88
Cambridge union list of serials 285
Camden Community Information Services 188
Camp, A.J. 165, 181
Campaigning handbook 201, 216
Campbell-Kease, J. *A companion to local history research* 145, 149, 177
Canada
  atlases 133
  bibliography of bibliographies 39
  biography 106
  business directories 238
  historical atlases 135
  national bibliography 22, 31
  national biographical dictionaries 101
  official publications 322
  road atlases 134
Canadian books in print 31
Canadian diaries and autobiographies 116
Canadian who's who 106

413

Index

Index

Index

431

Index

Index

441

Index

UNESCO, statistical publications 358
Unesco statistical yearbook 358
Union of International Associations 326
Union list of Commonwealth newspapers in London, Oxford and Cambridge 269
Union list of periodicals held in institute and school of education libraries 285
union lists
  of newspapers 269
  of periodicals 284–5
United Kingdom digital marine atlas 131–2
United Kingdom Serials Group 295
United Nations 335–9
  statistical publications 358–9
United Nations. *Multilateral treaties deposited with the Secretary-General* 328
United Nations bibliographic information system 338
United Nations documents index 338
United States
  almanacs 266
  business directories 238–9
  company information 232–3, 243
  gazetteers 140
  government publications 316–20
  historical atlases 135
  maps 126, 127
  national bibliography 22, 26–7, 29–30
  national biographical dictionaries 100–101
  news information sources 254, 257–8, 260
  newspaper directories 267
  non-official statistics 360
  official reports 368–9
  official statistics 356
  patents 380
  road atlases 134
  standards 378
  statistical sources 359, 360
  telephone directories 235
United States. Congress, publications 319
United States. Congressional Information Service 363
United States. President, publications 320
United States Defense Mapping Agency 128
United States Geological Survey 126, 127
United States Historical Documents Institute 315
United States Soil Conservation service 128

universal biographical dictionaries 95–8
Universal etymological English dictionary (1721) 44
Universalia 263
University of Cambridge, biography 112
University of London union list of serials 285
University of Nottingham Treaty Centre 328
University of Oxford, biography 112
University of Reading. *Catalogue of the collection of children's books* 34
University of Warwick. Library 361
urban history 153–4
Urban history yearbook 153, 178
Urdang, L. *The Oxford thesaurus* 59
Uruguay round of multilateral trade negotiations 345
US books 22
US Phonedisc 235
USA and Canada (Europa) 265
usage guides, language 60
Useful statistical addresses on the Internet 359
user groups, statistical sources 361–2
user training, statistical sources 361
Using old photographs: a guide for the local historian 174
UTET (Grand dizionario enciclopedico) 82

Van den Brink-Budgen, R. *How to survive divorce* 215
Van Nostrand's scientific encyclopedia 85
VDUs: an easy guide to the regulations 210
Venice Commission 331
Venn, J. and J.A. *Alumni cantabrigienses* 112
Verzeihnis lieferbarer Bücher 31
Victoria county histories 150, 177
Victorian periodicals
  bibliographies of 283
  indexes to 287
videodiscs, audiovisual materials 393
Videolog 402
videorecordings
  audiovisual materials 458
  bibliography 401–3
Village records 160
Visions of the future of social justice (ILO) 341
visual arts, slides 403–4
Visual dictionary 53

443